JAPAN

A Practical Guide for Independent Travelers

by

EIJI KANNO

NITCHI MAP-PUBLISHING CO., LTD.

Tokyo

JAPAN SOLO

© 1985 by Eiji Kanno
All rights reserved. No part of this book may be reproduced in any form
without permission in writing from the author.

Published by
    Nitchi Map-Publishing Co., Ltd.
    2-2-15, Nishi-Kanda, Chiyoda-ku, Tokyo 101, Japan
Printed in Japan by
    Shalom Printing Co., Ltd.

Text and maps by
    Eiji Kanno.
Text rewrite by
    Constance O'Keefe.
Editorial production services by
    Kazuo Daibo, Nitchi Map-Publishing Co., Ltd.
Text and cover design by
    Takayuki Okada, Shalom Printing Co., Ltd.

Photos by
    Eiji Kanno
Illustrations of Ms. Nitchi by
    Ms. Yasuko Matsumoto
Other illustrations by courtesy of
    the Japan National Tourist Organization.

A Message to the Readers of This Unusual Guide Book

Our former collegues, Mr. Eiji Kanno and Miss Constance O'Keefe, have just completed a new, very practical Japan guide, which, we feel, is the best answer to a guide book that we have ever seen.

Mr. Kanno, who has worked for the Japan National Tourist Organization for 12 years, has had an outstanding career with JNTO. It includes assignments for the New York Office as Deputy Director, Finance and the International Departments in Tokyo Head Office.

"JAPAN SOLO" reflects his extensive knowledge not only of Japan but also of what foreign travelers want to know about Japan. It is a fact that he traveled all the destinations introduced in his guide book and he has drawn up as many as 135 walking tour maps by himself. It is no wonder that "JAPAN SOLO" contains much practical and accurate information.

Miss O'Keefe first visited Japan in the guise of an English teacher over 10 years ago and has lived in Nagoya for more than two years. After returning to New York, she worked for JNTO's New York Office as well as for the Information Center of the Japanese Consulate and Japan Society. Her views of Japan as an American, together with her practical language experience has contributed greatly in making "JAPAN SOLO" an easy-to-read, easy-to-use guidebook.

Japan has a unique historical and cultural legacy, as well as beautiful natural surroundings and hospitable people of which she is very proud. As Mr. Kanno mentions in the text, with its uniform safety and convenient public transportation network, Japan is an ideal destination for independent travel.

The Japan National Tourist Organization has been making strenuous efforts to develop reception services for visitors to Japan. Good-will Guide System, a toll-free Travel-phone service and seminars on how to facilitate the staying of foreign visitors for owners of inexpensive accommodations are just a few examples of our activities of this kind.

We believe that tourism is a "Passport to Peace," and we hope that our public efforts and private efforts, as exemplified by Mr. Kanno, are combining effectively and will enhance international mutual-understanding.

Mr. Kanno has just begun his new career in a private tourism sector. I am confident of his success and prosperity in his new world.

Yasukuni Kajimoto
President
Japan National Tourist Organization

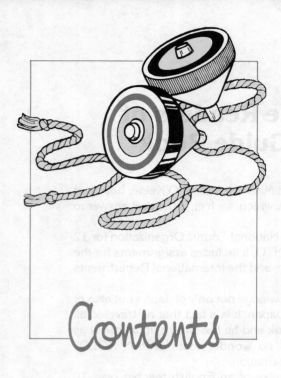

City/Resort Guides

Contents

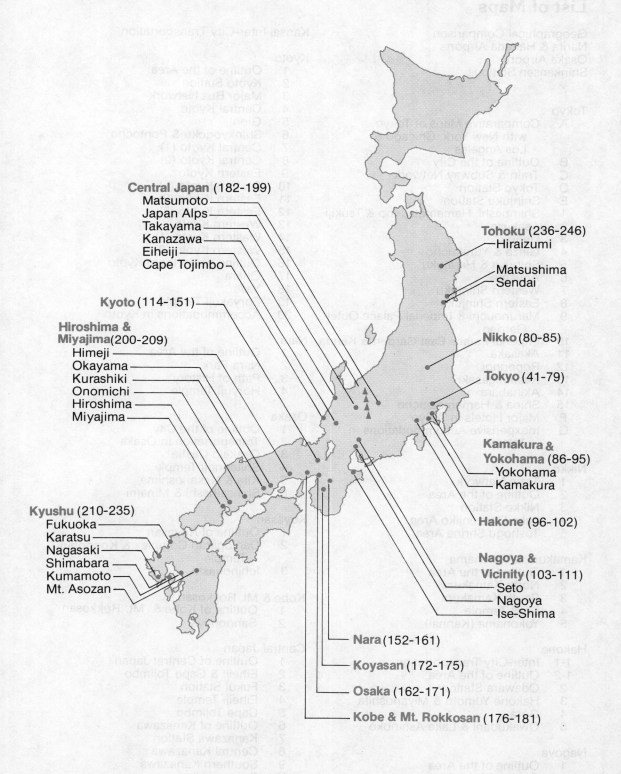

List of Maps

Introducing Ms. Nitchi

Your Personal Guide in Japan

A picture of Ms. Nitchi on horseback lets you know that a particular section explains public transportation to and within a destination. As emphasized throughout the text, good public transportation is one of Japan's biggest attractions.

With her telescope, Ms. Nitchi signals that a section contains a destination outline.

In her feudal era traveling costume, Ms. Nitchi indicates the beginning of a walking tour itinerary.

Get out of your hotel and track down an authentic Japanese dinner. A variety of restaurants are introduced in these sections. Soon you will be using chopsticks as well as Ms. Nitchi!

Both Western hotels and Japanese ryokans in a variety of price ranges are listed in these sections. You can select accommodations to suit your taste and your budget.

A wide variety of stores, carrying everything from antiques and handicraft items to modern electronic products, are introduced in these sections.

Ms. Nitchi's traditional festival costume indicates sections with information on Japan's great festival celebrations. Join in and enjoy the fun!

Why I Wrote This Book

This guidebook is designed to provide foreign tourists with the detailed practical information they need to travel in Japan independently. Business travelers will also find this book helpful for its detailed maps and practical information on how to use free time well. Even those who participate in group tours to Japan will find this book useful, because it contains detailed shopping information as well as guides to restaurants, coffee shops and pubs. Since tours are including fewer meals these days, group members can use this guide to plan their meals as well as their free time.

The greatest problem for foreign visitors to Japan is probably that of language. Japan's transportation system is world famous, and its railroad networks are a magnificently efficient and economical means of travel. But, paradoxically, the very superiority of this system makes it all that much more difficult for foreigners. The railroad networks are as complex as they are extensive. All major train stations are mazes served by several lines, usually including the Japanese National Railways, private railways and city subways. In addition to railway and subway services, street cars, buses and sometimes even boats, cable cars and ropeways are the best way to get around in some of the destinations included in this guide. For most visitors to Japan, the inability to speak and read Japanese makes using these marvelous facilities difficult, if not impossible.

To help foreign tourists overcome these difficulties, this guide incorporates three features never before used in travel books. They are designed to liberate foreign visitors to Japan from their linguistic prison, to give them the freedom to travel like the Japanese, and the ability to take advantage of the public transportation values available in all parts of Japan.

The **first** is detailed maps. This book contains a total of 135 maps. At the beginning of each chapter on a new city or resort, there is a map outlining the area. The locations of major places of interest, major accommodation facilities, and inter- and intra-city transportation networks are indicated. More detailed maps, picturing "downtown" sections and areas of the city with tourist attractions are also included. These contain the exact locations of train stations and bus stops, major hotels, restaurants, shops, etc. Wherever there are English language signs of any kind, I have indicated them on the maps to help you orient yourself in the area. Using these maps as walking tour guides you can really get off the "beaten track," and away from the traffic-clogged main streets to explore the back alleys where the real Japan is still concealed.

The **second** innovation is "Conversation Cards." To help you use public transportation to the various destinations described in the text, I have prepared nine types of Conversation Cards with requests for information/assistance in both Japanese and English. You can use the Conversation Cards to figure out train/subway fares (fare tables are written only in Japanese at most train and subway stations), to locate the right track for the particular train you want, or to make sure that you'll get off your train/subway at the right place. Several friends have tried this method. It works! Just fill in the particular information you need, show the card to a Japanese passerby, and help is on the way! It's much more efficient than trying to ask for help, because most Japanese have trouble listening to and speaking English, even though they can read it very well.

The **third** special feature is this guide's detailed fare information, train schedules, and timetables for other types of transportation. Some of my friends and colleagues have warned that it's foolish to include such detailed information because fares will go up, and because the schedules will soon be outdated. Fares, like taxes, it is true, are sure to go up, but the increases will never be as steep as the 20 - 30% per year increases I've seen in the United States. The listings are accurate as of October 1985, and will serve for many years thereafter as reliable benchmarks for travelers who are trying to calculate their transportation costs. Timetables in Japan are also very stable. In the 12 years I worked for the Japan National Tourist Organization, the only changes I saw in timetables were minor ones. In future years trains will operate at the same or similar intervals and with at least approximately the same frequency.

Seeing a city from a sightseeing bus or a taxi window is one thing. Taking public transportation and doing as the Japanese do is another experience — and it's far less costly!

Try it!! I hope you enjoy Japan and wish you good luck.

Eiji Kanno
October 1985
Tokyo

Bill Kanzo
October 1985
Tokyo

Remarks, Details and Survival Tips

How to Use This Book and its Maps

The destinations introduced in this guide are arranged in rough geographical order starting at Tokyo. The order in which they are introduced does not, however, reflect my priorities for the destinations. There is separate chapter below that introduces several suggested itineraries.

I've walked every one of the suggested itineraries in this book and have drawn maps for each itinerary that I believe are as complete and accurate as possible. At the beginning of each section on a city or resort, inter-city transportation is explained first so that readers can figure out the links between the various destinations. The suggested itinerary for the particular city or resort is then introduced and is followed by an explanation of intra-city transportation. Details on places of interest are then presented — in the order in which I think they should be visited. Restaurants, shops and accommodations are introduced at the end of each city/resort section.

Regional, city and district maps are placed to coordinate with the text. The regional maps are designed to help you understand inter-city transportation. The city maps outline intra-city transportation networks, the location of downtown areas, places of interest, etc. Once you understand how an area is laid out in general terms, proceed to the more detailed walking tour maps on the pages that follow. You can use them much more easily than the big city maps.

Each detailed walking tour map follows four basic principles:

— Places important for tourists, such as sightseeing destinations, hotels, restaurants and coffee shops are indicated with black dots and bold letters. E.g.: **Miyako Hotel●**

— The names of places to be used just as landmarks or for orientation purposes are indicated with red dots and regular letters (These are usually the most prominent English signs in any given location). E.g.: Shell●   Oriental Fine Arts●

— Where signs are written only in Japanese, they are indicated on the map with parentheses. English signs are indicated without parentheses.

— Suggested walking tour routes are indicated with shaded red. For the downtown areas, the busiest and most interesting streets are also shaded red.

Sounds pretty complicated, doesn't it? To make sure you understand the system, let's look at a sample map. For the purpose of illustration, we'll use Kyoto Map 10, which is actually much more complicated than most of the maps in this book.

On Kyoto Map 10, the suggested walking tour starts at the upper center, at Ginkakuji-michi bus stop, where the shaded red begins. (Bus stops are always indicated with the symbol ⚲). At the intersection where the bus stops there are three signs in English that will help you get oriented. They have no significance otherwise—they are not names of sightseeing destinations; they are not places to eat or shop; and they are not the names of accommodations. Because they are useful only as landmarks, they are indicated with regular letters and red dots: Dry Cleaning •; Pachinko •; and Kyoto Bank •.

The first stop on the walking tour is the Silver Pavilion. This is one of Kyoto's top sightseeing destinations, but it has no signs in English. It is therefore indicated on the map with bold letters (because of its significance), and is placed in parentheses (because there is no English sign): **(Silver Pavilion)** •.

After you visit the Silver Pavilion, you should double back to the path alongside the small creek pictured on the map (Rivers, creeks and even larger bodies of water are always pictured with the diagonal black lines.). Following the map, you should walk south, on the path shaded red on the map. Along the way you will pass several restaurants, coffee shops and souvenir shops. Matsuya • has an English sign, but is of no real interest to you except as an orientation aid. **Bobby Soxer** •, which is a combination pizza and coffee shop, has an English sign, and is a good place to stop for a coffee break or a light lunch. Because it has an English sign there are no parentheses, and because it is important for tourists, it is indicated with a black dot. Kazenoyakata • is good for orientation because of its English sign, and **Coffee & Tea Lounge Pino** •, which also has an English sign, is another good place to stop for a snack.

Coffee & Tea Lounge Pino is also indispensable for finding the entrance to the next destination on this walking tour itinerary—Honen-in Temple. Because the Temple has no English sign, it is placed inside parentheses, and it is of course written in bold letters because of its status as a major sightseeing destination: **(Honen-in Temple)** •. Because the Temple has beautifully arranged mounds of sand near its southern entrance, the walking tour itinerary suggests that you use the southern entrance to the Temple grounds. A phone box that is right by that entrance is pictured on the map: Phone Box •, to help you find the southern gate.

After your visit to Honen-in Temple go back to the path along the creek and continue your walking tour to the south.

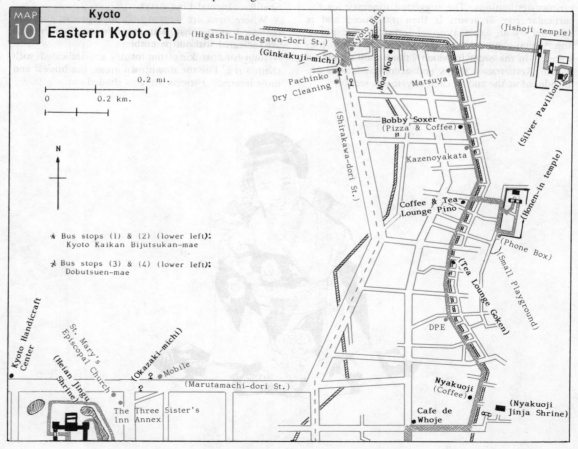

MAP
10

Kyoto
Eastern Kyoto (1)

(Higashi-Imadegawa-dori St.)

(Ginkakuji-michi)

(Jishoji temple)

Kyoto Bank

Noa Noa

Pachinko
Dry Cleaning

Matsuya

0.2 mi.

0   0.2 km.

(Silver Pavilion)

Bobby Soxer
(Pizza & Coffee)

Kazenoyakata

(Shirakawa-dori St.)

N

(Honen-in temple)

Coffee & Tea
Lounge Pino

(Phone Box)

(Small Playground)

✦ Bus stops (1) & (2) (lower left): Kyoto Kaikan Bijutsukan-mae

✦ Bus stops (3) & (4) (lower left): Dobutsuen-mae

(Tea Lounge Goken)

DPE

Kyoto Handicraft Center

St. Mary's Episcopal Church

(Okazaki-michi)

Mobile

(Marutamachi-dori St.)

Nyakuoji
(Coffee)

(Nyakuoji Jinja Shrine)

(Heian Jingu Shrine)

The Three Sister's Inn Annex

Cafe de Whoje

LEGEND

- **Bold Letters:** Places of interest or importance for tourists that have English signs. These include sightseeing destinations, hotels, restaurants, souvenir shops, etc. They are explained in the text.

- **(Bold Letters):** Places of interest or importance for tourists that do not have English signs. These too are explained in the text.

- Regular Letters: These places are not important for tourists for any reason. However, they have English signs that will help travelers get their bearings in unfamiliar surroundings.

- (Regular Letters): These places are not important for sightseeing, but the notations on the maps provide some additional information, such as river names, street names, etc. There are no English signs.

⬚⬚⬚⬚⬚ In the historical or walking tour areas, the roads shaded in red show the author's suggested walking tour routes. In the downtown areas, the busiest and most interesting streets are indicated in the same manner.

▨▨▨▨▨ Seas, lakes, rivers, creeks, and other bodies of water are indicated with diagonal black lines.

▬▬▬▬ ⎫
―――― ⎬ Names of railroads and subways are
- - - - ⎭ shown on each map. Where several different
etc.   lines are shown on one map, a legend is always included. ⬥

⚲ Bus stops

⛩ Torii gates (entrances to shrines)

⛩ Temple gates

(RR) Rest rooms

All city and walking tour maps are drawn to scale.

Safety & Security

Japan is one of the safest countries in the world. Robberies are very rare and impersonal violent crime is virtually unknown. Even pickpockets seem to avoid foreigners (perhaps because they are unfamiliar with the designs of foreign-made clothing?). It is because Japan is so safe that I could write this guidebook and encourage foreigners to travel there on their own.

Geography and Population

The Japanese archipelago stretches 1,860 miles (3,000 km.) from northeast to southwest along the eastern coast of the Asian Continent. The country has four major islands (from north to south — Hokkaido, Honshu, Shikoku and Kyushu), and about 4,000 small islands. The total area of Japan is about 146,000 square miles (378,000 square kilometers). Although it is one and a half times the size of the U.K., it is only one-twenty-fifth the size of the U.S. and the whole country is only about the size of the state of California. Three-fourths of Japan is mountainous and covered with forests. The highest peak is Mt. Fuji (12,388 feet or 3,776 m.). Japan's other high mountains are grouped in the middle of the main island of Honshu and form the "Japan Alps." Several volcanic ranges running through the archipelago have created unique topography and account for the large number of hotsprings located throughout the country. Only 15% of the land is arable, and residential areas account for only 3% of the total land of the country.

Some 117 million people (about half the size of the population of the U.S.) are crowded onto these mountainous islands. Post-war industrialization and housing shortages have resulted in incredibly high population density in all of the major cities. Ten cities have a population of more than one million. The nation's capital, Tokyo, has about 8.4 million people within its city limits, and an additional 3.1 million in its suburbs. Yokohama, the second largest city, with a population of 2.8 million, is located only 18 miles (29 km.) from Tokyo. Between these two giant cities is Kawasaki, the nation's 10th largest city, with a population of 1 million. These three cities form the world's largest megalopolis.

Climate

Map 1 overlays a map of Japan on a map of the East Coast of the United States, at the same latitude, so that readers can make easy comparisons. The climate of Japan is similar to that of the East Coast of the United States. Japan has four distinctively different seasons. Spring begins in March (April in northern Honshu and Hokkaido) and lasts until the middle of June. Plum and peach blossoms appear in March, heralding Japan's great springtime event, the blooming of the cherry trees in early April. The first cherry blossoms appear in the southern part of Kyushu around March 20. The "Cherry Blossom Frontier" then moves gradually toward the northeast. Full bloom in the Kyoto/Osaka and Tokyo areas is usually around April 5. The northern part of Japan is in full bloom by the middle of April. The cherry trees are easily affected by slight changes in temperatures, and the period of full bloom varies slightly from year to year. With warm temperatures and stable weather, April and May are very comfortable months for traveling in Japan. This comfortable weather usually continues until the second week of June, when the rainy season sets in.

Summer begins with the rainy season. With the exception of Hokkaido island, high humidity and temperatures, along with occasional showers, prevail over all of the country. This is not an ideal season for traveling, but many landscaped gardens are said to look most attractive during a light rain or just after a rainfall. The rainy season usually ends in the middle of July. Hot yet stable weather lasts until late August or early September. Areas of high altitude, such as Hakone, Nikko, Koyasan, the Japan Alps and Mt. Asozan, are pleasantly cool throughout the summer. September is typhoon season, but most of these

storms remain at sea with only about three or four a year coming ashore. Severe damage is rare.

Autumn is marked by occasional quiet showers in late September and early October. After this short rainy period, Japan has a two-month long period of stable, comfortable weather, with brilliant blue skies and pleasant temperatures. Japan's scenic beauty reaches its peak in the middle of November, when the country is bedecked with the intense hues of the autumn leaves.

Winter begins with cold western winds blown in by Siberian high pressure systems. The areas along the Japan Sea coast and the mountainous areas of the interior have heavy snowfalls throughout the winter, and become winter sports paradises. Even though walking tours are often difficult in these areas in winter, the rugged, snow-covered mountains are scenes of magnificent natural beauty. Most areas on the Pacific coast, especially those southwest of Tokyo, have clear skies and low humidity. Temperatures are mild and seldom fall below freezing. In these areas of

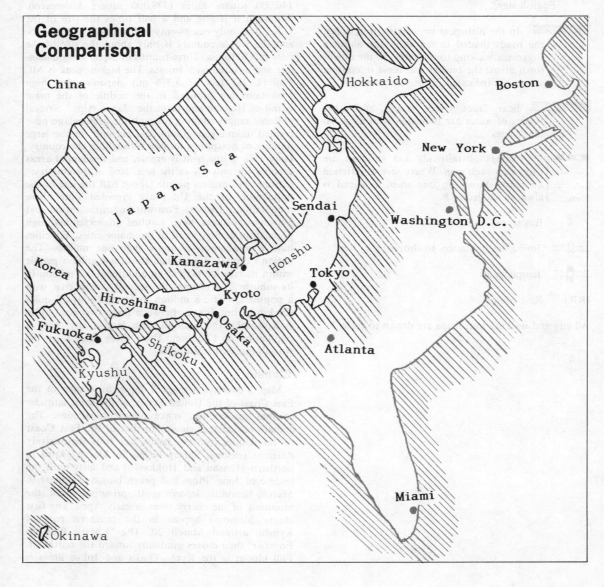

Geographical Comparison

the Pacific coast, winter is really not at all a bad time for sightseeing.

Average Temperatures in Major Cities

	April	July	October	January
Fukuoka				
High	66 (19c)	87 (31c)	73 (23c)	49 (9c)
Low	48 (9c)	74 (23c)	54 (12c)	35 (2c)
Average	57 (14c)	80 (27c)	63 (17c)	42 (5c)
Kanazawa				
High	62 (17c)	84 (29c)	69 (21c)	42 (6c)
Low	43 (6c)	70 (21c)	54 (12c)	32 (0c)
Average	52 (11c)	76 (25c)	60 (16c)	37 (3c)
Kyoto				
High	67 (19c)	89 (31c)	73 (23c)	48 (9c)
Low	46 (8c)	72 (22c)	54 (12c)	31 (-1c)
Average	56 (13c)	79 (26c)	62 (17c)	38 (4c)
Nagasaki				
High	66 (19c)	85 (29c)	74 (23c)	50 (10c)
Low	51 (11c)	75 (24c)	59 (15c)	37 (3c)
Average	58 (15c)	79 (26c)	65 (19c)	44 (6c)
Sendai				
High	58 (15c)	79 (26c)	66 (19c)	40 (5c)
Low	39 (4c)	67 (19c)	49 (10c)	25 (-4c)
Average	48 (9c)	72 (22c)	57 (14c)	32 (0c)
Tokyo				
High	65 (18c)	85 (29c)	70 (21c)	49 (9c)
Low	48 (9c)	72 (22c)	56 (14c)	31 (0c)
Average	56 (14c)	77 (25c)	62 (17c)	39 (4c)

Language

Pronunciation. Throughout this book I have used the Hepburn system of romanization because it is more helpful for foreigners who want to pronounce Japanese words correctly. There are only five vowels in Japanese — **a** (pronounced like "ah"), **i** ("i" of itch), **u** ("oo" of food), **e** ("e" of bet), and **o** (pronounced like "oh"). All consonants are pronounced the same as in English (If in doubt, you should use a hard rather than a soft sound). Japanese is a language of syllables, not individual letters. The five vowels are separate syllables. All other syllables combine the vowels with a consonant or a consonant blend, e.g., **Na, ri, ta, ryo,** and **shi.** Except for occasional doubling of consonants between syllables (e.g., Jakkoin), virtually the only exception is **n,** which can be a syllable all by itself. The name of the Japanese city Sendai has four syllables: **Se-n-da-i.** To pronounce it correctly be sure to pronounce each separate syllable. Even long words like Hachigaoka-cho become manageable when you separate them thusly: **Ha-chi-ga-o-ka-cho.** Remember that each Japanese vowel counts as a separate syllable and that long vowels in Japanese count as two syllables. For example, Tokyo and Osaka are each really four syllable words: **To-o-kyo-o** and **O-o-sa-ka.** Try it! Once you get used to it, you'll be able to hear the Japanese using it.

Japanese Suffixes. There is usually confusion on how to handle Japanese suffixes when translating into English. For example, "Kiyomizudera" is usually translated as Kiyomizu Temple ("Kiyomizu" is the name of the temple, and "dera" means temple), while "Nanzenji" is usually translated as Nanzenji Temple ("Nanzen" is the name of the temple, and "ji" is another suffix that means temple). To avoid this kind of confusion, this text leaves all Japanese suffixes attached, and adds explanatory English nouns. Therefore, Kiyomizudera is translated as Kiyomizudera Temple, and Nanzenji as Nanzenji Temple.

Nagoyajo (the castle in the city of Nagoya) is Nagoyajo Castle, and Asozan (an active volcano in Kyushu) Mt. Asozan. The only exception is Fujisan because the mountain is already world famous as "Mt. Fuji." When you talk with Japanese, delete the explanatory English word and use the full Japanese name. Your friends will be surprised and delighted at your proper use of Japanese names.

Japanese makes no distinction between singular and plural nouns or pronouns, or between present and future tenses. Many English sounds — such as "c", "f", "v", and especially the difference between "r" and "l", are very difficult for Japanese to say; it is also difficult for them to distinguish these sound when they hear them. Bear this in mind when conducting conversations. Speak slowly and distinctly, and be patient.

Conversation Cards

After World War II studying English became compulsory for all junior and senior high school students, and most university students. All Japanese under the age of about 45 have therefore studied English and can read it fairly well. However, because the average Japanese has few opportunities to practice, and because the schools place all their emphasis on grammar and translation, most Japanese have difficulty understanding spoken English. To make the situation worse, most of them are embarrassed that they're not good at spoken English, and believe that they don't understand anything at all. As a result, they often fail to understand even easy questions that they would be able to answer if they were not paralyzed by embarrassment and self-consciousness. To help you ask Japanese passersby simple questions when you need help during your travels in Japan, I have designed nine different kinds of Conversation Cards. Several copies of each card are attached at the end of this book so that readers can tear them out and use them while traveling. Remember to **print** your questions clearly on the cards. Handwriting is not easy for Japanese to read. A list of the different Conversation Cards and instructions on how to use them follows:

Train Rides
Looking for train and subway stations
Card 1 — Where is the following train/subway station?
Circle either train or subway and fill in the name of the station and the name of the line you are looking for.
You shouldn't have much difficulty finding train

stations. However, in some huge complexes that house several different lines — including JNR, city subways, and private railways — you'll need to use this card to locate the station for the particular line you want.

Card 1 Station	下の電車または地下鉄の駅を教えてください Where is the following train/subway station? (Circle either train or subway and fill in the name of the station and the name of the line.)		
	Circle either one	路線名 Line Name	駅名 Destination
	1 電車 地下鉄 Train Subway		
	2 電車 地下鉄		
	3 電車 地下鉄		
	4 電車 地下鉄		
	5 電車 地下鉄		

Purchasing tickets for subways and short-distance commuter trains
Card 2 — How much is the fare to the following station?

Fill in the name of your destination and the name of the line you want to take.

Tickets for subways and short-distance commuter trains are usually sold in vending machines. Because Japanese train and subway fares vary with the distance traveled, and because the fare tables are usually written only in Japanese, you will probably use this card frequently to make sure that the ticket you're purchasing is for the proper amount.

Card 2 Ticket	下の駅までの運賃を教えてください How much is the fare to the following station? (Fill in the name of your destination and the name of the line you want to take.)	
	路線名 Line Name	目的駅 Destination
	1	
	2	
	3	
	4	
	5	

Looking for train platforms
Card 3 — What is the platform number for the following train to the destination listed below?

Fill in the name of the line, the name of the train you plan to take, and the name of your destination. If the train is a local and does not have a name, write "Donko." The best person to show this card to is the railway employee at the entrance gate. Show him your ticket as well.

Card 3 Platform	下の電車の発車ホーム番号を教えてください What is the platform number for the following train to the destination listed below? (If the train is a local and does not have a name, write "Donko" in the train name column.)		
	路線名 Line Name	電車名 Train Name	目的駅 Destination
	1		
	2		
	3		
	4		
	5		

Purchasing a reserved ticket
Card 4 is designed so that you can easily fill in all the information necessary for purchasing a reserved seat ticket. Just fill in the columns and present it to the clerk at the ticket window.

Card 4 Reservation	座席指定申込書 Application for reserved seats		If you have a Rail Pass, you can request reservations for JNR trains free of charge. Show the Pass with this form. Your Rail Pass cannot be used for private railways.	
	乗車日 Date of Trip	月 (month) 日 (date)	人数 No. of Pans 大人 Adults 枚 子供 Children 枚	
	出発駅 Departure		目的駅 Destination	Station
	座席の種類 Class of Seat	(Check either one) □グリーン車 First Class □普通車 Coach Class	□禁煙席 Nonsmoking section, if available	
	第一希望 First Choice	電車名 Train Name	出発時間 Dep. Time	時 分 (hour) (minute)
	第二希望 Second Choice	電車名 Train Name	出発時間 Dep. Time	時 分 (hour) (minute)
	第三希望 Third Choice	電車名 Train Name	出発時間 Dep. Time	時 分 (hour) (minute)

Streetcars and Buses
Looking for a stop
Card 5 — Where is the stop for the streetcar (or bus) going to the following destination?

Circle either streetcar or bus and fill in the name of your destination.

Card 5 Streetcar Bus Stop	下の行先の市電またはバス乗場を教えてください Where is the stop for the streetcar (or bus) going to the following destination? (Circle either streetcar or bus and fill in the name of your destination.)	
	Circle either one	目的駅 Destination
	1 市電 バス Streetcar Bus	
	2 市電 バス	
	3 市電 バス	
	4 市電 バス	
	5 市電 バス	

Asking about the arrival of your train, streetcar or bus at your destination (for use while on the train, streetcar or bus).
Card 6 — I am going to the following place. Please let me know when we near the destination.

Fill in the name of your destination and show the card to a fellow passenger.

Card 6 Destination	私は下の目的地まで行きます 目的地が近づいたら教えてください I am going to the following place. Please let me know when we near the destination. (On the train, streetcar or bus) (Fill in the name of your destination and show the card to a fellow passenger.)		
	1		6
	2		7
	3		8
	4		9
	5		10

Taxis
Card 7 — Please take me to the following place.

Fill in the name of your destination.

Card 7 Taxi	下の目的地まで行ってください Please take me to the following place. (For a taxi driver) (Fill in the name of your destination.)		
	1		7
	2		8
	3		9
	4		10
	5		11
	6		12

Checking Baggage
Card 8 — Where are the coin lockers or a short-term baggage check room?

Train stations have either coin lockers (usually 200 yen per day) or a manned short-term baggage check room. The former can accommodate only carry-on size bags, and you'll need to find the latter for large bags. Manned check rooms are more convenient for tourists, but many of them are being replaced by coin lockers.

One More Important Question
Card 9—Where is a rest room?

All train stations have rest rooms. I have also pictured many of them along the suggested walking tour itineraries (They are indicated with the letter "RR" on the maps).

Travel Phone

The most important telephone number for you while traveling in Japan is **106.** This is the number of the toll-free telephone service operated by Japan National Tourist Organization to provide travel information free of charge, from 9 a.m. to 5 p.m. daily. Outside Tokyo and Kyoto you can call 106 toll free. In Tokyo you can reach the Tourist Information Center at 502-1461 (a 10 yen call), and in Kyoto you can reach the Information Center by calling 371-5649. To use the toll free number, pick up the receiver of a blue or yellow phone (there is no dial tone until you insert your money), insert a 10 yen coin, dial 106, and tell the operator "T.I.C." slowly and clearly. You will be connected to an Information Center and your 10 yen coin will be returned at the end of your call.

What to Pack

Clothes. Japan is located in the North Temperate Zone and has four distinct seasons. Jackets or sweaters are enough in the spring and autumn. Summer is hot and humid and only very light clothes are needed. In the winter a light overcoat or a raincoat with a liner will be enough. Casual clothes are fine for sightseeing, but Japanese usually get dressed up when they're going out to shop or to eat, so you'll probably want to be a little more formal yourself on these occasions.

Supplies at Japanese hotels and ryokans. A fresh nemaki (sleeping robe) is provided for your use every night. They are not giveaways. If you want to keep one as a souvenir, ask the hotel or ryokan clerk if it's possible to buy one. Towels, soap, washcloths, toothbrushes and toothpaste are standard supplies at all regular accommodations. Shampoo is usually not provided. If you are staying at inexpensive accommodations (i.e. where the charge is less than 14,000 yen for a twin room at a western style hotel, or less than 12,000 yen per person for a Japanese style room plus two meals), these items will not necessarily be supplied (but you'll always be able to purchase them at such places).

Shoes. Bring a pair of comfortable shoes for your walking tours. Don't expect to be able to purchase shoes in Japan. It'll probably be impossible to find any big enough. Because you have to take your shoes off when you enter most temples and shrines, socks are indispensable, especially in the winter when the wooden corridors of these old, unheated buildings are very chilly.

Medicines. Japan's medical services and facilities meet the highest international standards. If you have prescription medicines you should be sure to pack them. Hotels can help with emergencies.

Electrical products. Electric current in Japan is 100 volts. 50 cycles is the standard in Tokyo and to the northeast, and 60 cycles in Nagoya, Kyoto, Osaka and areas to the southwest. Most electrical products used by North American travelers, such as electric shavers and hair dryers will just run a little slower than they do at home. More sensitive instruments won't work properly unless they are adjusted. If you intend to use sophisticated equipment, try to bring models that work on batteries.

Others. Japanese always carry tissue paper and handkerchiefs because public toilets often don't have toilet paper or hand towels. It's also good to know that these items are always sold at the newsstands in train stations.

Shopping and Money

Tax Free Shopping. Foreign visitors to Japan can avoid taxes by patronizing the authorized stores that display "Tax-Free" signs. Be sure to carry your passport with you because the store clerks have to complete special forms and attach them to the passport. These forms will be collected by the customs officials when you leave Japan. Tax free shopping is available in major department stores, hotel arcades and other tourist locations. The tax exemptions vary from 5 to 40 percent, and the items available include precious and semi-precious gems, pearls, electronic goods, watches and cameras. However, when the dollar is very strong against other major currencies you might find with consumer goods that there's not much difference between the prices of the special tax free items sold in Japan and the export models you'd be able to buy at home.

Currency. The Japanese currency is the yen. There are three kinds of bills — 1,000 yen, 5,000 yen, and 10,000 yen — and several kinds of coins — 1 yen, 5 yen, 10 yen, 50 yen, 100 yen, and 500 yen. Because 500 yen coins were only introduced recently replacing 500 yen bills, most vending machines do not accpet them.

Banks at Narita (New Tokyo International) Airport and Osaka International Airport are open from 9 a.m. till the arrival of the last flight. You can also convert your foreign currency into Japanese yen at banks, hotels and other established tourist facilities that display an "Authorized Money Exchanger" sign. There is no currency black market in Japan. The conversion rate is always a bit more advantageous at banks than at other locations. There are no restric-

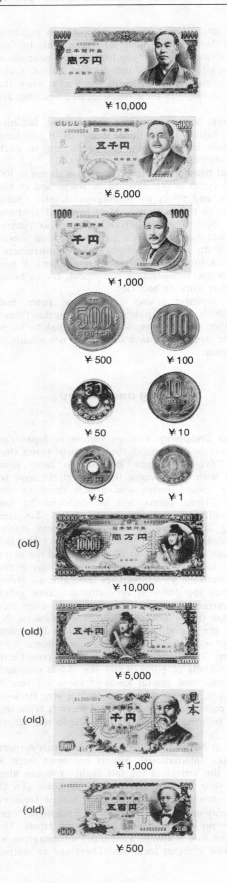

¥ 10,000

¥ 5,000

¥ 1,000

¥ 500   ¥ 100

¥ 50   ¥ 10

¥ 5   ¥ 1

(old)   ¥ 10,000

(old)   ¥ 5,000

(old)   ¥ 1,000

(old)   ¥ 500

tions on reconversion of unused yen to other international currencies. You can also take up to 5 million yen out of Japan. The Japanese yen fluctuates against other foreign currencies. In recent years, U.S. $1 has been worth something between 215 and 260 yen.

Credit Cards. Major credit cards, such as American Express, Master Card, Visa and Diners Club, are accepted at major tourist facilities, including hotels, restaurants and souvenir shops. Inexpensive facilities usually do not accept credit cards.

Travelers' Checks. Travelers' checks are accepted at established tourist facilities. However, inexpensive places which cater mainly to Japanese usually do not accept travelers' checks. You should exchange your travelers' checks for Japanese yen at banks.

Cash. Japan is still pretty much a cash society. Because it is safe to do so, people usually carry large amounts of cash, and most Japanese still prefer cash to credit cards.

Service Charge and Tax

Personal tipping is not customary in Japan. Instead of tipping, a 10-15% service charge is automatically added to your bill at most major restaurants and accommodations. However, many inexpensive restaurants do not add a service charge. Porters at airports and train stations (there are very few at most stations) work on a fee basis (200-300 yen per piece) rather than for tips.

If the charge at an accommodation is less than 5,000 yen per person per night, no tax is levied. If the charge is 5,000 yen or more, a 10% tax will be added to your bill. At restaurants, if your bill is 2,500 yen or more per person, a 10% tax is added. If you want to save money, don't charge your breakfast to your hotel bill. If you pay for your breakfast separately no tax will be levied (provided, of course, that the bill is less than 2,500 yen per person). If you charge your meal to your hotel bill and pay the entire amount when you check out, the total charge, which will include your breakfasts, will be subject to a 10% tax (except at Tokyo and Osaka hotels).

Water, Food and Drinks

Water. Tap water is safe everywhere in Japan.

Food. Food (even what's sold by street vendors) is also safe.

Drinks. A variety of soft drinks, including international and Japanese brands, are available, but diet soft drinks with saccharin are not allowed to be sold in Japan.

Major hotels have installed refrigerators in every room so that guests always have easy access to cold beer and soft drinks, but anything you take from one of these refrigerators will be very expensive. Inexpensive hotels usually have vending machines for soft drinks and beer in the lobby. Prices are tolerable, but still higher than prices in the stores. You might want to consider taking beverages out and bringing them to your room (see below). Alcoholic beverages are not unusually expensive, but this does not mean that they are cheap. If you drink alcohol regularly you should purchase some at an airport duty-free shop before you leave your own country. You can bring in up to three regular-sized bottles of any kind of alcoholic beverage duty free.

Take out. A variety of take out foods, canned soft drinks and alcoholic beverages are sold in the basements of department stores. If you feel like relaxing in your hotel room but don't want to spend the money for room service, you should buy food and beverages at these places. Many housewives shop for dinner for their families at these establishments, which have a wide selection at very inexpensive prices.

Morning Service. If you don't want a big breakfast at your hotel, find a coffee shop nearby. Most of them serve a "morning service" special for 350-500 yen. The special consists of coffee or tea, toast, a boiled egg, and a small salad or a piece of fruit.

Table Manners

As soon as you are seated at a restaurant or coffee shop you'll be presented with a hot towel (a cold one in summer). You can use the towel to clean your hands and wipe your face (Women should stop with the hands!). Napkins are not provided except at very expensive restaurants. At most restaurants, except those which specialize in Western food, disposable chopsticks, which are very clean because they are used just once, are provided; pull them apart at the top. If you ask for a knife, fork or spoon, don't be surprised if the restaurant doesn't have them. Don't eat your soup with a spoon. In Japan it's proper to "drink" your soup. Pick up the bowl and drink the broth; use your chopsticks for the contents. Don't be surprised if you hear Japanese slurping their soup or noodles (it's often quite loud!). Slurping is good manners in Japan, and demonstrates one's appreciation.

Useful Hints

Rest Rooms

In real emergencies you can always stop in a coffee shop and take a break. You'll probably find it well worth the 300-400 yen it will cost you for a cup of coffee or a soft drink. If you are in a city, department stores and hotels are good places to take refuge. All train stations have rest rooms but they are almost always dirty and are sometimes inside the ticket barriers (another advantage for holders of Japan Rail Passes, who have unlimited access to all JNR trains and platforms — for whatever the reason). Rest rooms in office buildings are not locked. I have indicated (with the letters "RR") a number of rest rooms along each suggested walking tour route. Public rest rooms are not clean, but will do in emergencies.

Hotels, department stores and fancy restaurants and coffee shops have Western-style toilets. But if you are traveling as the Japanese travel, you should expect to encounter a lot of Japanese-style toilets. Japanese style requires squatting rather than sitting. Actually, it's supposed to be better for you, and it's certainly cleaner. Once you get used to it you might find that you prefer Japanese style to Western style!

Baggage Handling

Trains in Japan are not equipped to accommodate the big bags popular with international travelers. Train stations in Japan are generally very large and have many staircases and underground passages connecting the various platforms and entrances/exits, but it's almost impossible to find a porter. It's torture trying to lug big bags through these huge, confusing and often very crowded stations. Plan a separate baggage transfer between major cities such as Tokyo and Kyoto. Even if you plan to travel extensively, consider arranging several side trips using Tokyo and Kyoto as your bases. There are more details in the Transportation and Suggested Itineraries Chapters below.

Traffic on the Left

Like the U.K., traffic on the left is the rule in Japan. Not only automobiles, but also trains and subways run on the left. Be careful when you're waiting for a train at a local station or for a bus on an empty street. If you don't think about it, you're likely to wait on the right-hand side facing your destination!

Japan has the largest number of cars per square foot in the world. Because of the heavy traffic many pedestrian bridges and underground passages have been constructed. Use these facilities and cross only at intersections. Don't jaywalk. Japanese obey traffic signals, and drivers usually aren't prepared for pedestrians who don't.

Why I Recommend That You Don't Drive in Japan

There are several reasons why I recommend that foreigners travel on the trains rather than by car. First of all, except on a few expressways, road signs are only in Japanese. If you can't read Japanese it is extremely difficult to drive in Japan. Secondly, many Japanese cities were laid out during the feudal era. For defensive purposes, the streets were arranged in complicated patterns. Even for Japanese it is not easy to get around in these cities by car. Thirdly, renting a car costs far more than taking trains. Even though car rentals themselves are not too expensive, gas costs about twice what it does in the U.S. and tolls are extremely expensive. For example, the one-way toll from Tokyo to Kyoto is 11,600 yen, which is almost the same amount as the Shinkansen fare for the same distance. The fourth reason is that trains are much faster than cars. For example, the Shinkansen takes a little less than three hours to make the trip from Tokyo to Kyoto, but driving the same distance usually takes eight hours, even on the expressway. Even if you have experience driving on the left and are able to manage manual shifts (which are standard on rental cars), it does not mean that you can drive in Japan enjoyably. Experiencing the efficiency and punctuality of public transportation while traveling in Japan should be, I believe, a part of your discovery of the country.

National Holidays

January 1 — New Year's Day (Only January 1 is a legal holiday, but government offices, corporations, museums and theaters are closed from December 29 through January 3).

January 15 — Adults' Day

February 11 — Founding of the Nation Day

March 21 — Vernal Equinox Day

April 29 — Emperor's Birthday

May 3 — Constitution Day

May 5 — Children's Day

Most Japanese take a long break at this time, bridging these three holidays with the weekends before or after them. As a result, the period from April 28 through May 6, called "Golden Week," is the period of the largest movement of people throughout the country.

September 15 — Respect for the Aged Day

September 23 — Autumn Equinox Day

October 10 — Health-Sports Day

November 3 — Culture Day

November 23 — Labor Thanksgiving Day

Business Hours

Department Stores are open from 10 a.m. to 6 p.m. (till 6:30 p.m. on Saturdays and Sundays). They are closed once a week on a weekday. Closing days differ from store to store, so in major cities at least one store is open on any given weekday.

Other Stores: Smaller stores are usually open from 10 a.m. to 8 p.m. (some are open till 10 p.m.). They usually close once a week or once every two weeks on a weekday.

Banks are open from 9 a.m. to 3 p.m. on weekdays and from 9 a.m. to 12 noon on Saturdays. They are closed on Sundays and on the second Saturday of each month. Banks at Narita (New Tokyo International) Airport and Osaka Airport are open from 9 a.m. till the arrival of the last flight.

Time Differences

All of Japan is in a single time zone. Japanese standard time is nine hours ahead of G.M.T., 14 hours ahead of New York, 15 hours ahead of Chicago and 17 hours ahead of Los Angeles. If it is 7 a.m. in New York it is 9 p.m. in Japan (plus 14 hours). If it is 4 p.m. in Los Angeles it is 9 a.m. the next day in Japan (plus 17 hours).

When you travel to Japan from the U.S. you lose one day (arriving in Japan the following day). When you return from Japan to the U.S. you gain one day (arriving in the U.S. on the same day — usually even before you left Japan!).

International Telephone Service

In major cities in Japan international telephone calls can be arranged at your hotel. Further information is available from KDD (International Telegram and Telephone Co.) at (03) 270-5111. When you call from Tokyo you don't have to use the (03) area code.

English Newspapers

Four English language newspapers are published — three in the morning and one in the evening. They are sold at newsstands in train stations and at major hotels. International news magazines (usually Asian editions) are also sold at major hotels and bookstores.

Massage Service at Accommodations

Japanese massseuses are renowned (justifiably) for their skill. Massages can be arranged at most accommodations — Western style hotels as well as Japanese inns. The charge is 2,000-3,000 yen for 30 minutes.

Guides and Hired Cars

If you plan to sightsee using a car and a guide, you'll have to hire a chauffeur-driven car and a guide separately, because these two services are completely separate in Japan. The standard charge for a tourist guide is 20,000-30,000 yen per day. You'll also have to pay for the guide's transportation. If you take a guide on an overnight trip, you'll also have to pay for the guide's accommodation and meals. The cost of a chauffeur-driven car varies from city to city. A typical rate is about 5,000-6,000 yen per hour. A guide and a hired car can be arranged for at your accommodations. You can also make arrangements through the Japan Guide Association. About 1,000 active licensed guides belong to the Association. The Association's telephone number in Tokyo is (03) 213-2706.

About Japanese

Japan's Roots

Archeological discoveries have confirmed that the Japanese archipelago was inhabited as long as 10,000 years ago. Contrary to the belief popular in Japan that the "Yamato race" is monotribal, recent studies indicate that the Japanese are a mixture of various Asian races, including Mongolians, Chinese, Koreans and Southeast Asians, who inhabited Japan before the archipelago split away from the continent. Even after the Japanese islands floated away from the continent, many Asian peoples, especially Koreans and Chinese, emigrated to Japan, adding new strains to Japanese native stock and creating the "Japanese" as they are today. Despite all the evidence to contrary, the myth that the Japanese are a monotribal people who conquered the uncivilized inhabitants of their islands still persists and is an important part of the view most Japanese have of themselves and of their nation. It was used to fan the flames of the nationalism that consumed Japan in the period between the Meiji Restoration and the end of World War II.

Japan is located only 110 miles (176 km.) from the Korean peninsula. Throughout its history, this proximity to the continent has enabled Japan to import advanced culture and technologies from various Asian countries, especially China. At the same time, the roughness of the Japan Sea and the primitive equipment and rudimentary navigational techniques of ancient times kept Japan relatively free from military and political interference by other countries. Japan created its own unique culture, based on the imports from the continent, adopting and "Japanizing" them, much as it has done in the modern era with its adoptions and modifications of Western cultures and technologies.

Religion

Japan's native religion is Shinto. Because it originated in the daily life of the people during the primitive era, all sorts of natural objects and phenomena were considered gods or the work of gods. A naturalistic religion, it does not involve belief in any specific creator and has no scriptures. After the Meiji Restoration (in 1868), Shinto was established as the national religion. The new government, organized in the name of the emperor, portrayed the Shinto gods as progenitors of the imperial family as a means of legitimating imperial authority. After World War II Shinto lost its official status.

Buddhism was introduced into Japan in the 6th century. It deeply influenced the philosophical life of the Japanese, introducing for the first time the belief in eternal life. Buddhism first spread among the aristocrats, and was used as the spiritual base of the unified nation. Zen is one of Buddhism's sects and was especially popular with the military classes. It emphasized serenity of mind and freedom from worldly desires, to be achieved not through the study of scripture, but rather through the practice of meditation. A number of Buddhist groups are active today, and most of them have, either formally or informally, a substantial influence on political affairs.

But neither Buddhism nor Shintoism has much real influence on the everyday life of today's Japanese. In Japan religion is usually regarded as merely the provider of social ceremonies. Ceremonies related to birth, maturation and marriage are usually performed according to Shinto rites, while those related to death utilize Buddhist rites: most Japanese do not think it at all strange to be involved with more than one religion at a time.

Christianity, introduced in the middle of the 16th century, but then banned during the period of Japan's isolation, was reintroduced after the Meiji Restoration. Despite great missionary efforts and the establishment by Christians of many useful social institutions, such as hospitals and schools, neither Catholicism nor Protestantism has attracted many followers. The total number of Christians is estimated to be 700,000 - 900,000.

Entrance Requirements, Airlines and Airport Transportation

Entrance Requirements

Visas

Citizens of the U.S. and Australia must obtain tourist visas to enter Japan (There is no charge for these visas). Canadians, New Zealanders and British subjects (except for those who obtained British passports in Hong Kong and other British Colonies) do not need visas. Citizens of other countries should check with the nearest Japanese Embassy or Consulate.

Customs

The following can be brought into Japan duty free:
— Up to three regular-sized bottles of alcoholic beverages.
— 20 packs of cigarettes (400 cigarettes), or 100 cigars, or 500 grams of pipe, powdered or chewing tobacco.
— Two ounces of perfume.
— In addition to the items listed above, souvenirs whose combined market value is less than 100,000 yen.

The following cannot be brought into Japan under any circumstances:
— Illegal drugs, including marihuana (Don't try it; you'll be in big trouble!). Properly labeled prescription drugs are OK.
— Pornographic books, pictures, films and other items.

Other Requirements

Vaccinations are not required unless you are visiting Japan after traveling in an affected area.

Security checks at Japanese airports are rather strict. You're likely to be frisked at the entrance gates to the departure wings.

There is no departure tax per se at Japanese airports. However, if you leave Japan from Narita (New Tokyo International) Airport, a 2,000 yen "airport utility charge" is levied.

Airlines

In addition to Japan Air Lines, the flag carriers of most nations serve Japan. From the United States, Pan American World Airways, Northwest Orient Airlines and United Airlines provide service between major American cities and Tokyo (Narita Airport).

Airport Transportation

NARITA AIRPORT (New Tokyo International Airport)

There are several means of public transportation between Narita Airport and the city of Tokyo:

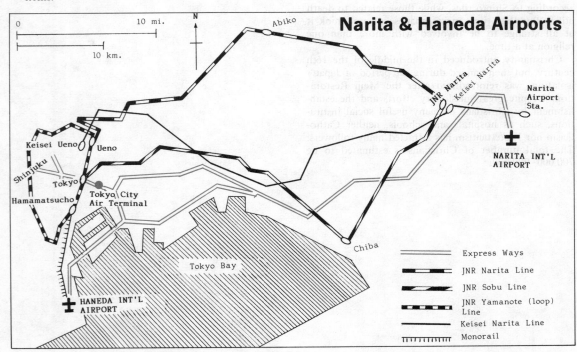

Narita & Haneda Airports

Legend:
- Express Ways
- JNR Narita Line
- JNR Sobu Line
- JNR Yamanote (loop) Line
- Keisei Narita Line
- Monorail

Map labels: Abiko, JNR Narita, Keisei Narita, Narita Airport Sta., NARITA INT'L AIRPORT, Keisei Ueno, Ueno, Shinjuku, Tokyo, Hamamatsucho, Tokyo City Air Terminal, Chiba, Tokyo Bay, HANEDA INT'L AIRPORT

Scale: 0 — 10 mi. / 10 km. N

Airport Limousine Bus

This is the most popular and the easiest way to get to Tokyo, especially when you have big suitcases. The Airport Limousine Bus information and ticketing counter is located in the arrivals lobby of the airport. You can't miss the counter because it has a huge orange English sign that you'll see as soon as you emerge from the Customs Hall. This company operates several bus routes as explained below. Depending on when you arrive, there might be direct service to major hotels in Tokyo. Check with the staff at the counter. The bus stop is right outside the lobby (Only about 100 feet from the ticket counter).

Between Narita Airport and Tokyo City Air Terminal (TCAT)

This is the main Airport Limousine Bus route. Buses operate two to eight times an hour, connecting with all flights. The ride takes 60-70 minutes, and the fare is 2,500 yen. From TCAT, most hotels are within a 1,000-2,000 yen taxi ride (10-20 minutes). At TCAT, the buses arrive on the third floor. Escalators take you down to the baggage claim area on the ground floor. Plenty of taxis are always waiting at the TCAT exit (again, 100 feet from the baggage claim area).

Between Narita Airport and Tokyo Station

A direct bus between the airport and Tokyo Station operates twice an hour from 2 p.m. to around 9:30 p.m. This service is especially convenient for those who are headed for other cities, such as Kyoto, by the Shinkansen. The ride takes 60-70 minutes, and the fare is 2,600 yen. Service from Tokyo Station to Narita Airport is available two or three times an hour from dawn to dusk. The bus stop at Tokyo station is pictured on Tokyo Map 9 (middle right).

Between Narita Airport and the Shinjuku District

There are direct buses three times an hour on this route, from 1 p.m. to 10 p.m. The buses stop at Shinjuku Station, the Keio Plaza Inter-Continental Hotel, the Century Hyatt Hotel and the Tokyo Hilton Hotel. The ride takes about 1 hour and forty minutes and the fare is 2,700 yen. Buses from the Shinjuku district (making the same stops) to Narita Airport run from early in the morning till late in the afternoon, about twice an hour (Some of these buses involve a transfer at TCAT).

Direct Buses Between Narita Airport and Major Hotels in Tokyo

In addition to the special service to the Shinjuku area hotels, there is also direct Airport Limousine Bus service to other major hotels in Tokyo. Most buses from the airport to the hotels operate in the early evening (from 4:30 p.m. to 9 p.m.), and their availability depends on your arrival time at Narita. Check at the counter. Several buses make the reverse trip from the major hotels to the airport, directly or via TCAT. Check with the hotel staff for times. The rides take 80-120 minutes, and the fare is 2,500-2,700 yen.

Between Narita Airport and Haneda Airport

Most domestic flights operate from Haneda Airport ("Old" Tokyo International Airport). The two airports (Narita and Haneda) are connected by Airport Limousine Bus service every 20-30 minutes, from morning till night. The ride takes 90 minutes and the fare is 2,700 yen.

Airport Express Bus

This second company (with a name frustratingly similar to the first) operates direct buses about once an hour to major hotels in Tokyo. It too has an information and ticketing counter with an English sign in the arrivals lobby at Narita Airport (not far from the Airport Limousine Bus counter). If you cannot find a convenient bus to your hotel with the Airport Limousine Bus service, check with this company for a direct bus to your hotel. If you can't find direct service with this company, you'll have to take the Airport Limousine Bus service to TCAT, or use one of the rail systems detailed below.

Keisei Line Skyliner Train

Keisei Electric Railway (private) operates limited express trains between Narita Airport Station and Ueno Station in Tokyo. The train is called Skyliner, and runs every 30 minutes. The ride takes exactly 61 minutes, and the fare is 1,490 yen, which includes a limited express reserved seat surcharge. The station is located in the airport grounds. Shuttle buses take you the short distance from the arrivals building to the station (170 yen). Stop at the Keisei Information Counter in the arrivals lobby if you decide to use this way of getting to Tokyo. Keisei is especially recommended for those staying in or near the Ueno area. Keisei Ueno Station is pictured on Tokyo Map 3 (middle center).

Japanese National Railways

JNR train service is less convenient than the other methods of transportation between the airport and Tokyo, and is recommended only for those who want to make maximum use of a Japan Rail Pass. JNR Narita Station is a 25-minute bus ride from Narita Airport. The connecting buses stop right outside the arrivals building—the shuttle bus fare is 370 yen, but it is covered by the Rail Pass (because the bus is a JNR bus). The Sobu Line runs between Narita Station and Tokyo Station, via Chiba. The Narita Line connects Narita with Ueno Station (via Abiko). Both trains operate about once an hour and both trips take about 80 minutes.

Taxis

Taxis are plentiful at Narita Airport, and the drivers are quite willing to take you the long distance to your hotel in Tokyo, but the ride costs about 20,000 yen.

HANEDA AIRPORT ("Old" Tokyo International Airport)
Limousine Bus between Haneda and Narita Airports

Explained above.

Monorail between Hamamatsucho and Haneda Airport

There is frequent monorail service between Haneda

Airport and Hamamatsucho Station in Tokyo. Because Hamamatsucho is located on the JNR Yamanote (Loop) Line, it can be reached easily from most hotels in Tokyo. The monorail ride takes only 15 minutes, and the fare is 270 yen.

Taxis

A taxi trip from Haneda Airport to any major Tokyo hotel will cost about 5,000 yen.

OSAKA AIRPORT
To and from Kyoto
Airport Bus from Osaka Airport to Kyoto

There is service three times an hour from early in the morning till late at night. The buses stop at major hotels in Kyoto and at the southern side of Kyoto Station. The ride takes 60-90 minutes, and the fare is 730-800 yen, depending on your destination.

Airport Bus from Kyoto to Osaka Airport

Buses operate at least once an hour from major hotels and from the southern side of Kyoto Station to the Airport. There is connecting service for all flights.

* Kyoto hotels served by the Airport Bus are:
Kyoto Hotel, Miyako Hotel, Kyoto Grand Hotel, International Hotel Kyoto, Kyoto Tokyu Hotel, and Hotel New Hankyu.

To and from Osaka

Because a taxi ride to major hotels in Osaka costs about only 4,000 yen, this is the most convenient and easiest method of transportation to Osaka. There is also frequent bus service to various points in the city of Osaka, including Osaka Station and Shin-Osaka Station (the Shinkansen station).

To and from Kobe
Airport But between Osaka Airport and Kobe (Sannomiya)

There is service three times an hour from dawn to dusk. The bus stop near Sannomiya station (the main train station in Kobe) is pictured on Kobe Map 2 (upper right). The ride takes 50 minutes and the fare is 600 yen.

Taxis

A taxi trip between Osaka Airport and major hotels in Kobe costs about 10,000 yen.

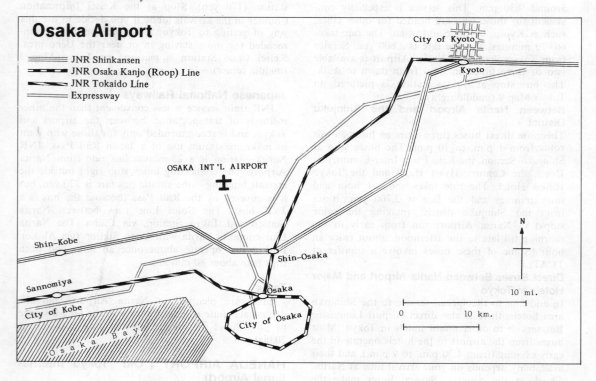

Osaka Airport

━━━ JNR Shinkansen
━━━ JNR Osaka Kanjo (Roop) Line
━━━ JNR Tokaido Line
━━━ Expressway

City of Kyoto

Kyoto

OSAKA INT'L AIRPORT

Shin-Kobe

Shin-Osaka

Sannomiya

Osaka

City of Kobe

City of Osaka

Osaka Bay

N

10 mi.

0   10 km.

Transportation within Japan

Some Advice — How to Use Japanese Common Sense

Trains are the most convenient and efficient method of travel in Japan. Most Japanese cities are conveniently linked by the Japanese National Railways (JNR) network. In the larger cities and major resort areas, private railways provide parallel and supplementary service.

All long distance trains (whether JNR or private) have reserved seats. To make your trip as comfortable as possible you should make reservations for the long distance trains as soon as you arrive in Japan. If you are not able to make reservations, don't worry because all long distance trains also have nonreserved cars, and you will usually be able to get a seat. The "Hikari" Shinkansen (bullet train) between Tokyo and Kyoto, for example, has 16 cars, five of which are nonreserved. On the slower "Kodama" Shinkansens on the same line, 9 of the 12 cars are nonreserved.

One nonreserved car and one reserved car on most long distance trains are nonsmoking cars. (The Shinkansen recently added two more non-smoking cars.) Smoking is prohibited on all short-distance and commuter trains.

Japanese trains are not designed to accommodate the large suitcases and bags that many international travelers use. Except in the Green Car (first class), there is no space for luggage other than on the overhead rack (though there is sometimes some space behind the last seat in a car). You can leave your big bags outside the door of the car. They will be safe (Japan really is as safe as all the promotional materials claim). If you feel uneasy, go to the door when the train stops at a station. This won't be too much of a bother because long distance trains only stop at major stations. Small and medium sized bags can be stored on the overhead racks.

If you want to travel light in Japan, you can easily arrange separate baggage delivery between hotels. It usually takes two days between major cities such as Tokyo, Nagoya, Kyoto, Osaka. It takes three days between smaller cities. In order to use this service it is important to have advance hotel reservations at your next destination. Separate delivery costs about 2,000-2,500 yen per bag, depending on the size of the bag and the distance involved.

When planning your itinerary, reduce the number of excursions on which you will have to travel with your large bags. For example, if you take the Tokyo — Kyoto — Inland Sea — Central Japan — Tokyo route, plan the trip as follows:

- Travel on the Shinkansen to Kyoto with your big bags (or arrange separate delivery).
- Then plan a two-night-three-day excursion to the Inland Sea area from Kyoto. You can check your large bags at your hotel in Kyoto, and just carry a smaller bag on the Inland Sea trip.
- Returning to Kyoto, plan another three-night-four-day excursion to the Central Japan area. Carry only a small bag, leaving your large bags at your hotel in Kyoto again.
- Return to Kyoto. After spending a few days in Kyoto and the Nara area, return to Tokyo with all your bags (or arrange for separate baggage delivery).

By arranging your trip this way, you move your large bags only twice, between Tokyo and Kyoto, while covering wide areas of interest. This is possible thanks to the extensive network of the ultra-fast Shinkansen and the Japan Rail Pass, which allows you unlimited train rides on all the trains in the JNR network.

During the following periods, trains are very crowded. Avoid them. When I say avoid, I mean it. These are major holiday periods, and most Japanese travel back to their original home towns for big family get-togethers. The inter-city trains at these times look something like the famous rush hour subways of Tokyo — the ones where professional pushers cram everyone into the car! Pick another time or stay in a major tourist destination such as Tokyo or Kyoto. Stay off the trains.

New Year's Holidays: December 28 — January 4
Golden Week: April 28 — May 6
Obon Period: August 12 — 18

Interior of an ordinary car on the Shinkansen. Note the capacity of the overhead rack.

JAPANESE NATIONAL RAILWAYS (JNR)

Types of JNR Trains

Shinkansen 新幹線

Popularly known as the bullet trains. Because all the English signs in the JNR stations refer to these as "Shinkansen" rather than "bullet train," I will use "Shinkansen" throughout this book when referring to this super express train. Only major cities have stations on the Shinkansen lines, in some cases separate from the stations for other lines, because the Shinkansen runs on its own special tracks.

There are now three Shinkansen lines operating in Japan:

West-bound from Tokyo (Tokaido & Sanyo Shinkansen 東海道・山陽新幹線)

This Shinkansen runs between Tokyo and Hakata (Fukuoka) via such major cities as Nagoya, Kyoto, Osaka, Kobe and Hiroshima. Most foreigners have this line in mind when they refer to the Shinkansen. In this book, when I refer to "the" Shinkansen, this is the line I mean.

North-bound from Ueno (Tohoku Shinkansen 東北新幹線)

This line connects Tokyo's Ueno Station with Morioka via Utsunomiya, Sendai, Ichinoseki, etc. I recommend this train for visits to Nikko and the Tohoku area (Sendai, Hiraizumi and Matsushima), and will refer to it as the Tohoku Shinkansen.

Japan Sea-bound from Ueno (Joetsu Shinkansen 上越新幹線)

This train runs from Tokyo's Ueno Station to Niigata on the Japan Sea Coast, via Minakami, etc. Because there is no major tourist destination along this line, I won't make any further reference to it.

Limited Express Trains 特急 and Express Trains 急行

These are the long distance trains that operate on regular tracks. A limited express makes fewer stops than an express. The extra charges are higher for a limited express than for an express, but the surcharge for a limited express is cheaper than that for a Shinkansen.

Local Trains 普通電車

Local trains operate over comparatively short distances and serve the everyday needs of the people. These trains are convenient for traveling around in the larger cities, or for making side trips from these larger cities. Only a basic fare is required on this type of train.

The fact that there are four types of train service does not mean that you can take any type of train for any trip. You should decide which type of train is best, depending on your destination and the time you have for the trip. When recommending itineraries, I have selected the most convenient trains, taking into consideration comfort, ease and speed as well as economy.

Classes of Service

There are two classes of service, first class and coach class, on Shinkansen trains, limited express trains, most express trains, and some local trains. There's an extra charge for the Green Car (the name JNR gives its first class cars).

Sleeping berth service is available on some long distance night trains, but I have not included any of these trains in this book. The berths are not big enough for most foreigners, and sleeping berth charges are not covered by the Japan Rail Pass.

The distinctive Green Car (First Class) symbol, here on the Shinkansen.

Fare Systems

Because there are four types of trains and two classes of service, calculating total train fares is pretty complicated. For example, if you use the Green Car on a limited express train, you have to pay:

— the basic fare;

— a limited express surcharge; and

— a Green Car surcharge.

Don't worry. I have calculated total fares for all the long distance train rides I have suggested in this guidebook and included them in the applicable sections.

How to Purchase and Use Tickets

If you are using a Japan Rail Pass, skip this section and proceed to the next section, Japan Rail Pass.

Reserved Seats

You can make reservations and purchase tickets at a JNR station. However, there are no English-speaking clerks at the ticket windows except in a few of the largest stations. Conversation Card 4 will help you manage in this situation. In large JNR stations there are special "Reservation Tickets" offices that are recognizable by their green signs. In these stations the regular ticket windows handle only nonreserved seat tickets. If the station does not have a green ticket office, you can purchase both reserved seat tickets and nonreserved seat tickets at the regular ticket windows.

Some of the travel agencies located in major hotels handle JNR tickets. Because these agency offices usually have English-speaking clerks, it will probably be more convenient to use them.

Reserved tickets office at a JNR station.

Nonreserved seats for longer distance trains

Purchase tickets at regular ticket windows in the stations.

Commuter train tickets

Because the fares are low, these tickets are usually sold in vending machines. Fares, which vary with the distance traveled, are usually listed only in Japanese (There are only a few English fare tables in all of Japan). If you can't figure out the fare, write the name of your destination on Conversation Card 2 and show it to a Japanese passerby.

JNR ticket vending machines.

Ticket Check

When you go through the entrance gate, your ticket will be punched. Keep the ticket with you. On long distance trains a conductor usually checks tickets, but they are usually not checked on commuter trains. All tickets have to be returned to the employee at the exit gate when you reach your destination.

Japan Rail Pass

For foreign visitors to Japan, the Japanese National Railways has made available the specially discounted Japan Rail Pass. The Pass entitles the bearer to unlimited travel on the entire JNR rail, bus and boat system.

Eligibility

A Japan Rail Pass voucher can be purchased by any foreign tourist visiting Japan on a tourist visa or a transit visa (Sorry, holders of business visas cannot use Japan Rail Passes). A Japan Rail Pass cannot be purchased in Japan. The Pass (actually a voucher which you exchange for a pass once you arrive in Japan) must be obtained before you leave for Japan.

Types of Japan Rail Passes and Prices

There are two types of Japan Rail Passes — ordinary car (coach class) and Green Car (first class). One week, two week and three week passes are available as follows:

Type	Seven Days	14 Days	21 Days
Ordinary Car	27,000 yen	43,000 yen	55,000 yen
Green Car	37,000 yen	60,000 yen	78,000 yen

How to Purchase a Japan Rail Pass

A voucher for a Japan Rail Pass can be purchased from your travel agent.

Exchanging Your Voucher for a Pass

Upon arrival in Japan, you can exchange your voucher for your Pass at any of the following JNR stations:

Tokyo, Yokohama, Nagoya, Kyoto, Osaka, Hiroshima, Hakata, Kumamoto, Nishi-Kagoshima, Niigata, Sendai, and Sapporo.

The offices are open from 10 a.m. to 6 p.m. If you land in Japan at Narita Airport, however, I definitely recommend that you change your voucher for your pass at the JNR counter right in the airport arrivals lobby. The JNR counter, which is open from 7 a.m. to 11 p.m. daily, is located on the concourse just outside the Customs Hall. When you exchange your voucher you can specify the date on which you'd like your one, two or three week pass to start running.

Seat Reservations

The Japan Rail Pass entitles its holder to make seat reservations for ordinary cars or Green Cars depending on the type of Pass. Plan your long distance train rides in advance and request reservations at the time you exchange your voucher (There's no additional charge for reservations). If you change your schedule while you are traveling, you can change your reservations at any of the major JNR stations, or just abandon your reserved seat and take a nonreserved seat on another train. Sleeping berths (all reserved) are not covered by the Japan Rail Pass. An additional surcharge will be collected if you request a sleeping berth reservation.

Details of the Shinkansen

The world famous Shinkansen bullet train runs west from Tokyo, connecting the major cities of Nagoya, Kyoto, Osaka, Kobe, Hiroshima and Hakata (Fukuoka) with the capital. There are two types of Shinkansens — one is called Hikari ("Light") and makes fewer stops than the Kodama ("Echo"), which stops at all stations on the Shinkansen line. Because only major cities have stations on the Shinkansen line, and because this super express runs on its own special tracks, even the Kodama is much faster than other JNR trains which run on regular lines. There are several different types of Hikaris depending on the number of station stops made. As the Shinkansen trains approach stations, an announcement is made in both Japanese and English. A detailed timetable for the Shinkansen is listed on the following pages.

The following are some useful tips for when you take the Shinkansen:

Arrangement of the Cars
Hikari

The Hikari Shinkansen consists of 16 cars. Car No. 1 is in the front when the train is traveling west (from Tokyo toward Kyoto and Hakata), and Car No. 16 is in the front on the trip east. Cars No. 1 through No. 5 have nonreserved seats (No. 1 and No. 2 are nonsmoking), Car No. 8 is the dining car, Cars No. 11 and 12 are Green Cars (No. 12 is nonsmoking) and the rest of the cars (No. 6 and No. 7, No. 9 and No. 10, and No. 13 through No. 16) are ordinary reserved cars (No. 10 is nonsmoking).

Kodama

The Kodama Shinkansen operates between Tokyo and Osaka, and Osaka and Hakata (Fukuoka). There is no through Kodama service to Hakata. Most Kodama Shinkansens consist of 12 cars. No. 1 is in the lead when the train is headed west, and No. 12 is in the front when the train goes east. Cars No.1 through No. 7 and cars No. 11 and No. 12 have nonreserved seats (No. 1 and No. 2 are nonsmoking cars, and half of No. 9 is a buffet car). Car No. 8 is the Green Car (nonsmoking), and Cars No. 9 and No. 10 have ordinary reserved seats (No. 10 is nonsmoking).

Finding Your Seat

If you have made a seat reservation, you will have a ticket that lists your car and seat number, e.g., Car 13, Seat 17A. Shinkansen platforms have signs — either written directly on the platform floor or on plastic signs hung from the ceiling — that show where each car will be when the train stops (Yes, it is that precise). The signs will help you to get on and find your seat with no trouble at all.

Catering Service

In addition to the dining or buffet car, there are vendors on every train who walk up and down the aisles with baskets or wagons (Keep your legs out of the aisle!). You can buy sandwiches, box lunches, coffee, soft drinks, Japanese tea, beer, whisky, and even local souvenirs from these vendors.

Rest Rooms

Almost every other car has a rest room.

Wise Use of the Kodama

It's useful to remember that the Kodama is always less crowded than the Hikari. So, if you are traveling from Kyoto to Tokyo without reservations and see long lines of people waiting for the nonreserved cars on the Hikari platform, move to the Kodama platform. You'll be sure to get a seat on the next Kodama, because the Kodama has nine nonreserved cars, as compared to five on the Hikari. The traveling time from Kyoto to Tokyo is only one hour longer — three hours by Hikari and four hours by Kodama. Also, because the Kodama is less crowded than the Hikari, there'll be more room on the Kodama for any big suitcases you might have with you. (This tip on the wise use of the Kodama actually originated with a friend who works for JNR).

The schedule and the fares of the Shinkansen follow. (Note: All Shinkansen stations are listed on Shinkansen Station Map, but only those relevant to the tourist destinations presented in this text are included in this schedule.).

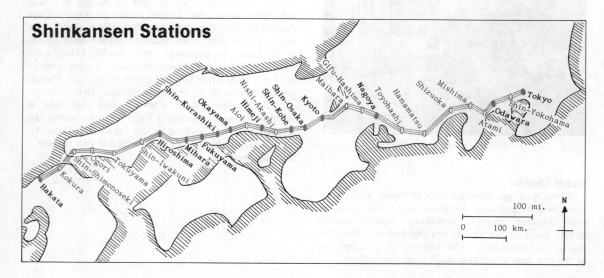

Shinkansen Stations

Shinkansen Fares

(upper fare : coach class,   lower fare : first class)

From \ TO	東京 Tokyo	小田原 Odawara	名古屋 Nagoya	京都 Kyoto	新大阪 Shin-Osaka	新神戸 Shin-Kobe	姫路 Himeji	岡山 Okayama	新倉敷 Shin-Kurashiki	福山 Fukuyama	三原 Mihara	広島 Hiroshima	博多 Hakata
東京 Tokyo	—	3,310 4,610	9,500 13,700	12,100 17,500	12,600 18,000	13,100 18,500	14,000 20,600	15,100 21,700	15,100 21,700	15,300 21,900	16,100 23,900	16,600 24,400	20,000 27,800
小田原 Odawara	3,310 4,610	—	7,800 12,000	11,100 16,500	11,400 16,800	12,100 17,500	12,900 18,300	14,000 20,600	14,000 20,600	14,800 21,400	15,100 21,700	16,100 23,900	19,000 26,800
名古屋 Nagoya	9,500 13,700	7,800 12,000	—	4,900 7,700	5,500 8,300	6,900 11,100	7,500 11,700	9,500 13,700	9,800 14,000	10,900 16,300	11,100 16,500	12,400 17,800	16,100 23,900
京都 Kyoto	12,100 17,500	11,100 16,500	4,900 7,700	—	1,310 3,310	2,870 4,170	4,600 7,400	6,600 10,800	7,200 11,400	7,500 11,700	8,800 13,000	9,800 14,000	14,000 20,600
新大阪 Shin-Osaka	12,600 18,000	11,400 16,800	5,500 8,300	1,310 3,310	—	1,370 3,370	3,310 4,610	5,200 8,000	6,600 10,800	6,900 11,100	7,500 11,700	9,100 13,300	13,800 20,400
新神戸 Shin-Kobe	13,100 18,500	12,100 17,500	6,900 11,100	2,870 4,170	1,370 3,370	—	2,850 4,150	4,900 7,700	5,200 8,000	6,600 10,800	6,900 11,100	8,800 13,000	13,100 18,500
姫路 Himeji	14,000 20,600	12,900 18,300	7,500 11,700	4,600 7,400	3,310 4,610	2,850 4,150	—	3,310 4,610	4,300 7,100	4,900 7,700	5,200 8,000	7,200 11,400	12,400 17,800
岡山 Okayama	15,100 21,700	14,000 20,600	9,500 13,700	6,600 10,800	5,200 8,000	4,900 7,700	3,310 4,610	—	1,230 3,230	2,850 4,150	3,310 4,610	5,200 8,000	11,100 16,500
新倉敷 Shin-Kurashiki	15,100 21,700	14,000 20,600	9,800 14,000	7,200 11,400	6,600 10,800	5,200 8,000	4,300 7,100	1,230 3,230	—	1,310 3,310	3,000 4,300	4,600 7,400	10,900 16,300
福山 Fukuyama	15,300 21,900	14,800 21,400	10,900 16,300	7,500 11,700	6,900 11,100	6,600 10,800	4,900 7,700	2,850 4,150	1,310 3,310	—	1,310 3,310	4,300 7,100	9,800 14,000
三原 Mihara	16,100 23,900	15,100 21,700	11,100 16,500	8,800 13,000	7,500 11,700	6,900 11,100	5,200 8,000	3,310 4,610	3,000 4,300	1,310 3,310	—	1,950 3,950	9,300 13,500
広島 Hiroshima	16,600 24,400	16,100 23,900	12,400 17,800	9,800 14,000	9,100 13,300	8,800 13,000	7,200 11,400	5,200 8,000	4,600 7,400	4,300 7,100	1,950 3,950	—	7,800 12,000
博多 Hakata	20,000 27,800	19,000 26,800	16,100 23,900	14,000 20,600	13,800 20,400	13,100 18,500	12,400 17,800	11,100 16,500	10,900 16,300	9,800 14,000	9,300 13,500	7,800 12,000	—

West-bound Shinkansens

(A : a.m.　N : noon　P : p.m.)

Train Name	Tokyo 東京	Odawara 小田原	Nagoya 名古屋	Kyoto 京都	Shin-Osaka 新大阪	Shin-Kobe 新神戸	Himeji 姫路	Okayama 岡山	Shin-Kurashiki 新倉敷	Fukuyama 福山	Mihara 三原	Hiroshima 広島	Hakata 博多
Hikari-71	×	×	×	×	6:00A	6:16A	→	7:01A	7:15A	→	7:38A	8:02A	9:40A
Hikari-81	×	×	×	×	7:00A	7:16A	→	8:01A	→	8:24A	→	8:57A	10:30A
Hikari-91	×	×	6:53A	7:46A	8:03A	8:21A	→	9:06A	→	→	→	9:57A	11:31A
Hikari-93	×	×	7:43A	8:36A	8:53A	9:11A	→	9:56A	→	→	→	10:47A	12:22P
Hikari-21	6:00A	→	8:01A	8:51A	9:08A	→	→	10:06A	→	→	→	10:57A	12:31P
Kodama-527	×	×	×	×	9:02A	9:17A	9:46A	10:18A	10:32A	10:46A	11:00A	11:23A	1:11P
Hikari-151	6:13A	6:52A	8:23A	9:13A	9:30A	9:47A	10:09A	10:38A	→	11:01A	→	11:33A	×
Hikari-1	7:00A	→	9:01A	9:51A	10:08A	→	→	11:06A	→	→	→	11:57A	1:26P
Kodama-407	7:21A	8:03A	10:05A	11:07A	11:26A	×	×	×	×	×	×	×	×
Kodama-531	×	×	×	×	11:02A	11:17A	11:46A	12:18P	12:32P	12:46P	1:00P	1:23P	3:11P
Hikari-3	8:00A	→	10:01A	10:51A	11:08A	→	→	12:06P	→	→	→	12:57P	2:26P
Kodama-411	8:21A	9:03A	11:05A	12:07P	12:26P	×	×	×	×	×	×	×	×
Hikari-201	8:47A	→	10:53A	11:43A	12:00N	12:17P	12:46P	1:18P	1:32P	1:46P	2:00P	2:24P	4:11P
Hikari-23	9:00A	→	11:01A	11:51A	12:08P	→	→	1:06P	→	→	→	1:57P	3:31P
Kodama-417	9:21A	10:03A	12:05P	1:07P	1:26P	×	×	×	×	×	×	×	×
Hikari-341	9:30A	→	11:39A	12:29P	12:46P	×	×	×	×	×	×	×	×
Kodama-419	9:51A	10:34A	12:31P	1:37P	1:56P	×	×	×	×	×	×	×	×
Hikari-5	10:00A	→	12:01P	12:51P	1:08P	→	→	2:06P	→	→	→	2:57P	4:26P
Kodama-533	×	×	×	×	1:02P	1:17P	1:46P	2:18P	2:32P	2:46P	3:00P	3:23P	5:11P
Hikari-245	10:17A	→	12:23P	1:13P	1:30P	1:47P	2:13P	2:46P	2:59P	3:13P	3:27P	3:51P	×
Kodama-421	10:21A	11:03A	1:05P	2:07P	2:26P	×	×	×	×	×	×	×	×
Hikari-7	11:00A	→	1:01P	1:51P	2:08P	→	→	3:06P	→	→	→	3:57P	5:26P
Kodama-425	11:21A	12:03P	2:05P	3:07P	3:26P	×	×	×	×	×	×	×	×
Hikari-25	12:00N	→	2:01P	2:51P	3:08P	→	→	4:06P	→	→	→	4:57P	6:31P
Hikari-205	12:47P	→	2:53P	3:43P	4:00P	4:17P	4:46P	5:18P	5:32P	5:46P	6:00P	6:24P	8:11P
Hikari-9	1:00P	→	3:01P	3:51P	4:08P	→	→	5:06P	→	→	→	5:57P	7:26P
Kodama-437	1:21P	2:03P	4:05P	5:07P	5:26P	×	×	×	×	×	×	×	×
Hikari-27	2:00P	→	4:01P	4:51P	5:08P	→	→	6:06P	→	→	→	6:57P	8:31P
Hikari-249	2:12P	→	4:23P	5:13P	5:30P	5:47P	6:13P	6:46P	6:59P	7:13P	7:27P	7:51P	×
Kodama-441	2:21P	3:03P	5:05P	6:07P	6:26P	×	×	×	×	×	×	×	×
Hikari-11	3:00P	→	5:01P	5:51P	6:08P	→	→	7:06P	→	→	→	7:57P	9:26P
Hikari-251	3:12P	3:52P	5:23P	6:13P	6:30P	6:47P	7:13P	7:46P	7:59P	8:13P	8:27P	8:51P	×
Kodama-449	3:51P	4:34P	6:31P	7:37P	7:56P	×	×	×	×	×	×	×	×
Hikari-107	4:00P	→	6:01P	6:51P	7:08P	7:25P	7:47P	8:16P	→	8:40P	→	9:17P	11:06P
Kodama-451	4:21P	5:03P	7:05P	8:04P	8:21P	×	×	×	×	×	×	×	×
Hikari-29	5:00P	→	7:01P	7:51P	8:08P	→	→	9:06P	→	→	→	9:57P	11:31P
Kodama-455	5:21P	6:03P	8:05P	9:07P	9:26P	×	×	×	×	×	×	×	×
Hikari-257	6:00P	→	8:01P	8:51P	9:08P	9:25P	9:51P	10:24P	10:37P	10:51P	11:05P	11:29P	×
Hikari-41	6:42P	→	8:43P	9:33P	9:50P	→	→	10:49P	→	→	→	11:40P	×
Hikari-367	7:30P	→	9:39P	10:29P	10:46P	×	×	×	×	×	×	×	×
Hikari-313	8:30P	→	10:36P	11:26P	11:43P	×	×	×	×	×	×	×	×

I have selected the Shinkansens most convenient for tourists and listed them above.

East-bound Shinkansens

(A : a.m.   N : noon   P : p.m.)

Train Name	Hakata 博多	Hiroshima 広島	Mihara 三原	Fukuyama 福山	Shin-Kurashiki 新倉敷	Okayama 岡山	Himeji 姫路	Shin-Kobe 新神戸	Shin-Osaka 新大阪	Kyoto 京都	Nagoya 名古屋	Odawara 小田原	Tokyo 東京
Hikari-310	×	×	×	×	×	×	×	×	6:46A	7:04A	7:51A	→	9:59A
Hikari-260	×	×	×	×	×	6:00A	6:33A	6:58A	7:14A	7:34A	8:21A	9:53A	10:34A
Hikari-262	×	×	×	×	×	6:30A	7:03A	7:28A	7:44A	8:04A	8:51A	→	11:04A
Kodama-406	×	×	×	×	×	×	×	×	8:20A	8:39A	9:43A	11:44A	12:25P
Hikari-240	×	6:04A	6:28A	6:42A	6:57A	7:09A	7:43A	8:08A	8:24A	8:44A	9:31A	→	11:34A
Hikari-40	×	7:06A	→	→	→	7:55A	→	→	8:54A	9:14A	10:01A	→	12:04P
Kodama-412	×	×	×	×	×	×	×	×	9:20A	9:39A	10:43A	12:44P	1:25P
Hikari-244	×	7:22A	7:46A	8:00A	8:18A	8:30A	9:03A	9:29A	9:44A	10:04A	10:51A	→	12:59P
Kodama-420	×	×	×	×	×	×	×	×	10:20A	10:39A	11:43A	1:44P	2:25P
Hikari-200	6:32A	8:20A	8:45A	8:59A	9:14A	9:26A	10:00A	10:28A	10:44A	11:04A	11:51A	→	1:59P
Hikari-22	7:45A	9:18A	→	→	→	10:09A	→	→	11:06A	11:26A	12:13P	→	2:16P
Kodama-424	×	×	×	×	×	×	×	×	11:20A	11:39A	12:43P	2:44P	3:25P
Hikari-272	×	×	×	×	×	10:26A	10:59A	11:24A	11:40A	12:00N	12:51P	→	2:59P
Hikari-202	8:02A	9:50A	10:15A	10:29A	10:44A	10:56A	11:30A	11:58A	12:14P	12:34P	1:21P	→	3:29P
Hikari-2	8:50A	10:18A	→	→	→	11:09A	→	→	12:06P	12:26P	1:13P	→	3:16P
Kodama-428	×	×	×	×	×	×	×	×	12:20P	12:39P	1:43P	3:44P	4:25P
Hikari-266	×	×	×	×	×	11:30A	12:08P	12:28P	12:44P	1:04P	1:51P	→	3:59P
Kodama-524	9:02A	10:50A	11:15A	11:29A	11:44A	11:56A	12:30P	12:58P	1:16P	×	×	×	×
Hikari-4	9:50A	11:18A	→	→	→	12:09P	→	→	1:06P	1:26P	2:13P	→	4:16P
Kodama-434	×	×	×	×	×	×	×	×	1:20P	1:39P	2:43P	4:44P	5:25P
Hikari-248	×	11:24A	11:48A	12:02P	12:17P	12:29P	1:03P	1:28P	1:44P	2:04P	2:51P	→	4:59P
Hikari-24	10:45A	12:18P	→	→	→	1:09P	→	→	2:06P	2:26P	3:13P	→	5:16P
Kodama-438	×	×	×	×	×	×	×	×	2:20P	2:39P	3:43P	5:44P	6:25P
Hikari-250	×	12:24P	12:48P	1:02P	1:17P	1:29P	2:03P	2:28P	2:44P	3:04P	3:51P	→	5:59P
Hikari-6	11:50A	1:18P	→	→	→	2:09P	→	→	3:06P	3:26P	4:13P	→	6:16P
Kodama-444	×	×	×	×	×	×	×	×	3:20P	3:39P	4:43P	6:44P	7:25P
Hikari-252	×	1:24P	1:48P	2:02P	2:17P	2:29P	3:03P	3:28P	3:44P	4:04P	4:51P	→	6:59P
Kodama-446	×	×	×	×	×	×	×	×	3:50P	4:09P	5:09P	7:14P	7:55P
Hikari-206	12:02P	1:50P	2:15P	2:29P	2:44P	2:56P	3:30P	3:58P	4:14P	4:34P	5:21P	→	7:29P
Hikari-8	12:50P	2:18P	→	→	→	3:09P	→	→	4:06P	4:26P	5:13P	→	7:16P
Hikari-254	×	2:24P	2:48P	3:02P	3:17P	3:29P	4:03P	4:28P	4:44P	5:04P	5:51P	→	7:59P
Hikari-26	1:45P	3:18P	→	→	→	4:09P	→	→	5:06P	5:26P	6:13P	→	8:16P
Hikari-256	×	3:24P	3:48P	4:02P	4:17P	4:29P	5:03P	5:28P	5:44P	6:04P	6:51P	→	8:59P
Hikari-208	2:02P	3:50P	4:15P	4:29P	4:44P	4:56P	5:30P	5:58P	6:14P	6:34P	7:21P	→	9:29P
Hikari-10	2:50P	4:18P	→	→	→	5:09P	→	→	6:06P	6:26P	7:13P	→	9:16P
Hikari-274	×	×	×	×	×	5:26P	5:59P	6:24P	6:40P	7:00P	7:51P	→	9:59P
Kodama-530	3:02P	4:50P	5:15P	5:29P	5:44P	5:56P	6:30P	6:58P	7:14P	×	×	×	×
Hikari-28	3:45P	5:18P	→	→	→	6:09P	→	→	7:06P	7:26P	8:13P	→	10:16P
Hikari-258	×	5:24P	5:48P	6:02P	6:17P	6:29P	7:03P	7:28P	7:44P	8:04P	8:51P	→	10:59P
Hikari-30	4:45P	6:18P	→	→	→	7:09P	→	→	8:06P	8:26P	9:13P	→	11:16P
Hikari-92	5:45P	7:18P	→	→	→	8:09P	→	8:55P	9:10P	9:30P	10:22P	×	×

An arrow in the column indicates that the Shinkansen does not stop at the station.

PRIVATE RAILWAYS

Private railways usually operate commuter trains in large cities and deluxe tourist trains from large cities to nearby resorts. In this guide I have introduced them when I believe they are more convenient than the JNR (Even in these situations I have also introduced parallel JNR service, if it exists, for the information of Japan Rail Pass holders). As with JNR, most commuter train tickets are sold in vending machines. Use Conversation Card 2 when you purchase tickets.

SUBWAYS

There are subways in Tokyo, Nagoya, Kyoto, Osaka, Hakata, and Yokohama (The Yokohama subway is not introduced in this guide because it is not at all useful for tourists). Tickets are sold in vending machines (To my surprise, all subway stations in Nagoya, which is not known as Japan's most cosmopolitan city, have at least one fare board in English). Except in Tokyo, subway stations are equipped with automatic entrance and exit gates like those in San Francisco and Washington, D.C. At the entrance, you have to insert your magnetized ticket in the slot at the front of the gate. The ticket is checked magnetically and the bar across the entrance retracts if the ticket is valid. Pick up your ticket from the slot at the rear of the gate. At your destination, you again insert your ticket into the machine. You can then exit, but the ticket does not come out this time. If the ticket you bought was for less that the required amount, an alarm bell sounds and a puzzled station clerk will arrive on the scene to settle the difference with you. Tokyo subways work like the trains. Have your ticket punched when you enter, make sure that you hold on to it, and turn it in when you exit. During rush hours (8 a.m. to 9:30 a.m.; 5 p.m. to 6:30 p.m.) Tokyo subways really are as horribly crowded as everyone says. It's probably best to avoid them then.

BUSES AND STREETCARS

Buses are especially important means of public transportation in Kyoto and Nara. Streetcars provide tourists with convenient and inexpensive transportation in Hiroshima, Kumamoto and Nagasaki. This book provides detailed information in the city sections on the bus networks and streetcar systems, and their fare collection systems. Don't hail taxis as a matter of course. Follow my suggestions and you will not only save money but also have many additional experiences available only when you travel as the Japanese travel.

TAXIS

Taxis are plentiful all over Japan. If you follow the suggestions in this book, you'll probably only need to use them when transferring your big suitcases from train stations to hotels. Empty taxis can be recognized by the red light in front of their windshields. Fares vary slightly from city to city. The average basic fare is 470 yen for the first 1.25 miles (2 km.), and 80 yen for each additional quarter mile (about 0.4 km.). There is a 20% surcharge added from 11 p.m. to 5 a.m. The maximum number of passengers is four. Taxi trunks can only accommodate two large suitcases. The left-hand side rear doors on all taxis are operated by the driver. When a taxi stops for you, wait for the door to open, and once you're inside wait for it to be closed. Keep your hands to yourself or you'll find your fingers closed inside the door! When you arrive at your destination, pay the exact amount shown on the meter (no tipping) and wait again for the door to open. When you get out you should just walk away (Don't worry about the door).

Accommodations

INTRODUCTION
Background

In 1949, the Japanese Diet passed a special law to encourage construction of high quality accommodations suitable for foreign guests. The law provided for low cost government loans to those who constructed hotels or ryokans (Japanese inns) which met official standards. Since then many facilities have benefited from this law. The number of government-registered hotels increased from 30 in 1950 to 464, and registered ryokans increased from 2 to 1,654. Hotel and ryokan operators have organized the Japan Hotel Association and the Japan Ryokan Association. Most member hotels have 300-1,000 rooms, and member ryokans generally have 15-50 rooms. The two associations represent Japan's top accommodations. The 1949 law was a manifest success.

The story, however, is unfortunately not so simple. Most of these accommodations, eager for the prestige and the profits connected with an international clientele, tried to extend their best courtesy to foreign guests. Many had good experiences and are still working to develop their international reputations. But others were discouraged by the inevitable problems — language barriers, differences in customs, no-shows, etc. — and gradually grew reluctant to accept foreign guests. Some just decided that it was less trouble and more profitable to cater to Japanese guests. So today, although membership in the Hotel or Ryokan Association usually indicates that the facilities are of good quality, it does not necessarily indicate a willingness to accept foreign guests.

Since this is the case, simply listing all the members of these Associations is at best meaningless, and at worst confusing. Instead, I have selected appropriate facilities and listed them at the end of each city/resort section. All of the facilities listed in this book are willing to accept foreign guests. Each listing includes price information, and the figure quoted includes service charges and tax. Most listings of hotel and ryokan rates do not include these charges, but all accommodations add them to your bill automatically. Hotels add a 10% service charge and ryokans add 10-15%, and the Japanese government, like most, is quite conscientious about collecting its additional 10% in tax. Because the prices quoted in this book include these additional charges, you'll be able to get a much more realistic idea of what accommodations will cost you. If you're interested, listings of members of the Hotel and Ryokan Associations are available from Japan National Tourist Organization.

Reservations

There are about 90,000 accommodations facilities of various types throughout Japan, ranging from five-room minshuku (small family-run inns) to giant first class hotels with more than 2,000 rooms. They are pretty crowded, especially during the tourist seasons in spring (from the middle of March to the end of May), in summer (from the middle of July to the end of August), and in autumn (October and November). Most hotels in large cities have high (more than 90%) occupancy rates throughout the year. Occupancy rates at accommodations in smaller cities and resorts fluctuate from 60-100%. If you are traveling during the busy seasons, I definitely recommend that you make reservations well in advance. Even in other cities, if you travel in Japan for less than 2-3 weeks, it is advisable to make reservations in advance.

The following are some tips:

It is possible to travel in Japan without reservations. Hotel and ryokan reservation offices are located in major train stations. Though the clerks probably won't speak English, they should be able to help you find an accommodation for the night. Needless to say, conveniently located, reasonable accommodations sell first. If you try to make reservations at the last minute, especially during the busy seasons, you may end up staying at a rather expensive accommodation or one that is inconveniently located. This is why I recommend that you make reservations in advance. Moreover, if you have reservations you won't have to worry about arriving at your destination early in the day. With reservations you'll be able to make the best use possible of your precious time in Japan. I have seen many foreign tourists in Japan whose main purpose each day seemed to be visiting the reservations office in the train station to find a place to stay for the night. "Keep your itinerary flexible" sounds like good advice, but doing so is not necessarily enjoyable. Careful advance planning is especially important when you are traveling extensively in a limited time period. Otherwise, you'll waste valuable sightseeing and leisure time trying to find places to stay.

Selecting Accommodations

When selecting accommodations, you should pay attention not only to the rates but also to the locations. Otherwise, even if you can find inexpensive accommodations, you'll end up spending your savings for long taxi rides. Combine Western style hotels and Japanese style ryokans in your itinerary. Even if you think that you are not interested in trying a ryokan, I really think that you should stay in one for at least one or two nights. As you will find in the detailed explanation of ryokans that follows, they are small properties where you can expect much more personalized service. You can experience Japanese life style and have closer contact with Japanese people while staying at a ryokan. If you are very interested in ryokans, allocate more nights for them. However, I do recommend that you stay at a Western style hotel occasionally to refresh yourself in familiar surroundings. Another reason why you should stay in Western style hotels occasionally is that ryokan rates usually include two meals (dinner and breakfast the next morning). Though it's a great way to experience authentic Japanese meals, eating in ryokans does deprive you of opportunities to eat out and to explore on your own. In the larger cities, where there are a variety of restaurants, Western style accommodations are recommended.

HOTELS

First-class Hotels (20,000 yen and up for a twin room, including service charge and tax)

First class hotels in Japan are designed to serve foreign visitors and Japanese VIPs. In polls of the world's best hotels many of them have ranked near the top. They are usually quite big and have fancy lobbies, large meeting and banquet rooms, and a variety of boutiques and shops. Most of the hotels in this category have more than 500 rooms (some of them have as many as 1,500 to 2,000 rooms). Travel agencies have offices in these hotels to assist guests in making travel arrangements. Pick-up service for guided tours is usually available. These hotels often maintain special "business service salons" to provide foreign business people with information, assistance and secretarial services. A variety of restaurants, bars and lounges are located in the hotels. Most of the hotels in this category have their own sales offices in the United States and other countries to accept overseas reservations.

Standard Hotels (14,000-20,000 yen for a twin room, including service charge and tax)

Hotels in this category are usually smaller (100-300 rooms) and do not have luxurious lobbies designed to impress. They don't have "business service salons" for foreign business people, and don't necessarily tailor their services for foreign visitors. However, each of these hotels has English-speaking employees and foreign guests shouldn't have any real communications problems. Standard features of these hotels include several restaurants, a coffee shop and a bar. Most of these hotels use representative agencies to accept reservations overseas.

Business Hotels (14,000 yen and less for a twin room, including service charge and tax)

Business hotels were developed to provide Japanese business travelers with convenient, inexpensive accommodations. They usually have 100-200 rooms, most of them singles. All the fancy elements of most hotels, such as spacious lobbies, room service, and even bellboys, are non-existent. Rooms are smallish, but each has its own pre-fab bath unit (The tubs aren't big enough for most foreigners, but taking a shower should be no problem). Though some business hotels have several restaurants, most of them have only one or two restaurants which do double or triple duty—as coffee shops in the morning, and as bars at night. The staff usually does not speak English, but regular check-in and check-out procedures shouldn't cause any problems. Currently there is no organized way to make reservations for individual hotels in this category. However, Pacific Select in New York recently announced that it has organized 61 hotels in a "Japan Hotel Pass" system and will make reservations for clients who plan to stay at member hotels.

RYOKANS

Eighty-three thousand of Japan's 90,000 accommodations facilities can be classified as ryokans. The name "ryokan" covers a wide variety of Japanese style facilities, from the very expensive to the very economical.

Common features of ryokans are:
— the number of rooms at each property is very small, usually 10-50 rooms;
— guest rooms have tatami mat floors — you have to remove your shoes;
— instead of beds, futon matresses are spread on the floor (and folded away in closets during the day);
— meals (dinner and breakfast the next day) are included in the rate, and the menu, which is selected by the chef rather than the guest, varies with the season;
— the entrance is locked up at night (usually after 11 p.m.).

Facilities and services vary greatly depending on price.

First-class Ryokans (20,000 yen and up per person on a double-occupancy basis, with two meals, including 10-15% service charge and 10% tax)

First class ryokans are expected to meet the following standards:
— Each guest room is decorated with a hanging scroll (often an antique) and arranged flowers, and is air conditioned and centrally heated (Central heating, which is technically difficult and very expensive in wooden buildings, is the exception rather than the rule).
— A small Japanese garden is maintained on the grounds. Guests can enjoy the view of the garden from their rooms and stroll about it in the evening.
— Each guest room has a private bath (even in hotspring resorts, where gigantic communal baths are the major attractions, really good ryokans have rooms with private baths for those who care for privacy).
— Meals are served to the guests in their rooms so they can be enjoyed in a private and relaxed atmosphere. The dinner served is an authentic Japanese full course meal, and breakfast is also Japanese style (Western breakfasts can be prepared if requested the night before). The china and lacquerware used to serve the meals are of the finest quality. You are expected to enjoy not only the taste of the food, but also the beauty of the

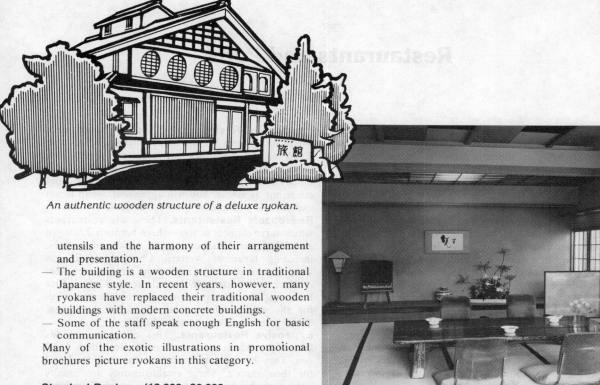

An authentic wooden structure of a deluxe ryokan.

A typical deluxe ryokan room.

utensils and the harmony of their arrangement and presentation.

— The building is a wooden structure in traditional Japanese style. In recent years, however, many ryokans have replaced their traditional wooden buildings with modern concrete buildings.

— Some of the staff speak enough English for basic communication.

Many of the exotic illustrations in promotional brochures picture ryokans in this category.

Standard Ryokans (12,000 - 20,000 yen per person on the same basis as above)

Standard ryokans are usually in modern buildings rather than traditional wooden structures and their rooms usually do not have private baths. Instead, they have large common baths (one for men and one for women). When you use a common bath, you have to wash before you get into the tub. Use the buckets provided, and water from the taps on the walls. When you are clean, get in the tub to soak and to warm your body, relax your muscles and soothe your nerves. Be careful, because the water temperature will probably be much hotter than what you're used to. Meals are usually served in a dining room, instead of guests' rooms. There is usually a small garden, and air conditioning and central heating are standard facilities.

Inexpensive Ryokans and Minshukus (12,000 yen or less per person on the same basis as above)

Ryokans in this category usually do not have central heating. In winter, guests snuggle into kotatsus (low tables covered with quilts and equipped with heaters) to keep warm. Some of the ryokans (but few of the minshukus) in this price range have air conditioning. Meals are simpler and are usually served in a dining room. Common baths are shared by all the guests. Few of these accommodations have gardens. Minshukus are small family-operated ryokans and were originally developed to provide extra accommodations in resort areas during busy seasons. Most minshukus are remodeled private homes, and the rooms are usually smaller than those of regular ryokans. Minshukus can be defined as inexpensive

ryokans of lesser quality. (Family operation is not a real distinguishing factor, because many small ryokans are also family-operated). Generally speaking, accommodations in this category cannot be booked overseas unless you pay handling charges and communications costs.

SHUKUBO

Shukubo are temple lodgings. Their facilities are very similar to those of standard or inexpensive ryokans. But there are two distinct differences:

— the lodgings are attached to temples, and are located in the temple precincts; and

— the meals served are vegetarian.

The best place to experience shukubo is Koyasan. There are about 50 accommodations available in Koyasan, and they are all temple lodgings.

Restaurants and Pubs

A number of restaurants and pubs, as well as several discos are introduced in this guidebook. All of them are clearly pictured on the detailed maps. I have also given sample menus and prices, especially for the inexpensive and reasonable restaurants. Most Japanese restaurants offer set-menu specials. They are usually good buys, but substitutions are not allowed. In addition to the main dish, a set-menu meal will typically include an appetizer, pickles, soup, green tea and rice — or soup, rice and one cup of coffee with dinners if the main dish is Western.

In this book restaurants are classified into the following categories: American Fast Food; Inexpensive Restaurants; Reasonable Restaurants; and Expensive Restaurants.

American Fast Food. Wherever I encountered them, I noted American fast food restaurants such as McDonald's, Kentucky Fried Chicken, Shakey's Pizza and Dunkin Donuts. I have done this because I think Americans in Japan feel like eating familiar food once in a while, especially for a quick lunch, just as I like to eat Japanese ramen noodles for lunch, even when I'm not in Japan. I also wanted to emphasize how popular these American fast food chains are in Japan today. Most important of all, the English signs of these chains are often very helpful when you're trying to get oriented in an unfamiliar area.

Inexpensive Restaurants. These are restaurants where most items on the dinner menu are less than 2,500 yen. They are inexpensive but not cheap. They serve meals that are quite good, and give value for money spent. They are used by budget and quality conscious Japanese. You will agree that Japan is not expensive if you dine at these restaurants.

Reasonable Restaurants. These are restaurants which serve dinners at somewhere between 2,500 yen and 5,000 yen. You can enjoy a variety of cuisines, including Japanese, Western, Chinese, etc. If you want a good dinner in a pleasant atmosphere, these restaurants are ideal. If they are located near office buildings, they also often serve special lunch menus for the white collar workers at 1,200-2,000 yen. These lunches are always good buys.

Expensive Restaurants. This category includes restaurants which serve dinners at more than 5,000 yen. They have great reputations for their food and for their service. These establishments are usually patronized by business people on expense accounts and by international travelers. In addition to those I have mentioned by name, all restaurants in major hotels belong to this category. Most Japanese use these places only on special occasions, such as wedding anniversaries, alumni reunions or very classy dates. Because they serve special delicacies, I think you should sample a few of them while you are in Japan. But if you dine at these places every night you will naturally think that Japan is an extremely expensive country. If you are the kind of person who always stays at the Helmsley Palace in New York, and who always eats your meals in the hotel, then by all means go ahead and patronize these "Expensive Restaurants" in Japan; you'll feel right at home. If you're not, use a combination of restaurants from the four categories according to your budget. "Expensive" means the same thing that it does at home; remember that, and remember that there are a lot of places in Japan where you can enjoy good meals at reasonable prices. If you don't follow these suggestions, you really won't be entitled to have anyone listen if you complain about Japan being expensive.

Coffee Shops. At several places in the text I've also mentioned coffee shops. Japanese love these establishments because customers are never hurried along. You might come to appreciate them too because they are good places to sit down, relax and rest your feet when you're tired. Coffee is still considered a bit of an exotic luxury in Japan. It's expensive, and you don't get automatic refills. If you order tea you have to ask for milk, or it will come with lemon. Many coffee shops are pretty utilitarian affairs, with rather standardized decor, but some

McDonald's, one of the most successful multi-national corporations.

have exotic atmospheres to go with the exotic beverage. You might, for example, find a "Viennese" coffee shop, a rock and roll coffee shop, or a space ship coffee shop. The whimsy adds to the charm. Coffee shops always have tea, coffee, "cake-sets" — tea or coffee plus a piece of fancy cake—, ice creams, sandwiches, and, sometimes, a few other light snacks. Most coffee shops (and many restaurants as well) have display cases out front with plastic models of the dishes they serve. If you have trouble making yourself understood you can always walk the waiter or waitress out front with you and just point to what you want.

Another way to get a quick lunch or snack is to buy a box lunch ("bento"). These are always Japanese style; the contents vary from town to town, and often include local specialties. The divided containers usually have a few portions of fish or meat along with vegetables, rice and Japanese pickles. You can buy bento in most large train stations, and, in the case of the Shinkansen and other long distance trains, on the train itself. They usually cost 600-1,200 yen (slightly higher on the Shinkansen).

Pubs. There is a remarkable difference in the clientele of Japanese style and Western style pubs (and wine houses). The former are usually used by groups of business colleagues, while the latter are often used by couples on dates. Beer halls occupy a middle ground. The atmosphere of Western style pubs is not too different from those you're used to at home. But if you go to a Japanese pub, you'll see lots of differences. First, you will note that 70-80% of the customers are men (the number of women has increased in recent years). Secondly, you will find that Japanese drink a lot — sometimes in pubs like this it seems that you've arrived in a nation of alcoholics. Thirdly, you will find that many of the drinkers are very eloquent. In the Japanese business world, it is considered rather uncouth to express one's opinion too clearly or to object to another's proposal openly. So after work Japanese businessmen often go drinking with their office colleagues. They discuss differences of opinion, seek compromises, and sound each other out before presenting proposals formally. Thus, pubs are places where a great deal of business is conducted, and where a great many decisions are made, before even the preliminary memos begin to make the rounds in the office. Once you know this you may understand why some groups in Japanese style pubs seem to carry on such serious conversations while they are drinking.

It is rather difficult to clearly separate Japanese pubs from Japanese restaurants. Even in restaurants much more alcohol is consumed than in regular Western restaurants. Those facilities which emphasize drinking have been classified here as pubs, and those which serve substantial meals have been labeled restaurants.

The following are typical popular dinner menus:
Tempura 天婦羅 is deep-fried seafood and vegetables. It usually includes shrimp, white fish, squid, eggplant, green pepper and onion. A special dipping sauce is also served.
Sukiyaki すきやき is probably the Japanese dish most popular with foreigners. Thinly sliced beef, and vegetables, tofu and Japanese vermicelli are cooked in an iron pan in a special broth. Raw egg is used as a dip.
Shabu-shabu しゃぶしゃぶ is a cousin of sukiyaki. A brass pot with a chimney in its center is placed on the table. Thinly sliced beef and ingredients similar to those used for sukiyaki are prepared on a large tray. Guests dip these ingredients into the boiling water in the pot for a few seconds to cook them, and then eat them after dipping them again in a special sauce which is served separately.
Sushi 寿司 is a Japanese invention. Various types of thinly sliced raw fish are served atop small rice patties. Fish and vegetables are also rolled up with rice in seaweed wrappers. A set menu sushi dinner usually includes about 10 different types of sushi. A la carte orders at sushi counters usually cost substantially more than the set menu meals.
Kaiseki 会席・懐石 is an authentic Japanese dinner. The meal usually consists of about 10 different courses, and features the delicacies of the season. The best way for foreign tourists to try a kaiseki meal in a relaxed atmosphere is to stay at a first class ryokan in a traditional city like Kyoto. Inexpensive ryokans seldom serve this type of full course Japanese dinner.

The following are typical side dishes served at Japanese pubs as accompaniments to the drinks:
Robatayaki 炉端焼: In any given area, the robatayaki pubs are usually the most popular. A variety of seafood, meats and vegetables are arranged in front of the counter where guests are seated. You can order whatever you want to have broiled on the hearth. Because you can just point, the language barrier is no problem.
Yakitori 焼鳥 is barbecued chicken shish kebab. This is one of the most popular snacks with alcoholic beverages.
Sashimi さしみ is thinly sliced raw fish. Unlike sushi, where the raw fish is served on top of small rice patties, sashimi is just the slices of fish. Another side dish popular with drinkers.
Nabemono 鍋物 means things cooked in an earthen bowl. Different kinds of ingredients and broth bases are used in the different kinds of this popular dish, and its name varies with the ingredients used. Chankonabe, for example, was concocted by sumo wrestlers. It uses fish, chicken and vegetables. Another nabemono dish — Ishikarinabe — uses salmon and vegetables. Nabemono dishes are a special treat on cold winter nights.

For many Japanese, eating and drinking at pubs is a substitute for dinner. After drinking a lot people will order **onigiri** おにぎり (rice balls that contain small pieces of broiled salmon, cod roe or pickled plums), or **ochazuke** お茶づけ (green tea poured over a bowl of rice and topped with broiled salmon, cod roe or pickled plums).

Suggested Itineraries

Five Two-week Itineraries

The Golden Route
(Intensive Exploration of Japan's Cultural Heritage)
Day 1. Arrive in Tokyo.
Day 2. Sightseeing in Tokyo.
Day 3. Sightseeing in Tokyo.
Day 4. One-day excursion to Nikko from Tokyo.
Day 5. One-day excursion to Kamakura from Tokyo.
Day 6. Sightseeing in Hakone (overnight stay in Hakone). I recommend that you arrange for separate delivery of your big bags from Tokyo to Kyoto and just carry an overnight bag with you.
Day 7. Transfer from Hakone to Kyoto.
Day 8. Sightseeing in Kyoto.
Day 9. Sightseeing in Kyoto.
Day 10. Sightseeing in Nara (overnight stay in Nara). Leave your big bags at your hotel in Kyoto.
Day 11. Sightseeing in Nara, and return to Kyoto.
Day 12. Sightseeing in Kyoto.
Day 13. Return to Tokyo.
Day 14. Leave Japan (If your flight leaves from Narita Airport in the late afternoon, you can spend the night of Day 13 in Kyoto and transfer to Narita via Tokyo on the last day).

Modified Golden Route
(Incorporating Hiroshima and Miyajima)
Day 1. Arrive in Tokyo.
Day 2. Sightseeing in Tokyo.
Day 3. One-day excursion to Nikko from Tokyo.
Day 4. One-day excursion to Kamakura from Tokyo.
Day 5. Sightseeing in Hakone (overnight stay in Hakone). I recommend that you arrange for separate delivery of your bags from Tokyo to Kyoto, and just carry an overnight bag with you.
Day 6. Transfer from Hakone to Kyoto.
Day 7. Sightseeing in Kyoto.
Day 8. Sightseeing in Kyoto.
Day 9. One-day excursion to Nara from Kyoto.
Day 10. Sightseeing in Kyoto.
Day 11. Morning transfer from Kyoto to Hiroshima, and afternoon sightseeing in the city of Hiroshima. I recommend that you arrange for separate delivery of your big bags from Kyoto to Tokyo, and just carry a small bag to Hiroshima.
Day 12. One-day excursion to Miyajima from Hiroshima.
Day 13. Transfer from Hiroshima to Tokyo.
Day 14. Leave Japan.

The Local Flavor
(Incorporating Central Japan)
Day 1. Arrive in Tokyo.
Day 2. Sightseeing in Tokyo.
Day 3. One-day excursion to Nikko from Tokyo.
Day 4. One-day excursion to Kamakura or Hakone from Tokyo. You can also stay overnight in either of these destinations and transfer to Kyoto from there on Day 5. In this case, separate delivery of your big bags from Tokyo to Kyoto is recommended.
Day 5. Transfer to Kyoto.
Day 6. Sightseeing in Kyoto.
Day 7. Sightseeing in Kyoto.
Day 8. One-day excursion to Nara from Kyoto.
Day 9. Kyoto to Kanazawa. On the way visit Eiheiji Temple and Cape Tojimbo. I definitely recommend that you arrange separate delivery of your big bags from Kyoto to Tokyo, and just carry a smaller bag for the trip to Central Japan.
Day 10. Sightseeing in Kanazawa.
Day 11. Morning transfer from Kanazawa to Takayama. Afternoon sightseeing in Takayama.
Day 12. Sightseeing in Takayama.
Day 13. Takayama to Tokyo, either via Nagoya or via the Japan Alps and Matsumoto.
Day 14. Leave Japan.

Unusual Route
(Incorporating Northern Japan and Koyasan)
Day 1. Arrive in Tokyo.
Day 2. Sightseeing in Tokyo.
Day 3. A trip to Tohoku. Morning Tohoku Shinkansen to Ichinoseki. Visit Chusonji and Motsuji Temples in Hiraizumi. Accommodations in Sendai.
Day 4. One-day excursion to Shiogama and Matsushima from Sendai.
Day 5. Morning sightseeing in Sendai. Afternoon return to Tokyo.
Day 6. Transfer from Tokyo to Kyoto.
Day 7. Sightseeing in Kyoto.
Day 8. Sightseeing in Kyoto.
Day 9. Sightseeing in Nara and overnight in Nara. Leave your big bags at your hotel in Kyoto.
Day 10. Morning transfer from Nara to Koyasan. Afternoon sightseeing in Koyasan.
Day 11. After morning sightseeing in Koyasan, return to Kyoto.
Day 12. Sightseeing in Kyoto.
Day 13. Transfer from Kyoto to Tokyo.
Day 14. Leave Japan.

Extensive Exploration

(Incorporating Kyushu)

I recommend backpacking for this itinerary because it is difficult to arrange separate baggage delivery along the route.

Day 1. Arrive in Tokyo.

Day 2. Sightseeing in Tokyo.

Day 3. Transfer from Tokyo to Hiroshima. Afternoon sightseeing in the city of Hiroshima.

Day 4. One-day excursion to Miyajima from Hiroshima.

Day 5. Transfer from Hiroshima to Kumamoto via Fukuoka. Afternoon sightseeing in the city of Kumamoto.

Day 6. One-day excursion to Mt. Asozan from Kumamoto.

Day 7. Transfer from Kumamoto to Nagasaki. Sightseeing in Shimabara on the way.

Day 8. Sightseeing in Nagasaki.

Day 9. Transfer from Nagasaki to Kyoto via Fukuoka.

Day 10. Sightseeing in Kyoto.

Day 11. Sightseeing in Kyoto.

Day 12. One-day excursion to Nara from Kyoto.

Day 13. Transfer from Kyoto to Tokyo.

Day 14. Leave Japan.

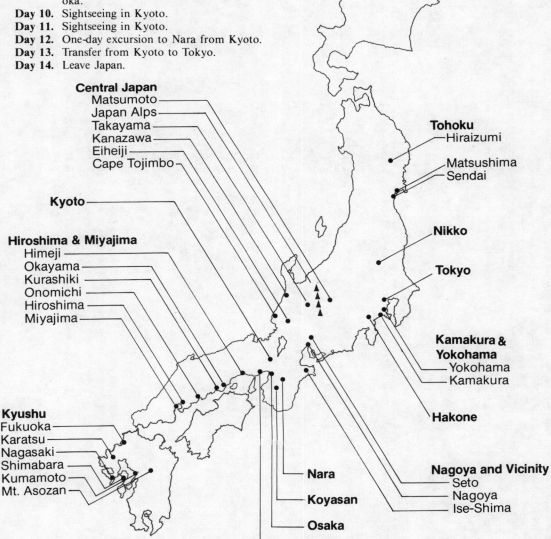

Central Japan
Matsumoto
Japan Alps
Takayama
Kanazawa
Eiheiji
Cape Tojimbo

Kyoto

Hiroshima & Miyajima
Himeji
Okayama
Kurashiki
Onomichi
Hiroshima
Miyajima

Kyushu
Fukuoka
Karatsu
Nagasaki
Shimabara
Kumamoto
Mt. Asozan

Tohoku
Hiraizumi
Matsushima
Sendai

Nikko

Tokyo

Kamakura & Yokohama
Yokohama
Kamakura

Hakone

Nagoya and Vicinity
Seto
Nagoya
Ise-Shima

Nara

Koyasan

Osaka

Kobe & Mt. Rokkosan

Tokyo

The city of Tokyo consists of 23 wards spread over an area of 230 square miles (590 square km.). It is two to four times larger than New York, Chicago or Los Angeles, and is divided into several subsections which are really cities within the city. Map A, which superimposes the central area of Tokyo on maps of New York, Chicago and Los Angeles, is good for getting an idea of the size of the city. "Tokyo" usually means the area inside or just outside the Japanese National Railways (JNR) Yamanote (Loop) Line — an area 4.5 miles (7 km.) from east to west, and 7.6 miles (12 km.) from north to south. The Yamanote Loop is the reference point for map A, and, as the key to transportation within the city, a reference point throughout much of the rest of this book as well.

MAP
A

Comparative maps of Tokyo with New York, Chicago & Los Angeles

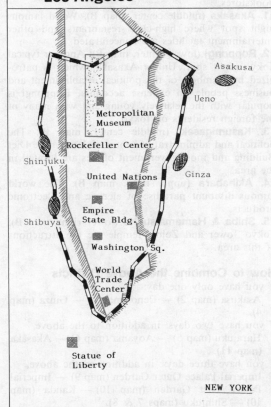

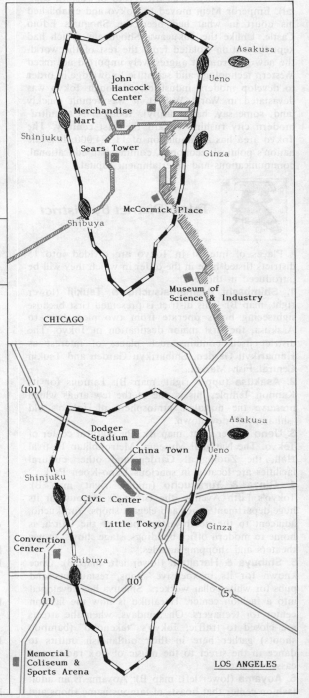

Tokyo is much newer than most Japanese cities. Its real development only began in 1603 when Ieyasu Tokugawa, the first Tokugawa Shogun, selected the town then known as Edo as headquarters for his military government. During the 265-year reign of the Tokugawas, Edo functioned as the nation's administrative center even though Koyto, the home of the emperors, remained the nominal capital. After the Imperial forces regained power in 1868 (the Meiji Restoration), Edo officially became the capital and was renamed Tokyo (eastern Kyoto or eastern capital). Emperor Meiji moved to Tokyo and established his court in what had been the Shogun's Edojo Castle. Unlike the Tokugawa Shogunate, which had kept the nation isolated from the rest of the world, the new government aggressively imported advanced Western technology and scientific knowledge in order to develop modern industries. Although Tokyo was devastated in World War II, it was rebuilt quickly (and, some say, haphazardly). Today it is an ultra-modern city rushing toward the 21st century. The Tokyo area has a population of 11,384,000. It is the nation's political, economic, commercial, educational, communications and entertainment capital.

Tokyo District by District

Places of interest in Tokyo are divided into 15 districts (listed here in the order in which they will be introduced in the text):

1. Shimbashi, Hamamatsucho & Tsukiji (lower right, map B): This district is presented first because sightseeing boats operate from two piers here to Asakusa, the first major destination in Tokyo. The district itself contains such places of interest as Hamarikyu Garden, Shibarikyu Garden and Tsukiji Central Fish Market.

2. Asakusa (upper right, map B): Famous for its Kannon Temple, this is one of the few areas which preserve the nostalgic atmosphere of Tokyo's old "shitamachi" downtown.

3. Ueno (upper right, map B): The cultural center of Tokyo. The National Museum, Metropolitan Festival Hall, the Zoological Garden and other cultural facilities are located in spacious Ueno-Koen Park.

4. Ginza & Yurakucho (middle right, map B): Tokyo's Fifth Avenue, the Ginza, is famous for its huge department stores and elegant shops. Yurakucho, adjacent to the northwestern part of the Ginza, is home to modern office buildings, stage shows, movie theaters and shopping arcades.

5. Shibuya & Harajuku (lower left, map B): Once known for its inexpensive shops, restaurants and pubs for white collar workers, Shibuya has developed into a fashion center. Harajuku is now the fashion center for teenagers. On Sundays, when the streets are closed to traffic, Tokyo's "takenoko" (bamboo shoots) gather here in their outlandish outfits to dance in the street to the music of box radios and cassette players.

6. Aoyama (lower left, map B): Aoyama is an adult fashion center that boasts of famous name shops and boutiques such as Hanae Mori, Issey Miyake, Paul Stuart and Brooks Brothers. Omotesando Boulevard, which connects Aoyama with Harajuku, is a lovely tree lined promenade, and an ideal place for a leisurely stroll.

7. Western Shinjuku (middle left, map B): An area of new urban development, home of most of Tokyo's new skyscrapers.

8. Eastern Shinjuku (middle left, map B): The southern part of the area is a fashionable shopping center with department stores, specialty shops and restaurants. The northern half is a bustling young people's playground where night never visits and where pornographic enterprises flourish.

9. Marunouchi & Imperial Palace Outer Garden (middle right, map B): Marunouchi is the nation's business center and home of the headquarters of most major Japanese corporations. The Imperial Palace Outer Garden is a spacious oasis in the midst of the busy city. The Palace moats and Nijubashi Bridge with a turret of the old Edojo Castle in the background is one of the most picturesque and typical of Japanese scenes, recorded by thousands on film every year.

10. Imperial Palace East Garden & Kanda (middle center, map B): The Palace's East Garden is a spacious park, incredibly quiet for Tokyo. A few of the old rock walls of Edojo Castle, including the base of the donjon, are still standing. To the north of the East Garden is the National Museum of Modern Art and other public institutions. Kanda, further north of the Palace moats, is famous for its innumerable bookstores.

11. Akasaka (middle center, map B): World famous night spot where high-class restaurants and other entertainment facilities are concentrated.

12. Roppongi (lower center, map B): Another typical Tokyo night spot. Unlike Akasaka, which is patronized by members of the political establishment and business people on expense accounts, Roppongi is popular with the relatively young and with many of the foreign residents of Tokyo.

13. Kasumigaseki (middle center, map B): The political and administrative center of Japan. The Diet Building and most government offices are located in the area.

14. Akihabara (upper right, map B): The world famous discount paradise of electric and electronic products.

15. Shiba & Hamamatsucho (lower right, map B): Tokyo Tower and Zojoji Temple are the attractions of this area.

How to Combine the Above Districts

If you have only one day:
   Asakusa (map 2) — Ueno (map 3) — Ginza (map 4).

If you have two days: in addition to the above,
   Harajuku (map 5) — Aoyama (map 6) — Akasaka (map 11).

If you have three days: in addition to the above,
   Imperial Palace Outer Garden (map 9) — Imperial Palace East Garden (map 10) — Kanda (map 10) — Shinjuku (maps 7 & 8).

If you have four days:

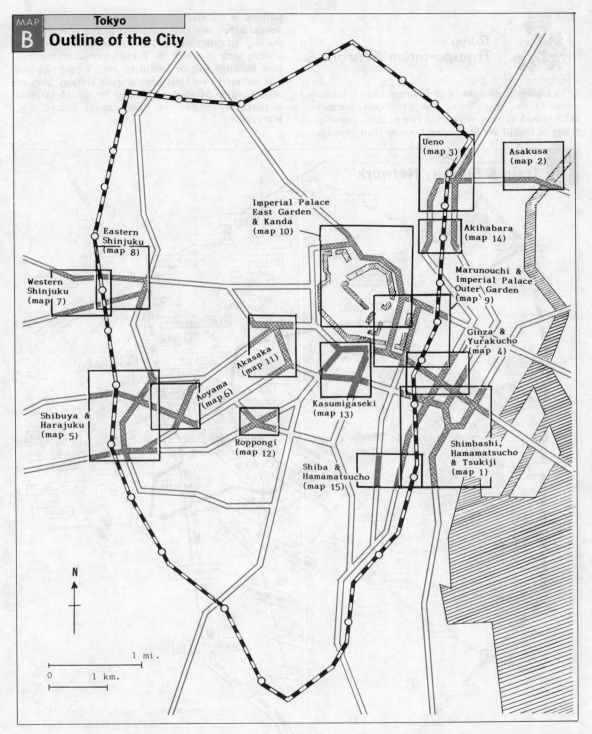

MAP
B
Tokyo
Outline of the City

(1) Hamarikyu (map 1) — Asakusa (map 2) — Ginza (map 4).

(2) Harajuku (map 5) — Aoyama (map 6) — Akasaka (map 11).

(3) Imperial Palace Outer Garden (map 9) — Imperial Palace East Garden (map 10) — Kanda (map 10) — Shinjuku (maps 7 & 8).

(4) Central Fish Market (map 1) — Ueno (map 3) — Akihabara (map 14) — Roppongi (map 12)

If you have five days or longer:

Read the following pages carefully and organize your additional days.

Tokyo's Transportation Network

To transport millions of commuters from suburban areas to the city, Tokyo has developed extensive railway and subway networks. For tourists, however, many of them have little value because their principal purpose is convenient connections to suburban residential areas, not easy access to places of interest in the city. In order to avoid confusion and to give you a clear idea of which of Tokyo's public transportation facilities will be useful to you, I have selected and pictured two JNR lines and six subway lines on map C. The 34 stations located in the 15 targeted districts are shown in bold capital letters, e.g., ROPPONGI

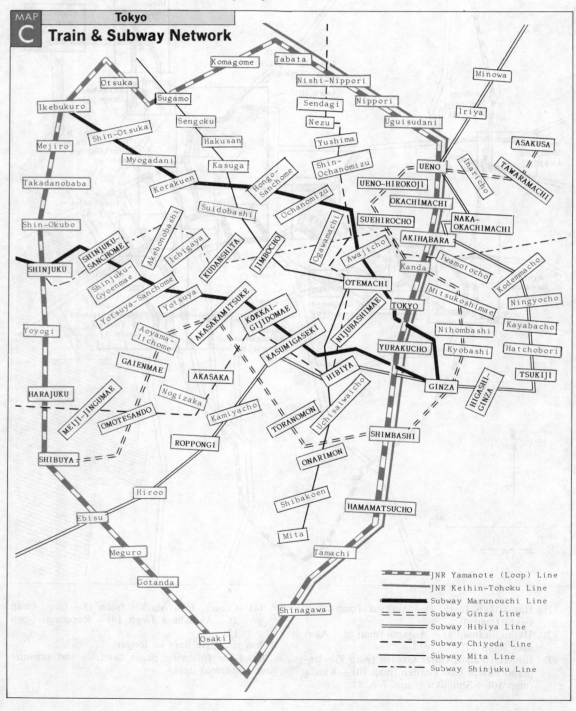

MAP C

Tokyo

Train & Subway Network

- ▨▨▨ JNR Yamanote (Loop) Line
- —— JNR Keihin-Tohoku Line
- ▬▬ Subway Marunouchi Line
- – – – Subway Ginza Line
- —— Subway Hibiya Line
- — — Subway Chiyoda Line
- —— Subway Mita Line
- —·—· Subway Shinjuku Line

JNR (Japanese National Railways)
How to Find Stations

All the stations you need to know in order to get around Tokyo easily are clearly pictured on the 15 district maps which appear on the following pages (Tokyo maps 1 through 15). Because the JNR stations are so important in the everyday life of Tokyo, you shouldn't have trouble recognizing the stations.

Bilingual sign on the platform at Harajuku station on the JNR Tokyo Yamanote (Loop) Line.

Two Convenient JNR Lines in Tokyo

Yamanote (Loop) Line (green colored): This line surrounds the central part of Tokyo. It takes about one hour to make the trip around the loop.

Keihin-Tohoku Line (blue colored): Between Tabata and Shinagawa this line runs parallel to the Yamanote (Loop) Line. At most stations, the Yamanote and Keihin-Tohoku trains headed in the same direction arrive and depart from the same platform, the Yamanote at one side and the Keihin-Tohoku at the other. For example, at Tokyo Station, the north-bound Keihin-Tohoku line uses Track No. 3 and the north-bound Yamanote uses Track No. 4. At the next platform, the south-bound Yamanote uses Track No. 5 on one side while the south-bound Keihin-Tohoku uses Track No. 6 on the other side. When you travel to and from stations located between Tabata and Shinagawa, you can therefore take either the Yamanote or Keihin-Tohoku line, whichever comes along first.

How to Find Platforms in a Station

The name of the line, e.g., "Yamanote Line" or "Keihin-Tohoku Line," and the direction of the train, e.g., "for Shibuya and Shinjuku" or "for Shimbashi and Tokyo," are written in both Japanese and English on many signboards in the JNR stations. At smaller stations you should not have any problem finding the track number of the train you want. Maps D and E of Tokyo and Shinjuku stations, the two largest stations in the city, should help.

Bilingual signs at JNR train station.

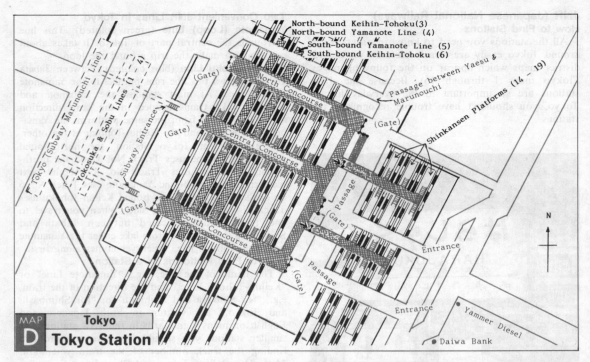

MAP D — Tokyo
Tokyo Station

North-bound Keihin-Tohoku(3)
North-bound Yamanote Line (4)
South-bound Yamanote Line (5)
South-bound Keihin-Tohoku (6)

Passage between Yaesu & Marunouchi

Shinkansen Platforms (14 – 19)

Tokyo (Subway Marunouchi Line)

Yokosuka & Sobu Lines (1 – 4)

Subway Entrance

North Concourse

Central Concourse

South Concourse

Passage

(Gate)

Entrance

Yammer Diesel

Daiwa Bank

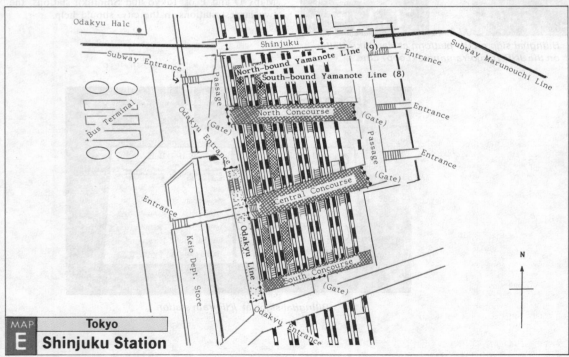

MAP E — Tokyo
Shinjuku Station

Odakyu Halc

Subway Entrance

Shinjuku

North-bound Yamanote Line (9)

South-bound Yamanote Line (8)

Subway Marunouchi Line

Entrance

Bus Terminal

Odakyu Entrance

Passage

North Concourse

(Gate)

Central Concourse

Keio Dept. Store

Odakyu Line

South Concourse

(Gate)

Odakyu Entrance

N

Subways
How to Find Stations

All the stations essential for tourist travel in Tokyo are clearly pictured on the 15 district maps. Entrances are clearly marked "subway" in both Japanese and English. At large stations, such as Shinjuku, Ginza and Otemachi, long underground passages connect the platforms of the various lines. In stations which are served by more than two subway lines, in addition to small English signs indicating the line names, signs — actually circles of various colors — are posted to help passengers find the proper platforms. There is a different color for each line, and even the cars used on the trains are painted in accordance with this color-coordinated scheme, as follows:

Marunouchi Line (red cars) — indicated by **red** circles.
Ginza Line (yellow cars) — indicated by **yellow** circles.
Hibiya Line (stainless steel cars) — indicated by **gray** circles.
Chiyoda Line (dark green cars) — indicated by **dark green** circles.
Mita Line (stainless steel cars with blue stripes) — indicated by **blue** circles.
Shinjuku Line (stainless steel cars with pale green stripes) — indicated by **pale green** circles.

If you ever have difficulty finding the subway you want, you should go back to the surface and walk to the approximate location of the station as pictured on the district map. You will find the entrance to the line you want around that area.

Bilingual signs and color-coordinated circles indicating subway stations.

Special Directions

The following two lines cover most places of interest in Tokyo and are used most frequently by tourists:

Marunouchi Line: Major stations such as Shinjuku, Akasakamitsuke, Kasumigaseki, Ginza and Tokyo are on this line. From Shinjuku it takes only nine minutes to Akasakamitsuke, and 16 minutes to Ginza.

Ginza Line: Asakusa, Ueno, Ginza, Shimbashi, Akasakamitsuke and Shibuya are the major stations served by this line. From Asakusa, it takes five minutes to Ueno, 18 minutes to Ginza and 25 minutes to Akasakamitsuke.

At Akasakamitsuke Station, easy interchange between these two lines is possible. The west-bound Ginza Line (for Shibuya) uses Track No. 1 and the west-bound Marunouchi Line (for Shinjuku) uses Track No. 2, the two sides of one platform. In the same way, the east-bound Ginza Line (for Ginza and Asakusa) uses Track No. 3 and the east-bound Marunouchi Line (for Ginza and Tokyo) uses Track No. 4, the two sides of another platform. For example, if you want to go to Asakusa from Shinjuku, you should take the Marunouchi Line to Akasakamitsuke, then transfer to the Ginza Line at the opposite side of the same platform to continue your trip to Asakusa.

Remarks

To help you get familiar with the subway system, the same symbols used on map C are used on the 15 district maps (Tokyo maps 1 through 15).
For example:
The **Marunouchi Line** is always represented by a bold solid line: ▬▬▬▬
The **Ginza Line** is always represented by double dotted lines: = = = = = = =
The **Hibiya Line** is always represented by double solid lines: ═══════

Refer back to map C whenever you want to check subway or train connections as you move from one district to another.

Bilingual signs at the entrance of the Tokyo subways.

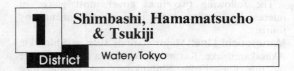

1

District   Watery Tokyo

Shimbashi, Hamamatsucho & Tsukiji

This area is introduced first because taking a Sumidagawa River boat from here to Asakusa is an unusual experience. You can see the ragged hems of sophisticated Tokyo's skirts, and travel to Asakusa Kannon Temple (formally, Sensoji Temple), the top

of the list of "must-see" places in Tokyo, in a very enjoyable way. Another advantage of this route to Asakusa is that on your way to the boat pier you can visit either Hamarikyu or Shibarikyu Gardens, beautiful Japanese-style gardens on the waterfront.

Boat to Asakusa

There are two piers from which boats to Asakusa operate, Hamarikyu Pier (middle center, map 1) and Takeshiba Pier (lower center). Boats from Hamarikyu Pier operate seven times daily, at 10:20 a.m., 11:05 a.m., 11:50 a.m., 12:40 p.m., 1:25 p.m., 2:15 p.m., and 3 p.m. From Takeshiba Pier the boats operate

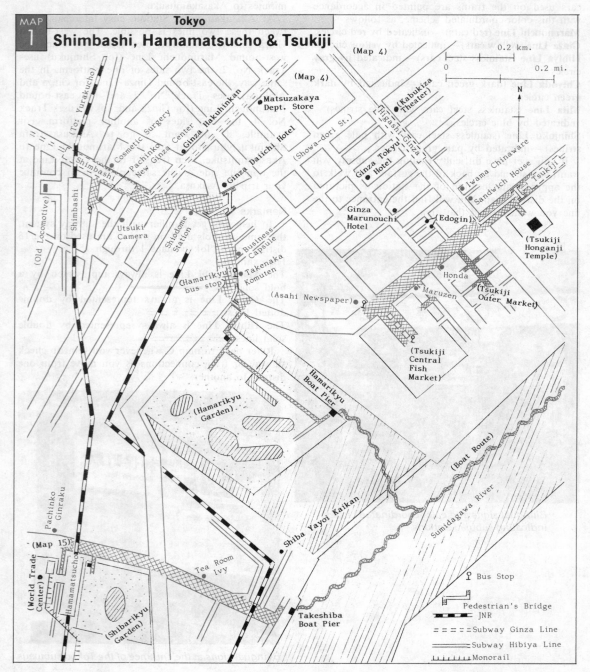

MAP 1

Tokyo

Shimbashi, Hamamatsucho & Tsukiji

nine times daily, at 9:50 a.m., 10:25 am., 11 a.m., 12 noon, 12:50 p.m., 1:30 p.m., 2:20 p.m., 3:10 p.m., and 3:55 p.m. I recommend that you take the boat from Hamarikyu Pier because nearby Hamarikyu Garden is lovely and retains many of its original features. However, the boat pier is closed when the Garden is closed (Every Monday. If Monday is a holiday, the Garden and pier are open on Monday and closed on Tuesday). The alternative is the boat from Takeshiba Pier. From either Hamarikyu or Takeshiba the boat ride to Asakusa costs 480 yen and takes about 40 minutes. The Sumidagawa River provided the main means of transportation in the Edo Era (17th —19th centuries), and the areas along the river were, at that time, the most prosperous in the city. The center of Tokyo moved west only with the development of the railroad and other surface transportation. The view from the boat is not particularly noteworthy, but the ride is an interesting way to see the face this huge city never shows to the casual tourist.

Places of Interest

Hamarikyu Garden 浜離宮庭園 (middle center, map 1)

This garden was built about 330 years ago at the order of Tsunashige Matsudaira, a feudal lord. Later, it was ceded to the sixth Tokugawa Shogun, Ienobu, who used it for duck hunting. After the Meiji Restoration the garden became the property of the Imperial Household Agency and was used for outdoor parties for the nobles and for receptions for foreign guests of honor. General Ulysses S. Grant, the 18th President of the United States, was entertained here when he visited Japan. Later, the garden was given to the Tokyo Metropolitan Government and opened to the public (9 a.m. to 4:30 p.m. Admission 200 yen).

Shimbashi is the station closest to Hamarikyu Garden (0.5 miles or 0.8 km.). If you are too lazy to walk the 0.5 miles, you can take a bus. The stop is located on the eastern side of Shimbashi Station (upper left, map 1). Take the No. 1 bus (every five minutes) to Hamarikyu, the first stop (140 yen. Put your fare in the box near the driver upon boarding).

Shibarikyu Garden 芝離宮庭園 (lower left, map 1)

This garden was built about 300 years ago as part of the private residence of Tadaasa Okubo, a top Shogunate official. After the Meiji Restoration, the garden belonged to the imperial family for a time, and then was given to the Tokyo Metropolitan Government. Its oddly shaped pine trees are especially delightful (9 a.m. to 4:30 p.m. Admission 100 yen. Closed every Monday. When Monday is a holiday, open on Monday and closed on Tuesday).

The station closest to Shibarikyu Garden is Hamamatsucho, which is served by the JNR Yamanote and Keihin-Tohoku Lines. Passing under the elevated tracks, the Garden is just on the right-hand side. Takeshiba Pier is only 0.3 miles (0.5 km.) from Shibarikyu Garden. If you are staying at a hotel in the Hamamatsucho area, take the boat from Takeshiba Pier.

Other places of interest if you are in Tokyo for an extended period

Tsukiji Central Fish Market 築地中央卸売市場 (middle right, map 1): This wholesale market handles all the fish and meat consumed in the Tokyo area. Because of the overwhelming volume of trade in fish and fish products (much greater than that in meat and meat products), it is popularly called the Central Fish Market. The business between producers and wholesalers is conducted early in the morning, between 5:20 a.m. and 6 a.m. From 6 a.m. the market is crowded with purchasers from retail stores and restaurants. There are many small restaurants in the market which serve sushi, tempura, noodles, etc. for these traders. The restaurants are busy, noisy, no-frills affairs, but the food is excellent and they are very inexpensive (The market is closed on Sundays and holidays, on August 15 & 16, and for the New Year's Holidays).

If you want to see the early morning trading, take a taxi from your hotel. If you visit the market a little later, you can take the No. 1 bus from Shimbashi Station (explained above for visits to Hamarikyu Garden). Pay 140 yen upon boarding and tell the driver "Tsukiji Fish Market" slowly.

Tsukiji Outer Market 築地場外市場 (middle right, map 1): Small retail stores which handle fish, other foodstuffs and various consumer products crowd the small lanes near the Central Fish Market. The Outer Market is for members of the general public who want small quantities of the freshest food and other inexpensive items. This is one of the two best places to learn about what goes home in shopping baskets to the kitchens of typical Tokyoites, with Ameya-Yokocho near Ueno (introduced in District 3) being the other one.

Tsukiji Honganji Temple 築地本願寺 (upper right, map 1): Near Tsukiji subway station on the Hibiya Line is an Indian-style temple, the only one of its kind in Japan. This massive stone structure, built in 1935 after the 1680 original was destroyed by the Kanto Earthquake, is the main hall of Tsukiji Honganji Temple. There are Japanese-style rooms at both sides of the altar. The temple combines traditional atmosphere and modern practicality to provide busy Tokyoites with a place of worship.

Restaurant in the Area

Edogin. If you want to enjoy excellent sushi at a reasonable price, this is the place. The restaurant is busy, and not fancy at all. At lunch time Deluxe Sushi is your best bet (2,000 yen). Even the bargain 1,200 yen lunch gives you a good sampling of marvelously fresh sushi. In the evening, 5,000 yen is usually enough to cover a good a la carte sampling (plus drinks). The restaurant does not have an English sign, but the paper lanterns at its entrance are a good landmark.

2
Asakusa

District | Nostalgic Tokyo

Sensoji Temple 浅草寺 (upper right, map 2)

Asakusa has prospered as a temple town all through Japanese history. Sensoji Temple (popularly known as Asakusa Kannon Temple) is the oldest temple in Tokyo. Until recently Asakusa was also the entertainment center of Tokyo, and was especially famous for its comedies and girls' revue. Though the entertainment centers have shifted to other areas, Asakusa has stubbornly preserved the nostalgic atmosphere of the traditional "shitamachi" downtown of the common people.

Kaminarimon Gate 雷門 (middle right, map 2) is the entrance to the main approach to the Temple. Gods of Wind and Thunder stand in the niches on both sides of the Gate, and an 11-foot (3.3 m.) tall red lantern hangs from it. Both sides of the main approach, called **Nakamise Street** 仲見世, are lined with souvenir shops decorated with colorful small lanterns.

For transportation to Asakusa, the boat ride from Hamarikyu or Takeshiba is recommended. If you're only staying in Tokyo for three days or less and want to see as much as possible, skip the boat ride and take the Ginza subway line to Asakusa Station, the last stop on the line. The station is pictured at the lower right of map 2.

Other Places of Interest in Asakusa

Shin-Nakamise Street 新仲見世 is a shopping arcade lined with modern stores, restaurants and traditional souvenir shops. At the end of the arcade are many movie houses and other theaters reminiscent of the old Asakusa.

Asakusa Flea Market 浅草のみの市 is famous for its inexpensive consumer products such as clothes, shoes, watches, accessories, etc. You should take a look at the market if you pass here on your way to Kappabashi Street.

Kappabashi Street 合羽橋商店街 : Both sides of this street are lined with shops which handle various restaurant products, such as lacquer ware, pottery, small decorative objects like lanterns and umbrellas, the menu stands found in authentic Japanese restaurants, and the plastic displays of foods used in the windows of many restaurants and coffee shops. Though the primary clients of these stores are restaurant owners, retail sales to the general public are also made. The southern part of Kappabashi Street is especially interesting. Many items much more interesting than what you can find in regular souvenir shops are available here. Because Kappabashi is within easy walking distance of the Ginza subway line's Tawaramachi Station, you can stop back here to shop for souvenirs on the last days of your stay in Japan.

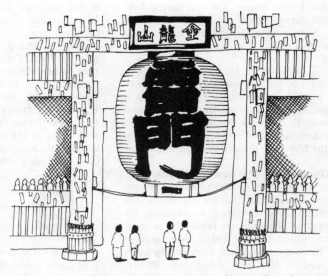

Kaminarimon Gate, the main entrance to Sensoji Temple.

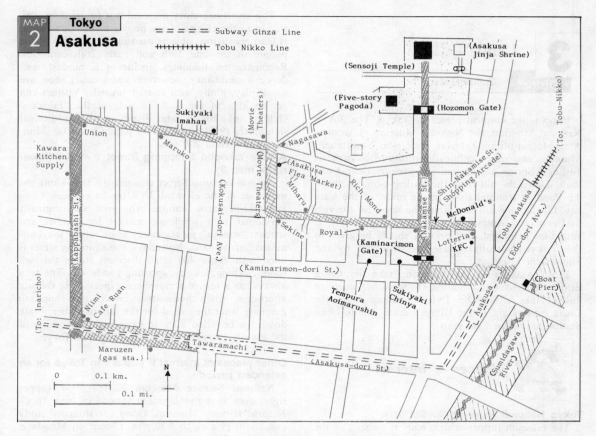

MAP 2 Tokyo Asakusa

- ===== Subway Ginza Line
- +++++++ Tobu Nikko Line

(Asakusa Jinja Shrine)
(Sensoji Temple)
(Five-story Pagoda)
(Hozomon Gate)
Sukiyaki Imahan
(Movie Theaters)
Nagasawa
(To: Tobu-Nikko)
Union
Maruko
Kawara Kitchen Supply
(Asakusa Flea Market)
Rich Mond
Shin-Nakamise St. Shopping Arcade)
(Movie Theaters)
Miharu
(Kokusai-dori Ave.)
McDonald's
Sekine
(Nakamise St.)
Tobu Asakusa
(Kappabashi St.)
Royal
Lotteria
KFC
(Edo-dori Ave.)
(Kaminarimon Gate)
(Boat Pier)
Niimi
Cafe Ruan
(Kaminarimon-dori St.)
Tempura Aoimarushin
Sukiyaki Chinya
(To: Inaricho)
L Asakusa
(Sumidagawa River)
Maruzen (gas sta.)
Tawaramachi
N
0   0.1 km.
0.1 mi.
(Asakusa-dori St.)

For Information Purposes Only. North of Asakusa (about five minutes by taxi) is Yoshiwara, the former licensed quarters. The area was formerly a "Toruco (Turkish) Baths" mecca, but because the Turkish Embassy protested loud and long against this defamation, the industry recently decided to switch to the name "soapland." Though prostitution is illegal in Japan, this traditional business is openly conducted here. Hotel clerks can provide good information about individual facilities in the area. The existence of the "soapland" establishment is a good example of the contradiction between "tatemae," ideal, and "honne," reality, which governs so many aspects of Japanese social behavior.

Restaurants

American Fast Food: McDonald's and Kentucky Fried Chicken (abbreviated KFC on map 2, middle right).

Do as Japanese do — authentic food in the traditional town

Sukiyaki Chinya (middle right, map 2). Famous for sukiyaki and shabu-shabu (2,400-3,800 yen). A special 1,400 yen lunch is served in the basement.

Tempura Aoimarushin (middle right, map 2). The name Aoimarushin is famous throughout Japan as the home of quintessential tempura. The higher up you go in this seven-story restaurant, the better the facilities become, and the higher the prices go. Set menu meals range from 1,350 to 2,800 yen.

Sukiyaki Imahan (upper center, map 2). Another big-name sukiyaki restaurant. Authentic sukiyaki costs 2,600 yen to 4,000 yen. A sukiyaki lunch is only 1,300 yen. Katsudon (a bowl of rice topped with a fried pork cutlet) is only 700 yen.

3 Ueno

District | Cultural Tokyo

Ueno is the cultural center of Tokyo. The Tokyo National Museum, the National Museum of Western Art, Metropolitan Festival Hall, the Shitamachi Museum and other cultural institutions as well as Toshogu Shrine are located in spacious Ueno-Koen Park. Down the hill from the Park is Shinobazu-no-ike Pond, a tranquil oasis in the midst of the busy city. Ideally, one full day should be saved for the visit to Ueno (and Ameya-Yokocho Shopping Street). If your time is limited, first priority should be given to the Tokyo National Museum, followed by the Shitamachi Museum.

From Asakusa or Tawaramachi, take the Ginza subway line to Ueno Station. From other parts of Tokyo, take either the JNR Yamanote Line, the Ginza subway line or the Hibiya subway line to Ueno Station as pictured on map 3.

Places of Interest

Tokyo National Museum 東京国立博物館

The museum (upper center, map 3) consists of the following halls:

The Main Hall, which houses Japanese fine and applied arts; **The Gallery of Oriental Antiquities,** which features historical and artistic objects of China, India and other Asian countries; **The Hyokeikan Gallery,** which specializes in Japanese archeological relics; and **The Gallery of Horyuji Treasures,** which contains the priceless Buddhist treasures of Nara's Horyuji Temple.

The Museum is open from 9 a.m. to 4:30 p.m. Closed on Mondays. The Gallery of Horyuji Treasures is open only on Thursday. Even on Thursday, if it is rainy or very humid the Gallery may be closed in order to protect the fragile relics. The 250 yen admission charge covers all four halls.

Toshogu Shrine 東照宮 **(middle left, map 3)**

This shrine was built in 1627 to honor the spirit of Ieyasu Tokugawa, the first Tokugawa Shogun. The structure is painted vermilion red and decorated with gold foil and numerous carvings. Both sides of the approach are lined with many stone lanterns (9:30 a.m. to 5 p.m. Admission 100 yen).

Shinobazu-no-ike Pond 不忍池 **(middle left, map 3)**

On your way down the hill to Shinobazu-no-ike Pond, you will pass through numerous small red torii gates which lead to the precincts of Hanazono Jinja Shrine. On an island in the center of the pond stands a small hall called Bentendo. This hall contains the image of Benzaiten, the goddess of wealth. Don't forget to pay your respects!

Shitamachi Museum 下町博物館 **(lower center, map 3 near the Pond)**

This small two-story museum was founded in 1980 thanks to the efforts of the people of the Ueno area. It features various objects used in the daily life of the people in the late 19th and early 20th centuries. Reconstructed buildings, including a modest residence, a merchant's showroom and a candy shop, are on display, along with related utensils. Visitors can get an idea of the lost life style of the "Edokko" children of Tokyo who lived in the traditional shitamachi (9:30 a.m. to 4:30 p.m. Closed on Mondays. Admission 200 yen).

Ameya-Yokocho Shopping Street アメヤ横丁 **(lower right, map 3)**

Ameya-Yokocho Street is a narrow lane along the west side of the elevated JNR tracks between Ueno and Okachimachi Stations. The area was originally developed as a wholesale market for candies and snacks. "Ameya" means candy store, and "Yokocho" means narrow lane. Nowadays, the shopping street is lined with about 400 retail discount stores that sell food, clothing, jewelry, sporting goods, etc. The area always has a festive atmosphere, especially in the late afternoon, when housewives crowd the shops to purchase what they need for the family dinner. Walk down the crowded alley to experience something of the casual, everyday life of the people of Tokyo.

Other places of interest if you are in Tokyo for an extended period

National Science Museum 国立科学博物館 (upper right, map 3) is the Japanese version of New York's Natural History Museum. Good for students' study excursions (9 a.m. to 4:30 p.m. Closed on Mondays. Admission 250 yen).

National Museum of Western Art 国立西洋美術館 (middle right, map 3) contains carvings and statues, many of them by Rodin, on the first floor. The second floor features paintings, most of them of the French Impressionist school (9:30 a.m. to 5 p.m. Closed on Mondays. Admission 250 yen).

Metropolitan Art Museum 東京都美術館 (upper center, map 3) is a huge modern structure used mainly for exhibitions of the works of younger Japanese artists (9 a.m. to 4 p.m. Admission varies depending on the exhibition).

Metropolitan Festival Hall 東京文化会館 (middle right, map 3) has two concert halls. The large one is used for concerts, operas and ballets, and the smaller one for chamber music and recitals. Concerts usually start at 6:30 p.m.

Ueno Zoo 上野動物園 (middle left, map 3) is home to about 8,300 animals from all over the world. The most popular animals here are the pandas presented by the Chinese government. A monorail connects the Aquarium with the main grounds (9:30 a.m. to 4:30 p.m. Closed on Mondays. Admission 300 yen. Aquarium 200 yen).

Restaurants

American Fast Food: McDonald's is at the corner near the Ueno-Hirokoji Station of the Ginza subway line. Kentucky Fried Chicken ("KFC") is near the JNR Okachimachi Station (both lower center, map 3).

Restaurants

Ueno Seiyoken (middle center, map 3). This restaurant opened right after the Meiji Restoration in 1868 and introduced Western cuisine to Japan. The grill is located in a quiet corner of Ueno-Koen Park and overlooks Shinobazu-no-ike Pond. Rather expensive (3,000 yen for lunch), but the quality is excellent.

Totenko (lower left, map 3). This eight-story Chinese restaurant is proud of its fantastic view of Shinobazu-no-ike Pond and the thickly wooded Ueno-Koen Park. The 7th floor grill serves a fine 2,000 yen lunch.

Ueno Fugetsudo (lower center, map 3). Famous for its sponge cake (which is also retailed all over Japan). You can enjoy this famous delicacy in the first floor cafe. The second floor serves Western food, such as beef stew (2,300 yen) and salmon steak (2,500 yen).

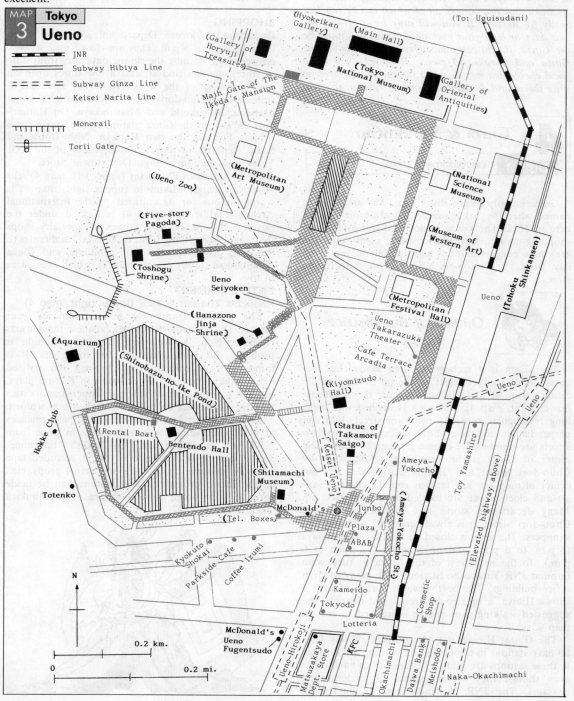

Suggestions for the evening

If you start your day in Hamarikyu Park and visit Asakusa, it will be late afternoon by the time you finish in the Ueno area. You can just go back to your hotel, or you can enjoy an evening stroll and dinner in one of Tokyo's three renowned night spots (Ginza, Akasaka and Roppongi), all of which can be reached easily by subway. If you will only be in Tokyo for two days or less, your evening destination should be the Ginza. If you can allocate one extra day for the Ginza and Yurakucho areas, Roppongi will be a good choice, leaving Akasaka for the second evening since the second day itinerary ends at nearby Aoyama.

4 Ginza & Yurakucho

District Establishment Tokyo

Ginza literally means silver mint. The area was so named when the Tokugawa Shogunate built its mint here in 1612. The Ginza is now Tokyo's established shopping district. Instead of minting silver coins, the area now collects millions and millions of yen every day from the customers who patronize its many stores.

Outline of the District

The Ginza is a rectangular area sandwiched between Sotobori-dori Street on the northwest (middle center, map 4) and Showa-dori on the southeast (lower right, map 4). The area is divided into eight long rectangular zones by narrower streets that run perpendicular to these boundaries; these narrow streets are numbered 1-chome through 8-chome. The center of Ginza is the large intersection made by Chuo-dori Street and Harumi-dori Street (in the center of map 4.). The famous round building (San-ai) and clock tower are located at this intersection. Many department stores and specialty shops line Chuo-dori Street; it is always crowded with window shoppers. The area is closed to traffic on Saturdays (3 p.m. to 6 p.m.) and on Sundays (12 noon to 6 p.m.). To the northwest of the Ginza is Yurakucho (around JNR Yurakucho Station), with many modern office buildings. The northwestern corner of map 4 shows Hibiya, a theater and restaurant district. The suggested walking tour course is marked in red on map 4.

The Ginza, Hibiya and Marunouchi subway lines all have stations in the Ginza. As you can see on map 4, these stations are quite a distance from each other even though they are connected by underground passages. The JNR Yamanote and Keihin-Tohoku Lines serve Yurakucho Station.

Places of Interest

The Japanese government's free **TOURIST INFOR-MATION CENTER** is located on Harumi-dori Street near the elevated JNR tracks ("TIC(?)," upper left, map 4).

SHOPPING

Department Stores: Department stores are open from 10 a.m. to 6 p.m. They are closed once a week on weekdays. Because the closing days vary from store to store, you can find at least a few stores open on any given day of the week. There are three major stores along Chuo-dori Street — from north to south, **Matsuya, Mitsukoshi** and **Matsuzakaya.** On Harumi-dori Street near the Ginza Station on the Marunouchi subway line are the two **Hankyu, Nishi-Ginza** and **Seibu** Department Stores. To the north of the JNR Yurakucho Station is **Sogo** Department Store.

Others: American Pharmacy (upper left, map 4) sells American drugs; **Mikimoto** (upper right, map 4) is world famous for its cultured pearls; **International Arcade** (middle left, map 4) is located under the elevated JNR tracks and houses 24 specialty shops that handle everything from traditional handicrafts to the most advanced electronic products; and **Ginza Hakuhinkan** (lower center, map 4), which specializes in toys.

ENTERTAINMENT

Kabukiza Theater 歌舞伎座 **(lower right, map 4)**

The Kabuki drama has a four hundred year history. Of the many traditional Japanese theater arts (Kabuki, Noh, Kyogen and Bunraku), Kabuki is probably the most accessible for foreigners. It is famous for its colorful stage settings and stylized acting style. There are no actresses in Kabuki plays, but it is often said that the female impersonators who take these roles are more feminine than real women. Matinees start at 11 a.m., and evening performances at 4:30 p.m. Admission tickets range in price from 1,500 yen to 10,000 yen. An English "Earphone-Guide" can be rented for 600 yen. A recorded tape provides information on the story, actors props, etc., as the drama progresses. Reservations can be made through your hotel, or you can call the Kabukiza Theater at 541-8597.

Kabuki performance.

Restaurants & Pubs

American Fast Food: The main street of the Ginza (Chuo-dori) is lined with many American fast food shops — from north to south, **Dunkin Donuts, Shakey's Pizza, Wendy's,** and **McDonald's** at the southern end of the Ginza. McDonald's also has one more shop in Hibiya (upper left, map 4).

Inexpensive Restaurants (2,500 yen or less for dinner)

Western: Italian (middle center, map 4): Spaghetti 750 yen, pizza 800 yen, beef stew 1,800 yen. **Americana** (second floor of **Food Center,** upper center, map 4): American style restaurant. Hamburger steak 800 yen, beef steak 2,500 yen.

Japanese: Tsukiji Tamazushi (4th — 6th floors of **Love Skirt** manufacturing Bldg., middle center, map 4): Set menu sushi 800 - 1,500 yen. If you order a la carte, be prepared to pay 3,000 - 5,000 yen. **Tsukiji Uemura** (5th floor of **Ginza Hakuhinkan,** lower center, map 4): Japanese set menu dinner 1,800 - 2,500 yen.

Others: Keiraku (middle left, map 4) serves good Chinese food at 600 - 800 yen per plate. **Maharao** (basement of **Mitsui Bldg.,** upper left, map 4): My favorite Indian restaurant. Indian chefs. Shrimp curry 950 yen, Tandori mixed grill 1,070 yen, Maharaja delight (full course) is as inexpensive as 1,480 yen.

Moderate Restaurants (2,500 - 5,000 yen for dinner)

These restaurants serve special set menu lunches at 1,000 - 1,500 yen for white collar workers from the nearby offices. They are always good buys.

Western: Jardin (middle center, map 4): French home-style cuisine. Especially famous for mussels. **Suehiro** (lower center, map 4): Famous for its good quality, inexpensive steaks. Sukiyaki is also served. **Maison de France** (B2 of **Twin Tower Bldg.,** upper left, map 4): French.

Japanese: Tenkuni (middle center, map 4, on the basement floor): Famous tempura restaurant. **Unkai** (second floor of **Ginza Kokusai Hotel,** lower left, map 4): Shabu-shabu. 3,900 yen for as much as you can eat.

Others: Totenko (third floor of **Twin Tower Bldg.,** upper left, map 4): A Chinese chain restaurant. **Ashoka** (lower center, map 4): Indian (Try this if you can't get into Maharao).

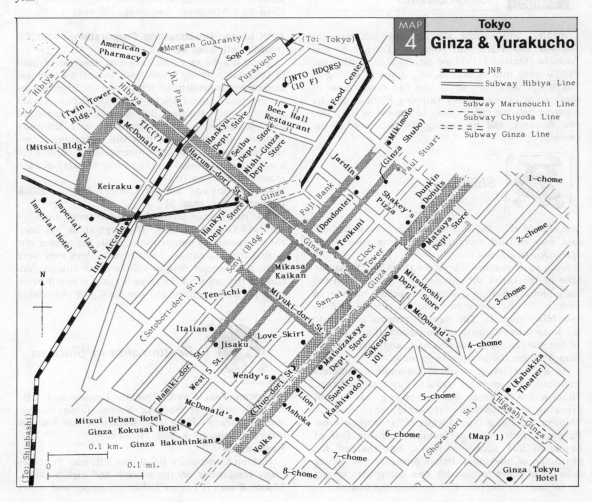

MAP 4

Tokyo

Ginza & Yurakucho

JNR
Subway Hibiya Line
Subway Marunouchi Line
Subway Chiyoda Line
Subway Ginza Line

Expensive Restaurants (5,000 - 10,000 yen, or up)

Ten-Ichi (middle center, map 4): A renowned tempura restaurant. **Jisaku** (middle center, map 4): Authentic Japanese cuisine; **Haruna** (second floor of **Mikasa Kaikan,** middle center, map 4): Excellent French food; **Yamato** (seventh floor of Mikasa Kaikan): Steak and seafood restaurant.

Inexpensive Pubs & Beer Halls

Japanese-style Pubs: Dondontei (middle center, map 4): Yakitori and sake or beer. **Ginza Shubo** (middle center, map 4): Robatayaki. **Kashiwado** (second floor of Suehiro, lower center, map 4): Chankonabe.

Beer Halls: Beer Hall Restaurant (upper center, map 4): The first floor is a beer hall popular with the staff of Japan National Tourist Organization. The second floor is a restaurant that's an especially good bargain for lunch. **GGC — Asahi Beer Hall** (second floor of **Food Center,** upper center, map 4). **Lion — Sapporo Beer Hall** (lower center, map 4).

5 Shibuya & Harajuku

District Fashionable Tokyo

Ideally, you should allocate one full day for Shibuya and Harajuku. Aoyama (District 6) and Akasaka (District 11) should be allocated another full day. If your time is limited, i.e., if you're staying in Tokyo for only four days, you can cover most of these areas in one day by skipping Shibuya and by selecting only the major places of interest in Harajuku and Aoyama, and by visiting Akasaka only in the evening.

Shibuya

You should skip this section if your time is limited, and you should start your walking tour from Harajuku (see below).

Shibuya is reached by either the JNR Yamanote Line or the Ginza subway line (the last stop on the line). Shibuya Station is very complicated because, in addition to the above two lines, it is also used by four other rail lines. The major attractions of Shibuya are located to the north of the station. If you get lost in the station, walk out any exit, and then refer to map 5 to get the landmarks in view.

As a large terminal where suburban commuters transfer from commuter trains to city transportation, Shibuya has a great many shopping, eating and drinking establishments. However, until recently Shibuya was just a typical white collar workers area. Parco, a new concept fashion building full of boutiques and accessory stores, has changed the character of the area. Parco attracted the young ladies, and other fashionable new enterprises sprang up to cater to the new traffic. With the completion

of the new headquarters of NHK (Japan Broadcasting Corporation), Koen-dori Street has become a promenade for young couples, connecting Shibuya, National Yoyogi Sports Center, Meiji Jingu Shrine and Harajuku.

Shopping in Shibuya

Tokyu Plaza (lower center, map 5), Fashion Community 109 (lower left, map 5), Seibu Department Store, Marui Fashion, Parco, Parco Part II, and Parco Part III are the major shopping buildings in the area. Tokyu Hands (middle left, map 5, near Parco) is a new department store that specializes in various do-it-yourself products for Sunday carpenters and hobbyists.

Tobacco & Salt Museum たばこと塩の博物館 **(middle left, map 5)**

This is probably the only museum of its kind in the world, and exists here only because the tobacco and salt businesses in Japan are administered by a monopolistic government agency. The first and second floors display objects related to smoking. Especially interesting are the numerous packages collected from all over the world. The third floor displays a huge salt rock imported from Poland. The fourth floor features wood-block prints featuring smoking, and a number of smoking devices (10 a.m. to 5:30 p.m. Closed on Mondays. Admission 100 yen).

NHK (Japan Broadcasting Corporation 日本放送協会 **(middle left, map 5)**

There is a 0.4 mile (0.6 km.) long observation path in the main building which leads visitors past several studios and panel displays featuring popular programs of the past. Sound tricks and film techniques are demonstrated. Because the displays are explained only in Japanese, foreigners may have difficulty understanding them, but it is still interesting to see the workings of a popular contemporary industry (10 a.m. to 5 p.m. Closed on the fourth Monday of each month. Admission free).

National Yoyogi Sports Center 国立代々木競技場 **(upper center, map 5)**

The two indoor arenas here were constructed for the 1964 Olympic Games. The large arena was used for the swimming competitions, while the smaller one hosted the ball games. Twenty years since they were built, their unique designs still fascinate visitors. You can see the inside of the large arena if it is not being used for a competition (10 a.m. to 4 p.m. Admission free).

Restaurants in Shibuya

American Fast Food: Dunkin Donuts and McDonald's are near Shibuya Station (lower center, map 5). Shakey's Pizza is on Koen-dori Street across from the Tobacco & Salt Museum.

Restaurants

Fashion Community 109 (lower left, map 5) houses many restaurants on the seventh and eighth floors. **Monte Rosa** (7F) is an Italian restaurant and serves spaghetti at 800-1,000 yen. **Tsunahachi** (7F) serves a good tempura set menu meal at 1,000-3,000 yen. **Vega** (8F) is a regular Western restaurant. Seafood salad is 1,500 yen and beef stew is 2,200 yen.

Parco (middle left, map 5) also has a number of restaurants on its sixth through eighth floors. **Shabutei** (6F) is a good place to taste shabu-shabu (only 1,500-2,400 yen). **El Domingo** (6F) has a 1,380

yen paella. **Inagiku** (8F) is a famous expensive tempura restaurant, but at this branch prices have been adjusted for the young customers (1,000-2,800 yen for set menus). **Rozan Hanten** (8F) is a Chinese restaurant. A typical dish costs 1,000-1,500 yen.

Steak House Volks (middle left, map 5) serves steak lunch at only 980 yen (a good value!). Steak dinner is 2,500 yen.

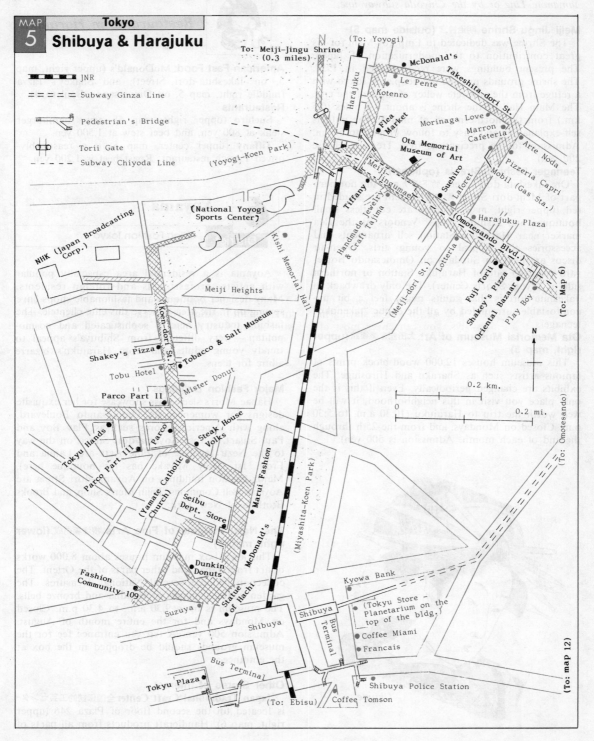

MAP 5

Tokyo
Shibuya & Harajuku

JNR
Subway Ginza Line
Pedestrian's Bridge
Torii Gate
Subway Chiyoda Line

Harajuku

Visitors with limited time should start their walking tours here. Harajuku can be reached by the JNR Yamanote Line or by the Chiyoda subway line.

Meiji Jingu Shrine 明治神宮 (outside map 5)

The Shrine was dedicated to Emperor Meiji for his great contribution to the modernization of Japan. The present buildings were reconstructed in 1958. The shrine grounds provide the people of Tokyo with a refuge from the concrete welter of most of the city. The Main Hall of the shrine is about 0.3 miles (0.5 km.) from the northern end of map 5. The path is self-explanatory and easy to follow (9 a.m. to 5 p.m. Admission to the precincts is free. Treasure House 200 yen).

Teenager Fashion Streets (optional)

On Takeshita-dori Street 竹下通り and the northern part of Meiji-dori Street 明治通り (both are shaded in red, upper right, map 5) there are countless small boutiques and fashion shops. Vendors at the flea market near Harajuku Station sell ornaments and accessories that appeal to young girls. Open-air discos are held on Sundays on Omotesando Boulevard (western side of Harajuku Station or northern side of Yoyogi Sports Center). The only drawback to Takeshita-dori is that adults might feel a bit uncomfortable surrounded by all the exotic "takenoko" teenagers.

Ota Memorial Museum of Art 太田記念美術館 (upper right, map 5)

This museum houses 12,000 wood-block prints of famous artists such as Sharaku and Hiroshige. The exhibits are changed periodically. Even if this is the only place you visit in this neighborhood, it will be well worth the trip to Harajuku (10:30 a.m. to 5:30 p.m. Closed on Mondays, and from the 25th through the end of each month. Admission is 500 yen).

Ukiyoe

Towards Aoyama

Omotesando Boulevard is lined with lovely gingko trees and, in my opinion, is the most beautiful street in Tokyo. After crossing Meiji-dori Street, there are two antique stores — **Fuji Torii** and **Oriental Bazaar.** Once you pass these two shops you've entered Aoyama (District 6).

Restaurants in Harajuku

American Fast Food: McDonald's (upper right, map 5, on Takeshita-dori Street), and Shakey's Pizza (middle right, map 5, on Omotesando Boulevard).

Restaurants

Suehiro (upper right, map 5) serves hamburger steak at 800 yen, and beef stew at 1,500 yen.

Tiffany (upper center, map 5) is a reasonably-priced French restaurant. Roast beef is 1,200 yen.

6

District   **Aoyama**

High Fashion Tokyo

Aoyama is a residential area especially popular with artists, professionals and foreign residents. Many designer boutiques and fashionable shops have sprung up in the area to serve this elite clientele. The fashion industry here is sophisticated and cosmopolitan — very different from Shibuya's appeal to trendy young adults and from Harajuku's bizarre allure for teens.

Major Fashion Buildings

Hanae Mori's sleek glass showcase for her exquisite designs for women is on Omotesando Boulevard, along with American stores such as Play Boy and Paul Stuart. Across Aoyama-dori Street, on the way to the Nezu Institute of Fine Arts are Lamia and From 1st (Issey Miyake has his boutique here). Major Fashion buildings on Aoyama-dori Street are Aoyama Bell Commons, Teijin Men's Shop, and Brooks Brothers of New York.

The Nezu Institute of Fine Arts 根津美術館 (lower right, map 6)

This jewel-box museum houses about 8,000 works of art from Japan and other parts of the Orient. The collection includes several National Treasures. The garden features images of Buddha and bronze bells. The museum is open 9:30 a.m. to 4:30 p.m. Closed on Mondays and for the entire month of August. Admission 500 yen. A ten yen entrance fee for the museum grounds should be dropped in the box at the entrance.

Other Stores of Interest

Japan Traditional Craft Center 全国伝統的工芸センター is located on the second floor of Plaza 246 (upper right, map 6). Handicraft products from all parts of

Japan, including lacquer ware, pottery, silk clothing and accessories, are displayed and sold here. Even if you don't purchase anything, just browsing through the lovely displays is quite enjoyable.

Crayon House クレヨン・ハウス (middle left, map 6, on Omotesando Boulevard) has a small book store on the second floor that stocks children's picture books from around the world.

Restaurants

American Fast Food: Wendy's and Kentucky Fried Chicken (middle center, map 6) are on Aoyama-dori Street. There is no McDonald's in this area yet.

Restaurants

Leger is a French restaurant located on the ground floor of **Diamond Hall** (middle center, map 6). The lunch special is 1,300 yen. Dinners range in price from 5,000 to 7,000 yen. **Anjou** is another popular French restaurant located on the fifth floor of Aoyama Bell Commons (upper right, map 6.). Lunch is 2,000 yen and dinner 5,000 yen. **Gooseberry** (middle right, map 6) is an American style sandwich shop. **Tempura Miyagawa** (lower right, map 6),

located near the Nezu Museum, serves a set menu tempura meal at 1,000-2,000 yen. **Genrokuzushi** (middle left, map 6). This automated, self-service restaurant is a lot of fun. It's also one of the few places where a la carte sushi is reasonably priced. Small plates with two pieces of sushi each revolve on a conveyor belt, and guests take their pick. Each plate costs 120 yen, so 20 pieces of sushi (10 plates) will only be 1,200 yen. There are many of these conveyor belt shops in Japan, but the quality of the fish they serve is usually very poor. This shop, however, is exceptional and I recommend that this is the place to choose if you're interested in trying one of these Japanese automats.

Suggestions for your next destination

After Aoyama, Akasaka is the logical destination for the evening. Take the Ginza subway line from either Omote-Sando or Gaiénmae Station to Akasakamitsuke (only a five minute ride). As explained below in the District 11 section, there are a few good places to visit before dark.

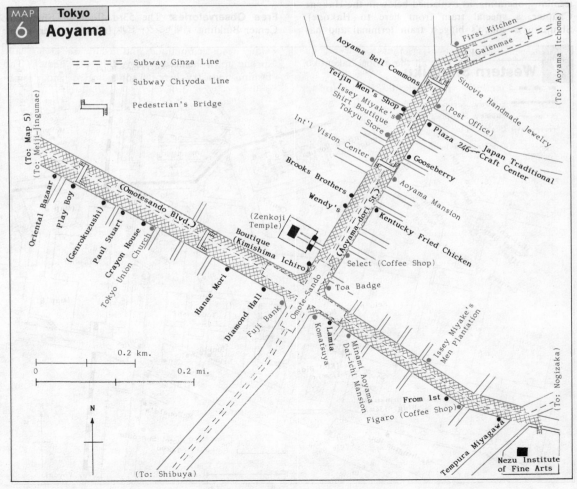

7 Western Shinjuku

In the last ten years Western Shinjuku has undergone the most drastic changes of any area of Tokyo. The area used to be nothing more than a sleepy small town whose only claim to fame was that it was the location of the reservoirs that provided millions of Tokyoites with their water. But starting with the completion of the Keio Plaza Hotel, more than 10 skyscrapers have been constructed in the area, and development is planned to continue into the 21st century.

How to Get to and from Shinjuku

The JNR Yamanote Line, and the Marunouchi and Shinjuku subway lines serve Shinjuku Station (The Odakyu private line also uses Shinjuku as its terminus, operating, as explained below in the Hakone Chapter, a special train from here to Hakone). Shinjuku is Tokyo's biggest train terminal and has extensive, confusing underground passages and shopping malls. When you arrive at Shinjuku, walk towards the West Exit. Don't stay underground. Go up onto the surface and use map 7 to get oriented. The broad bus terminal area and the four huge cylindrical air vents are good landmarks.

Leaving the Shinjuku area can present even more of a problem. If you are taking the JNR Yamanote Line from Shinjuku, you shouldn't have any trouble because all the entrances to the station building lead to the JNR station. But if you want to take the Marunouchi subway line, don't go into the station building. Walk instead to the north, past the Odakyu Department Store until you come to the big English "subway" sign as pictured on map 7 (middle right); from there many English signs will lead you to the ticket machines and the subway entrance. If you want the Shinjuku subway line stay on the surface until you arrive at the approximate location of the station (lower right, map 7) where you will find English "Shinjuku Station" sings indicating the entrance. Refer to map E for details of the Station.

Places of Interest

Free Observatories: The 53rd floor of Shinjuku Center Building 新宿センタービル (middle center, map

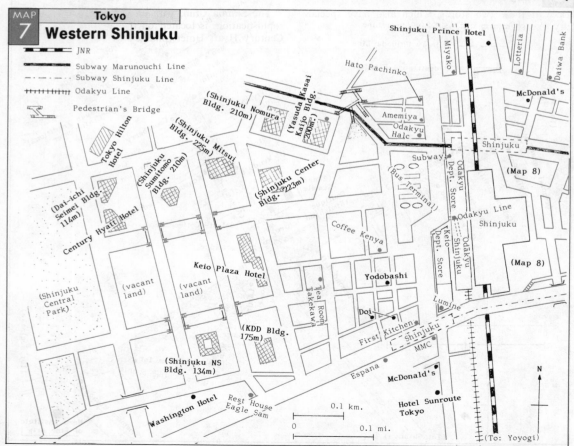

7), the 50th floor of Shinjuku Nomura Building 新宿野村ビル (upper center) and the 51st floor of Shinjuku Sumitomo Building 新宿住友ビル (middle left) have free observatories.

Togo Seiji Museum 東郷青児美術館: About 100 works of Seiji Togo, a great master of paintings of girls, are displayed on the 42nd floor of Yasuda Kasai Kaijo Building 安田火災海上ビル (upper center, map 7). The museum also has an observatory gallery overlooking the Shinjuku area (9:30 a.m. to 4:30 p.m. Closed on Saturdays, Sundays and holidays. Admission 300 yen).

Shinjuku NS Building 新宿NSビル **(lower center, map 7)**

At only 440 feet or 134 m., this building is dwarfed by many of its neighbors, but its unique interior — with an atrium topped with a glass roof — opened a new chapter in Japanese architecture. A 24-foot (7 m.) tall antique clock stands in the first floor lobby. The basement exhibition hall is one of Tokyo's largest. Nineteen computer companies have showrooms on the fifth floor.

Discount Camera Shops

Tokyo's two leading discount camera shops, Yodobashi and Doi (both middle center, map 7) are located near the station. Recently the Japanese have been bored with large professional type cameras, and are now more interested in compact, automatic-focus electronic models. All the models of many different camera makers are displayed and sold at discount prices at these two stores, which also have special duty free shopping.

Restaurants & a Disco

As a general rule, the higher up the floor on which restaurants are located, the more expensive their prices. However, all of the following restaurants serve good food at reasonable prices, and have magnificent views of Tokyo as well.

Shinjuku NS Building

Orizuru-tei (30F) is a good choice if you want to sample an authentic Japanese full course meal. The full course set menu lunch (Orizuru Kaiseki) is 3,500 yen and the full course set menu dinner (Take Kaiseki) is 6,000 yen. **Suehiro** (29F) serves a steak lunch for 800 yen. Steak dinner is 2,500 yen. **Ise** (29F) specializes in tonkatsu (pork cutlet) (1,000-1,500 yen). **The Old Kitchen** has a varied continental menu (around 1,000 yen average). **Hakkaku** is a robatayaki pub. This is a good place to sample Japanese seafood and sake (480 yen per item).

Shinjuku Nomura Building

Tempura Tsunahachi (49F) serves set menu tempura meals at 1,000-4,000 yen. **Miyoshitei** (49F) serves a combination of Japanese and Chinese food. Several dishes are available for less than 1,000 yen. **Swiss Chalet** (50F) serves dinners that start at 2,200 yen.

Disco

The Samba Club, with an atmosphere of studied sophistication, is located on the ground floor of the Century Hyatt Hotel (middle left, map 7).

Skyscrapers in Shinjuku.

8 Eastern Shinjuku

District | Eternally Confusing Tokyo

Everything new under the rising sun, especially everything new with young people, makes its first appearance in Eastern Shinjuku. If the behavior of young people is a barometer of future societal trends, Eastern Shinjuku is certainly the place to get an idea of where Japanese society is headed, for better or worse.

Outline of the District

There are two distinct areas in Eastern Shinjuku. The southern part, from Shinjuku-dori Street south (middle center and middle right, map 8), is a traditional shopping and restaurant area. The northern part, to the north of Yasukuni-dori Street (upper left, map 8), called Kabukicho 歌舞伎町, is Tokyo's biggest amusement center. It is estimated that Kabukicho's population during the day time is only 3,000, but that its night time population is 400,000. Even at midnight, the stream of people headed toward Kabukicho from the station is much larger than that of those going toward the station on their way home. Kabukicho is drinking places, discos, snack shops, trysting places for young couples, and pornographic salons. It crackles with the energy of the young people who throng its streets. It is alluring, seductive, enticing, gaudy, tawdry, vulgar, exhilarating and exciting all at once. The destination of desires, it is a place where the veils that usually mask human emotions are torn aside. A lot of scams and bunco schemes are in operation here but violent crimes are seldom heard of. Kabukicho is especially safe for foreign tourists because the denizens of the street are afraid to even talk to foreigners. Don't be afraid to walk on the streets shaded in red on map 8, but if you are a woman, don't stay in the area alone after 8 p.m. After then most of the men will be drunk and, inspired by alcohol, quite likely to make propositions that you probably won't find welcome.

How to Get There

As explained in the Western Shinjuku district section, Shinjuku is the biggest train terminal in Tokyo, served by the JNR Yamanote Line, the Marunouchi and Shinjuku subway lines, etc. If you visit Shinjuku by either subway line, the Shinjuku-Sanchome Station is also convenient for Eastern Shinjuku. When leaving Shinjuku, again, it's best to stay on the surface and walk to the approximate location of the station to find an entrance with an English sign.

Stores

Isetan (middle right, map 8) is a huge department store especially popular with young people.

Kinokuniya Bookstore (middle center, map 8) has an inventory of 400,000 books. Believe it or not, 40,000 of them are foreign books, most of them in English.

Sakuraya and **Yodobashi** (both middle center, map 8) are two more discount camera stores.

JC Tax-Free (lower center, map 8) handles electric and electronic products, and other souvenir items, and caters to foreign tourists.

An **antique flea market** is held on the first Saturdays and on the third Sundays of each month in the precincts of Hanazono Jinja Shrine (from dawn till dusk) (middle right, map 8).

Restaurants, Pubs & Discos

American Fast Food: McDonald's has three locations in Eastern Shinjuku, one right in the heart of Kabukicho (upper left, map 8), the second on the way to Shinjuku Station from Kabukicho (middle left, map 8), and the third in the shopping area (lower center, map 8). Kentucky Fried Chicken is located at the southern end of Kabukicho ("KFC", upper left, map 8), and Wendy's is in the shopping area across from McDonald's (lower center, map 8).

Inexpensive Restaurants (2,500 yen or less for dinner)
Western: Jack & Betty Club (middle center, map 8) is an American-style sandwich shop (500-700 yen). **Stew Ukraine** (middle center, map 8) serves a variety of Russian stews at 1,000 to 1,300 yen.
Japanese: Tempura Tsunahachi (basement of **Studio Alta**, middle center, map 8) serves tasty set menu tempura meals at 990-1,400 yen. **Hinodezushi** (also in the basement of Studio Alta) has set menu sushi at 1,200 yen. **Funabashiya** (middle center, map 8) is an authentic tempura restaurant. The 2,000 yen selection is good. The restaurant does not have an English sign but is easily recognized by its Japanese-style entrance located right at the intersection.
Others: Korean Barbecue (Tokaien) (middle center, map 8) serves an as-much-as-you-can-eat barbecue dinner at only 1,800 yen (Make sure to go to the 6F. The 7th to 9th floors are the same restaurant, but serve only an a la carte menu.).

Moderate Restaurants (2,500-5,000 yen for dinner)
Essen (5F of **Takayama Land Kaikan,** middle right, map 8) is a popular German restaurant. **Suehiro** (6F of Takayama Land Kaikan, the same as the above) serves sukiyaki and shabu-shabu at reasonable prices. **Amimoto** (upper center, map 8) is famous for its fresh seafood. Sukiyaki is also served here (No

English sign, but many red lanterns at the entrance). **Chinese Restaurant Baien** (upper center, map 8) is next to Amimoto. **Yarozushi** (upper center, map 8) is a very small sushi bar. If you are ready to pay 5,000 yen, you can eat sushi to your heart's content (but don't order too many pieces of "toro" or "uni", the most expensive items). People usually pay 2,000-2,500 yen here for 12-16 pieces (remember that in sushi bars each individual order consists of 2 pieces).

Inexpensive Pubs

Jazz Club Pit Inn (middle center, map 8). Live jazz performances. **Pub Sherlock Holmes** (6F of **American House,** middle center, map 8) is an English-style pub. **Shinjuku Wine House** (5F of **Saison Plaza,** middle right, map 8) is a good place to sample Japanese wines at reasonable prices. Imported wines are also served. **Haikara Hida** (first basement of **Takayama Land Kaikan,** middle right, map 8) is a Japanese-

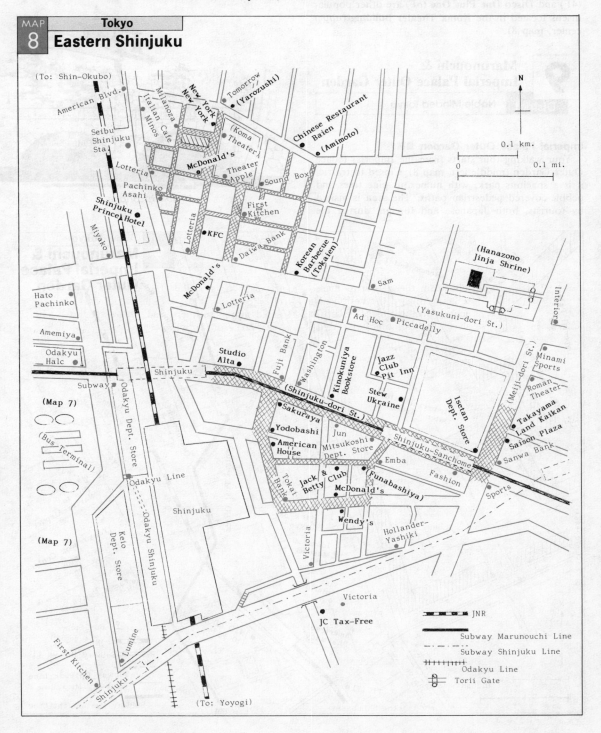

MAP 8 Tokyo
Eastern Shinjuku

style pub which serves skewered fish, meat and vegetables. No English sign, but this is the only shop on the first basement.

Discos

All the discos in Eastern Shinjuku are filled with youngsters. **New York New York** (upper center, map 8) is on the fourth floor of Joy Pac Building. Though not pictured on map 8, **Disco Studio Xenon** (4F) and **Disco One Plus One** (6F) are other popular discos located in the **Koma Theater Building** (upper center, map 8).

9
Marunouchi & Imperial Palace Outer Garden
District Noble-Minded Tokyo

Imperial Palace Outer Garden 皇居外苑

Your walking tour starts from the Imperial Palace Outer Garden (middle left, map 8). Closed to traffic, it is a spacious park, with numerous pine trees and pebble-covered pedestrian paths. The area is visited by tourists, both Japanese and foreign, during the

daytime, and by amorous couples in the evening. If you are a camera fan, the shot of Nijubashi Bridge with the Palace's turret and moats behind it is not to be missed. The Palace itself is not open to the public.

Many kinds of public transportation are available to reach the Outer Garden: the Chiyoda subway line's Nijubashimae Station 二重橋前 and the Mita

Nijubashi Bridge

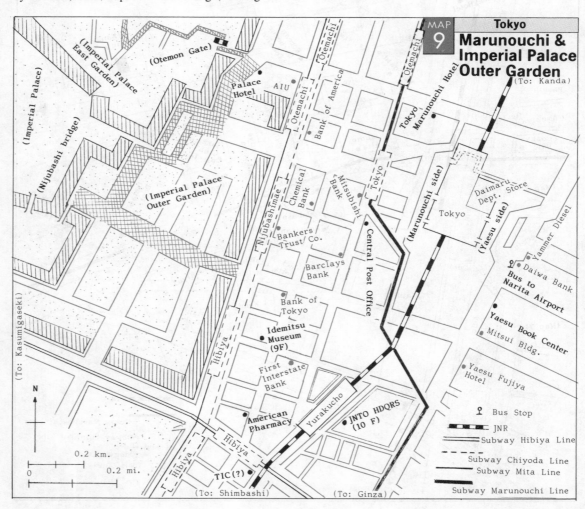

subway line's Hibiya Station 日比谷 are the closest. If you are walking to the Garden from the Hibiya subway line's Hibiya Station or from JNR's Yuraku-cho Station 有楽町, Idemitsu Museum is on the way. If you approach the Garden from the Marunouchi subway line's Tokyo Station 東京 or from JNR's Tokyo Station, you will pass through the Marunouchi business district on your way.

Other places of interest in the area (if you have extra time)

Marunouchi 丸の内 is the area sandwiched between the JNR lines and the Imperial Palace moats. To the south of Marunouchi are Yurakucho and Hibiya (see District 4 section above). Marunouchi is Japan's business headquarters, and many conglomerates, especially the companies of the Mitsubishi conglomerate, have company headquarters here. (Before it was developed, the area was known as Mitsubishi Meadow). Many foreign financial corporations also have Japanese subsidiaries here. For tourists Marunouchi is really nothing more than rows of modern concrete and glass office buildings. However, it is here that you can see what the members of Japan's business elite look like.

Idemitsu Museum 出光美術館 (middle center, map 9) is located on the ninth floor of Kokusai building. The entrance to the museum is clearly marked in English at ground level. The museum specializes in Japanese and Oriental (especially Chinese) antiquities, and is especially renowned for its collection of pottery and ceramics (10 a.m. to 5 p.m. Admission 500 yen).

Yaesu Book Center 八重洲ブックセンター (middle right, map 9) is on the other side of Tokyo Station, in the Yaesu area. This five-story bookstore contains as many as one million books. If you tire of looking at the books, you can take a coffee break on the mezzanine. It's not worth making a detour to visit this bookstore because the District 10 section below introduces Kanda, Japan's bookworm's paradise. Ideally, Kanda should be visited after the Imperial Palace. But if you happen to be in the Yaesu area for some other reason, drop in here.

After visiting Nijubashi Bridge, proceed to Otemon Gate (upper center, map 9).
If your time is really limited, you can go to this Gate directly, skipping the Outer Garden. Continue to District 10.

10 District
Imperial Palace East Garden & Kanda

Bookaholic Tokyo

Imperial Palace East Garden 皇居東御苑 (continued from District 9)

What is now the Imperial Palace East Garden used to be the main grounds of Edojo Castle. Otemon Gate (lower right, map 10) was the main entrance to the castle grounds. Though most of the castle buildings were lost to repeated fires, the garden grounds still contain the Hundred-guard Office, huge old stone walls, and neatly maintained ponds, flower-beds and pine trees. The stone base of the donjon is at the northwestern end of the grounds. The grounds are open to the public from 9 a.m. to 4 p.m., but visitors are not admitted after 3 p.m. Closed on Mondays and Fridays, but if a Monday or a Friday is a holiday, the Garden is open. At the entrance visitors receive numbered cards that have to be turned in when exiting. There are three gates — Otemon, Kita-Hanebashimon and Hirakawamon. The visitor can enter and exit at any of the three. Admission free.

Kitanomaru-Koen Park 北ノ丸公園 (upper left, map 10)

Kitanomaru was also part of Edojo Castle. The Park is now open to the public 24 hours a day. Coming out of the East Garden through Kita-Hanebashimon Gate and using the pedestrian bridge to cross the wide street, you will reach the entrance to the Park. Four museums are located in the southern part of the Park.

My first recommendation is the **Craft Gallery of the National Museum of Modern Art** 国立近代美術館工芸館 (middle left, map 10). This brown brick museum displays the highest quality craft works of contemporary masters. The displays include textiles, ceramics, glass ware, lacquer ware, wood ware, bamboo ware, metal works, etc. (10 a.m. to 5 p.m. Closed on Mondays. Admission 300 yen).

The National Museum of Modern Art 国立近代美術館 often holds special exhibitions of the works of modern and contemporary painters and sculptors (10 a.m. to 5 p.m. Closed on Mondays. Admission 250 yen, higher for special exhibitions).

The Science Museum 科学技術館 is always crowded with school children. The exhibits are not particularly interesting for adults, but this is a good place to get an idea of how the scientific education of Japanese children is organized and conducted. (9:30 a.m. to 4:50 p.m. Closed only during New Year's Holidays. Admission 500 yen).

Yasukuni Jinja Shrine 靖国神社

At the northern end of the Park is Tayasumon Gate — the northernmost gate of Edojo Castle. Yasukuni Jinja Shrine (outside map 10, a few minutes walk to the west after crossing Yasukuni-dori Street) enshrines the spirits of the 2.5 million soldiers who died in the wars since the Meiji Restoration. The shrine has been controversial for a long time. Left-wing political groups have accused the conservative parties of disregarding the tragedy these wars brought to the nation and of trying to revitalize Japanese militarism by putting too much emphasis on this shrine and the chauvinism they say it encourages. In spite of all this, the shrine grounds are famous as one of the best places in Tokyo to enjoy cherry blossoms in early April.

Kanda

The Kanda district, the center of which is **Jimbocho** 神保町, is about 0.6 miles (1 km.) from Tayasumon Gate. If you are tired of walking, you can take the Shinjuku subway line to Jimbocho (only one stop). Kanda (Jimbocho) is a scholars' and students' area, especially famous as a mecca for bookstores, particularly second-hand books. More than 50 bookstores line the southern side of Yasukuni-dori Street, on both sides of Jimbocho Station. Traditionally, Japan has absorbed advanced cultures, science and technology by way of written documents, from China and other Asian countries in olden times, and from European countries and the U.S. in modern times. The Japanese love of books developed as a result of these experiences, and still endures even though TV and other audio-visual media have, in recent years, diminished what used to be the overwhelming popularity and power of the written word.

Some bookstores of interest: Sanseido (upper right, map 10) has the greatest floor space of any Japanese bookstore. If you want to take a look at just one Japanese bookstore, this is the place. **Ohya-Shobo** handles an extensive inventory of old Japanese books, hand-written documents (calligraphy) and wood-block prints. **Charles E. Tuttle** deals in new Western (mostly English language) books. **Hara Shobo** has a good inventory of wood-block prints. **Shogakudo** and **Kitazawa** handle second-hand European and American literature.

Komingu Kottokan 古民具骨董館 (upper right, map 10): This is a sort of headquarters for all the antique dealers in Japan. More than 50 dealers are located in this building. Most of the antique flea markets held throughout Japan are operated by these dealers (10 a.m. to 7 p.m. Open year round).

Place for Lunch

Iroha near Jimbocho Station is an all purpose restaurant. Typical Japanese foods, such as sushi and tempura are served on the first floor, and Japanized western food, such as pork cutlet and fried shrimp, is served on the second floor. Prices range from 700 to 1,300 yen. There is no English sign, but its large window display of plastic models makes it easy to find.

Suggestions

You can easily spend a whole day in the Imperial Palace area and Kanda. If your time is limited, I recommend that you visit Shinjuku after Kanda because the subway connection is so easy. Take the Shinjuku subway line from Jimbocho straight to Shinjuku.

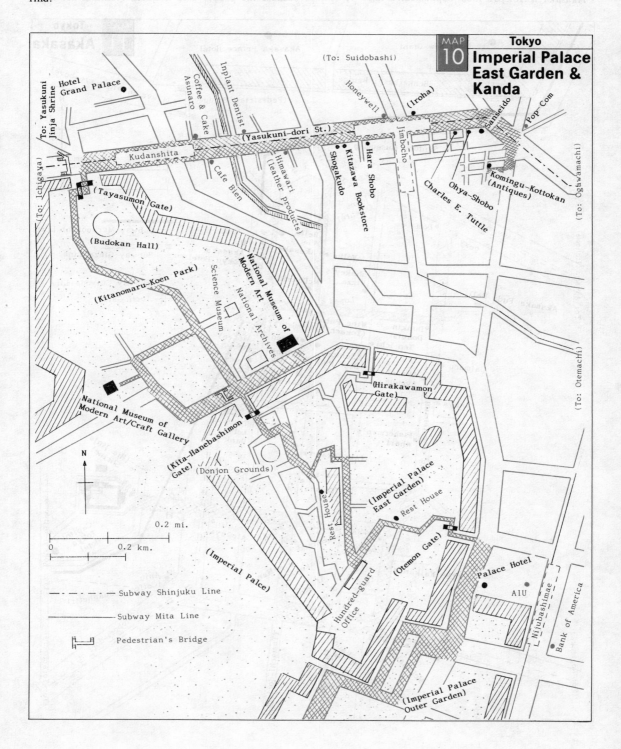

MAP 10 Tokyo

Imperial Palace East Garden & Kanda

(To: Suidobashi)

To: Yasukuni Jinja Shrine

Hotel Grand Palace

Coffee & Cake Asunaro

Inplant Dentist

(To: Ichigaya)

Honeywell

(Iroha)

Sanseido

Pop-Com

(Yasukuni-dori St.)

Kudanshita

Cafe Bien

Himawari (leather products)

Shogakudo

Kitazawa Bookstore

Hara Shobo

Jimbocho

Charles E. Tuttle

Ohya-Shobo

Komingu-Kottokan (Antiques)

(To: Ogawamachi)

(Tayasumon Gate)

(Budokan Hall)

(Kitanomaru-Koen Park)

Science Museum

National Art Museum of Modern

National Archives

National Museum of Modern Art/Craft Gallery

(Kita-Hanebashimon Gate)

(Donjon Grounds)

N

0.2 mi.

0 0.2 km.

(Imperial Palace)

(Hirakawamon Gate)

(To: Otemachi)

Rest House

(Imperial Palace East Garden)

Rest House

(Otemon Gate)

Hundred-guard Office

Palace Hotel

AIU

Niiubashimae

Bank of America

—·—·— Subway Shinjuku Line

——— Subway Mita Line

Pedestrian's Bridge

(Imperial Palace Outer Garden)

11

District

Akasaka

International Tokyo

Akasaka is Tokyo's most sophisticated night spot.

Because the area is patronized mainly by politicians and bureaucrats who are busy arranging their next maneuvers, by businessmen on company expense accounts, by high society people, and by foreign VIPs visiting Tokyo, prices are generally quite high. Foreign visitors often say that they feel most comfortable in Akasaka. This is probably because the area is accustomed to taking care of foreigners, and because the people who frequent Akasaka are more

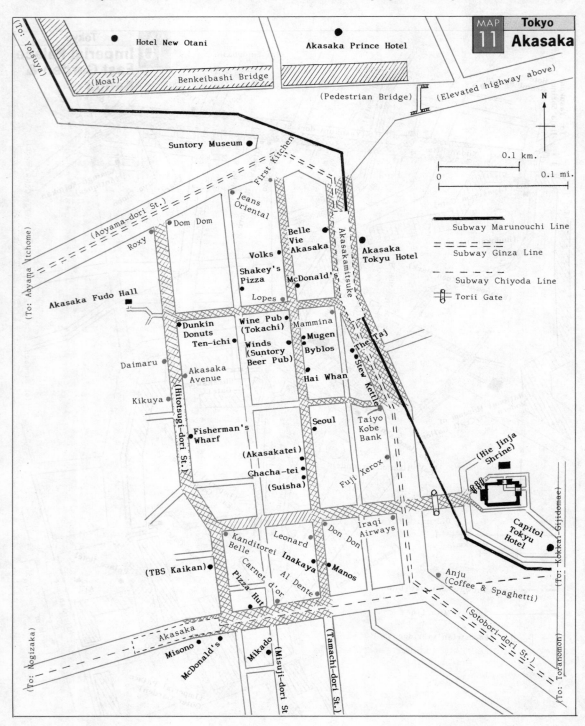

international minded than the average Japanese. In Akasaka foreigners are never objects of curiosity.

The Marunouchi and Ginza subway lines serve Akasakamitsuke Station and the Chiyoda subway line stops at Akasaka Station.

Be forewarned that after midnight, when the subway service ends, it is extremely difficult to find an empty taxi in Akasaka. Call it a night while the subway is still in operation (by 11:30 p.m.).

If You Get to Akasaka before Dusk

Suntory Museum サントリー美術館 (upper center, map 11) is located on the 11th floor of the Suntory Building. The museum houses about 2,000 traditional Japanese art objects, including paintings, lacquer ware, glass ware and women's ornaments, several of which are National Treasures. A real tea house is attached to the museum, and, if it's not occupied by a group, you can enjoy real tea-ceremony powdered green tea there (300 yen). The spectacular view of Akasaka and Shinjuku from the windows is a nice bonus (10 a.m. to 5 p.m. Until 7 p.m. on Fridays. Closed on Mondays. Admission 500 yen; 300 yen on Sundays).

Hie Jinja Shrine 日枝神社 (lower right, map 11) is another place you should visit in Akasaka. The entrance is marked by a big torii gate. At the end of the street are steep stone steps lined with numerous small red torii gates. Watch your head when passing under them. This authentic shrine is quite impressive, and the precincts are unexpectedly quiet despite the shrine's location right next to the bustling play town.

Restaurants & Night Spots

Tamachi-dori 田町通り and **Hitotsugi-dori** 一ッ木通り streets are crowded with all sorts of restaurants, pubs, discos and pachinko pinball parlors (both streets are shaded in red on map 11). Misuji-dori Street, located between them, is a rather quiet street that is home to many extremely expensive Japanese-style restaurants. These restaurants have many private rooms which are used for business negotiations and for entertaining real VIPs. Geisha are often called to these establishments to enhance the party atmosphere. Stay away from these places unless you are invited by Japanese business associates. No one can afford these places on one's own; they are strictly for expense accounts only.

American Fast Food: There are five American fast food shops in the prestigious night zone. They are two McDonald's (lower center and middle center, map 11), Pizza Hut (lower center), Dunkin Donuts (middle left) and Shakey's Pizza (middle center).

Reasonable Restaurants (5,000 yen or less for dinner)

Western: Stew Kettle (middle center, map 11) has a full line of stew dishes. **Al Dente** (7F of **Belle Vie Akasaka,** upper center, map 11) is an Italian spaghetti restaurant. **Volks** (upper center, 2F) is famous for its inexpensive steaks. **Manos** (lower center) serves authentic Russian dishes.

Japanese: Tsunahachi (8F of Belle Vie Akasaka, upper center, map 11) is a tempura restaurant. **Fukusuke** (7F of the same building) is a sushi restaurant. An a la carte dinner may cost about 3,000 - 5,000 yen.

Others: Seoul (middle center, map 11) is a Korean barbecue restaurant, probably the best place to eat your fill of beef at a reasonable price in this area. **Nangokushuka** (8F of Belle Vie Akasaka) is great if you're hungry for Chinese food. **The Taj** (middle center, map 11) is known for its authentic Indian curry.

Expensive Restaurants (5,000 yen to 10,000 yen or more)

Western: Fisherman's Wharf (middle left, map 11) is an American-style seafood restaurant. **Granata** is Italian, and **Shido** French. Both are located in the basement of the **TBS Kaikan Building** (middle left, map 11). TBS is Japan's largest private TV broadcasting network. **Misono** (lower left, map 11) is a renowned steak restaurant.

Japanese: Ten-ichi (middle center, map 11) is a tempura house well prepared for foreign guests. **Zakuro** (basement of the TBS Kaikan Building, middle left, map 11) serves superb sukiyaki and shabu-shabu dinners.

Others: Hai Whan (middle center, map 11) is famous for its Chinese-style seafood dishes.

Pubs

Western-style: Wine Pub Tokachi (middle center, map 11) serves Japanese wine produced in the Tokachi area of Hokkaido island. The wine has a reputation as the best in Japan. **Winds** (middle center) is a Suntory beer hall.

Japanese-style: Chacha-tei (middle center, map 11) serves oden (fish cakes, sliced radish, eggs, tofu, etc. boiled together in a soup). **Akasakatei** (2F of Chacha-tei) is a yakitori pub. **Suisha** (middle center, map 11) and **Inakaya** (lower center, map 11) are robatayaki pubs. Inakaya has an English sign. Though Suisha has no English sign, it does have a watermill ("suisha") signs at its entrance.

Discos

Mugen and **Byblos** (middle center, map 11) are well known discos often frequented by foreign visitors.

Cabaret

Mikado (lower center, map 11) is famous for the waterfalls and lavish displays of its small garden. Foreign entertainers often perform in Mikado's live shows. Expensive.

One final place of interest in Akasaka

If you have a chance to walk on Hitotsugi-dori Street, visit **Akasaka Fudo Hall** 赤坂不動尊 (middle left, map 11). Although the Hall itself is only a small structure housing an image of the god Fudo, the narrow path leading to the hall is illuminated by many small lanterns, and is especially exotic and romantic in the evening.

12 Roppongi

District | Night Owl Tokyo

Roppongi is popular among Tokyo's young sophisticates and "artistes." It also appeals to many foreign residents because it is easily accessible from the embassies located in nearby Azabu, and because a liberal atmosphere pervades the neighborhood. This has helped to give Roppongi an international flavor. Even former President Carter, during his stay in Tokyo, slipped away from his hotel and visited Roppongi (incognito, he believed!). Roppongi in recent years has become so caught up in its night life that it's no longer much of a residential area, but it is a very enjoyable place for urban owls.

The Hibiya subway line (Roppongi Station) is the only method of public transportation to Roppongi.

As is the case with Akasaka it is extremely difficult to find an unoccupied taxi after midnight in Roppongi. Finish your day while the subway is still available.

Shopping

Folkcraft Tsukamoto (upper right, map 12) has a good inventory of small handicraft items suitable for souvenirs. **Toshikane Art Porcelain** (lower left, map 12) handles innovative porcelain products such as pins and pendants. **Wave** (lower left, map 12) is a music store. Records, tapes, scores and musical literature from around the world are on sale here.

Restaurants & Night Spots

American Fast Food: McDonald's (upper center, map 12) and Kentucky Fried Chicken ("KFC") (middle center, map 12) are located in Roppongi, too.

Reasonable Restaurants (less than 5,000 yen for dinner)
Western: Berni Inn (middle right, map 12) serves good quality steaks at 2,000 to 3,200 yen. **Stew Kettle** (middle right, map 12) is a stew specialist (1,800 yen). **Double Ax** (middle center, map 12) is a Greek restaurant — Greek dances are performed twice nightly (dinner 7,000 yen for two). **Tokyo Swiss Inn** (upper right, map 12) is a renowned Swiss restaurant (entrees range from 1,800-4,500 yen).

Japanese: Inagiku (basement of **Sunroser,** upper center, map 12) is the Roppongi branch of the world famous Inagiku tempura restaurant. An a la carte dinner costs about 5,000 yen.

Others: Tokyo-en (upper center, map 12) is a Korean barbecue restaurant. **Raja** (middle left, map 12) is an Indian restaurant. **Bungawan Solo** (lower left, map 12) is an Indonesian restaurant.

Expensive Restaurants (5,000 - 10,000 yen and up)
Seryna is a famous, elegant shabu-shabu restaurant (middle center, map 15). **Hai-Kung** is a Chinese-style restaurant renowned for its seafood (middle right, map 12).

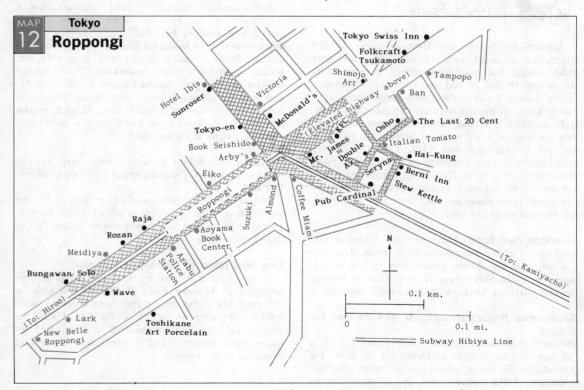

MAP 12 Tokyo **Roppongi**

Tokyo Swiss Inn
Folkcraft Tsukamoto
Shimojo Art
Tampopo
Hotel Ibis
Sunroser
Victoria
McDonald's
Ban
(Elevated highway above)
KFC
Osho
The Last 20 Cent
Tokyo-en
Mr. James
Double Ax
Italian Tomato
Book Seishido
Hai-Kung
Arby's
Seryna
Berni Inn
Eiko
Roppongi
Suzuki
Almond
Coffee Miami
Stew Kettle
Pub Cardinal
Raja
Rozan
Aoyama Book Center
Meidiya
Azabu Police Station
Bungawan Solo
Wave
(To: Kamiyacho)
(To: Hiroo)
Lark
New Belle Roppongi
Toshikane Art Porcelain
N
0.1 km.
0   0.1 mi.
Subway Hibiya Line

Pubs

Mr. James (middle right, map 12) is a pub with live Dixie and Country and Western music. **Pub Cardinal** (middle center, map 12) is popular among foreign residents.

Disco

"The Last 20 Cent" (middle center, map 12) is one of the most popular in Roppongi. There are several discos located on the upper floors of the same building.

THE LAST TWENTY CENT

Disco

13 Kasumigaseki

District Governmental Tokyo

Kasumigaseki is the central area of Tokyo. Most governmental institutions are concentrated here, including the National Diet, most Ministries and the Supreme Court. Because the area can be reached easily by many subways, you can visit here whenever you find some extra time (see map 13 for details).

Japan's modern government, established after World War II, was founded on the new Constitution, which was promulgated on November 3, 1946 and came into effect six months later. Under the new Constitution, the Emperor, who had had sovereign power, became a symbol of the State, and sovereign power is declared to rest with the people. Three independent governmental branches, the legislative, the executive and the judiciary, operate on checks-and-balances principles.

Legislative 立法

The Diet consists of two Houses, the House of Representatives 衆議院 (511 seats) and the House of Councillors 参議院 (252 seats). The members of both Houses are elected by the votes of those 20 years of age and older. The term of office for the Representatives is four years, but the House can be dissolved by the Prime Minister before the term is completed. The term of office for Councillors is six years, and half of the members are elected every three years (no dissolution). The House of Representatives has much more real power than the House of Councillors. More than seven parties have seats in the Diet. The Liberal Democratic Party 自由民主党 has held the majority in both Houses since 1955. The Socialists 日本社会党 Komeito 公明党 (Clean Government), Democratic Socialists 民主社会党 and Communists 日本共産党 are the other major political parties.

Executive 行政

Executive power rests with the Cabinet. The Prime Minister is elected by the Diet. Typically, the chairman of the majority party is elected Prime Minister. The other ministers who form the Cabinet are selected by the Prime Minister 内閣総理大臣 . The following are the major ministries and agencies: Ministry of Justice 法務省, Ministry of Foreign Affairs 外務省, Ministry of Finance 大蔵省, Ministry of International Trade & Industry 通商産業省 (the famous, or, in the eyes of some, the notorious MITI), Ministry of Education 文部省, Ministry of Health & Welfare 厚生省, Ministry of Agriculture, Forestry & Fisheries 農林水産省, Ministry of Transport 運輸省, Ministry of Postal Services 郵政省, Ministry of Labor 労働省, Ministry of Construction 建設省, Ministry of Home Affairs 自治省, and Prime Minister's Office 総理府. Under the supervision of the Prime Minister's Office are: Defense Agency 防衛庁, Science & Technology Agency 科学技術庁, National Police Agency 警察庁, Environment Agency 環境庁, Imperial Household

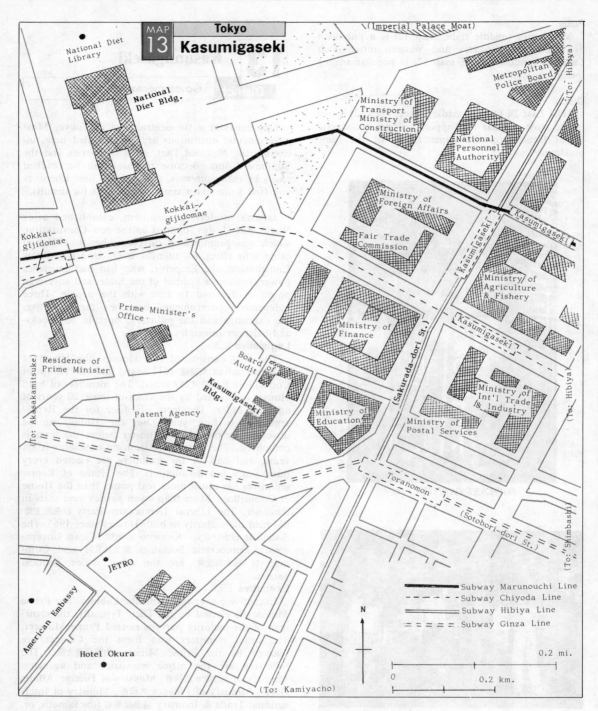

MAP 13 Tokyo Kasumigaseki

(Labels on map:)

National Diet Library

National Diet Bldg.

(Imperial Palace Moat)

Metropolitan Police Board

(To: Hibiya)

Ministry of Transport
Ministry of Construction

National Personnel Authority

Kokkai-gijidomae

Kokkai-gijidomae

Ministry of Foreign Affairs

Fair Trade Commission

Kasumigaseki

Kasumigaseki

Ministry of Agriculture & Fishery

Kasumigaseki

Prime Minister's Office

Ministry of Finance

(Sakurada-dori St.)

Ministry of Int'l Trade & Industry

(To: Hibiya)

Residence of Prime Minister

Board of Audit

(To: Akasakamitsuke)

Kasumigaseki Bldg.

Patent Agency

Ministry of Education

Ministry of Postal Services

Toranomon

(Sotobori-dori St.)

(To: Shimbashi)

JETRO

American Embassy

Hotel Okura

(To: Kamiyacho)

N

Subway Marunouchi Line
Subway Chiyoda Line
Subway Hibiya Line
Subway Ginza Line

0.2 mi.
0   0.2 km.

Agency 宮内庁, etc.

Judiciary 司法

The court system consists of the Supreme Court 最高裁判所, regional high courts, district courts and a number of summary courts. Three full appeals are granted if either the plaintiff or the defendant is not satisfied with the initial judgment and decides to proceed to higher courts. The final decision is made by the Supreme Court.

Take a Break

If you are in the Kasumigaseki area during lunch time, a variety of restaurants are available in the basement of **Kasumigaseki Building** 霞ヶ関ビル (middle center, map 13). For high altitude fans, a free observatory is located on the 36th floor of the building.

14

District   **Electronified Tokyo**

Akihabara

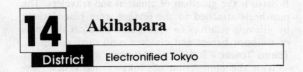

Akihabara 秋葉原 is world famous as Japan's bargain basement for electrical and electronic products. When you arrive in Akihabara you'll be confronted with a confusing jumble of colorful signs inviting you to sample the various wares of this electronic bazaar. Most of them are written in Japanese, but you may find familiar words and letters such as "Big," "Discount," "4" or "5." "Big" is

followed by "bargain" in Japanese, and "discount" is followed by "below-cost" in Japanese. "4" or "5" means 40 or 50 percent discount. The area is always bustling with bargain hunters, and the busy streets always have a bit of the air of a festival.

The JNR Yamanote and Keihin-Tohoku lines serve Akihabara Station. Because the station is rather complicated, just go out any exit, and then find one of the landmarks pictured on map 14 to get yourself oriented. The Ginza subway line's Suehirocho Station is located at the northern end of the shopping street.

Shopping

Many small stores are clustered along the narrow streets named **My Way 1** and **My Way 2** (lower center, map 14). The larger stores are indicated with

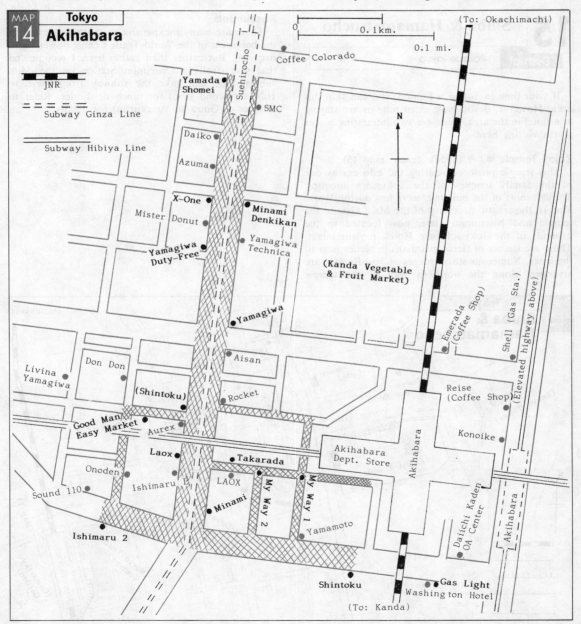

bold letters on map 14. These offer duty-free shopping and cater to foreign customers. Most stores are open daily from 10 a.m. to 7:30 p.m.

In Addition to Shopping

The **Kanda Vegetable and Fruit Market** 神田中央卸売市場 is located near Akihabara Station (middle center, map 14). This wholesale market is open from 6 a.m. to 9 a.m.

Restaurant

Gas Light is a good restaurant located in the basement of the Washington Hotel (lower right, map 14). The prices are very reasonable. Lunch table d'hote is only 1,000 yen and Washington Steak is 1,300 yen (higher for dinner).

15

District Parque Tokyo

Shiba & Hamamatsucho

If your time in Tokyo is limited, you can skip this area. However, if you have extra time or are staying at a hotel in the area, there are two interesting places worth visiting here.

Zojoji Temple 増上寺 (middle center, map 15)

This temple prospered during the Edo era as one of the family temples of the Tokugawa shoguns. Though most of the buildings were lost during World War II, the artistic structures of the Main Gate to the temple and Nitemmon Gate, now located in the grounds of the Tokyo Prince Hotel, remain intact. There are statues of fierce guardians in niches next to the gates. Numerous stone images of Jizo-Bosatsu are arranged along the northern wall of the temple precincts (marked with dots on map 15). Jizo-Bosatsu is the guardian of children and travelers. The pinwheels attached to the images were placed there by grieving relatives to soothe and comfort the souls of stillborn babies and children who died young.

Tokyo Tower 東京タワー (middle left, map 15)

With the completion of Tokyo's many new skyscrapers, the observatories of this radio tower have lost their popularity. But the **Special Observatory,** located at an altitude of 820 feet (250 m.) is still the highest point in Tokyo and commands an extensive view of the city and Tokyo Bay. The entrance to the **Main Observatory** (492 feet or 150 m.) costs 600 yen, and an additional 400 yen is necessary to reach the Special Observatory. Though it is expensive, it is a must-see for those who enjoy high altitude views.

Restaurants

There are many inexpensive restaurants located in the basement of the World Trade Center (lower right, map 15). But rather than eating here, I recommend that you stroll to Onarimon Station on the Mita subway line and take the subway from there to Hibiya (second stop) for lunch or dinner. Refer to District 4 (Ginza & Yurakucho) for details.

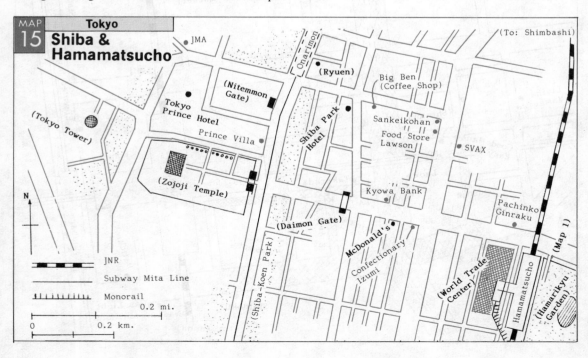

MAP 15 Tokyo
Shiba & Hamamatsucho

JMA · Onarimon (To: Shimbashi)

(Ryuen) · Big Ben (Coffee Shop)

(Nitemmon Gate) · Sankeikohan · Food Store · Lawson · SVAX

Tokyo Prince Hotel · Prince Villa · Shiba Park Hotel

(Tokyo Tower)

(Zojoji Temple) · Kyowa Bank · Pachinko Ginraku

(Daimon Gate)

McDonald's · Confectionary Izumi

(Shiba-Koen Park)

(World Trade Center) · Hamamatsucho · (Hamarikyu Garden) · (Map 1)

N

JNR
Subway Mita Line
Monorail
0.2 mi.
0   0.2 km.

Major Festivals in Tokyo

January 6: Dezomeshiki New Year Parade by firemen at Harumi near Ginza. Firemen in traditional uniforms perform acrobatic stunts atop tall bamboo ladders.

February 3: Setsubun Festival at Sensoji Temple in Asakusa. Bean-throwing ceremonies are held to ensure good fortune throughout the year.

April 8: Hanamatsuri Festival at Sensoji Temple in Asakusa celebrates the birthday of Shakya.

April 21 — 23: Spring Festival at Yasukuni Jinja Shrine.

Middle of May: Kanda Matsuri Festival in the Kanda area and Sanja Matsuri Festival in the Asakusa area both feature processions of miniature shrines.

Middle of June: Torigoe Jinja Festival near Asakusa and Sanno Matsuri Festival in Akasaka (Hie Jinja Shrine) feature processions of miniature shrines.

July 13 — 16: Mitama Matsuri Festival at Yasukuni Jinja Shrine.

Middle of July: Shoro Nagashi Festival: a number of paper lanterns with lighted candles are floated on the Imperial Palace moat near Kitanomaru-Koen Park.

Last Saturday of July: Fireworks Festival on the Sumidagawa River near Asakusa.

Beginning of August: Takigi Noh (open-air Noh performance) at Hie Jinja Shrine in Akasaka.

Middle of October to Middle of November: Kiku Matsuri Chrysanthemum Show at Sensoji Temple in Asakusa.

October 27 — November 3: Flea market of second-hand books in Kanda (Jimbocho).

Beginning of November: Meiji Jingu Shrine Festival features performance of traditional arts and demonstrations of martial arts.

Middle of December: Gasaichi flea market features New Year decorations (at Sensoji Temple in Asakusa).

Procession of a miniature shrine.

Accommodations

HOTELS

First-class Hotels (20,000 yen and up for a twin room)

Imperial Hotel 帝国ホテル (middle right, map F)
Address: 1-1-1, Uchisaiwaicho, Chiyoda-ku, Tokyo; Phone: (03) 504-1111. 1,135 deluxe rooms. The older main building has a better reputation than the new tower.

Hotel Okura ホテル・オークラ (middle center, map F)
Address: 2-10-4, Toranomon, Minato-ku, Tokyo; Phone: (03) 582-0111. 980 deluxe rooms. Especially popular among business executives.

New Otani Hotel & Tower ホテル・ニューオータニ (middle center, map F)
Address: 4-1, Kioicho, Chiyoda-ku, Tokyo; Phone: (03) 265-1111. The Tower provides deluxe rooms and the main building first-class rooms. 2,057 room.

Akasaka Prince Hotel 赤坂プリンスホテル (middle center, map F)
Address: 1-2, Kioicho, Chiyoda-ku, Tokyo; Phone: (03) 234-1111. 760 deluxe rooms. The flagship hotel of the Prince Hotel Group.

Century Hyatt Hotel センチュリー・ハイアット・ホテル (middle left, map F)
Address: 2-7-2, Nishi-Shinjuku, Shinjuku-ku, Tokyo; Phone: (03) 349-0111. 800 luxurious rooms. One of the best buys in this price range.

Keio Plaza Inter-Continental Hotel 京王プラザホテル (middle left, map F)
Address: 2-2-1, Nishi-Shinjuku, Shinjuku-ku, Tokyo; Phone: (03) 344-0111. Rooms in the south wing are deluxe and those in the main building are first class.

Palace Hotel パレスホテル (middle right, map F)
Address: 1-1-1, Marunouchi, Chiyoda-ku, Tokyo; Phone: (03) 211-5211. 404 luxurious rooms are always filled with regular customers.

Capitol Tokyu Hotel キャピトル東急ホテル (middle center, map F)
Address: 2-10-3, Nagatacho, Chiyoda-ku, Tokyo; Phone: (03) 581-4511. Formerly the Tokyo Hilton. Now the flagship hotel of the Tokyu Hotel Chain. 468 deluxe rooms.

New Takanawa Prince Hotel 新高輪プリンスホテル (lower center, map F)
Address: 3-13-1, Takanawa, Minato-ku, Tokyo; Phone: (03) 442-1111. Fancy resort-style. 1,010 rooms. At a bit of a distance from major downtown areas. Quiet surroundings.

Takanawa Prince Hotel 高輪プリンスホテル (lower center, map F)
Address: 3-13-1, Takanawa, Minato-ku, Tokyo; Phone: (03) 447-1111. Very quiet. 386 superior rooms. Suitable for serious business people.

Tokyo Prince Hotel 東京プリンスホテル (middle center, map F)
Address: 3-3-1, Shiba-Koen, Minato-ku, Tokyo; Phone: (03) 432-1111. 484 superior rooms in a quiet location. Patronized by many regular customers.

Tokyo Hilton Hotel 東京ヒルトンホテル (middle left, map F)
Address: 6-6-2, Nishi-Shinjuku, Shinjuku-ku, Tokyo; Phone: (03) 344-5111. A newly opened 858-room deluxe hotel.

Miyako Hotel Tokyo 都ホテル東京 (lower center, map F)
Address: 1-1-50, Shiroganedai, Minato-ku, Tokyo; Phone: (03) 447-3111. Excellent quality for the prices. Location a little inconvenient. 483 deluxe rooms.

Hotel Pacific ホテル・パシフィック (lower center, map F)
Address: 3-13-3, Takanawa, Minato-ku, Tokyo; Phone: (03) 445-6711. 854 first-class rooms. In front of JNR Shinagawa Station.

Hotel Grand Palace ホテル・グランドパレス (upper center, map F)
Address: 1-1-1, Iidabashi, Chiyoda-ku, Tokyo; Phone: (03) 264-1111. 480 first-class rooms. Convenient for sightseeing but a little away from night spots.

Ginza Tokyu Hotel 銀座東急ホテル (middle right, map F)
Address: 5-15-9, Ginza, Chuo-ku, Tokyo; Phone: (03) 541-2411. 445 comfortable rooms. Very convenient to the Ginza shopping center.

Standard Hotels (14,000 - 20,000 yen for a twin room)

Akasaka Tokyu Hotel 赤坂東急ホテル (middle center, map F)
Address: 2-14-3, Nagatacho, Chiyoda-ku, Tokyo; Phone: (03) 580-2311. 566 cozy rooms. Good location for enjoying Akasaka nightlife.

Tokyo Marunouchi Hotel 東京丸の内ホテル (middle right, map F)
Address: 1-6-3, Marunouchi, Chiyoda-ku, Tokyo; Phone: (03) 215-2151. 210 cozy rooms. Only a few-minute walk to Tokyo Station. Unknown but a good buy.

Shiba Park Hotel 芝パークホテル (middle right, map F)
Address: 1-5-10, Shiba-Koen, Minato-ku, Tokyo; Phone: (03) 433-4141. 370 comfortable rooms. Especially popular with Australian tourists.

Ginza Daiichi Hotel 銀座第一ホテル (middle right, map F)
Address: 8-13-1, Ginza, Chuo-ku, Tokyo; Phone: (03) 542-5311. The flagship hotel of the Daiichi Hotel Chain. 812 cozy rooms.

Ginza Marunouchi Hotel 銀座丸の内ホテル (middle right, map F)
Addess: 4-1-12, Tsukiji, Chuo-ku, Tokyo; Phone: (03) 543-5431. A 114-room compact hotel. Walking distance to Central Fish Market.

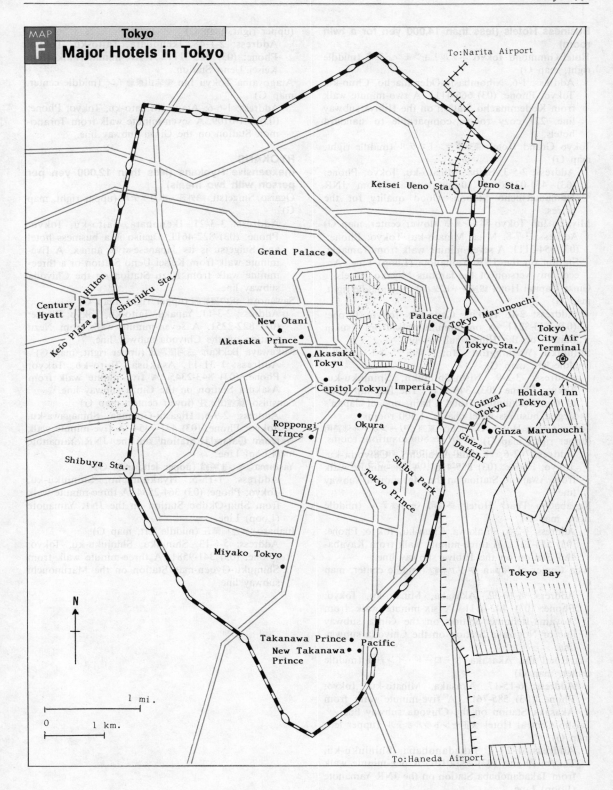

MAP
F

Tokyo

Major Hotels in Tokyo

To:Narita Airport

Keisei Ueno Sta.

Ueno Sta.

Grand Palace

Century Hyatt

Hilton

Keio Plaza

Shinjuku Sta.

New Otani

Akasaka Prince

Palace

Tokyo Marunouchi

Tokyo Sta.

Tokyo City Air Terminal

Akasaka Tokyu

Capitol Tokyu

Imperial

Holiday Inn Tokyo

Ginza Tokyu

Roppongi Prince

Okura

Ginza Daiichi

Ginza Marunouchi

Shibuya Sta.

Shiba Park

Tokyo Prince

Miyako Tokyo

Tokyo Bay

N

Takanawa Prince

Pacific

New Takanawa Prince

1 mi.

0   1 km.

To:Haneda Airport

Business Hotels (less than 14,000 yen for a twin room)

Hotel Gimmond Tokyo ホテル・ギンモンド東京 (middle right, map G)

Address: 1-6, Nihombashi-Odemmacho, Chuo-ku, Tokyo; Phone: (03) 666-4111. A two-minute walk from Kodemmacho Station on the Hibiya subway line. 221 cozy rooms comparable to standard hotels.

Tokyo Grand Hotel 東京グランドホテル (middle right, map G)

Address: 2-5-3, Shiba, Minato-ku, Tokyo; Phone: (03) 454-0311. A 10-minute walk from JNR Hamamatsucho Station. Good quality for the prices.

Miyako Inn Tokyo 都イン東京 (lower center, map G)

Address: 3-7-8, Mita, Minato-ku, Tokyo; Phone: (03) 454-3111. A seven-minute walk from Tamachi Station on the JNR Yamanote (Loop) Line. An economy version of the famous Miyako Hotels.

Ginza Capital Hotel 銀座キャピタルホテル (middle right, map G)

Address: 2-1, Tsukiji, Chuo-ku, Tokyo; Phone: (03) 543-8211. A one-minute walk from Tsukiji Station on the Hibiya subway line.

Shinjuku Washington Hotel 新宿ワシントンホテル (middle left, map G)

Address: 3-2-9, Nishi-Shinjuku, Shinjuku-ku, Tokyo; Phone: (03) 343-3111. The flagship hotel of the Washington Hotel Chain, one of Japan's largest business hotel chains. 1,300 rooms.

Tokyo Green Hotel Awajicho 東京グリーンホテル淡路町 (upper right, map G)

Address: 2-6, Kanda-Awajicho, Chiyoda-ku, Tokyo; Phone: (03) 255-4161. A one-minute walk from Awajicho Station on the Marunouchi subway line.

Kayabacho Pearl Hotel 茅場町パールホテル (middle right, map G)

Address: 1-2-5, Shinkawa, Chuo-ku, Tokyo; Phone: (03) 553-2211. A three-minute walk from Kayabacho Station on the Hibiya subway line.

Asia Center of Japan アジア会館 (middle center, map G)

Address: 8-10-32, Akasaka, Minato-ku, Tokyo; Phone: (03) 402-6111. A six-minute walk from Aoyama-Itchome Station on the Ginza subway line or Nogizaka Station on the Chiyoda subway line.

MarRoad Inn Akasaka マーロード・イン赤坂 (middle center, map G)

Address: 6-15-17, Akasaka, Minato-ku, Tokyo; Phone: (03) 585-7611. A five-minute walk from Akasaka Station on the Chiyoda subway line.

Taisho Central Hotel 大正セントラルホテル (upper left, map G)

Address: 1-27-7, Takadanobaba, Shinjuku-ku, Tokyo; Phone: (03) 232-0101. A one-minute walk from Takadanobaba Station on the JNR Yamanote (Loop) Line.

Shiba Yayoi Kaikan 芝弥生会館 (middle right, map G)

Address: 1-10-27, Kaigan, Minato-ku, Tokyo; Phone: (03) 434-6841. A five-minute walk from JNR's Hamamatsucho Station.

Hokke Club (Ueno Ikenohata) 法華クラブ上野池之端 (upper right, map G)

Address: 2-1-48, Ikenohata, Taito-ku, Tokyo; Phone: (03) 822-3111. A five-minute walk from Keisei Ueno Station.

Atagoyama Tokyu Inn 愛宕山東急イン (middle center, map G)

Address: 1-6-6, Atago, Minato-ku, Tokyo; Phone: (03) 431-0109. A seven-minute walk from Toranomon Station on the Ginza subway line.

RYOKANS

Inexpensive Ryokans (less than 12,000 yen per person with two meals)

Ogaiso/Suigetsu 鷗外荘・水月ホテル (upper right, map G)

Address: 3-3-21, Ikenohata, Taito-ku, Tokyo; Phone: (03) 822-4611. Ogaiso is a business hotel and Suigetsu is its Japanese-style annex. A five-minute walk from Keisei Ueno Station or a three-minute walk from Nezu Station on the Chiyoda subway line.

Sawanoya 沢の屋旅館 (upper right, map G)

Address: 2-3-11, Yanaka, Taito-ku, Tokyo; Phone: (03) 822-2251. A seven-minute walk from Nezu Station on the Chiyoda subway line.

Mikawaya Bekkan 三河屋別館 (upper right, map G)

Address: 1-31-11, Asakusa, Taito-ku, Tokyo; Phone: (03) 843-2345. A five-minute walk from Asakusa Station on the Ginza subway line.

Sansuiso 旅館山水荘 (lower center, map G)

Address: 2-9-5, Higashi-Gotanda, Shinagawa-ku, Tokyo; Phone: (03) 441-7454. A five-minute walk from Gotanda Station on the JNR Yamanote (Loop) Line.

Yashima やしま旅館 (upper left, map G)

Address: 1-15-5, Hyakunincho, Shinjuku-ku, Tokyo; Phone: (03) 364-2534. A three-minute walk from Shin-Okubo Station on the JNR Yamanote (Loop) Line.

Inabaso 旅館稲葉荘 (middle left, map G)

Address: 5-6-13, Shinjuku, Shinjuku-ku, Tokyo; Phone: (03) 341-9581. A three-minute walk from Shinjuku-Gyoen-mae Station on the Marunouchi subway line.

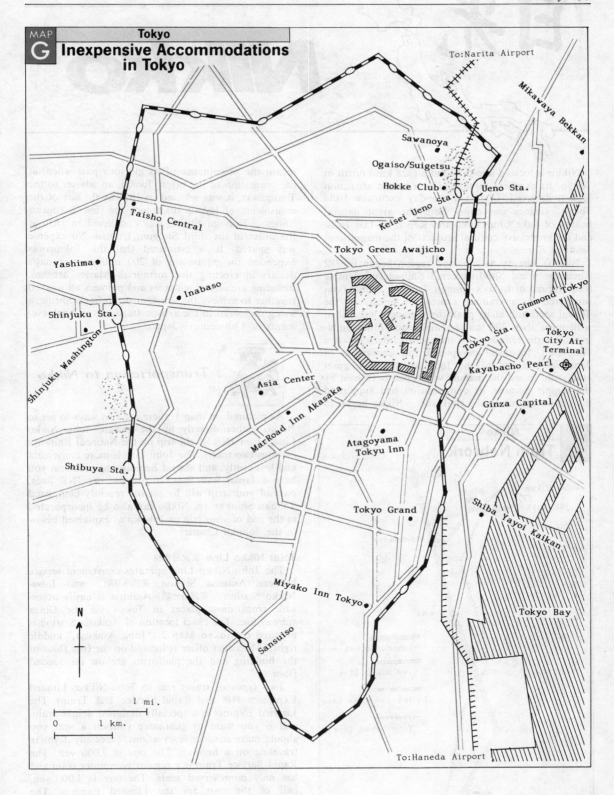

MAP
G

Tokyo
Inexpensive Accommodations in Tokyo

To: Narita Airport

Mikawaya Bekkan

Sawanoya

Ogaiso/Suigetsu

Hokke Club

Ueno Sta.

Keisei Ueno Sta.

Taisho Central

Tokyo Green Awajicho

Yashima

Gimmond Tokyo

Inabaso

Shinjuku Sta.

Tokyo Sta.

Shinjuku Washington

Tokyo City Air Terminal

Kayabacho Pearl

Asia Center

Ginza Capital

MarRoad Inn Akasaka

Atagoyama Tokyu Inn

Shibuya Sta.

Tokyo Grand

Shiba Yayoi Kaikan

Miyako Inn Tokyo

N

Tokyo Bay

Sansuiso

1 mi.

0   1 km.

To: Haneda Airport

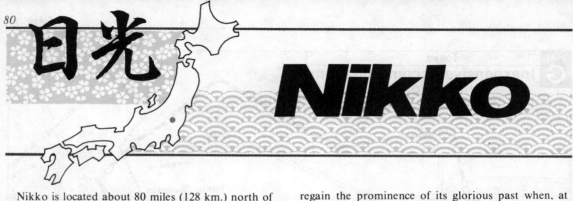

日光 Nikko

Nikko is located about 80 miles (128 km.) north of Tokyo. Its excellent reputation as a tourist attraction is well deserved: in just a one-day excursion from Tokyo, visitors can enjoy both the great natural beauty of Lake Chuzenjiko and Kegon-no-Taki Falls, and the impressive cultural artifacts of the magnificent Toshogu Shrine.

Nikko's history as a sacred region began in 782 when the priest Shodo erected Shihonryuji Temple (the original of today's Rinnoji Temple). Shihonryuji prospered as a training center for priests of the Tendai sect, and at its peak the precincts were filled with more than 300 minor temples and other buildings. But the temple went into serious decline when Hideyoshi Toyotomi completed the unification of Japan at the end of the 16th century. The great Hideyoshi seized the manors which had been held by the temple because its congregation had supported his opponent during the civil wars. Nikko began to

regain the prominence of its glorious past when, at the suggestion of the priest Tenkai, an adviser to the Tokugawas, it was selected in 1617 as the site of the mausoleum of Ieyasu Tokugawa, the first Tokugawa Shogun. Toshogu Shrine was completed in 1636 at the order of the third Shogun, Iemitsu. No expense was spared. It is estimated that the Tokugawas expended the equivalent of 200 million of today's dollars in erecting this memorial. Master artisans, including architects, sculptors and painters all worked together to achieve the splendor of Toshogu Shrine, a living memorial to the artistic standards and achievements of 17th century Japan.

Transportation to Nikko

As pictured on map 1, there are two ways to get to Nikko, either directly by the private Tobu Nikko Line, or on JNR — the trip on the National Railways involves two trains. The Tobu Line is more convenient and less costly, and should be your choice unless you have a Japan Rail Pass. If you use the JNR lines, part of your trip will be on the recently completed Tohoku Shinkansen. Nikko can also be incorporated at the end of your trip to Tohoku as explained below in the Tohoku Chapter.

Tobu Nikko Line 東武日光線

The Tobu Nikko Line operates convenient service between Asakusa Station 東武浅草駅 and Tobu-Nikko Station 東武日光駅. Asakusa is easily accessible from most places in Tokyo via the Ginza subway line. The exact location of Asakusa Station is pictured on Tokyo Map 2 ("Tobu Asakusa," middle right). The ticket office is located on the first floor of the building and the platforms are on the second floor.

Two types of trains run to Tobu-Nikko: Limited Expresses 特急 and Rapid Service 快速 Trains. The Limited Express is a specially designed deluxe train, and if you want to guarantee yourself a seat you should make advance reservations, especially if you're traveling on a holiday. The fare is 2,000 yen. The Rapid Service Train is a regular commuter train and has only nonreserved seats. The fare is 1,000 yen, half of the cost for the Limited Express. The schedule of morning and early afternoon trains is as follows:

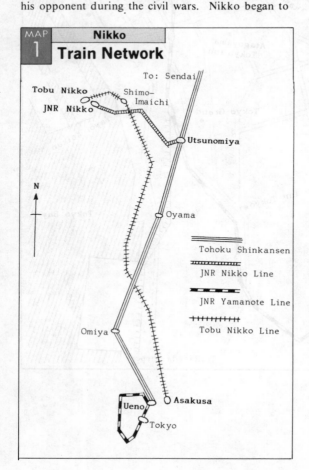

MAP 1

Nikko
Train Network

To: Sendai

Tobu Nikko
JNR Nikko

Shimo-Imaichi

Utsunomiya

N

Oyama

━━━━━ Tohoku Shinkansen

━━━━━ JNR Nikko Line

━━━━━ JNR Yamanote Line

++++++++ Tobu Nikko Line

Omiya

Asakusa

Ueno

Tokyo

Asakusa to Tobu-Nikko

Type of Train	Name of Train	Lv. Asakusa	Ar. Tobu-Nikko
Rapid Service	—	7:10 a.m.	9:13 a.m.
Limited Express	Kegon-1	7:20 a.m.	9:06 a.m.
Limited Express	Kegon-3	8:00 a.m.	9:43 a.m.
Rapid Service	—	8:10 a.m.	10:15 a.m.
Limited Express	Kegon-9	9:00 a.m.	10:41 a.m.
Rapid Service	—	9:10 a.m.	11:17 a.m.
Limited Express	Kegon-13	10:00 a.m.	11:43 a.m.
Rapid Service	—	10:20 a.m.	12:19 p.m.
Rapid Service	—	11:20 a.m.	1:28 p.m.
Rapid Service	—	12:20 p.m.	2:28 p.m.

If you plan to visit both the Lake area and the Shrine area, you should leave Asakusa by 9 a.m. at the latest. If you are visiting only the Shrine area, you can take a later train.

The schedule of return trains is as follows:

Tobu-Nikko to Asakusa

Type of Train	Name of Train	Lv. Tobu-Nikko	Ar. Asakusa
Rapid Service	—	3:45 p.m.	5:55 p.m.
Limited Express	Kegon-26	4:40 p.m.	6:25 p.m.
Rapid Service	—	4:50 p.m.	6:55 p.m.
Limited Express	Kegon-28	5:00 p.m.	6:45 p.m.
Limited Express	Kegon-32	5:40 p.m.	7:25 p.m.
Rapid Service	—	5:50 p.m.	7:58 p.m.
Rapid Service	—	6:55 p.m.	8:54 p.m.

Japanese National Railways

There is no convenient direct train to Nikko from Tokyo on the JNR. The fastest way to reach Nikko by JNR is the combination of the Tohoku Shinkansen (Tokyo's Ueno Station 上野駅 to Utsunomiya 宇都宮駅), and the JNR Nikko Line (Utsunomiya 宇都宮駅 to Nikko 日光駅).

The Tohoku Shinkansen 東北新幹線: As with the Shinkansens that run southwest from Tokyo, there are two types of trains. The faster one, which makes fewer station stops, is called "Yamabiko" やまびこ (Mountain Echo), while the slower one, which stops at all the stations on the line, is called "Aoba" あおば (Green Leaf). All the Aobas and most of the Yamabikos stop at Utsunomiya.

The following is the schedule of major Tohoku Shinkansens between Ueno and Utsunomiya:

Ueno to Utsunomiya

Name of Train	Lv. Ueno	Ar. Utsunomiya
Aoba-203	7:18 a.m.	8:11 a.m.
Yamabiko-39	8:00 a.m.	8:47 a.m.
Aoba-205	8:18 a.m.	9:11 a.m.
Yamabiko-41	9:00 a.m.	9:47 a.m.
Aoba-207	9:18 a.m.	10:11 a.m.
Yamabiko-21	9:40 a.m.	10:23 a.m.
Yamabiko-45	10:00 a.m.	10:47 a.m.
Aoba-209	10:18 a.m.	11:11 a.m.
Yamabiko-49	11:00 a.m.	11:47 a.m.

Utsunomiya to Ueno

Name of Train	Lv. Utsunomiya	Ar. Ueno
Aoba-214	3:18 p.m.	4:22 p.m.
Yamabiko-52	3:48 p.m.	4:34 p.m.
Aoba-216	4:29 p.m.	5:22 p.m.
Yamabiko-58	4:48 p.m.	5:34 p.m.
Aoba-218	5:29 p.m.	6:22 p.m.
Yamabiko-62	5:48 p.m.	6:34 p.m.
Yamabiko-22	6:13 p.m.	6:57 p.m.
Aoba-220	6:30 p.m.	7:22 p.m.
Yamabiko-64	6:48 p.m.	7:34 p.m.
Aoba-222	7:29 p.m.	8:22 p.m.

Because the ride takes less than one hour, I recommend that you travel without advance reservations.

The Nikko Line 日光線 is a commuter line. All seats are unreserved, and the trains leave Utsunomiya from track No. 5. The schedule of the trains you're likely to take is as follows:

Utsunomiya to Nikko		Nikko to Utsunomiya	
Lv.Utsunomiya	Ar. Nikko	Lv. Nikko	Ar. Utsunomiya
8:25 a.m.	9:10 a.m.	2:01 p.m.	2:41 p.m.
9:56 a.m.	10:43 a.m.	3:01 p.m.	3:41 p.m.
10:56 a.m.	11:42 a.m.	3:48 p.m.	4:37 p.m.
11:56 a.m.	12:42 p.m.	4:33 p.m.	5:13 p.m.
12:56 p.m.	1:42 p.m.	5:25 p.m.	6:10 p.m.
1:56 p.m.	2:42 p.m.	6:00 p.m.	6:45 p.m.
2:56 p.m.	3:42 p.m.	6:37 p.m.	7:18 p.m.

Utsunomiya is the first and Nikko the last station on the Nikko Line. There are five intermediate stations. Just for your information, the fare on this JNR route is about 4,500 yen one way from Tokyo.

Yomeimon Gate of Toshogu Shrine.

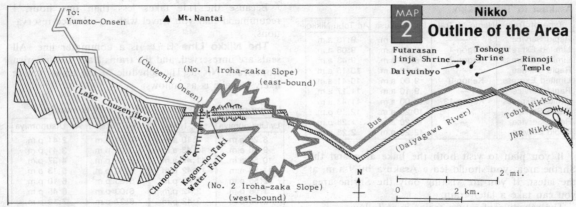

MAP 2 — Nikko
Outline of the Area

Futarasan Jinja Shrine
Daiyuinbyo
Toshogu Shrine
Rinnoji Temple

To: Yumoto-Onsen
▲ Mt. Nantai
(No. 1 Iroha-zaka Slope) (east-bound)
(Chuzenji Onsen)
(Lake Chuzenjiko)
Chanokidaira
Kegon-no-Taki Water Falls
(No. 2 Iroha-zaka Slope) (west-bound)
Bus
(Daiyagawa River)
Tobu Nikko
JNR Nikko
N
0   2 km.   2 mi.

Outline of Nikko

As pictured on map 2, Nikko's major cultural and historical attractions are located about 1.3 miles (2 km.) from the train stations. The area's natural wonders are on the eastern side of the Lake Chuzenjiko. The train stations are at an altitude of about 2,000 feet (600 m.), the surface of the Lake at 4,163 feet (1,269 m.), and Mt. Nantai at 8,150 feet (2,484 m.). "Nikko" thus encompasses not only a wide area but also an area with great differences in altitude. To facilitate the flow of traffic on the mountainous roads of the area, special one-way roads have been constructed to and from the Lake. The southern road, No. 2 Iroha-zaka Slope, is used for the west-bound traffic up to the lake, while the northern road, No. 1 Iroha-zaka Slope, is used for

the east-bound traffic back down from the lake. "Iroha" is the name of the 48 character Japanese syllabic alphabet. The roads were so named because of the many (but not exactly 48!) hairpin curves on the slopes.

Suggested Itinerary

Nikko Station to Chuzenji-Onsen (near the Lake) by bus

Nikko buses have both Japanese and English signs. In order to get to Chuzenji-Onsen you can take a bus headed for either Chuzenji-Onsen 中禅寺温泉 or Yumoto Onsen 湯元温泉. At the JNR Nikko Station the bus for Chuzenji-Onsen uses stop No. 2 (see map 3), and the bus for Yumoto-Onsen uses stop No. 3. Departure times of the buses are coordinated with the arrival times of the JNR Nikko Line trains.

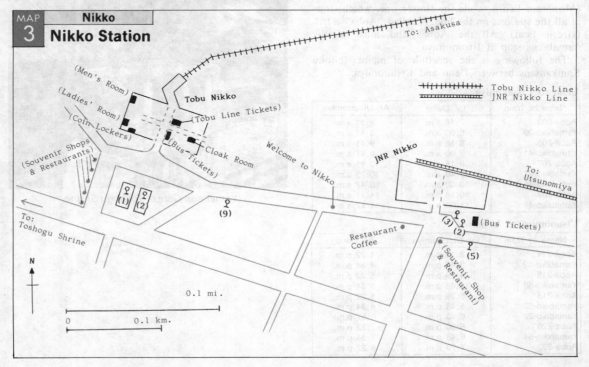

MAP 3 — Nikko
Nikko Station

To: Asakusa
Tobu Nikko Line
JNR Nikko Line
(Men's Room)
Tobu Nikko
(Ladies' Room)
(Tobu Line Tickets)
(Coin Lockers)
(Souvenir Shops & Restaurants)
(Bus Tickets)
Cloak Room
Welcome to Nikko
JNR Nikko
To: Utsunomiya
To: Toshogu Shrine
(1) (2)
(9)
Restaurant Coffee
(3) (2) (Bus Tickets)
(5)
(Souvenir Shop & Restaurant)
N
0   0.1 km.   0.1 mi.

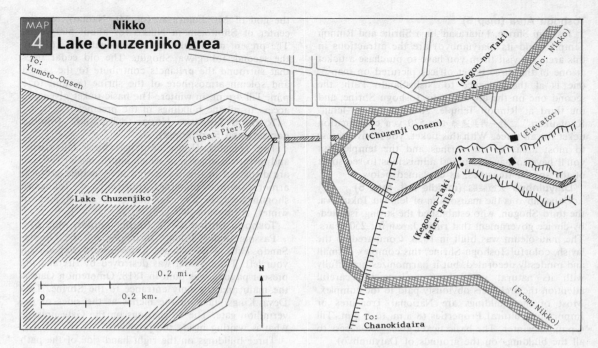

If you plan to visit only the Toshogu Shrine area, you can also take the bus headed for Nishi-Sando 西参道, from stop No. 5. Nishi-Sando stop is pictured at the lower left of map 5.

At Tobu-Nikko Station the bus for Chuzenji-Onsen uses stop No. 2 (map 3), and the bus for Yumoto-Onsen uses stop No. 1.

The bus for Nishi-Sando uses stop No. 9.

Because the Tobu Nikko Line trains arrive more frequently than the JNR trains, there are more buses out of Tobu-Nikko Station. The fare to Chuzenji-Onsen is 800 yen. The ride takes about 45 minutes. *The fare to Nishi-Sando is 220 yen and the ride takes about 10 minutes.*

Chuzenji-Onsen Area (map 4)

Chanokidaira 茶ノ木平 (5,308 feet, or 1,618 m.) commands a great view of Lake Chuzenjiko 中禅寺湖 and the 8,200-foot (2,500 m.) high mountains surrounding the Lake. To reach the observatory you take a ropeway from Chuzenji-Onsen. The short six minute trip (0.6 miles, or 1 km.) costs 320 yen one way, or 600 yen round trip.

A sightseeing boat (optional) operates on the Lake every hour from the Boat Pier pictured on map 4. The cruise takes 55 minutes and costs 700 yen. If you want to take the boat ride, you have to leave Tokyo as early in the morning as possible.

The Observatory of Kegon-no-Taki Water Falls

華厳ノ滝展望台 is reached by an elevator that is only a five-minute walk from Chuzenji-Onsen bus stop. The dynamic 325-foot (99 m.) high water falls are known as the best in Japan. The falls are especially impressive in the spring when the snow melts and the run off from the lake swells them far beyond their normal size. The elevator trip (round trip) costs 500 yen.

Chuzenji-Onsen to Nishi-Sando 西参道

Catch a bus headed for Nikko Station at either Chuzenji-Onsen or Kegon-no-Taki bus stop. These buses run about once every 30 minutes, and the ride to Nishi-Sando takes about 30 minutes (700 yen).

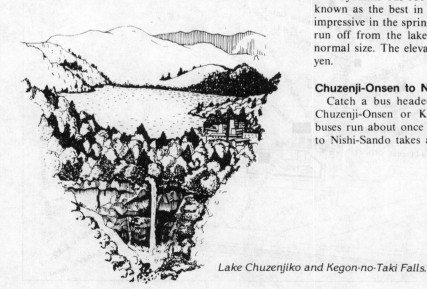

Lake Chuzenjiko and Kegon-no-Taki Falls.

Toshogu Area (map 5)

Toshogu Shrine, Futarasan Jinja Shrine and Rinnoji Temple, (and its Daiyuinbyo) are the attractions in this area. To visit them you have to purchase a ticket at one of the three ticket offices pictured on map 5; one is at the entrance to Nishi-Sando Path; the second one on the approach to Toshogu Shrine; and the third at Rinnoji Temple. Ask for "Nisha-Ichiji-Kyotsuken," 二社一寺共通券 the 530 yen combination ticket for all three. With this ticket, you'll have access to most areas of the shrines and the temple, but you'll have to pay additional admissions to see some of the special treasures, as explained below.

Daiyuinbyo 大猷院廟 (middle left, map 5)

Daiyuinbyo is the mausoleum of Iemitsu Tokugawa, the third Shogun, who established the strong, isolated-by-choice government that ruled Japan for 250 years. The mausoleum was built in 1653. Compared to the lavish, colorful Toshogu Shrine, this complex is small and modestly decorated, but it harmonizes beautifully with its natural setting and reflects the careful attention the architects obviously paid to the complex. Most of the buildings are National Treasures or Important Cultural Properties (8 a.m. to 5 p.m. Till 4 p.m. in winter. The basic ticket gives you access to all the buildings on the grounds of Daiyuinbyo).

Futarasan Jinja Shrine 二荒山神社 (upper left, map 5)

Futarasan Jinja Shrine is only a short walk northeast from Daiyuinbyo. Until Toshogu Shrine was constructed, Futarasan Jinja Shrine, dedicated to

the god of Mt. Futarasan (or Mt. Nantai), was the center of Shintoism in Nikko for about 800 years. The present main buildings were donated in 1619 by the second Tokugawa Shogun. The old cedar trees that surround the precincts contribute to the sacred and solemn atmosphere of the shrine (8 a.m. to 5 p.m. Till 4 p.m. in winter. The basic ticket gives you access to all the buildings in the precincts).

Toshogu Treasure House 東照宮宝物館 (middle center, map 5, optional)

The Treasure House contains about 250 artistic and historical objects, of which approximately 60 - 70 are displayed in turn. The treasures include samurai armor, swords, paintings, portraits of Tokugawa shoguns, etc. (9 a.m. to 4:30 p.m. Till 4 p.m. in winter. Admission 300 yen).

Toshogu Shrine 東照宮 (upper center, map 5)

Passing under a huge torii gate on the Omote-Sando Path, you will see a Five-Story Pagoda on your left. The original was destroyed by fire and the present pagoda was built in 1818. Omotemon Gate is the main and the only entrance to the Shrine. Two Deva Kings stand in the niches at the sides of the vermilion gate. The 66 carvings on the Gate presage what is waiting inside the precincts.

Three buildings on the right hand side of the path are warehouses for the costumes and equipment used each spring and fall for the Festival of the Procession of the Warriors (May 18 and October 17). On the walls of Kami-Jinko are two rather strange carvings of elephants. When Tanyu Kano, a master painter of

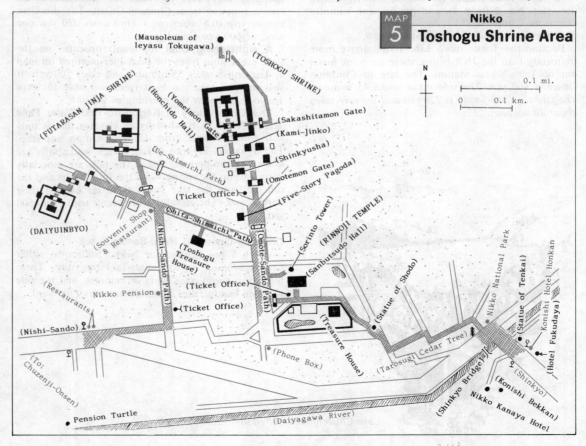

MAP 5 — Nikko
Toshogu Shrine Area

the Kano School, drew the original design, there were no elephants in Japan; he had only read about them. Walls of the Shinkyusha (Stable for Sacred Horses) feature eight carvings that depict the life of monkeys (as an allegory of human existence). The second scene is the famous "hear-no-evil, see-no-evil, speak-no-evil" three monkeys. Passing through the torii gate, you will see Yomeimon Gate (National Treasure) at the top of the stone steps. The 36-foot (11 m.) tall gate is entirely covered with innumerable (actually, more than 400) carvings painted brilliant shades of gold, vermilion red, blue, and green. Corridors (National Treasures) stretch in both directions from Yomeimon Gate and surround the main buildings (National Treasures). On the western side of the Yomeimon Gate is Honchido Hall, which is famous for the dragon painting on its ceiling. The original building was lost to fire in 1961 and the present one was completed in 1963. The dragon was painted from the original design by Nampu Katayama, a modern master. If you clap your hands under the head of the dragon, the resulting echo is said to resemble the sound of the dragon roaring (An additional 200 yen admission is required). Each of the main buildings boasts of its own carvings; especially famous is the Sleeping Cat (very small) in the East Corridor. You can see it on the upper left hand side as you cross the East Corridor toward Sakashitamon Gate. The mausoleum of Ieyasu Tokugawa is located to the north of Toshogu Shrine at the end of the long stone stairway (An additional 300 yen is collected at Sakashitamon Gate).

Rinnoji Temple 輪王寺 (lower center, map 5)

Walking down Omote-Sando Path you will come to the impressive Sanbutsudo Hall of Rinnoji Temple on your left. Until the 17th century, most religious activity in Nikko took place in this temple. Though the glory days of the temple, when thousands of priests were housed in its precincts, vanished with Hideyoshi Toyotomi's suppression, the temple still plays a leading role for Buddhism in the Nikko area. The Sanbutsudo Hall contains three Buddha images (Entrance to this Hall is included in the basic ticket). Sorinto Tower is an impressive golden structure decorated with 24 golden bells. Entrance to the Treasure House and the attached garden requires an additional 300 yen admission (optional).

"Hear-no-evil, see-no-evil, speak-no-evil" three monkeys.

To Nikko Station

When you emerge from the temple precincts, you will see a statue of the priest Shodo. Stone steps lead you down to the main street. On the northern side of the main street stands "Tarosugi," a huge cedar tree. Several years ago the Ministry of Construction insisted that Tarosugi be cut down in order to facilitate the flow of traffic, and this venerable giant was spared only after a long court battle between the Temple and the Ministry. As you cross Daiyagawa River, look to your right to see the "Shinkyo" (Sacred Bridge). On the other side of the Daiyagawa River stands a statue of the priest Tenkai. The stop for buses to Nikko Station is in front of Konishi Hotel Honkan. Most buses go to Tobu-Nikko Station first, and then to the JNR Station. Some of them terminate at Tobu-Nikko Station, but the JNR Station is only a few minutes walk from Tobu Station (140 yen).

Accommodations

HOTEL
First-class Hotel (20,000 yen and up for a twin room)
Nikko Kanaya Hotel 日光金谷ホテル (lower right, map 5)
   Address: 1300, Kami-Hachiishicho, Nikko; Phone: (0288) 54-0001. A renowned traditional hotel with 85 rooms. Lower rates are available in colder seasons.

RYOKANS
Standard Ryokans (12,000-20,000 yen per person with two meals)
Hotel Fukudaya ホテル福田屋 (lower right, map 5)
   Address: 1036, Kami-Hachiishicho, Nikko; Phone: (0288) 54-0389. A convenient location for sightseeing (31 rooms).
Konishi Bekkan 小西別館 (lower right, map 5)
   Address: 1115, Kami-Hachiishicho, Nikko; Phone: (0288) 54-1105. A typical Japanese-style inn with 24 rooms.

Inexpensive Ryokan (less than 12,000 yen per person with two meals)
Pension Turtle ペンション・タートル (lower left, map 5)
   Address: 2-16, Takumicho, Nikko; Phone: (0288) 53-3168. A small property with five Japanese-style rooms and seven Western rooms.

Kamakura & Yokohama

Outline of the Area

As pictured on map 1, Kamakura (lower left) is located about 30 miles (48 km.) southwest of Tokyo. Foreign tour groups usually skip this city or visit only the Great Buddha. But Kamakura is definitely worth exploring and has much more to offer visitors. This once prosperous feudal city is on a direct train line from Tokyo and is an ideal day-excursion from the capital.

Yokohama is included here as an additional destination for those who stay in Tokyo for a longer period. Located between Tokyo and Kamakura, Yokohama stretches northeast to southwest, with Tsurumi Station (middle right, map 1) at the northeastern end of the city, and Hongodai (lower left) at its southwestern border. The center of the city, both geographically and functionally, is the area around Yokohama, Sakuragicho and Kannai stations. With a population of 2,774,000, Yokohama is Japan's second largest city — larger than Osaka, Nagoya and Kyoto. Kannai has been an international port since the middle of the 19th century, and there are still many traces of Western influence in this area. The area around Yokohama Station is a modern shopping and business district, but because there is little of special interest there only the Kannai area is detailed below. In addition to Kannai, I have also included some information on Tsurumi, because Sojiji Temple, headquarters of Soto Zen Buddhism, is located there.

Transportation

Between Tokyo and Kamakura

As shown on map 1, JNR's Yokosuka Line 横須賀線 operates between Tokyo and Kurihama via Ofuna and Kamakura (All the stations on the Yokosuka Line are pictured on the map — The trains on this line usually run beyond Tokyo, as the Boso Line 房総線, to Chiba, east of Tokyo). The Yokosuka Line operates every 10-20 minutes from 5 a.m. to 11:30 p.m., and stops at three Yamanote (Loop) Line stations — Tokyo 東京, Shimbashi 新橋 and Shinagawa 品川. Therefore, you can take the Yokosuka Line from whichever of these three stations is closest to your hotel. "Yokosuka Line" or "Yokosuka-Boso Line" is clearly posted in English at these stations.

The ride to Kamakura takes one hour from Tokyo, 57 minutes from Shimbashi, and 50 minutes from Shinagawa. There are two important stations in Kamakura, Kamakura 鎌倉 and Kita-Kamakura 北鎌倉. Before you get on the train decide what your

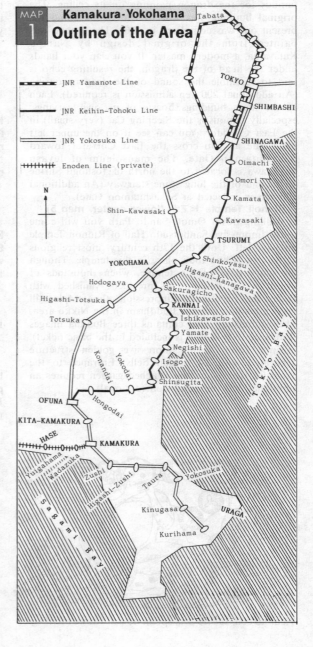

MAP 1 — Kamakura-Yokohama — Outline of the Area

- ▢▢▢ JNR Yamanote Line
- —— JNR Keihin-Tohoku Line
- —— JNR Yokosuka Line
- ++++ Enoden Line (private)

Tabata
TOKYO
SHIMBASHI
SHINAGAWA
Oimachi
Omori
Kamata
Kawasaki
Shin-Kawasaki
TSURUMI
Shinkoyasu
YOKOHAMA
Higashi-Kanagawa
Hodogaya
Sakuragicho
Higashi-Totsuka
KANNAI
Ishikawacho
Totsuka
Yamate
Negishi
Komandai
Isogo
Yokodai
Shinsugita
OFUNA
Hongodai
KITA-KAMAKURA
HASE
KAMAKURA
Yuigahama
Wadazuka
Zushi
Higashi-Zushi
Taura
Yokosuka
Kinugasa
URAGA
Kurihama

Tokyo Bay
Sagami Bay

first destination will be so you'll know which of these stations you want. Fares from Tokyo are 740 yen to Kita-Kamakura and 850 yen to Kamakura; from Shimbashi 740 yen to either station; and from Shinagawa 660 yen to either station. You can use your Rail Pass if you have one.

On the way to Kamakura, you can see an 82-foot (25 m.) tall Kannon (Goddess of Mercy) statue from the right-hand side of the train on a hill near Ofuna Station. As the train leaves the station, look back to get a good look at her merciful face.

In Kamakura

Kamakura's major temples and shrines are located between Kita-Kamakura and Kamakura. A walking tour is the ideal way to visit these places.

The Great Buddha and Hasedera Temple are located near Hase Station (lower left, map 1) on the Enoden (the Enoshima Dentetsu) Line. This line originates at Kamakura Station; Hase is the third stop, and the ride from Kamakura takes only five minutes (140 yen). You cannot use a Rail Pass on this line.

Between Tokyo and Yokohama (Kannai Station)

JNR's blue colored commuter line between Omiya (to the north of Tokyo, outside of map 1), and Yokohama is called the Keihin-Tohoku Line 京浜東北線, and the Negishi commuter line 根岸線 runs from Yokohama further south to Ofuna. Though the names of the lines are different, most of the trains from the Tokyo area run through Ofuna via Yokohama and Kannai. In Tokyo, the Keihin-Tohoku Line runs parallel to the Yamanote (Loop) Line at the 14 major stations located between Tabata and Shinagawa. Tsurumi, the site of Sojiji Temple in Yokohama, is also located on this line. The Keihin-Tohoku Line operates every 2-10 minutes from 4:40 a.m. to 12:30 midnight. The ride from Tokyo takes 33 minutes to Tsurumi 鶴見 and an additional 16 minutes to Kannai 関内. The fare is 360 yen from Tokyo to Tsurumi and 200 yen from Tsurumi to Kannai (The through fare from Tokyo to Kannai is 510 yen). You can use your Japan Rail Pass. Some trains terminate at stations along the way: at Kamata (very rare) and Sakuragicho (occasionally). If this happens, just wait for a few minutes for the next train going in the same direction.

Between Kamakura and Yokohama (Kannai Station)

If your time is limited, it is a good idea to visit Kannai on your way back to Tokyo from Kamakura and enjoy authentic Western or Chinese cuisine in this international port area. The ride on the Yokosuka Line from Kamakura to Ofuna 大船 takes only 7 minutes. The Keihin-Tohoku (Negishi) Line will take you from Ofuna to Kannai in another 27 minutes (360 yen for a Kamakura-Kannai through ticket).

Kamakura   鎌倉

The first military government in Japanese history was established in Kamakura by Shogun Yoritomo Minamoto in 1192. Before the Minamoto family seized control of the country, the Taira family, another powerful military clan (which the Minamotos destroyed) had already played an influential role in the imperial government in Kyoto. The Minamotos made history by establishing a government independent, both geographically and structurally, from Kyoto. The second and the third Minamoto shoguns were assassinated, and political power shifted to the family of Yoritomo's wife, the Hojos. Succeeding generations of the Hojo family installed puppet shoguns, reserving for themselves the powerful office of regent. The military government of Kamakura lasted until 1333. During these 141 years, Kamakura prospered as Japan's political, economic, cultural and religious center. Zen Buddhism was especially popular among the samurai class, and flourished here in the stronghold of the Shoguns.

Japan was attacked by the forces of the Yuan Dynasty of China twice, in 1274, and again in 1281. The Kamakura government, led by Regent Tokimune Hojo, successfully defeated the Mongolian invaders, thanks in part to fortuitous typhoons (Kamikaze, or Divine Wind), but these wars caused the Kamakura Shogunate great financial difficulties. The local lords whose military support had made the victories possible expected recognition, gratitude and hard cash in return for their contributions, and felt that the Shogunate was not supplying any of them. Emperor Godaigo capitalized on this situation, rallying these dissatisfied lords to his cause. With their support the imperial forces defeated the Kamakura forces and the Emperor was restored to political power in 1333. The Emperor's ascendancy was, however, very short lived, and in 1336, the Ashikaga family seized power and established a new Shogunate.

After the fall of the Hojos, Kamakura never reappeared on the historical scene. It remained a sleepy temple town with agriculture and fishing being its only industries. Since World War II it has become a classy residential district. Its many carefully preserved cultural relics testify to the glory the area enjoyed in the medieval era.

Places of Interest

The full day walking tour starts from Kita-Kamakura Station as explained below. If you want to see just the highlights of Kamakura, take a train to Kamakura Station and visit Tsurugaoka Hachimangu Shrine, the Hasedera Temple, and finally the Great Buddha.

Engakuji Temple 円覚寺 (upper center, map 2)

Engakuji Temple was built in 1282 to honor the victims of the wars against the Mongolian invaders. In the Kamakura of the time, Engakuji was second in importance only to Kenchoji Temple, and, at the peak of its prosperity, its precincts contained more than 50 minor temples and other buildings. Even though most of the original buildings were lost in fires, the reconstructions preserve the atmosphere of a powerful Zen temple. What might be the original Shariden 舎利殿 (National Treasure) still stands, and is Engakuji's most important historical relic. You can't go through the gate in front of Shariden, but you can get a glimpse of part of this famous building. The garden of Butsunichian 仏日庵 and Obaiin 黄梅院 are open to the public. Obaiin is the mausoleum of Tokimune Hojo and has a well-maintained garden located at the foot of a steep cliff. Japanese powdered tea is served in the garden of Butsunichian (350 yen, including a 100-yen admission). If you are interested in tasting real Japanese tea ceremony tea (it's green and bitter!), Butsunichian is a good place to enjoy it in a casual atmosphere. The entrance to Butsunichian is a small wooden door (Don't hit your head!). The precincts of Engakuji Temple are open to the public from 8 a.m. to 5 p.m. Admission is 100 yen.

Tokeiji Temple 東慶寺 (middle left, map 2)

Tokeiji Temple was a nunnery until the Meiji Restoration, and was popularly known as the "Divorce Temple." In the feudal era, women were not allowed to initiate divorces, no matter how cruel their husbands. A special law promulgated by the wife of Tokimune Hojo designated Tokeiji Temple as the place where unhappily married women could, as a last resort, seek refuge. Once a woman escaped into the precincts, no one was allowed to remove her. The temple still has a bit of the delicate atmosphere of a nunnery and the precincts are filled with the flowers of the season (8:30 a.m. to 5 p.m. Admission 50 yen). The Treasure House in the temple's precincts is open from 10 a.m. to 3 p.m. (Closed on Mondays). Admission is 300 yen.

Jochiji Temple 浄知寺 (middle left, map 2) (optional)

Kamakura-Kaido Street is the main road connecting Kita-kamakura and Kamakura. The traffic is always heavy and there's only a narrow sidewalk —be careful!

The entrance to Jochiji Temple is at the top of a long moss-covered stone stairway. The unique gate houses a temple bell on its second floor. All the temple's magnificent original buildings were destroyed by fires over the course of history, and the present buildings were constructed about 50 years ago. There is a neatly trimmed garden behind the Main Hall. Statues of the Seven Gods of Fortune stand at the northern end of the precincts (marked with an asterisk on map 2) (9 a.m. to 4:30 p.m. Admission 100 yen).

Meigetsuin Temple 明月院 (middle center, map 2) (optional)

Meigetsuin Temple is known as the Temple of Hydrangeas because of the thousands of these bushes in its grounds. It is especially beautiful in June when they are all in bloom. Japanese find them particularly appealing in the rain, which is fortunate since the rainy season begins in mid-June. Thousands visit Kamakura just to see the hydrangeas in bloom. Even though Meigetsuin Temple is bit off the walking tour route, I recommend that you visit here if you are in Japan in June (8:30 a.m. to 5 p.m. Admission 100 yen).

Kenchoji Temple 建長寺 (middle right, map 2)

Chojuji Temple (Long Life Temple, middle center, map 2) is located on the way to Kenchoji. Despite the temple's small entrance, its grounds are quite extensive, but they are not open to the public.

Kenchoji, erected in 1253 as a training center for Zen priests, is the most important Zen temple in Kamakura. At the peak of its prosperity, the grounds contained more than 50 buildings, but all the original buildings were lost in successive fires. The present reconstructions were based on the original models. The bronze bell in the belfry near Sanmon Gate is a National Treasure. The precincts are at complete harmony with nature and are filled with the solemn atmosphere of Zen Buddhism. The huge buildings, arranged in a straight line and surrounded by a thick pine forest, are on a grand scale that helps one image how magnificent Kamakura must have been when the Shoguns ruled from here (8:30 a.m. to 4:30 p.m. Admission 200 yen).

Ennoji Temple 円応寺 (middle center, map 2) (optional)

Steep, narrow stone steps set between stone walls lead to the gate of Ennoji Temple, which is also known as "Temple of the Ten Kings of Heaven." In the Kamakura era people believed that Ten Kings of Heaven sat in judgment on all souls after death, admitting them to heaven or damning them to hell. Wooden statues of these Kings are housed in this small temple. Unless you are especially interested in sculpture, you should skip this temple (9 a.m. to 5 p.m. Admission 100 yen).

Tsurugaoka Hachimangu Shrine 鶴ガ岡八幡宮 (lower right, map 2)

Passing under the covered portion of the road, the street turns right, and you will see the modern Kanagawa Prefectural Museum of Modern Art 神奈川県立近代美術館. The slow downward slope leads to the back gate of Tsurugaoka Hachimangu Shrine. The long flight of stone steps that begins at the torii gate leads you to the highest point of the precincts and the Main Hall. The Shrine was built in 1180 at the order of Yoritomo Minamoto, the first Kamakura Shogun. It is especially popular among Japanese because it is associated with the tragic story of two brothers of the Minamoto family, Yoritomo and his younger brother, Yoshitsune, who are both credited with establishing the Kamakura Shogunate. As a matter of fact, Yoritomo did not participate in even one of the clashes with the Tairas, and Yoshitsune fought all the battles. However, once the Minamoto

forces had triumphed, it was Yoritomo, as the elder brother, who would, in the normal course of events, have assumed all the power won through the military clashes. To keep Yoritomo from exercising what would have been, in effect, absolute power over the entire nation, supporters of the imperial court in Kyoto moved to destabilize the situation by maneuvering to have Yoshitsune appointed to high office. Learning of this plot, Yoritomo sent retainers to Kyoto to assassinate his younger brother. Yoshitsune managed to escape from Kyoto and took refuge in

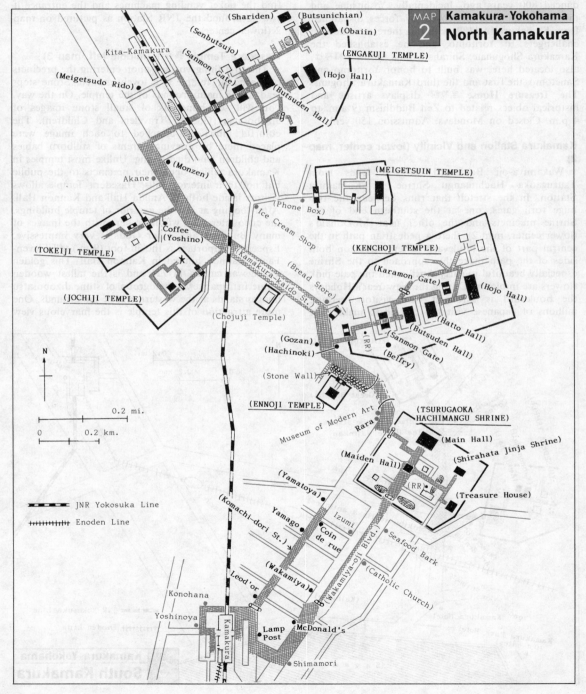

MAP 2 **Kamakura-Yokohama**
North Kamakura

Hiraizumi, which was governed by the Fujiwara family. But Yoshitsune's lover, Shizu, did not escape and was arrested by Yoritomo's force and taken to Kamakura. Because she had been a famous dancing girl when she met Yoshitsune, Yoritomo ordered Shizu to entertain him and his wife. Enduring the humiliation involved, Shizu made the forced performance an emotional expression of her love for Yoshitsune and her anxiety about his fate in his remote exile. Maiden Hall 舞殿, located at the foot of the stone steps to the Main Hall, is where Shizu danced 800 years ago. Incidentally, Yoshitsune and the Fujiwaras were destroyed by forces dispatched from Kamakura in 1189; with this there remained no challengers to Yoritomo, and he established the Kamakura Shogunate. Shirahata Jinja Shrine 白幡神社, also located here, was built to honor Yoritomo and Sanetomo, the first and the third Kamakura Shoguns. **The Treasure House** 宝物館 displays artistic and historical objecs related to Zen Buddhism (9 a.m. to 4 p.m. Closed on Mondays. Admission 150 yen).

Kamakura Station and Vicinity (lower center, map 2)

Wakamiya-oji Boulevard 若宮大路 leads from Tsurugaoka Hachimangu Shrine to Kamakura Station. In the stretch that runs between the two huge torii gates, one at the southern end of the Shrine precincts and the other near McDonald's (lower center, map 2), there a pedestrian path in the central part of the boulevard. Cherry trees on both sides of the path make this approach to the Shrine especially beautiful in early April when the pale pink flowers are in bloom. During the New Year's Holidays the boulevard is thronged with visitors because millions of Japanese visit this Shrine to make their

New Year's Resolutions. There are many souvenir shops and restaurants along the boulevard. Komachi-dori Street 小町通り runs to the west of Wakamiya-oji Boulevard. This street represents the modern face of Kamakura with many (perhaps too many) Western restaurants, souvenir shops, coffee shops and boutiques.

To Hase 長谷

The Enoden Line's 江ノ電 Kamakura Station is at the western side of the JNR Station. It is easier to find the ticket vending machines and the entrance if you go around the JNR Station as pictured on map 2 (lower center).

Hasedera Temple 長谷寺 (middle left, map 3)

The first thing you see upon entering the precincts of Hasedera Temple is a lovely garden. Stone steps lead to the main grounds of the temple. On the way, you will see hundreds of small stone images of Jizobosatsu (God of Travelers and Children). The colorful pinwheels attached to each image were placed there by grieving parents of stillborn babies and children who died young. Unlike most temples in Kamakura which open their precincts to the public but not their interior halls, Hasedera Temple allows visitors inside both its Amida Hall and Kannon Hall. After looking at just the exterior of temple buildings, the encounters you will have here with the images of many Buddhas and other Gods is very impressive. Especially important is the 30-foot (9 m.) tall Eleven-Faced Kannon housed in Kannon Hall. This golden image was carved in 721 and is the tallest wooden statue in Japan. Another group of stone Jizobosatsu images stands at the western end of the grounds. One more attraction of this temple is the marvelous view

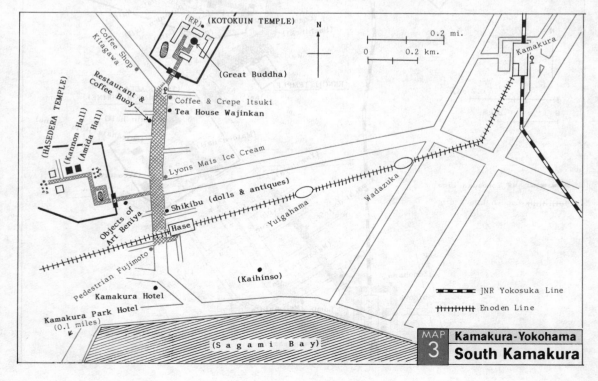

of Sagami Bay from the southern part of the grounds (7 a.m. to 5:40 p.m. Admission 100 yen).

Great Buddha 鎌倉大仏 (upper left, map 3)

The Great Buddha, the main object of worship at Kotokuin Temple 高徳院, is popular world-wide, and attracts visitors all year round. The 37-foot (11.3 m.) tall bronze image was cast in 1252. It is Japan's second largest statue (The largest is the Great Buddha of Todaiji Temple in Nara). This Buddha was originally housed in a wooden hall, which was swept away by a tidal wave in 1495. Since then the Buddha has sat in the open air. There's an entrance to the interior of the statue at the right side of its base (as you face the Buddha). Steep ladders go up to a small window at the top of the back of the statue (additional 20 yen) (7 a.m. to 5:45 p.m. Admission 100 yen).

To Kamakura Station

A bus to Kamakura Station 鎌倉駅 stops right in front of the grounds of the Great Buddha. (The bus stop is pictured on map 3). Take a numbered ticket when you get on the bus. The fare is displayed on a chart above and to the left of the driver's seat. When you get off, pay the amount shown on the chart under the number corresponding to your ticket. Of course, you can also walk back to Hase Station and take an Enoden train to Kamakura.

Restaurants and Coffee Shops

American Fast Food: McDonald's is located near Kamakura Station on Wakamiya-oji Boulevard (lower center, map 2). This shop established a one-day sales record when millions of worshippers visited Tsuruga-oka Hachimangu Shrine on New Year's Day several years ago.

Coffee Shops (from north to south): Meigetsudo Rido, near Kita-Kamakura Station (upper left, map 2). **Coffee Yoshino,** near Tokeiji Temple (middle left, map 2). **Gozan,** near Kenchoji Temple (middle center, map 2), **Leo d'or,** near Kamakura Station (lower

The Great Buddha, Kamakura's most famous citizen.

center, map 2). **Tea House Wajinkan,** near the Great Buddha (upper left, map 3). **Restaurant & Coffee Buoy** (same as the above).

In addition to coffee, tea and soft drinks, these coffee shops serve light snacks - sandwiches, pizza and curry.

Reasonable Restaurants: Monzen, near Tokeiji Temple (upper left, map 2), and **Hachinoki,** near Kenchoji Temple (middle center, map 2), serve authentic Japanese lunches for about 4,000 yen. **Coin de rue** on Komachi-dori Street (lower center, map 2) is a famous French restaurant. Lunch may cost anywhere between 2,000 and 3,000 yen.

Souvenir Shops

Yamago on Komachi-dori Street (lower center, map 2) deals in bamboo handicrafts. **Wakamiya** on Wakamiya-oji Boulevard (lower center, map 2) has a good inventory of Kamakura-bori, a special Kamakura craft. (Carved wooden items lacquered and relacquered many times in either black or vermilion). **Yamatoya** on Komachi-dori Street (lower center, map 2) sells various handicraft items. **Shikibu** near Hase Station (middle left, map 3) is known for its Japanese dolls and antiques. **Objects of Art Beniya** near Hasedera Temple (middle left, map 3) is an authentic antique store.

Accommodations

HOTEL
Standard Hotel (14,000 - 20,000 yen for a twin room)

Kamakura Park Hotel 鎌倉パークホテル (lower left, map 3)

> Address: 33-6, Sakanoshita, Kamakura; Phone: (0467) 25-5121. A small resort hotel with 29 Western rooms and 12 Japanese rooms. An eight-minute walk from Hase Station.

RYOKANS
Standard Ryokans (12,000 - 20,000 yen per person with two meals)

Kamakura Hotel 鎌倉ホテル (lower left, map 3)

> Address: 2-22-29, Hase, Kamakura; Phone: (0467) 22-0029. A renowned establishment with 15 Japanese rooms and eight Western rooms.

Kaihinso 海浜荘 (lower center, map 3)

> Address: 4-8-14, Yuigahama, Kamakura; Phone: (0467) 22-0960. Another traditional property with 11 Japanese rooms and three Western rooms.

Inexpensive Ryokan (less than 12,000 yen per person with two meals)

Shindotei 新道亭

> Address: 2-10-3, Zushi, Zushi; Phone: (0468) 71-2012. A three-minute walk from Zushi Station on the JNR Yokosuka Line. Zushi Station is one stop from Kamakura (refer to map 1).

Yokohama 横浜

In the feudal era Yokohama was a small village that depended on fishing and agriculture. In the middle of the 19th century, when the Tokugawa Shogunate reluctantly abandoned its policy of isolation and opened several Japanese ports to Western traders, Yokohama was selected as one of them. At that time nearby Kanagawa was the main port in the area, but it was too busy a place for the authorities to be able to adequately protect the Western traders against assassins, so the Shogunate had a new port constructed at Yokohama, which was a rather isolated place. Yokohama was the only place the Western traders were allowed to live and work. Moats were constructed to make the area unassailable, and check-points were set up on all the bridges to keep out the fanatics who wanted no foreigners in their country. The area inside the moats was Kannai (Inside the Checkpoints), while the rest of the area

was called Kangai (Outside the Checkpoints). After the Meiji Restoration, the new imperial government emphasized international trade. Yokohama grew rapidly and became Japan's largest port. Kannai became the center of the new city. Once Yokohama was opened to the traders many Chinese also took up residence in the city and today part of Kannai is a bustling Chinatown. Kannai is a living display of Japanese, Western and Chinese cultures, and has an exotic and rather cosmopolitan air quite different from other Japanese cities.

General Advice

Among the many places of interest in and around Tokyo, Yokohama is only sixth or seventh priority as a tourist attraction. Therefore, unless you are staying in Tokyo for an extended period or happen to be in Yokohama for some reason, you really should skip the city. Visiting Yokohama for an evening stroll and dinner on your way back to Tokyo from Kamakura, as suggested before, is the solution if your time is limited but you still want to see this international port city. If you have enough time in Japan and can allocate one day for Yokohama, I recommend the following itinerary:

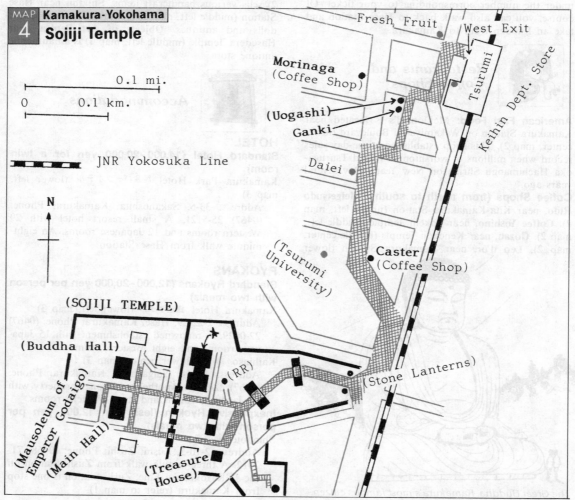

MAP 4 **Kamakura-Yokohama** **Sojiji Temple**

0.1 mi.

0   0.1 km.

JNR Yokosuka Line

N

Fresh Fruit

West Exit

Tsurumi

Keihin Dept. Store

Morinaga (Coffee Shop)

(Uogashi)

Ganki

Daiei

(Tsurumi University)

Caster (Coffee Shop)

(SOJIJI TEMPLE)

(Buddha Hall)

(RR)

(Stone Lanterns)

(Mausoleum of Emperor Godaigo)

(Main Hall)

(Treasure House)

Sojiji 総持寺 in Tsurumi (map 4)

Instead of going directly to Kannai, you should stop first at Sojiji. The Soto sect of Zen Buddhism used to have its headquarters on the Japan Sea coast — at Sojiji Temple in Ishikawa and at Eiheiji Temple in Fukui Prefecture. When the complex at Ishikawa was destroyed by fire at the end of the 19th century, a new Sojiji Temple was erected in Yokohama. Eiheiji Temple in Fukui (which is introduced in the Central Japan Chapter) is still the Soto sect's other headquarters. Though the structures of Sojiji Temple are comparatively new, the precincts are good example of the design of an important Zen temple. The large wooden building marked with an asterisk on map 4 is used as a resthouse for visitors and a lodging for trainees. You can go inside if you are interested in getting a good look at the complicated structure. Be aware that more than 200 trainees and visitors live in the building, and refrain from disturbing them. Buddha Hall and Main Hall are big concrete buildings of traditional temple design. Emperor Godaigo's mausoleum is located at the northern end of the grounds (Remember? He rallied the lords against the Kamakura Shogunate, and thus brought to an end the Kamakura era). The mausoleum is not open to the public. The variety of images of Buddha in the Treasure House are especially impressive (10 a.m. to 4:30 p.m. Admission 300 yen). The entrance to the temple precincts is free.

Coffee Break: At either **Morinaga** (upper center, map 4), or **Caster** (middle center).

Lunch: **Genki** (upper right, map 4) serves Japanese-style lunch specials at 1,400 yen. **Uogashi** (upper right) is a tiny no-frills sushi restaurant. The set menu sushi lunch is only 500-600 yen. Even a la carte should not cost more than 3,000 yen.

Zen meditation.

Kannai 関内
Kannai Station to Kanagawa Prefectural Museum on Bashamichi Street

The sidewalks along Bashamichi 馬車道 are paved with bricks, which is very unusual in Japan, and the buildings still have the atmosphere of the late 19th and early 20th centuries, when Japan first embraced Westernization. Kanagawa Prefectural Museum 神奈川県立博物館, a Western style building distinguished by its dome, is on the left side of Bashamichi Street (middle left, map 5). The first floor of the Museum features nature displays, the second floor archaeologoy, and the third sculptures and paintings of medieval and modern times (9 a.m. to 4:30 p.m. Closed on Mondays. If Monday is a holiday, closed on Tuesday. Admission 100 yen).

The Museum to Silk Center (middle center, map 5)

In 1854, Japan ended its more than 200 year long period of isolation by signing its first treaty of friendship with the United States. A monument commemorating the signing of this important docu-

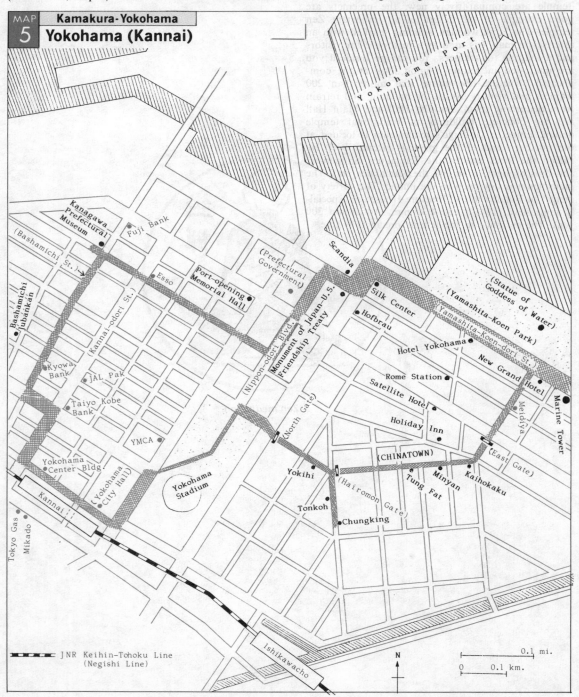

MAP 5 Kamakura-Yokohama
Yokohama (Kannai)

JNR Keihin-Tohoku Line
(Negishi Line)

ment is near the Silk Museum シルク博物館 (middle center, map 5). The Silk Museum, located on the second and third floors of the Silk Center Building, has displays that explain the silk production process. Fine silk products are also displayed here (9 a.m. to 4:30 p.m. Admission 200 yen).

Yamashita-Koen Park and Marine Tower (middle right, map 5)

Yamashita-Koen Park 山下公園 is a green oasis for urbanites during the daytime and a refuge for couples in the evening. In the center of the park are water fountains and a Statue of the Goddess of Water which was presented to Yokohama by San Diego, its sister city. The Marine Tower マリンタワー (348 feet, or 106 m. tall) was built to commemorate the 100th anniversary of the opening of Yokohama Port. Its Observatory is at an altitude of 328 feet (100 m.). If the weather permits, visitors can enjoy a panoramic view in all directions, even as far as Mt. Fuji (10 a.m. to 7:30 p.m. Till 8 p.m. in summer and till 6 p.m. in winter).

Chinatown

Chinatown 中華街 starts at East Gate (middle right, map 5) and stretches to North Gate via Hairomon Gate. About 100 Chinese restaurants are located along the main street and the alleys and lanes that branch off from it.

East Gate of Chinatown.

Restaurants in Kannai

The following are restaurants with good reputations for authentic international cuisines. You can have a good dinner for around 3,000 yen; for 5,000 yen you can get particularly good value for your money.

Western Food

Scandia is a Scandinavian restaurant, **Hofbrau** is a German beer hall restaurant (both of them are pictured in the middle center of map 5, near Silk Center). **Rome Station** (middle right, map 5) specializes in Italian food.

Bashamichi Jubankan (middle left, map 5) is a red brick building. The first floor is a coffee shop, the second an English-style bar, and the third a grill. The grill is a little more expensive than the other three restaurants listed above.

Chinese Food

You can pick any one of the hundreds of restaurants in Chinatown. The following have good reputations: **Kaihokaku, Minyan, Tung Fat, Chungking, Tonkoh,** and **Yokihi** (all of them are pictured on map 5).

Hakone

Hakone is a National Park and mountain resort about 50 miles (80 km.) southwest of Tokyo. Volcanic activity is responsible for the area's beautiful, complex topography. The many "hells" emitting steam and sulfur fumes found amid the 4,300-foot (1,300 m.) mountains testify to the great geological forces still at work underfoot. The calm surface of Lake Ashinoko reflects the symmetrical figure of Mt. Fuji as it rises to 12,399 feet (3,776 m.) northwest of the Lake. Japanese think this is one of the world's most beautiful natural sights; I'm sure you'll agree. For visitors, just sampling the various types of transportation available in the area — mountain trains, cable cars, ropeways and boats — is itself a lot of fun. Hakone is an easy day trip from Tokyo, but if you have a night to spare, linger in this hotspring resort and treat yourself to an experience you won't soon forget.

Transportation

To Hakone From Tokyo (map 1-1)

The usual gateway to Hakone is Odawara. As pictured on map 1-1, Odawara is easily accessible by the JNR Shinkansen or the Odakyu Line from Tokyo.

Shinkansen 新幹線

The Kodama Shinkansen stops at Odawara Station. Odawara 小田原 is the second stop from Tokyo. The ride from Tokyo Station takes only 42 minutes. Refer to the Transportation within Japan Chapter for details on the Shinkansen and its timetable. The layout of Tokyo Station is pictured on Tokyo Map D.

Odakyu Line 小田急線

This private railway operates frequent service between Shinjuku Station 小田急新宿駅 (in Tokyo) and Odawara Station, including a special limited express train called the "Romance Car," which features attendants and luxurious seating. Most Romance Cars go beyond Odawara, to Hakone-Yumoto Station 箱根湯本駅 , but some terminate at Odawara. Because Hakone-Yumoto is on the (private) Hakone Tozan Testsudo Line, which originates at Odawara Station, and which you will use for transportation within the Hakone area, you can get off at either Odawara or Hakone-Yumoto. The schedule of the Romance Cars is as follows:

Train Name	Lv. Shinjuku	Ar. Odawara	Ar. Hakone-Yumoto
Sagami-1	7:00 a.m.	8:15 a.m.	—
Sagami-3	7:30 a.m.	8:45 a.m.	9:00 a.m.
Hakone-7	8:50 a.m.	10:08 a.m.	10:25 a.m.
Hakone-9	9:30 a.m.	10:40 a.m.	10:55 a.m.
Hakone-11	10:00 a.m.	11:09 a.m.	11:25 a.m.
Sagami-7	10:10 a.m.	11:27 a.m.	—
Hakone-13	10:30 a.m.	11:38 a.m.	11:55 a.m.
Hakone-15	11:00 a.m.	12:08 p.m.	12:25 p.m.
Hakone-17	11:30 a.m.	12:38 p.m.	12:55 p.m.
Hakone-19	12:00 noon	1:07 p.m.	1:25 p.m.
Ashigara-55	12:10 p.m.	1:22 p.m.	—
Hakone-21	12:30 p.m.	1:38 p.m.	1:55 p.m.
Hakone-23	1:00 p.m.	2:07 p.m.	2:25 p.m.
Sagami-9	1:10 p.m.	2:26 p.m.	—
Hakone-25	1:30 p.m.	2:39 p.m.	2:55 p.m.
Hakone-27	2:00 p.m.	3:08 p.m.	3:25 p.m.

The Romance cars operate at similar intervals until 7:30 p.m. If you visit Hakone in a one-day excursion, you should leave Shinjuku by 9:30 a.m. at the latest. If you plan to stay the night in Hakone, you should try to leave Shinjuku before 2 p.m. (The layout of Shinjuku Station is pictured on Tokyo Map E). The Romance Cars have only reserved seats. If there are no seats available on the Romance Cars (though this is very rare), you can take one of Odakyu's regular express trains. These are designed to serve commuters and operate about once every 30 minutes. The ride to Odawara Station takes about 1 hour and 50 minutes. All the express trains terminate at Odawara Station. The fare to Odawara on the regular express is 550 yen. For the Romance Car, the fare to Odawara is 1,050 yen and 1,280 yen to Hakone-Yumoto. If you intend to return to Tokyo on the Romance Car you should purchase your return ticket before you leave Shinjuku.

Mt. Fuji and Lake Ashinoko.

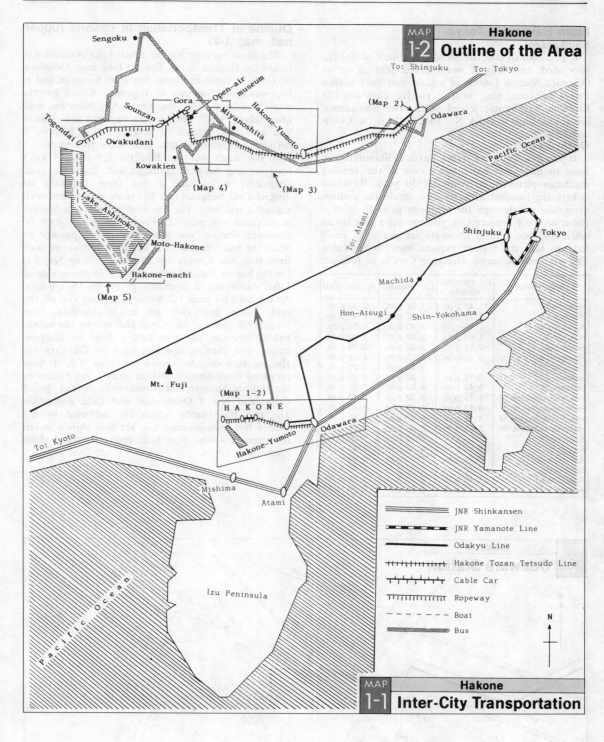

From Hakone to Tokyo
Shinkansen

If you plan to take the Shinkansen back to Tokyo, you need only buy a nonreserved seat ticket at Odawara Station (unless of course you have a Rail Pass) because nine of the twelve cars on the Kodama have non-reserved seats. The Shinkansen for Tokyo stops at track No. 14 (No. 13 is for Kyoto and Osaka).

Odakyu Line

If you did not buy a return ticket at Shinjuku, you have to buy your basic fare ticket at the vending machines pictured on map 2 (550 yen). Reserved tickets are handled at a window inside the station, after you go through the entrance gate. If there is room on the Romance Car, you can get a seat for an additional 500 yen. If no seats are available, you'll have to take the regular express back to Shinjuku. The schedule of major Romance Cars is as follows:

Train Name	Lv. Hakone-Yumoto	Lv. Odawara	Ar. Shinjuku
Hakone-16	12:43 p.m.	1:02 p.m.	2:10 p.m.
Hakone-18	1:13 p.m.	1:32 p.m.	2:40 p.m.
Ashigara-58	—	1:40 p.m.	2:53 p.m.
Hakone-20	1:43 p.m.	2:02 p.m.	3:10 p.m.
Hakone-22	2:13 p.m.	2:32 p.m.	3:39 p.m.
Hakone-24	2:43 p.m.	3:02 p.m.	4:09 p.m.
Sagami-10	—	3:10 p.m.	4:27 p.m.
Hakone-26	3:13 p.m.	3:32 p.m.	4:39 p.m.
Hakone-28	3:43 p.m.	4:02 p.m.	5:09 p.m.
Hakone-Ashigara-30	4:13 p.m.	4:32 p.m.	5:47 p.m.
Hakone-Ashigara-32	4:43 p.m.	5:02 p.m.	6:13 p.m.
Hakone-Ashigara-34	5:13 p.m.	5:32 p.m.	6:45 p.m.
Hakone-Ashigara-36	5:43 p.m.	6:02 p.m.	7:15 p.m.
Sagami-14	—	6:10 p.m.	7:28 p.m.
Ashigara-38	6:13 p.m.	6:32 p.m.	7:47 p.m.
Ashigara-40	6:43 p.m.	7:02 p.m.	8:14 p.m.
Sagami-42	7:13 p.m.	7:32 p.m.	8:48 p.m.
Ashigara-44	7:43 p.m.	8:02 p.m.	9:09 p.m.
Ashigara-46	8:13 p.m.	8:32 p.m.	9:44 p.m.

Outline of Transportation in Hakone (upper half, map 1-2)

The most exciting way to reach Lake Ashinoko is to use the Hakone Tozan Tetsudo Line from Odawara to Gora, a cable car from Gora to Sounzan and a ropeway from Sounzan to Togendai. If you go this way, you can visit the Open-Air Museum and Owakudani "Hell" on the way to the Lake. Unless you are really afraid of heights and ropeways, I definitely recommend that you follow this route.

If you don't want to take the 2.5 mile (4 km.) ropeway trip between Sounzan and Togendai, your alternative is to take a bus from Odawara to Togendai via Sengoku (the bus route is indicated with a shaded red line). The bus stop at Odawara Station is pictured on map 2. From the south exit of Odawara Station, use the underground passage to reach the bus terminal. The bus to Togendai operates from stop No. 4 every 15-20 minutes. Stop No. 3 is for the bus to Hakone-machi, at the southern side of Lake Ashinoko; it operates every 10-15 minutes. As pictured on map 1-2, these two buses run on the same route until they get to Miyanoshita, then branch off, one to the north and one to the south. From Togendai you can take a boat to Hakone-machi, and then take a bus back to Odawara via Hakone-Yumoto. As shown on map 1-2, I have prepared three detailed district maps — No.3 features the Hakone-Yumoto and Miyanoshita district, No. 4 Gora, and No. 5 Owakudani and Lake Ashinoko. The two bus routes, which are indicated by the shaded red lines on map 1-2, are also shown in red on maps 3, 4 and 5 to help you understand these maps more easily.

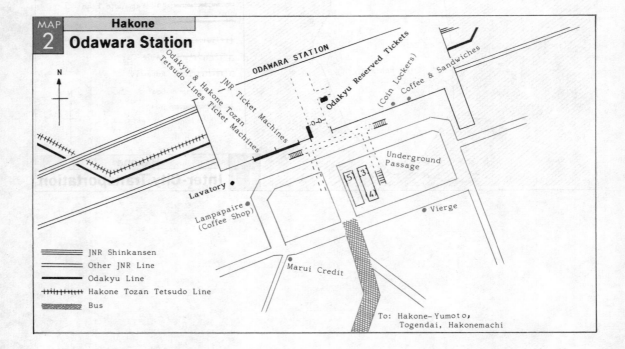

MAP 2 **Hakone**
Odawara Station

N

ODAWARA STATION

Odakyu & Hakone Tozan Tetsudo Lines Ticket Machines

JNR Ticket Machines

Odakyu Reserved Tickets

(Coin Lockers)

Coffee & Sandwiches

Underground Passage

Lavatory

Lampapaire (Coffee Shop)

5 3 4

Vierge

Marui Credit

To: Hakone-Yumoto, Togendai, Hakonemachi

- JNR Shinkansen
- Other JNR Line
- Odakyu Line
- Hakone Tozan Tetsudo Line
- Bus

Suggested Itinerary

Odawara (or Hakone-Yumoto) to the Open-Air Museum by Train

The Hakone Tozan Tetsudo Line 箱根登山鉄道 operates about once every 20 minutes. After Hakone-Yumoto Station, the mountain train goes up hills switchbacking, as pictured on map 3, three times on the way. Your first stop is Chokokunomori Station 彫刻の森駅 (middle right, map 4). The Hakone Open-Air Museum is only a few minutes walk from the station. If you are not interested in the museum, you can take the train directly to Gora Station 強羅駅, the next stop after Chokokunomori. The ride to Chokokunomori takes about 50 minutes from Odawara (650 yen) and about 35 minutes from Hakone-Yumoto (450 yen). The fares to Gora from Hakone-Yumoto and Odawara are the same as the fares from either of those starting points to Chokokunomori.

The Hakone Open-Air Museum 彫刻の森美術館

(middle right, map 4) displays many fine works of contemporary Japanese and Western sculptors in a spacious open-air setting. An indoor exhibition hall features paintings and sculptures of Picasso, Takamura, etc. Harmoniously matched to its natural surroundings, the Museum attracts hundreds of thousands of visitors every year (Open year round. 9 a.m. to 5 p.m. Till 4 p.m. in winter. Admission 1,000 yen).

Gora (upper center, map 4)

Gora is located at an altitude of 2,000 feet (600 m.), on the eastern slope of Mt. Sounzan (3,730 feet or 1,137 m. above sea level). If you are staying the night in Hakone, the following are optional sites to be visited in the Gora area.

Gora-Koen Park 強羅公園 (upper left, map 4) is a French-style rock garden. The Park also contains the Hakone Natural Museum, the Alpine Botanical Garden and the Tropical Bird House (Open year round. 9 a.m. to 5 p.m. Till 9 p.m. in summer. Admission 600 yen).

Hakone Museum 箱根美術館 (upper left, map 3) displays many priceless Japanese, Chinese and Korean ceramic and porcelain masterpieces. The museum's garden is also famous for its refined design (9 a.m. to 4 p.m. Closed on Thursdays. Admission 500 yen).

Places for Lunch

There are many reasonably priced restaurants near the Open-Air Museum and around Gora Station. However, (if you can hold out for another 30 minutes, especially if the weather is fine), I recommend that you wait to eat until you reach Owakudani ropeway station.

Gora to Sounzan by Cable Car (upper left, map 4)

The cable car station is in the same building as the train station. The cable car operates every 15 minutes, and the ride to Sounzan 早雲山 takes 9 minutes. There are four intermediate stations. With a through ticket from Gora to Sounzan (280 yen) you can stop over at any one of them. For example, Hakone Museum, mentioned above, is only a one-minute walk from Koen-Kami Station.

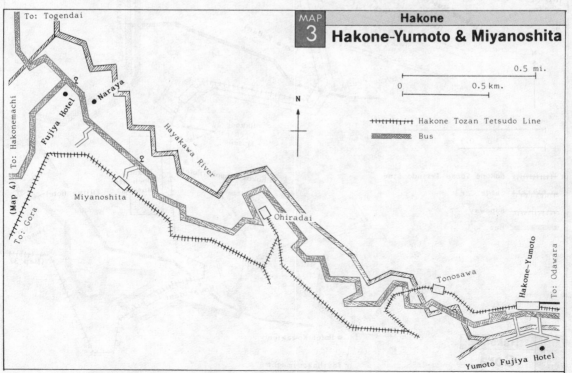

MAP 3 — Hakone — Hakone-Yumoto & Miyanoshita

Sounzan to Owakudani by Ropeway (map 5)

Small cabins, each with a capacity of only 12 persons, operate at one minute intervals from 9:30 a.m. to 4 p.m. between Sounzan and Togendai 桃源台, a distance of 2.5 miles (4 km.). There are two intermediate stations — Owakudani 大湧谷 and Ubako. The fare for the whole route is 1,050 yen. If you have a through ticket, you're allowed to stop over at an intermediate station. The ride takes 10 minutes from Sounzan to Owakudani, and an additional 25 minutes from Owakudani to Togendai. If you want to get off the ropeway at Owakudani Station (and I recommend that you do), signal the station employee, who will open the cabin door from the outside. The highlight of the ropeway ride is when it passes over Owakudani Valley just before it arrives at the Owakudani Station. Far below you can see steam escaping from the rugged mountains.

The second floor of the **Owakudani Station** houses a **restaurant** which commands a grand view of Hakone National Park. If the weather permits, you can see Mt. Fuji rising above the lower mountains to the northwest. Unfortunately, the menu of the restaurant is not nearly as special as the view. But because the 1,000-1,500 yen lunch includes the view it has to be classified as a real bargain.

Places of Interest in Owakudani (detailed map in the center of map 5)

Owakudani Natural Science Museum 大湧谷自然科学博物館, a modern three-story building near the station, displays various objects featuring the history, flora and fauna of Hakone (Open year round. 9 a.m. to 5 p.m. Admission 300 yen).

Owakudani Nature Exploration Path 大湧谷自然探勝路 goes through volcanic "hells." The circular path is about 0.4 miles (680 m.) long and the walk takes about 30 minutes. At the entrance to the Path, a vendor sells black eggs that have been boiled in one of the "hells": yolks are hard, the whites are soft, and the shells are black. Try one if you're interested in volcanic cuisine.

Owakudani to Togendai by Ropeway (upper center, map 5)

Continue your ride to Togendai via the ropeway. Because Owakudani is the highest point on the route, the cabin descends slowly toward Lake Ashinoko. The view of the Lake beneath your feet is breathtaking.

Togendai (upper left, map 5)

I have placed a detailed map of Togendai in the upper left hand corner of map 5 for those who have to go back to Odawara (or Hakone-Yumoto) from

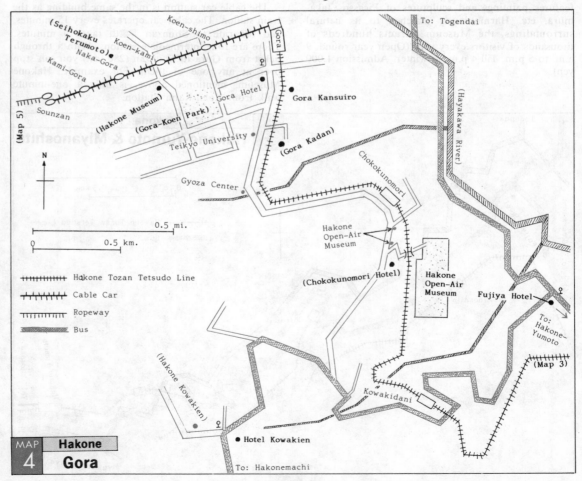

here. The bus going to Odawara originates at Togendai at the bus stop pictured on the map, and runs every 10-25 minutes. The ride to Hakone-Yumoto takes about 45 minutes (800 yen), and the ride to Odawara takes exactly one hour.

If you skip the ropeway ride and take a bus from Odawara to Togendai, your itinerary will begin here.

Togendai to Hakone-machi by Boat

Togendai Pier 桃源台船着場 is only a few minutes walk from the ropeway station. Boats leave every 30-

40 minutes, and all boats that originate at Togendai go to Hakone-machi. Usually they go to Hakone-machi 箱根町 first and then to Moto-Hakone 元箱根, but a few stop at Moto-Hakone first, and then continue to Hakone-machi. The cruise takes 30 to 40 minutes, and the fare is 800 yen or 900 yen, depending on the type of boat.

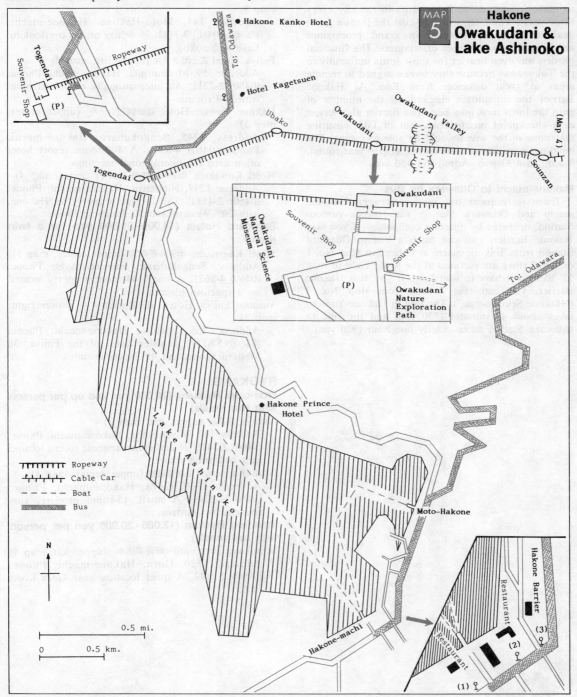

MAP 5 Hakone
**Owakudani &
Lake Ashinoko**

Ropeway

To: Odawara

● Hakone Kanko Hotel

Togendai

Souvenir Shop

(P)

● Hotel Kagetsuen

Ubako

Owakudani

Owakudani Valley

Sounzan

(Map 4)

To: Odawara

Owakudani

Souvenir Shop

Owakudani Natural Science Museum

Souvenir Shop

(P)

Owakudani Nature Exploration Path

Togendai

● Hakone Prince Hotel

Moto-Hakone

┬┬┬┬┬┬ Ropeway
┼┼┼┼┼┼ Cable Car
- - - - Boat
▨▨▨▨ Bus

Lake Ashinoko

N

Hakone Barrier

Restaurant

Restaurant

Restaurant

(3)

(2)

(1)

0.5 mi.

0 0.5 km.

Hakone-machi

Hakone-machi (lower center, map 5) (detailed map on lower right corner of map 5)

If you still have time before you have to go back to Odawara (or Hakone-Yumoto) to catch your train, you should visit **Hakone Barrier** 箱根関所跡 , a five-minute walk from the boat pier. In the Edo era, the main road between Tokyo and Kyoto (the "Tokaido" so vividly illustrated in Hiroshige's woodblock prints) ran through Hakone. To keep the minor feudal lords from rebeling, the Tokugawa shoguns forced the lords' wives to live in Edo, and the lords themselves to make formal, compulsory visits to the city every three years. These trips to Edo cost the lords a great deal because they traveled in grand processions accompanied by hundreds of retainers. The financial burden was even heavier for those lords unfriendly to the Tokugawas because they were assigned to remote areas at great distances from Edo. At Hakone Barrier the Shogunate checked on the number of guns the lords took into Edo. The Barrier also served as a checkpoint on the route out of Edo, ensuring that none of the wives would be able to escape. The buildings here are reconstructions. (Open year round. 9 a.m. to 4:30 p.m. Admission 150 yen).

Hakone-machi to Odawara by Bus

There is frequent bus service between Hakone-machi and Odawara Station via Hakone-Yumoto Station, operated by different companies. If you skip Hakone Barrier, you can catch a bus to Odawara Station from Hakone-machi at either bus stop No. 1 or No. 2 (they are pictured at the lower right of map 5). You won't have to wait long. If you visit Hakone Barrier, you can take a bus from stop No. 3 ("Hakone Sekisho-mae"). The ride to Hakone-Yumoto takes about 40 minutes (730 yen) and the ride to Odawara Station takes exactly one hour (920 yen).

Accommodations

HOTELS
First-class Hotels (20,000 yen and up for a twin room; lower rates are available on weekdays and in colder seasons)
Hakone Prince Hotel 箱根プリンスホテル(middle center, map 5)
> Address: 144, Moto-Hakone, Hakone-machi; Phone: (0460) 3-7111. 96 deluxe rooms overlooking Lake Ashinoko.

Fujiya Hotel 富士屋ホテル (upper left, map 3)
> Address: 359, Miyanoshita, Hakone-machi; Phone: (0460) 2-2211. An internationally renowned hotel with 149 rooms.

Hakone Kanko Hotel 箱根観光ホテル (upper center, map 5)
> Address: 1245, Sengokuhara, Hakone-machi; Phone: (0460) 4-8501. A 100-room resort hotel often used for international meetings.

Hotel Kowakien ホテル小湧園 (lower center, map 4)
> Address: 1297, Ninotaira, Hakone-machi; Phone: (0460) 2-4111. The largest property in Hakone, with 207 Western and 50 Japanese rooms.

Standard Hotels (14,000-20,000 yen for a twin room)
Hotel Kagetsuen ホテル花月園 (upper center, map 5)
> Address: Sengokuhara, Hakone-machi; Phone: (0460) 4-8621. A small, 44-room property located on a spacious plateau.

Yumoto Fujiya Hotel 湯元富士屋ホテル (lower right, map 3)
> Address: 256, Yumoto, Hakone-machi; Phone: (0460) 5-6111. A sister hotel of the Fujiya. 36 Western rooms and 49 Japanese suites.

RYOKANS
First-class Ryokans (20,000 yen and up per person with two meals)
Naraya 奈良屋 (upper left, map 3)
> Address: 162, Miyanoshita, Hakone-machi; Phone: (0460) 2-2411. 26 authentic Japanese rooms located in a hotspring resort.

Gora Kansuiro 強羅環翠楼 (upper center, map 4)
> Address: 1300, Gora, Hakone-machi; Phone: (0460) 2-3141. A small, 15-room property surrounded by gardens.

Standard Ryokan (12,000-20,000 yen per person with two meals)
Seihokaku Terumoto 静峰閣照本 (upper left, map 4)
> Address: 1320, Gora, Hakone-machi; Phone: (0460) 2-3177. A quiet location near Gora-Koen Park.

Nagoya & Vicinity

Major attractions in the Nagoya area include the city itself, Ise-Shima National Park and three pottery villages (Seto, Tajimi and Tokoname).

Transportation

Connections with Other Cities

Nagoya 名古屋 (upper center, map 1) is located on the Shinkansen, and is thus conveniently linked with other major cities such as Tokyo, Kyoto and Osaka.

Between Nagoya and Ise-Shima National Park

The Kintetsu Ise-Shima Line 近鉄伊勢志摩線 (private) operates limited express trains between Nagoya and Kashikojima (lower center, map 1) (some trains terminate at Toba) every 15 to 40 minutes. The ride from Nagoya takes about one and a half hours to Iseshi 伊勢市駅 (1,820 yen), one hour and 40 minutes to Toba 鳥羽駅 (2,020 yen) and two hours and 10 minutes to Kashikojima 賢島駅 (2,420 yen). The Kintetsu Nagoya Station 近鉄名古屋駅 is a few minutes walk from JNR's Nagoya Station (See map 3, middle center).

You can also combine two JNR lines — the Kise Line 紀勢線 between Nagoya and Taki 多気 (lower left, map 1), and the Sangu Line 参宮線 between Taki and Iseshi (lower center, map 1), though the number of trains is limited. The following is the schedule of major trains:

Nagoya to Toba via Taki

(1) Nagoya to Taki

Name of Train	Lv. Nagoya	Ar. Taki
Nanki-1	8 : 33 a.m.	10 : 00 a.m.
Nanki-3	10 : 03 a.m.	11 : 31 a.m.
Nanki-5	1 : 55 p.m.	3 : 21 p.m.

(2) Taki to Toba via

Name of Train	Lv. Taki	Ar. Iseshi	Ar. Toba
"Donko" (local)	10:23 a.m.	10:46 a.m.	11:15 a.m.
Shima	11:40 a.m.	11:55 a.m.	12:17 p.m.
"Donko" (local)	4 : 05 p.m.	4 : 29 p.m.	4 : 51 p.m.

Toba to Nagoya via Taki

(1) Toba to Tki via Iseshi

Name of Train	Lv. Toba	Ar. Iseshi	Ar. Taki
"Donko" (local)	10:29 a.m.	11:00 a.m.	11:25 a.m.
"Donko" (local)	2:33 p.m.	2:56 p.m.	3:19 p.m.
"Donko" (local)	5:43 p.m.	6:04 p.m.	6:30 p.m.

(2) Taki to Nagoya

Name of Train	Lv. Taki	Ar. Nagoya
Nanki-4	12:02 p.m.	1:30 p.m.
Nanki-6	4:04 p.m.	5:32 p.m.
Nanki-8	6:52 p.m.	8:20 p.m.

Between Toba and Kyoto

One JNR train a day connects Toba and Kyoto. Japan Rail Pass holders might be interested to know that this train exists.

Kyto to Toba

Name of Train	Lv. Kyoto	Ar. Iseshi	Ar. Toba
Shima	9:22 a.m.	11:59 a.m.	12:21 p.m.

Toba to Kyoto

Name of Train	Lv. Toba	Ar. Iseshi	Ar. Kyto
Shima	4:27 p.m.	4:52 p.m.	7:33 p.m.

The Kintetsu Railways (private) also operates deluxe service between Kashikojima and Kyoto via Toba and Iseshi about once an hour. The ride to Kyoto from Kashikojima takes 3 hours (3,040 yen), and the trip from Toba to Kyoto takes 2 hours and 2 minutes, and costs 2,640 yen.

Between Nagoya and Seto

The Meitetsu Seto Line 名鉄瀬戸線 (private) operates between Sakae-machi Station 栄町駅 in Nagoya and Owari-Seto Station 尾張瀬戸駅 (upper right, map 1) every 10 - 15 minutes (360 yen). The ride takes 40 minutes. The exact location of Sakae-machi Station is pictured on map 2 (middle center) and map 4 (middle right).

Between Nagoya and Tajimi

The JNR Chuo Line 中央本線 originates at Nagoya and operates to the northeast, stopping at Tajimi 多治見 (upper right, map 1). Local trains operate every 20-30 minutes 590 yen), and the ride takes 46 minutes. If you have a Japan Rail Pass, you can also take a limited express train; these operate about once an hour (The ride takes only 24 minutes).

Between Nagoya and Tokoname

The Meitetsu Tokoname Line 名鉄常滑線 (private) operates between Shin-Nagoya Station 新名古屋駅 (near JNR's Nagoya Station) and Tokoname Station 常滑駅 (middle center, map 1) every 15 minutes (460 yen). The ride takes 57 minutes. The Meitetsu Line's Shin-Nagoya Station is in an independent building, which is pictured on map 3 (middle center).

Ise-Shima National Park
伊勢志摩

Places of Interest

Ise Jingu Shrine 伊勢神宮 consists of two major shrines (Outer Shrine and Inner Shrine) and many minor buildings. The Outer Shrine 外宮, a seven minute walk from Iseshi Station, honors the Goddess of the Harvest. The Inner Shrine 内宮 is located 3.9

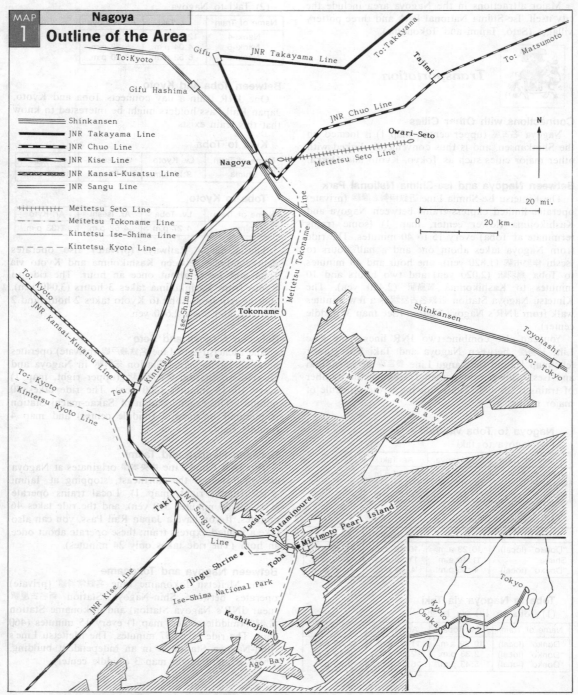

MAP 1 Nagoya
Outline of the Area

miles (6.2 km.) to the southeast of the Outer Shrine. The Shrines are connected by a bus that runs every 15 minutes (280 yen). The Inner Shrine is dedicated to the Goddess of the Sun, mythological ancestress of the imperial family. Because the main worship hall of both Shrines are reconstructed every 20 years in accordance with Shinto practice and tradition, the structures are new. They are, however, considered good examples of simple design and make the best possible use of the natural beauty of the wood. Buses operate from the Inner Shrine to major train stations, such as Iseshi, Toba and Futaminoura, every 15-30 minutes.

Futaminoura 二見浦 is famous for two rocks the sea has eroded in a distinctive way. They are called the Husband-Wife rocks, and are joined by a thick straw rope.

Mikimoto Pearl Island 御木本真珠島 (admission 500 yen) is only a five minute walk from Toba Station. Kokichi Mikimoto started his experiments with cultured pearls here in the late 19th century. He succeeded in culturing pearl hemispheres in 1893 and round pearls in 1905. A variety of pearl products are on display in the museum and the women pearl divers give demonstrations every 40-60 minutes.

Kashikojima 賢島 is on the southern side of Shima Peninsula. Ago Bay, with a number of small islands and pearl beds, provides the most beautiful marine scenery in the area. A one-hour boat tour operates frequently, connecting with the arrival of the Kintetsu Ise-Shima Line trains (1,400 yen).

Accommodations

HOTELS
First-class Hotels (20,000 yen and up for a twin room)
Toba Hotel International 鳥羽国際ホテル (three minutes by car from Toba Station)

Address: 1-23-1, Toba, Mie Pref.; Phone: (0599) 25-3121. Famous for its great view of the sea and many islands (102 rooms). There are 45 Japanese rooms in the wooden annex (also first class).

Shima Kanko Hotel 志摩観光ホテル (a five-minute walk from Kashikojima Station)

Address: Kashikojima, Agocho, Mie Pref.; Phone: (05994) 3-1211. A great location overlooking picturesque Ago Bay.

RYOKANS
First-class Ryokans (20,000 yen and up per person with two meals)
Futamikan 二見館 (three minutes by car from Futaminoura Station)

Address: 569-1, Ko, Futamimachi, Mie Pref.; Phone: (05964) 3-2003. An authentic Japanese ryokan located on the scenic coast (43 rooms).

Toba Kowakien 鳥羽小湧園 (10 minutes by car from Toba Station)

Address: 1061, Koshikake, Anrakujimamachi, Toba, Mie Pref.; Phone: (0599) 25-3251. A large modern property overlooking the sea. 95 Japanese rooms and 21 Western rooms.

Women pearl divers.

Solemn Ise Jingu Shrine.

Nagoya

名古屋

In the civil war period (the 15th-16th centuries), the Nagoya vicinity was the scene of major battles of feudal lords such as Nobunaga Oda and Ieyasu Tokugawa. At the beginning of the 17th century, when the Tokugawa Shogunate gained control over the entire country and incorporated Nagoya into the area under its direct administration, the real development of the area began. Nagoyajo Castle, a massive symbol of the power of the Tokugawa family, was completed in 1612. Most of the city, including the Castle, was destroyed during World War II. Ironically, this destruction hastened the development of Nagoya as a modern city. Wide streets were laid out in the center of the city to accommodate heavy modern traffic. To keep a bit of green within the city, each of these streets was designed with a grassy median strip with trees. Nagoyajo Castle was reconstructed in 1959 as the spiritual symbol of the city. Nagoya is often called Chukyo (Central Capital) because it is located between the modern capital, Tokyo (Eastern Capital), and the ancient capital, Kyoto (Western Capital). Though the city has never been the official capital of Japan, it has always been the focal point for the Central Japan district.

Outline of the City

Nagoya's downtown area, Sakae (middle center, map 2), is about 1.5 miles (2.5 km.) from Nagoya Station, but the station district, and especially its underground shopping and restaurant malls, has itself become another city center. Many office buildings are located around the station. Governmental offices of both Nagoya City and Aichi Prefecture are southeast of Nagoyajo Castle (upper center, map 2). There are five major places of interest in Nagoya — Nagoyajo Castle (upper center, map 2), the Noritake China Factory (upper left, map 2), the TV Tower (middle center, map 2), Atsuta Jingu Shrine (lower center, map 2), and the Tokugawa Museum (upper right, map 2).

Transportation in the City

There are four subway lines in the city. They provide tourists with an easy means of public transportation to all major places of interest. The **Higashiyama** subway line (No. 1) 地下鉄東山線 runs east to west, and connects Nagoya Station with Fushimi and Sakae, the major downtown area of Nagoya. The **Meijo** subway line (No. 2) 地下鉄名城線 and a second Meijo subway line (No. 4) run north to south on the same tracks between Ozone (upper right, map 2) and Kanayama (lower center, map 2) via Shiyakusho (the stop closest to Nagoyajo Castle) and Sakae. At Kanayama Station the No. 2 subway branches off to the south for Nagoya Port, and the No. 4 heads toward the suburbs in the southeast. Between Ozone and Kanayama the No. 2 and No. 4 trains alternate — i.e., if a No.`2 train is the first to come along, a No. 4 will be next. The **Tsurumai** subway line 地下鉄鶴舞線 runs from the northwest to the southeast. This line is probably not of much use to tourists.

All signs at the subway stations are written in both Japanese and English. If you refer to map 2, you should not have any difficulty at all getting around the city. At all the major subway stations I checked, at least one fare table was written in English. Nagoya's is the most courteous to foreigners of all the subway systems in Japan.

Places of Interest

Nagoyajo Castle 名古屋城 (upper center, map 2)

The Castle is a five minute walk from Shiyakusho Station 市役所駅 on the Meijo subway line. The original castle was famous for the twin gold dolphins on the top of the donjon as well as for the grandeur of its structure. The present donjon was reconstructed in 1959, and two new golden dolphins were placed atop its roof. These replacements are the symbol of the Castle. The donjon's modern conveniences include elevators that take you to the top of the building. The observatory affords an extensive view of Nagoya City and Nobi Plain. The lower floors of the donjon house a museum that displays various artistic and historical objects rescued from the fire which destroyed the original castle. Ninomaru Garden, to the east of the donjon, is typical of the refined castle gardens for which Japan is so famous (9:30 a.m. to 4:30 p.m. Admission 250 yen).

Atsuta Jingu Shrine 熱田神宮 (lower center, map 2)

To reach the Shrine, you can take the Meijo Line subway (No. 4) to Jingu-Nishi Station 神宮西駅, or either the JNR Tokaido Line (to Atsuta Station 熱田駅) or the Meitetsu Tokoname Line (to Jingu-mae Station 神宮前駅), as pictured on map 2.

Atsuta Jingu, set in densely wooded grounds, is one of the most important shrines in all of Japan. It was erected in the third century. The Shrine is especially famous as the repository of one of the emperor's three sacred symbols, the Kusanagi-no-Tsurugi (Grass Mowing Sword). The other two, the Mirror and the Jewel, are preserved at Ise Jingu Shrine and at the Imperial Palace respectively. These three sacred objects were, according to Japanese myth, brought to earth by the grandson of the Goddess of the Sun, ancestress of the nation's imperial family. Atsuta Shrine is still an object of deep respect among the people, and millions of worshippers visit here during the New Year's Holiday. Amateur groups often stage performances in Noh Hall on the weekends.

Tokugawa Museum 徳川美術館 (upper right, map 2)

Tokugawa Museum is a 10 minute walk from Ozone Station 大曽根駅 on the Meijo subway line, the JNR Chuo Line, or the Meitetsu Seto Line. It was built on the grounds of the former mansion of a high-ranking retainer of the Tokugawa family. The grounds themselves are a beautiful garden, and the Museum is the repository of works of art owned by the Tokugawa family. Although the Museum houses 10,000 treasures, such as swords, suits of armor, paintings, pottery, lacquerware and other works of art, only a limited number of them can be displayed in the Museum's three small chambers. The world famous scroll of the story of Prince Genji (Genji Monogatari) is displayed only once a year, and unless you happen to be in Nagoya during the time of this special exhibition, it is probably not worth allocating precious time to this Museum.

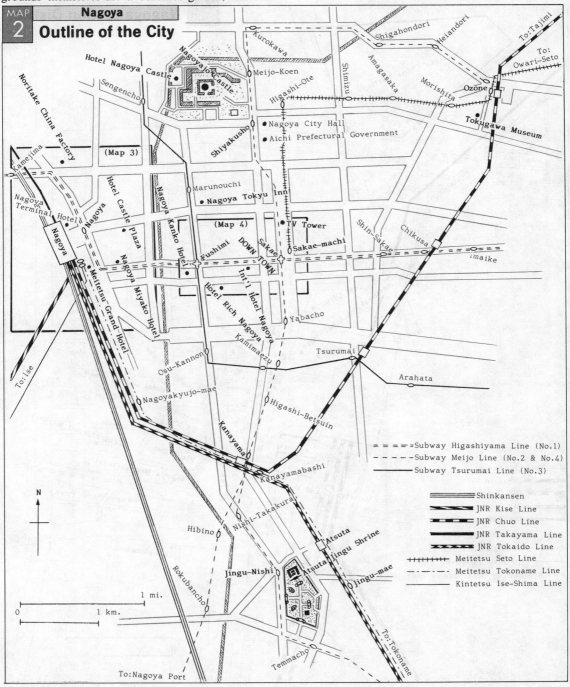

MAP 2 Nagoya
Outline of the City

Legend:
- ═ ═ ═ ═ Subway Higashiyama Line (No.1)
- ─ ─ ─ Subway Meijo Line (No.2 & No.4)
- ──── Subway Tsurumai Line (No.3)
- Shinkansen
- JNR Kise Line
- JNR Chuo Line
- JNR Takayama Line
- JNR Tokaido Line
- Meitetsu Seto Line
- Meitetsu Tokoname Line
- Kintetsu Ise-Shima Line

Scale: 0 — 1 mi. / 0 — 1 km.

Noritake China Factory ノリタケ・チャイナ (upper left, map 3)

The factory is a ten minute walk from Nagoya Station. Noritake is Japan's largest ceramics company, and its refined products are popular all over the world. The company welcomes foreign tourists to its factory to observe the manufacturing process. An English-speaking guide escorts you and explains details (twice a day at 10 a.m. and 1 p.m.). Before visiting, please make a telephone reservation to the Welcome Center (052-562-5072). The factory and tours are closed on Saturdays, Sundays and holidays.

Nagoya Station Vicinity

To the east of Nagoya Station there is a huge underground shopping center, the total length of

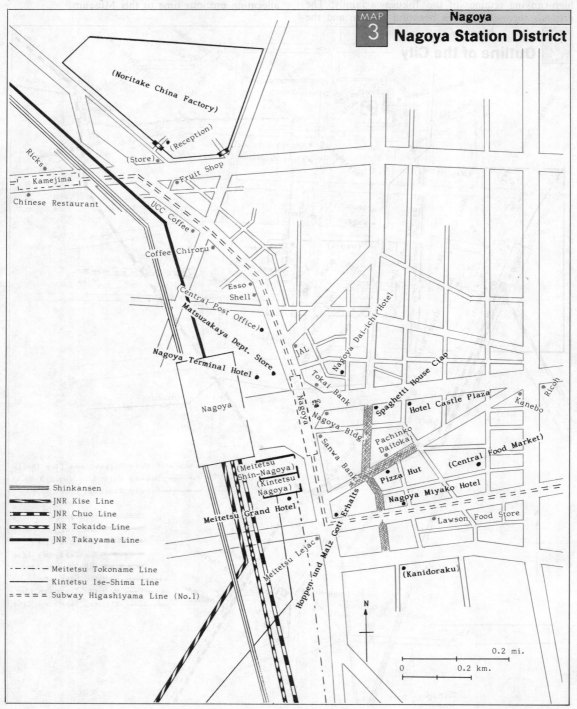

| MAP | Nagoya |
| 3 | **Nagoya Station District** |

(Noritake China Factory)

(Reception)

(Store)

Ricks

Kamejima

Chinese Restaurant

Fruit Shop

UCC Coffee

Coffee Chiroru

(Central Post Office)

Esso Shell

Matsuzakaya Dept. Store

Nagoya Terminal Hotel

Nagoya

JAL

Tokai Bank

Nagoya Dai-ichi Hotel

Spaghetti House Ciao

Hotel Castle Plaza

Ricoh

Kanebo

Nagoya Bldg

Nagoya

Sanwa Bank

Pachinko Daitoka

Pizza Hut

(Central Food Market)

Nagoya Miyako Hotel

(Meitetsu Shin-Nagoya)

(Kintetsu Nagoya)

Meitetsu Grand Hotel

Lawson Food Store

Meitetsu Lejac

Hoppen und Malz Gott Erhalts

(Kanidoraku)

Shinkansen
JNR Kise Line
JNR Chuo Line
JNR Tokaido Line
JNR Takayama Line

—·—·— Meitetsu Tokoname Line
——— Kintetsu Ise-Shima Line
==== Subway Higashiyama Line (No.1)

N

0.2 mi.

0   0.2 km.

which is 3.75 miles (6 km.). It's so extensive that natives of the city as well as foreign visitors can easily get lost. Above the bustling underground center is a business area. Although the district is busy during the day, it is rather quiet in the evening. Eating and drinking places, as well as numerous pachinko pinball parlors crowd the streets indicated on the map 3 with shaded red. (Pachinko, by the way, was invented in Nagoya, and is still a hometown favorite).

American Fast Food: Pizza Hut (lower center, map 3) is the only one I could find in the district. There may be a McDonald's in the maze of the underground shopping malls.

Restaurants and a Pub:

Spaghetti House Ciao building (middle center, map 3) houses several restaurants. **Europe,** on the second floor, serves spaghetti and pilaf at 1,000 yen and fondue at 1,800-3,000 yen. **Dohatsu Chinese Restaurant** is on the third floor (2,000-3,000 yen for set menu dinner). The fifth and sixth floors are **Kisoji,** an authentic Japanese restaurant. Shabu-shabu is 3,000-3,600 yen, and a set menu Japanese dinner is around 2,000 yen. **Kanidoraku** (lower right, map 3) has a huge mechanical crab for a sign. A set menu crab dinner is 4,000 yen. **Hoppen und Malz Gott Erhalts** (lower center, map 3) is an inexpensive beer hall for white collar workers in the district.

Downtown

Sakae ✳ is Nagoya's version of Tokyo's Ginza. Shopping, eating and drinking establishments are clustered on the streets here. There's another extensive underground shopping area around the Sakae subway stations and the Meitetsu Seto Line's Sakae-machi Station (which are themselves underground). In the center of the 238-foot (100 m.) wide Hisaya-dori Street is a park and the city's 590-foot (180 m.) tall TV Tower (upper right, map 4). The tower has an observatory at an altitude of 295 feet (90 m.).

American Fast Food: McDonald's and Kentucky Fried Chicken ("KFC") (both at lower center, map 4), and Pizza Hut (middle center, map 4) are located in downtown Nagoya.

Inexpensive Restaurants (2,500 yen or less for dinner)

Riviere (upper right, map 4) is a seafood restaurant. The dishes range in price from 1,000 to 2,000 yen. **Kaen** (middle center, map 4) is a Korean barbecue restaurant. Standard prices are 800-1,200 yen. **Akbar** (lower center, map 4) is located in the basement of a modern building. This Indian restaurant has a variety of curry dishes at 800-1,300 yen.

Reasonable Restaurants (2,500-5,000 yen for dinner)

Chinese Yamucha Miramar (not pictured on map 4, but at the same location as **Akbar** above) serves Chinese set menu dinners at 2,500-4,000 yen. **Kitahachi** (middle center, map 4) is a typical sushi bar restaurant. An a la carte dinner may cost 3,000-5,000 yen. **Kisoji** (middle center, map 4) is an authentic Japanese restaurant. Shabu-shabu is served at 3,000-3,600 yen. The Japanese set menu dinner is 5,800 yen. This restaurant has several set menu lunches at 1,000-1,500 yen. **Kanidoraku** (lower center, map 4) also has a branch restaurant in this district. A set menu crab dinner is 4,000 yen.

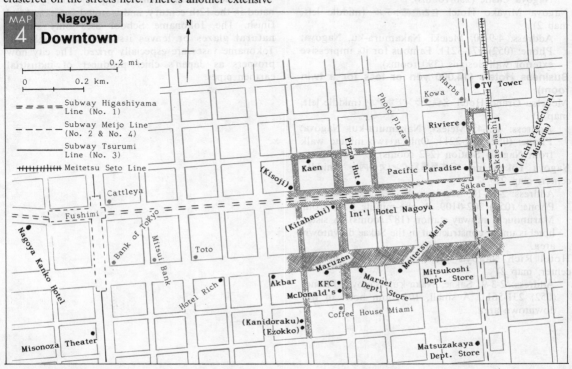

MAP 4 — Nagoya Downtown

Pubs

Ezokko (lower center, map 4) is a robatayaki pub. Typical dishes are 300-600 yen. **Pacific Paradise** (middle right, map 4) is a wine house. A bottle of wine is priced at 1,500-2,000 yen, and accompanying dishes are 700-1,000 yen.

Accommodations

HOTELS

First-class Hotels (20,000 yen and up for a twin room)

Hotel Nagoya Castle ホテル・ナゴヤキャッスル (upper left, map 2)

Address: 3-19, Hinokuchicho, Nishi-ku, Nagoya; Phone (052) 521-2121. Popular among foreign business people and tourists (250 rooms).

Nagoya Kanko Hotel 名古屋観光ホテル (middle center, map 2)

Address: 1-19-30, Nishiki, Naka-ku, Nagoya; Phone: (052) 231-7711. Another of Nagoya's guest houses for international travelers (505 rooms).

Standard Hotels (14,000-20,000 yen for a twin room)

International Hotel Nagoya 名古屋国際ホテル (middle center, map 2)

Address: 3-23-3, Nishiki, Naka-ku, Nagoya; Phone: (052) 961-3111. A high-standard hotel in the heart of downtown (254 rooms).

Hotel Castle Plaza ホテル・キャッスルプラザ (middle left, map 2)

Address: 4-3-25, Meieki, Nakamura-ku, Nagoya; Phone: (052) 582-2121. A sister hotel of the Hotel Nagoya Castle (258 rooms).

Nagoya Miyako Hotel 名古屋都ホテル (middle left, map 2)

Address: 4-9-10, Meieki, Nakamura-ku, Nagoya; Phone: (052) 571-3211. Famous for its impressive exterior wall designs (390 rooms).

Business Hotels (14,000 yen or less for a twin room)

Meitetsu Grand Hotel 名鉄グランドホテル (middle left, map 2)

Address: 1-2-4, Meieki, Nakamura-ku, Nagoya; Phone: (052) 582-2211. Only a two minute walk from Nagoya Station (242 rooms).

Nagoya Tokyu Inn 名古屋東急イン（丸の内） (middle center, map 2)

Address: 2-17-18, Marunouchi, Naka-ku, Nagoya; Phone: (052) 202-0109. A one-minute walk from Marunouchi subway station (187 rooms). A sister hotel is under construction in the Sakae downtown area.

Hotel Rich Nagoya ホテル・リッチ名古屋 (middle center, map 2)

Address: 2-3-9, Sakae, Naka-ku, Nagoya; Phone: (052) 231-5611. A small, 101-room hotel in the downtown area.

Pottery Villages
陶器村

In Japan, ceramics are popularly called "Seto-mono" (objects of Seto). It is believed that pottery production started in Seto (upper right, map 1) in the 8th century, and that Japan's first glazed pottery was produced here in the middle of the 9th century. The development of artistic pottery was advanced when new Chinese technology was introduced by Toshiro Kato in the 13th century, but the civil wars scattered the skilled potters to remote areas and Seto suffered a long stagnant period. The city was revitalized by Tamikichi Kato, who introduced advanced ceramic technology in the early 19th century. Today Seto is prosperous as Japan's largest producer of everyday ceramic products. Seto is the most typical of all Japanese pottery centers and has a long history as such. I have therefore selected Seto as the most representative of the three major pottery villages in the Nagoya vicinity and have included details on Seto in the pages that follow. The other Nagoya-area pottery villages are only sketched briefly as follows:

Tajimi (upper right, map 1) is the center of Mino Pottery, which originated with craftsmen from Seto who took refuge in the Tajimi area during the civil wars. The simple yet refined designs and color schemes used by this school of pottery have long been favored for the tea ceremony.

Tokoname (middle center, map 1) pottery originated in the 12th century, and is noted for its natural finish. The Tokoname School uses only simple, natural glazes or leaves its products unglazed. Tokoname vases are especially prized. The city now prospers as Japan's chief producer of industrial earthen pipes.

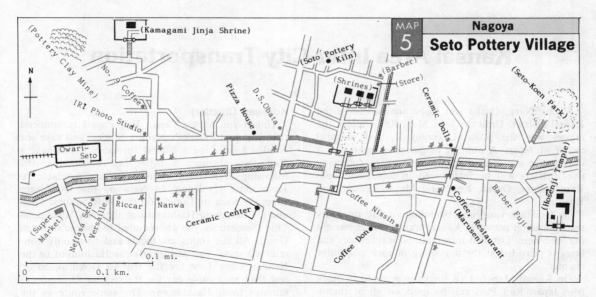

MAP 5 **Nagoya Seto Pottery Village**

Seto

Of the many pottery villages located all over Japan, Seto is proud that it has the longest history. The river running in the middle of the city is dark white from all the pottery clay, and the major streets are crowded with shops that display the products of the workrooms. Seto's Pottery Festival, which is held on the third Saturday and Sunday of September, is the largest open air market of this kind and attracts hundreds of thousands of visitors to the city. On map 5, I have pictured the major pottery stores with red stars.

Ceramic Center 陶磁器センター **(middle center, map 5)** is a Seto pottery museum. About 250 fine works, both old and new, are displayed on the second floor. The first floor is a souvenir shop and sells a variety of products at prices that range from about 250 yen to more than 1 million yen.

Hosenji Temple 宝泉寺 **(lower right, map 5, optional)** has an impressive two-story pagoda.

Seto-Koen Park 瀬戸公園 **(middle right, map 5)** is located in an elevated place. The hexagonal hall, made itself of pottery, contains a monument to Toshiro Kato, founder of Seto pottery. The 11-foot (3.3 m.) tall hall, built in 1866, is the largest pottery product in Japan, and a very impressive structure.

Toningyo Juhachibankan 陶人形十八番館 **(middle right, map 5),** a pottery shop specializing in pottery dolls, has an English sign **"Ceramic Dolls."** This store is always up on new trends in pottery making and is a good place to look for small souvenir items.

Soto Pottery Kiln 創陶 **(upper center, map 5)** teaches pottery making to amateurs. All visitors are invited to join in the work on Sundays and holidays (10 a.m. to 3 p.m.).There is a nominal charge (1,000-2,000 yen) to cover materials. On weekdays the kiln is open only to registered members (1 p.m. to 3 p.m.), but visitors can still observe the potters at work.

Kamagami Jinja Shrine 窯神神社 **(upper left, map 5)** is located on a small hill atop a long flight of stone steps. The Shrine has several ceramic lion dogs (Guardians of the Shrine). A statue of Tamikichi Kato, who revitalized the city in the early 19th century, is located in the Shrine's precincts. There is a good view of the city from the grounds.

Pottery Clay Mine (upper left, map 5): This source of the clay used by the city's potters is to the west of Kamagami Jinja Shrine.

Flower arrangement.

Kansai Area Inter-City Transportation

Kyoto, Nara, Osaka and Kobe are located in the Kansai district. Until the 1868 Meiji Restoration, the region was the political, economic, and cultural center of Japan. A number of places of interest and importance are located in the region. The following five districts will be introduced in this guidebook: Kyoto; Nara; Osaka; Kobe and Mt. Rokkosan; and Koyasan.

To facilitate your understanding of the inter-city transportation network, Kansai train connections are outlined here. Detailed information on schedules and fares is provided at the beginning of each respective chapter.

On Kansai Map 1, JNR lines are pictured in black (the Japan Rail Pass can be used on all of them), while private railways, the city subway, cable cars, and the ropeway routes are indicated with red lines.

Between Kyoto and Nara (details in the Nara Chapter)

The JNR Nara Line 奈良線 runs commuter trains between Kyoto and Nara (The ride takes 60 minutes).

The Kintetsu Kyoto Line 近鉄京都線 (private) operates deluxe cars for tourists between these cities.

Between Kyoto and Osaka (details in the Osaka Chapter)

There are three train lines available between these two cities:

The JNR Tokaido-Sanyo Line 東海道・山陽本線 operates commuter trains between Kyoto and Nishi-Akashi (to the west of Kobe, outside map 1) which stop at Osaka and Sannomiya (the main station in Kobe). The ride between Kyoto and Osaka takes 50 minutes.

If you have a Japan Rail Pass, you can take the Shinkansen 新幹線. The ride between Kyoto and Shin-Osaka takes only 17 minutes. If you don't have a Pass, the ride is too costly. From Shin-Osaka Station, you can take the Tokaido-Sanyo commuter train to Osaka Station. If you are going to Osaka's Namba area, the Midosuji subway line 地下鉄御堂筋線 is available from Shin-Osaka Station.

The Hankyu Kyoto Line 阪急京都線 (private) connects downtown Kyoto (Kawaramachi) and Umeda (The private railways and the city subways use the name Umeda for their stations near JNR's Osaka Station). If you are staying at a hotel in downtown Kyoto, this private railway is more convenient. The ride on the limited express takes 38 minutes.

Between Kyoto and Kobe (details in the Kobe & Mt. Rokkosan Chapter)

The JNR Tokaido-Sanyo Line is available for this connection. The ride between Kyoto and Sannomiya takes about one and a half hours.

If you have a Japan Rail Pass, you can also take the Shinkansen between Kyoto and Shin-Kobe. The ride takes only 35 minutes.

Between Kyoto and Koyasan (details in the Koyasan Chapter)

Unless you have a Japan Rail Pass I recommend that you go to Osaka's Namba Station and take the Nankai Koya Line 南海高野線 (private). If you have a Rail Pass, though a little time consuming, the following JNR train connections are available to Hashimoto: (1) Kyoto to Nara on the JNR Nara Line; (2) Nara to Takada on the JNR Sakurai Line; and (3) Takada to Hashimoto on the JNR Wakayama Line (Sometimes you are required to change trains at Gojo). All the trains are locals and have only non-reserved seats. You can transfer at Hashimoto to the Nankai Koya Line for the trip to Gokurakubashi, and then to a cable car for the trip to Koyasan (45 minutes from Hashimoto). The same route as the above is available for the return trip to Kyoto/Nara. (Details are included in the Koyasan Chapter below). An alternative is to take the Nankai Koya Line to Namba in Osaka, transfer there to the Midosuji subway line, and then transfer to JNR (either the Tokaido-Sanyo Line or the Shinkansen) for the trip back to Kyoto.

Between Osaka and Nara (details in the Nara Chapter)

As is the case with Kyoto-Nara connection, the JNR Kansai Line 関西本線 and the Kintetsu Nara Line 近鉄奈良線 (private) operate parallel service.

The JNR Kansai Line operates between Nara Station and Minatomachi Station in Osaka in the morning and in the evening (The ride takes about 40 minutes). The same commuter trains run between Nara Station and Osaka Station during the day (about a 50 minute trip). If you plan to visit Horyuji Temple in Nara, you should take this line because it stops at Horyuji Station (a 15 minute walk to the Temple) on the way to Nara.

The Kintetsu Nara Line operates deluxe cars specially designed for tourists. The ride between Namba Station and Nara Station takes about 30 minutes.

Between Osaka and Kobe (details in the Kobe & Mt. Rokkosan Chapter)

The JNR Tokaido-Sanyo Line connects these two cities (Osaka Station and Sannomiya Station) in 35 minutes.

The Hankyu Kobe Line 阪急神戸線 (private) operates between Umeda Station and Sannomiya Station. The ride takes 27 minutes by express and 42 minutes by local.

Between Osaka and Koyasan (details in the Koyasan Chapter)

The Nankai Koya Line (private) provides the most convenient transportation between Osaka (Namba Station) and Koyasan (Gokurakubashi Station). The limited express, which uses deluxe "tourist" cars, takes one and a half hours, and the express, which uses commuter cars, takes one hour and 45 minutes. Namba Station in Osaka can be reached easily on

Kansai Inter-City Transportation

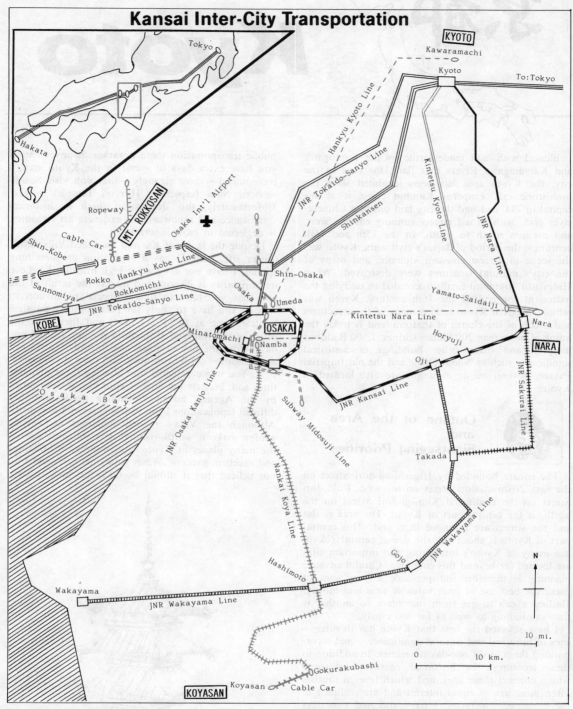

the Midosuji subway line.

Mt. Rokkosan (details in the Kobe & Mt. Rokkosan Chapter)

Bus service is available from JNR's Rokkomichi Station and Hankyu's Rokko Station to the cable car station. Refer to the information above for the best train connections from the city where you are staying.

JUST FOR YOUR INFORMATION
Train Service between Kyoto and Ise-Shima

National Park
(details in the Nagoya & Vicinity Chapter)

Though Ise-Shima National Park is not in the Kansai region, there are two train lines available between Kyoto and the Ise-Shima area:

One JNR express train a day connects Toba and Kyoto each way. The ride takes about three hours.

The Kintetsu Railways (private) operates more convenient train service about once an hour. The ride takes about two hours.

Kyoto

Blessed with land made fertile by the Kamogawa and Katsuragawa Rivers that flank the core of the city, the Kyoto area has been inhabited since the prehistoric era. Emperor Kammu chose it as his capital in 794, and had the city laid out in a Chinese-style grid, with broad streets running east to west, and avenues north to south. In the 15th and 16th centuries, the period of Japan's civil wars, Kyoto was the scene of almost constant violence, and many of the city's cultural treasures were destroyed. When Hideyoshi Toyotomi finally succeeded in unifying the nation at the end of the 16th century, Kyoto was rebuilt. Modern Kyoto retains many of the structures and much of the charm of that era, and is today the home of more than 200 Shinto shrines, 1,500 Buddhist temples, and many other buildings of historical significance such as Nijojo Castle and the old Imperial Palace. Several major museums are also located in Kyoto.

Outline of the Area and Sightseeing Priorities

The square bounded by Higashi-oji-dori Street on the east, Nishi-oji-dori Street on the west, Kujo-dori Street on the south and Kita-oji-dori Street on the north, is the central part of Kyoto. The area is flat and the streets are arranged in a grid. This central part of Kyoto is about half the size of central Tokyo, but many of Kyoto's interesting and important sites are located far beyond this core area. Careful advance planning is therefore indispensable if you want to make the best use of your valuable time and money. Hailing a cab to get from one place to another is time consuming as well as far too costly.

I have selected the best that Kyoto has to offer — sites of historical and cultural significance — and incorporated them in six one-day itineraries. In addition to these treasures, the historical narrow backstreets which connect these sites, and which foreign tourists often miss, are of equal interest and are included in the suggested itineraries. I have allocated two days each for Eastern and Western Kyoto and one day each for Central and Northern Kyoto. Though a two-day itinerary is ideal for Eastern and Western Kyoto, I have also suggested how you can select major sites in these areas to make decent one-day itineraries. So even if you stay in Kyoto for only four days, you can cover most major sites. Southern Kyoto also has several interesting destinations, but I have not included them because the average stay of most foreign tourists in Kyoto is only 2-3 days, and because

public transportation there is rather inconvenient. If you have extra days to spend in the Kyoto area, I recommend — most strongly — that you visit South-western Nara (especially Horyuji Temple) instead. Unfortunately, this destination, high in historical significance and renowned for exquisite art treasures, is neglected in most itineraries.

Despite the fact that Katsura Detached Villa 桂離宮 (lower left, map 1) has a reputation as something special, I have not assigned it high priority. I believe its popularity is illusory and merely the result of the fact that you have to obtain special permission to visit it. You have to apply for permission in advance by telephone at (075) 211-1211, and then visit the office of the Imperial Household Agency at least one day before the day of your visit, in order to fill out an application form. You must also present your passport. You waste valuable time making these preparations and, because the time of your visit is determined by the Agency, advance planning becomes rather difficult (applications from overseas are not accepted). Although the Villa's refined buildings and lovely garden make it worth visiting, it is still only one of the many places in Kyoto with impressive buildings and excellent gardens. When your time is limited I do not believe that it should be taken up making such

A five-story pagoda.

arrangements. The Villa is closed on Saturday afternoons and Sundays, and during the New Year's holidays. Applicants must be over 20 years of age, and the maximum size of groups admitted is four persons. The location of the Imperial Household Agency's Koyto Office 宮内庁京都事務所 is pictured on map 7.

Another temple in the southwestern portion of the city, Saihoji 西芳寺 (lower left, map 1), has the same kind of reputation as Katsura Detached Villa — for the same reasons, I believe. Popularly called Kokedera, or Moss Temple, Saihoji Temple does have a lovely garden, but permission to visit can only be obtained by means of advance application to the temple by mail (Saihoji Temple, Matsuo-Kamigaya-cho, Ukyo-ku, Kyoto). A maximum of five applications are accepted at once. Once permission is obtained, you must make your visit at the time set by the temple. All visitors to the temple are required to listen to a one hour lecture — in Japanese only — before they are allowed to see the garden, and are expected to make a donation of 3,000 yen before they leave. Again, in terms of the time and money involved, it's simply not worth it.

Central Kyoto is introduced first, and then Eastern, Western and Northern Kyoto. This order is designed merely to promote easy understanding of the layout of the city for those who read this guide, and does not reflect my priorities. I suggest that you spend your time in Kyoto as follows:

• If you have only one day: visit Eastern Kyoto (combining the two one-day itineraries as I suggest in the text that follows).

• If you have two days: add Central Kyoto and Gold Pavilion.

• If you have three days: add Western Kyoto (combined itinerary).

• If you have four days: add Northern Kyoto.

• If you have five days: split Eastern Kyoto into two days.

• If you have six days: Congratulations! Follow all the itineraries as written.

• If you have more than six days: Write to me!

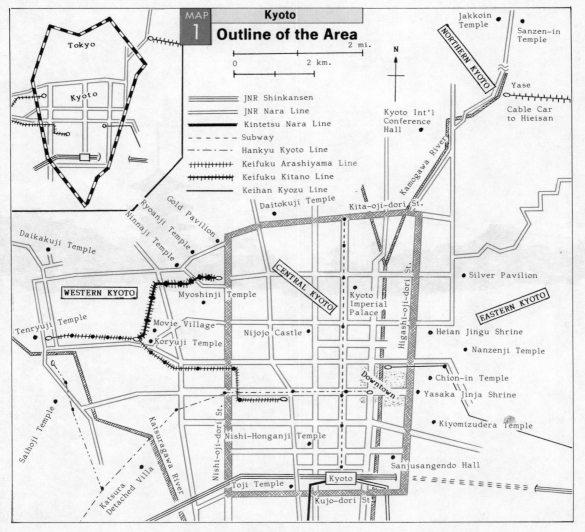

MAP 1

Kyoto
Outline of the Area

2 mi.

0   2 km.

——————— JNR Shinkansen
——————— JNR Nara Line
——————— Kintetsu Nara Line
– – – – – Subway
–·–·–·– Hankyu Kyoto Line
++++++++ Keifuku Arashiyama Line
++++++++ Keifuku Kitano Line
——————— Keihan Kyozu Line

Tokyo

Kyoto

N

NORTHERN KYOTO

Jakkoin Temple
Sanzen-in Temple
Yase
Cable Car to Hieisan

Kyoto Int'l Conference Hall

Kamogawa River

Daitokuji Temple

Kita-oji-dori St.

Ryoanji Temple
Gold Pavilion
Ninnaji Temple

Daikakuji Temple

WESTERN KYOTO

Myoshinji Temple

Movie Village
Koryuji Temple

Tenryuji Temple

CENTRAL KYOTO

Kyoto Imperial Palace

Higashi-oji-dori St.

Silver Pavilion

EASTERN KYOTO

Heian Jingu Shrine

Nanzenji Temple

Nijojo Castle

Downtown

Chion-in Temple
Yasaka Jinja Shrine

Kiyomizudera Temple

Saihoji Temple

Katsuragawa River

Nishi-oji-dori St.

Nishi-Honganji Temple

Sanjusangendo Hall

Katsura Detached Villa

Toji Temple

Kyoto

Kujo-dori St.

Transportation

Connections with Other Cities

Kyoto can be reached from all major Japanese cities by Shinkansen. Refer to the "Transportation within Japan" Chapter for details on the Shinkansen. The Shinkansen platforms, as pictured on map 2, are located at the southernmost side of Kyoto Station, on the second floor. When you arrive at Kyoto by Shinkansen, you have to go through two exits. The first exit is before you reach one of the connecting passages — the bridge on the western side or the underground passage on the eastern side. Your Shinkansen surcharge ticket is collected here. You keep your basic fare ticket with you, and it is collected at the second, general exit (if you used a Japan Rail Pass and traveled in a non-reserved seat, or if you have one ticket for both the Shinkansen charge and the basic fare, just show it at the first exit). Most major places of interest and most major hotels are located to the north of Kyoto Station, so you should walk through the connecting passage to the general exits on the north side of the station. However, if you are staying at the New Miyako Hotel, or have big bags and do not want to carry them through the station, you can go out through the southern exit (Kujo-guchi 九条口), which is just next to the Shinkansen platforms, and catch a taxi right in front of the exit. Your fare will be a little higher, but sparing yourself a long trek with your luggage is probably worth it.

Platform No. 5 is for the JNR rapid service commuter train for Osaka, and No. 8 for the JNR train to Nara. The Kintetsu private railway operates trains to Nara from the southwestern corner of the station. If you are planning to take this train, you can walk through the JNR passage all the way to the Kintetsu platform just by showing your Kintetsu ticket.

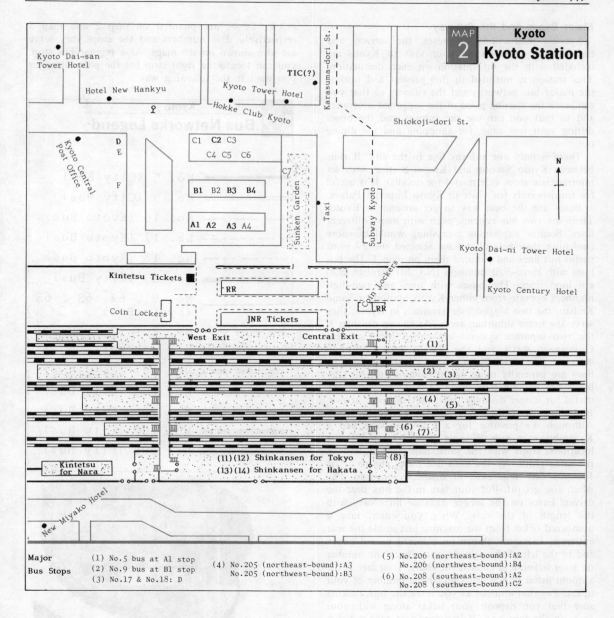

MAP 2

Kyoto

Kyoto Station

Kyoto Dai-san Tower Hotel

Hotel New Hankyu

Kyoto Tower Hotel

Hokke Club Kyoto

TIC(?)

Karasuma-dori St.

Shiokoji-dori St.

N

Kyoto Central Post Office

D
E
F

C1 **C2** C3
C4 C5 C6
C7

B1 B2 **B3 B4**

A1 A2 A3 A4

Sunken Garden

Taxi

Subway Kyoto

Coin Lockers

Kyoto Dai-ni Tower Hotel

Kyoto Century Hotel

Kintetsu Tickets

RR

Coin Lockers

JNR Tickets

RR

Coin Lockers

West Exit   Central Exit

(1)

(2) (3)

(4) (5)

(6)
(7)

Kintetsu for Nara

(11)(12) Shinkansen for Tokyo
(13)(14) Shinkansen for Hakata

(8)

New Miyako Hotel

**Major
Bus Stops**

(1) No.5 bus at A1 stop
(2) No.9 bus at B1 stop
(3) No.17 & No.18: D

(4) No.205 (northeast-bound):A3
No.205 (northwest-bound):B3

(5) No.206 (northeast-bound):A2
No.206 (northwest-bound):B4
(6) No.208 (southeast-bound):A2
No.208 (southwest-bound):C2

Major Buses and the Subway

Specific instructions on buses, the subway and trains to be used during your visit to Kyoto are included with the information on each destination. This section is intended to just present and outline the major bus networks and the subway so that you can reach the starting point of the suggested itineraries and so that you can use the subway and the buses during your free time, for shopping and for dining out.

There is only one subway line in the city. It runs between Kyoto Station and Kitaoji Station with six intermediate stops (see map 4 for details). It is useful for tourists only for visits to Kyoto Imperial Palace.

Buses are the best way to get around in Kyoto. There are two bus systems, each with many different lines. Because explaining everything would be more confusing than helpful, I have selected the 17 most useful bus lines and pictured them on map 3. The bus lines with three-digit numbers (No. 201 through 208) are loop lines. The buses with one- and two-digit numbers operate from either Kyoto Station or Sanjo Keihan, the two biggest bus terminals in Kyoto; they serve the outer suburban areas. As shown on map 3, the two separate systems are called the City Bus Company 市バス and the Kyoto Bus Company 京都バス. The City Bus Company is larger and its lines are generally more useful for tourists. All City buses are painted pale green. The Kyoto buses are useful for longer distance trips; they are pale brown. Both buses have the route number posted on front. Although it's possible for a City bus stop and a Kyoto bus stop with the same name to be in different locations, stops with the same name are usually in the same place. All the loop line buses charge a flat 140 yen fare regardless of distance you ride. Pay when you get off. Put your fare in the box near the driver. Fares on the longer distance lines vary with the length of the ride. When you enter, take a numbered ticket from the machine just inside the rear entrance. Fares are shown on a board posted above and to the left of the driver's seat. Check the number on your ticket, and consult the chart. Your fare is the amount listed on the chart under the number of your ticket. Pay that amount as you leave the bus, making sure that you deposit your ticket along with your coins in the fare box. If you forget to take a ticket when you get on or if you lose your ticket while you are on the bus, you will be charged the maximum fare, so pay attention, and when you get on a bus make sure you check to see whether there is a ticket machine.

A book of tickets, with eight 140-yen tickets and one 70-yen ticket, can be purchased from the driver for 1,000 yen (a 190 yen discount). If you get a book of tickets you won't have to worry about carrying change all the time. Ask the driver for "kaisu-ken 回数券" while he is waiting for a traffic light. The "kaisu-ken" tickets are valid for all buses in the Kyoto area.

If you change buses to continue your trip in a different direction, you cannot get a trasfer; you have to pay for each ride separately.

The two biggest bus terminals, Kyoto Station 京都駅前バスターミナル and Sanjo Keihan 三条京阪 バスターミナル, are pictured on map 2 and map 5 respectively. Bus numbers and the stops they serve are also shown on the maps. At a regular bus stop, you can locate the right stop for the particular bus you want in the following way:

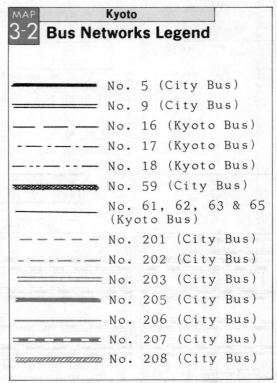

MAP 3-2	Kyoto Bus Networks Legend
▬▬▬▬	No. 5 (City Bus)
═══════	No. 9 (City Bus)
— — — —	No. 16 (Kyoto Bus)
—·—·—·	No. 17 (Kyoto Bus)
—··—··—	No. 18 (Kyoto Bus)
▰▰▰▰▰▰➤	No. 59 (City Bus)
▬▬▬▬▬	No. 61, 62, 63 & 65 (Kyoto Bus)
- - - - -	No. 201 (City Bus)
—·—·—·—	No. 202 (City Bus)
══════	No. 203 (City Bus)
▬▬▬▬▬	No. 205 (City Bus)
───────	No. 206 (City Bus)
▭▭▭▭▭	No. 207 (City Bus)
⫽⫽⫽⫽⫽⫽	No. 208 (City Bus)

Kyoto bus stop signs.

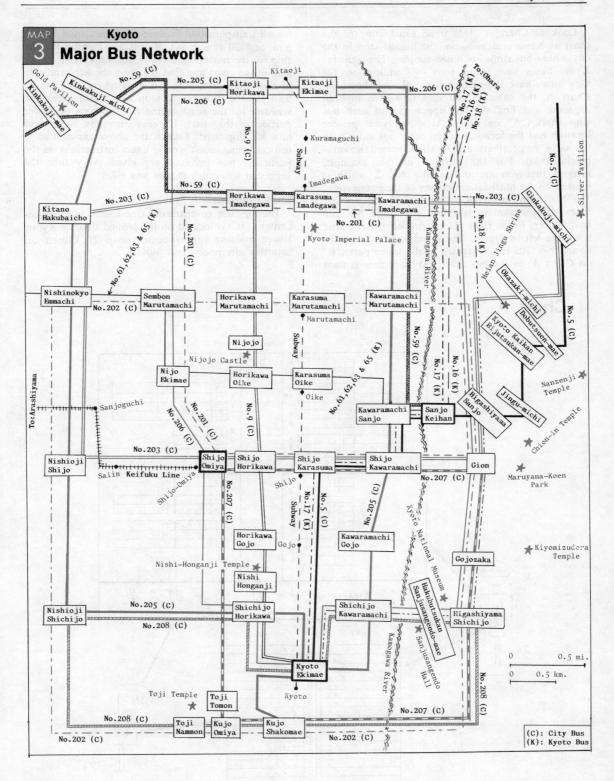

MAP 3

Kyoto

Major Bus Network

Look at Chart A. This is an exact copy of the chart at Kawaramachi-Sanjo, the busiest stop in the city. Other bus stops are much simpler. The signs for Kyoto buses have round tops -♀- while those for City buses have flag-shaped tops -ᖰ. As shown on Chart A, the name of the stop is written in both Japanese and English. The upper part of each bus stop chart ("A" on Chart A) shows your present location and the location of the other bus stops with the same name (there are 10 stops named Kawaramachi-Sanjo). For the purpose of this example, imagine that you are at bus stop No. 2, which is located on the northeastern corner of the intersection. The No. 2 stop is served by the No. 17 and No. 205 buses. If you want to take a south-bound No. 205 bus, you are in the right place (remember that traffic is on the left in Japan). The schedule for the south-bound No. 205 bus is written in the lower part ("B" on Chart A) of the bus chart. (Military time is used for all transportation facilities in Japan, thus 13 is 1 p.m. and 20 is 8 p.m.). If you are looking for the stop for the northbound No. 5 bus, look at the upper part of the chart and find No. 5 on the left-hand side of the street. Yes, stop No. 6 is where you should wait for the bus. Go to stop No. 6 and check the schedule for the north-bound No. 5 bus on the lower portion of the chart. It's easy once you understand how it's organized. Even if the above explanation is too confusing, don't worry. Exact instructions on the particular bus involved are given every time the suggested itineraries require bus rides.

Tourist Information

The Japanese government's free Tourist Information Center (TIC) is located on the ground floor of Kyoto Tower building (upper center, map 2). Closed on Saturday afternoons and Sundays.

Chart A

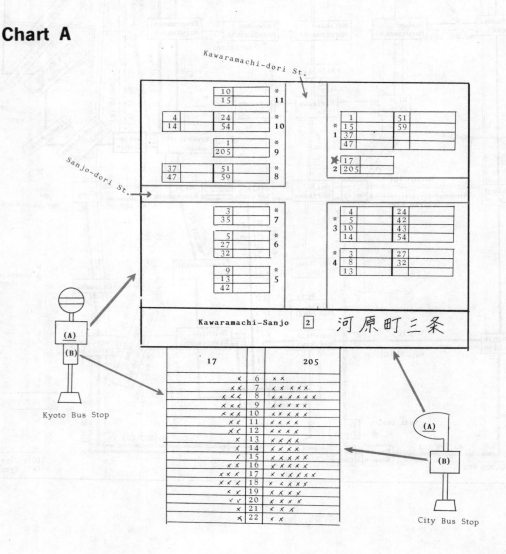

Shopping & Night Life

Kyoto's main shopping area and night life establishments lie on both sides of the Kamogawa River along Shijo-dori Street (indicated with many small red dots on map 4). **Gion** is on the eastern side and **Pontocho and Shinkyogoku** on the western side of the river.

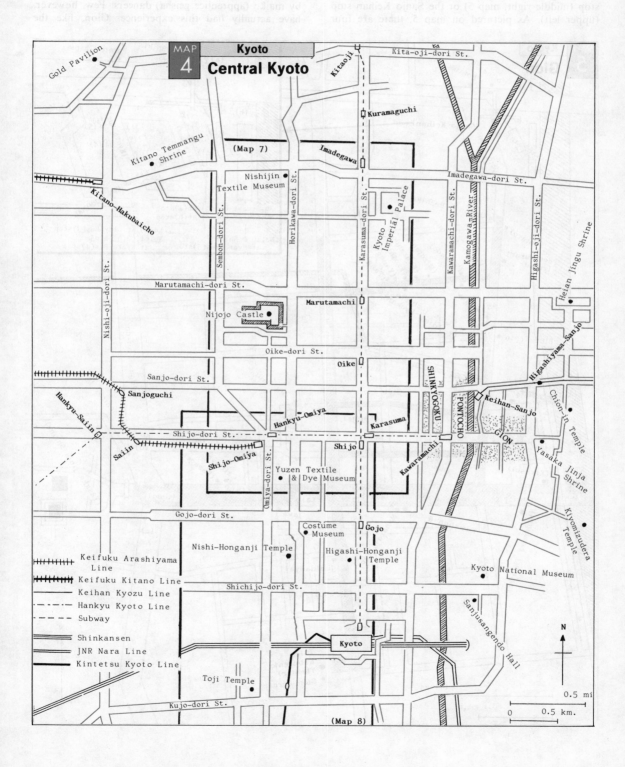

| MAP 4 | Kyoto Central Kyoto |

- Gold Pavilion
- Kita-oji-dori St.
- Kitaoji
- Kuramaguchi
- Kitano Temmangu Shrine
- (Map 7)
- Imadegawa
- Imadegawa-dori St.
- Nishijin Textile Museum
- Horikawa-dori St.
- Kitano-Hakubaicho
- Sembon-dori St.
- Karasuma-dori St.
- Kyoto Imperial Palace
- Kawaramachi-dori St.
- Kamogawa River
- Higashi-oji-dori St.
- Heian Jingu Shrine
- Nishi-oji-dori St.
- Marutamachi-dori St.
- Nijojo Castle
- Marutamachi
- Oike-dori St.
- Oike
- Sanjo-dori St.
- Hankyu-Saiin
- Sanjoguchi
- Higashiyama-Sanjo
- SHINKYOGOKU
- PONTOCHO
- Keihan-Sanjo
- Chion-in Temple
- Saiin
- Shijo-dori St.
- Hankyu-Omiya
- Karasuma
- GION
- Yasaka Jinja Shrine
- Shijo-Omiya
- Omiya-dori St.
- Shijo
- Kawaramachi
- Kiyomizudera Temple
- Yuzen Textile & Dye Museum
- Gojo-dori St.
- Costume Museum
- Gojo
- Nishi-Honganji Temple
- Higashi-Honganji Temple
- Kyoto National Museum
- Shichijo-dori St.
- Sanjusangendo Hall
- Kyoto
- Toji Temple
- Kujo-dori St.
- (Map 8)

Legend:
- Keifuku Arashiyama Line
- Keifuku Kitano Line
- Keihan Kyozu Line
- Hankyu Kyoto Line
- Subway
- Shinkansen
- JNR Nara Line
- Kintetsu Kyoto Line

N

0.5 mi

0 0.5 km.

Gion

Map 5 features details of the Gion 祇園 area. To reach Gion you can take a bus to either the Gion stop (middle right, map 5) or the Sanjo Keihan stop (upper left). As pictured on map 5, there are four bus stops named Gion. When you are ready to go back to your hotel, check to find the right stop for the bus you want by referring to the explanation given on the previous pages.

For Japanese the name "Gion" still conjures up images of fantastic, authentic, traditional establishments where guests (usually men) enjoy drinks and sophisticated Japanese dishes while being entertained by maiko (apprentice geisha) dancers. Few, however, have actually had this experience. Gion, like the

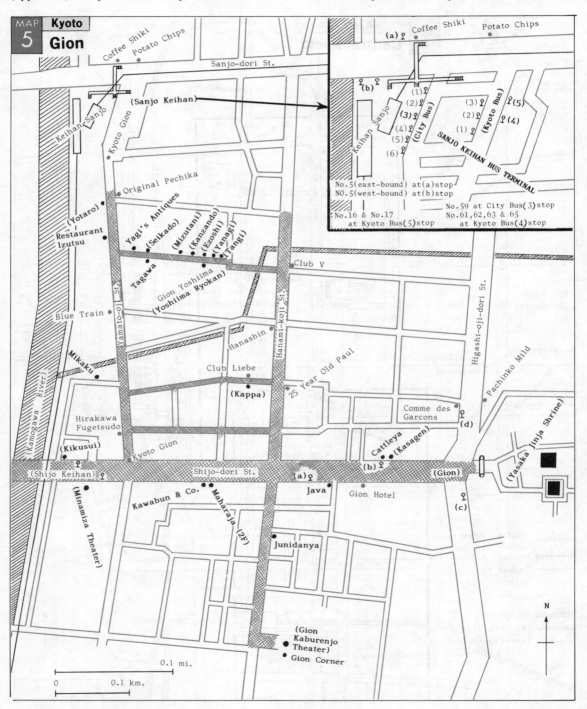

No.5(east-bound) at(a)stop
NO.5(west-bound) at(b)stop

No.16 & No.17 at Kyoto Bus(5)stop
No.59 at City Bus(3)stop
No.61,62,63 & 65 at Kyoto Bus(4)stop

traditional entertainment areas in most Japanese cities, has changed a great deal in modern times, and many traditional drinking places have been replaced by contemporary, convenient, but rather character-less cabarets and bars. However, some areas in Gion have stubbornly preserved the atmosphere of the ancient capital. There are also many good restaurants in Gion (a little more expensive than those on the other side of the Kamogawa River). Gion is a great place for a leisurely evening stroll and a good dinner.

Strolling in Gion

The southern part of Hanami-koji Street between Shijo-dori Street and Gion Corner is still lined with traditional buildings with wooden lattice windows and lanterns hung at the entrance. Walking here is one of the best ways to get an idea of what the old entertainment quarters were like. The narrow street between Yamato-oji Street and Hanami-koji Street (upper left, map 5, shaded in red), called **Shinmonzen Shopping Street,** is also full of wooden houses crowded together, most of which house art and antique shops. The names of eight of these shops are shown on map 5. If you are interested in taking a look at good antiques or interested in experiencing the authentic backstreets atmosphere of Kyoto, go there before 6 p.m. **Kasagen** (middle right on Shijo-dori Street next to Cattleya coffee shop) is another good place to look for souvenirs. Its specialty is traditional paper umbrellas (which are much more useful for decoration than for actual use).

Theaters

Minamiza Theater 南座 (lower left, map 5, near the Kamogawa River) is the oldest theater in Japan. During the feudal era, entertainers, whose social status was very low, performed in public on the dry bed of the Kamogawa River. When Kabuki was created, in the early part of the Edo era, it was first performed there as well. This new drama became so popular with the general public in Kyoto that Japan's first permanent theater was established where Minamiza Theater stands today. Three or four Kabuki programs are performed at Minamiza Theater each year (each run lasts 20-25 days).

Gion Kaburenjo Theater 祇園歌舞練場 (lower center, map 5) is a training center for the maiko of the Gion area. Once a year, in April, a public dance performance is given. 1984 marked the 112th occasion of this annual event.

Gion Corner ギオン・コーナー : This is a small theater (250 seats) attached to Gion Kaburenjo Theater. It was especially designed to introduce foreign tourists to a variety of traditional Japanese arts. Gion Corner is not the place to go if you expect high artistic standards, but it does allow you to sample a bit of everything, including Japanese dance, Bunraku puppet theater, Gagaku court dance and music, tea ceremony, etc. in just one hour. The theater is open from March 1 through Nov. 29. Two performances are held daily, at 8 p.m. and 9:10 p.m. Admission is 2,000 yen.

Restaurants and Coffee Shops
Coffee Shops

Java (middle center, map 5, on Shijo-dori Street) and **Cattleya** (middle right, map 5, on Shijo-dori Street) are good places to take a coffee break during your evening stroll.

American Fast Food — Sorry, I could not find any in the Gion area! A first!

Restaurants

Kikusui (middle left, map 5, near the Kamogawa River) is a Western restaurant in a four-story building. The restaurant on the first floor serves a "Service Steak Dinner" at 1,700 yen. The excellent grill on the second floor charges more than 5,000 yen for dinner.

Yotaro (upper left, map 5, Yamato-oji Street) is a tempura restaurant. The set menu tempura dinner is 3,000 yen. If you eat a la carte, be prepared to pay twice as much.

Junidanya (lower center, map 5) is located in the midst of the traditional quarter. A tempura dinner is 2,300 yen, and steak is 4,500 yen.

Kappa (middle center, map 5) has plastic food displays outside the entrance. This Japanese restaurant serves shabu-shabu at 3,000 yen. "Kappa Gozen," a Japanese-style set menu dinner is a treat for both the eyes and the taste buds. (3,000 yen).

Restaurant Izutsu (upper left, map 5) and **Mikaku** (middle left) are both steak restaurants. The former is rather Westernized while the latter is Japanese style. A steak at Izutsu costs around 5,000 yen and one at Mikaku about 6,000 yen. Sukiyaki and shabu-shabu are also served at Mikaku at 5,500 yen and 6,000 yen respectively.

Disco

Maharaja is located on the second floor of a modern building and is the most popular of Kyoto's few discos (middle center, map 5).

Shinkyogoku & Pontocho

Map 6 features the details of Shinkyogoku 新京極 and Pontocho 先斗町 . Major streets of interest are shaded in red.

Strolling in Shinkyogoku & Pontocho

The intersection of Kawaramachi-dori and Shijo-dori Streets (lower right, map 6) is Kyoto's version of the Ginza. Three large department stores, **Hankyu, Takashimaya,** and **Fujii-Daimaru,** and modern as well as traditional specialty shops line Shijo-dori Street. **Jusanya** (lower center, map 6, near the entrance to Shinkyogoku) deals in all sorts of exotic combs and hair ornaments. **Tachikichi** (lower center) is the main store of a famous Kiyomizu-yaki pottery chain. Even if you have no interest in purchasing anything, a visit to Tachikichi is a good opportunity to see the quality products of this famous, typically Japanese pottery. **Tanakaya** (lower left, map 6, on Shijo-dori Street) sells Kyoto pottery dolls. It is marvelous to see the variety of these clay dolls, especially those representing maiko.

Northeast of the main intersection are Pontocho-dori and Kiyamachi-dori Streets, two more of Kyoto's typical night life areas. **Pontocho-dori Street** has more old buildings, while **Kiyamachi-dori Street,** which runs along the narrow Takasegawa River, features modern buildings with colorful neon signs.

Shinkyogoku is the name given to the two shopping arcades that run north from Shijo-dori Street. The arcades display innumerable souvenir items in reasonable price ranges. Most of the stores close around 8 p.m. There are also many movie theaters in the area.

Nishikikoji-dori Street 錦小路通り runs west from Shinkyogoku. A torii gate, pictured on map 6, is a good landmark to help you find the entrance. This narrow covered street is Kyoto's food market. There are more than 150 stores, all of which handle food or food-related items; you will find a lot of products which you have never seen before.

Theater

Pontocho Kaburenjo Theater 先斗町歌舞練場 (middle right, map 6, near the Kamogawa River), like the Gion Kaburenjo, is a training center for the maiko of the area. This theater stages two programs of maiko dances a year, from May 1 — 24 and from October 15 to November 7, and as with the Gion dances, these have been a tradition for 112 years.

Restaurants and a Pub

American Fast Food: I found two of them. McDonald's is on the first floor of Fujii-Daimaru Department Store and Shakey's Pizza is at the northern end of the Shinkyogoku arcades (on the second floor).

Inexpensive Restaurants (2,500 yen or less for dinner)

Ashoka (lower center, map 6, at the entrance to Shinkyogoku) is an Indian restaurant. A variety of curries and shish kebab are served (1,000-1,500 yen).

Zuiun-en (lower right, map 6, off Kawaramachi-dori Street) is a Chinese restaurant with many 500-1,000 yen items on its menu.

Lipton Tea House (lower center, map 6) serves Western food, cakes and good tea at reasonable prices (about 2,000 yen for dinner).

Java (lower right, map 6, off Kawaramachi-dori Street) serves curry and Western foods (1,500-2,500 yen).

Izumo (middle center, map 6, in the Shinkyogoku arcades) is an excellent, very inexpensive sushi bar. Even though the restaurant does not have an English sign, you shouldn't have any trouble locating it once you find Daishodo book store. The restaurant has a number of plastic sushi displays outside its entrance. Guests seldom pay more than 2,000 yen for 10-15 pieces of sushi (depending on what kind of fish you order). It is very difficult to eat more than 4,000 yen's worth at this restaurant. If you want sushi a la carte, this is the place!

Reasonable Restaurants (5,000 yen or less)

Okinatei (middle right, map 6, to the east of Shinkyogoku) features sukiyaki and shabu-shabu (3,000 yen for each dinner). Yakitori is also served as

an appetizer to accompany Japanese sake or beer.

Manyoken (lower center, map 6, on Shijo-dori Street) is an authentic French restaurant. Dinners are 4,000-4,500 yen.

Lyon is another well known French restaurant located on the 9th floor of the modern **Asahi Kaikan Building** (upper right, map 6, on Kawaramachi-dori Street). Dinners start at 3,500 yen.

Suehiro (lower right, map 6, on Kawaramachi-dori Street) is a Japanese-style steak house. A steak dinner costs about 5,000 yen.

Cipolla (upper center, map 6, on Oike-dori Street) is a deluxe Italian restaurant. The three set menu dinners are priced at 4,000, 6,000 and 8,000 yen.

Pub

Yorunomado (middle right, map 6, off Kawaramachi-dori Street) is an inexpensive pub restaurant. Foods to accompany drinks cost 500-1,000 yen.

Central Kyoto

Glorious Kyoto

Sightseeing

As is the case with Japan's other large cities, the central part of Kyoto has developed into a thoroughly modern city, and to a great extent the atmosphere of the ancient capital has been lost. However, several important historical jewels, including Kyoto Imperial Palace, Nijojo Castle, Nishi-Honganji Temple and Toji Temple, have been preserved. There are also several interesting museums scattered throughout the area. To search out these treasures you should use map 4 and follow the one-day Central Kyoto itinerary detailed below. The walking tour starts at Kyoto Imperial Palace (upper center, map 4), and goes next to the Nishijin Textile Museum (upper center, to the west of the Palace).

If you have fewer than five days in Kyoto, the Gold Pavilion, as suggested earlier, should be visited today. You should go to the Gold Pavilion (upper left, map 4) after the Imperial Palace, and then come back to the Nishijin Textile Museum.

Nijojo Castle (middle center, map 4) is the next destination, followed by the Costume Museum and Nishi-Honganji Temple (lower center, map 4). You will probably run out of time at Nishi-Honganji Temple.

If you still have time, your last visit of the day should be to Toji Temple (bottom center, map 4). Note that Toji Temple closes at 4 p.m. If, after reading the following pages, you find that you are really interested in Toji Temple, your alternative is to skip Nishijin Textile Museum and the Costume Museum and visit Toji Temple instead.

Yuzen Textile & Dye Museum is located between Nijojo Castle and Nishi-Honganji Temple. Because this museum can be reached easily on foot from

Shijo-Omiya Station on the Keifuku Line, it will be introduced and explained in conjunction with Western Kyoto.

Avoid Sundays and Mondays for this itinerary because the Imperial Palace is closed on Sundays and Nijojo Castle is closed on Mondays.

Kyoto Imperial Palace 京都御所 (upper right, map 7)

Even though Japanese must apply in advance for permission to visit the Imperial Palace, foreign visitors are given special privileges, but you will only be admitted if you arrive at the office of the Imperial Household Agency in the Palace grounds by 9:40 a.m. (bring your passport). To get to the Palace you can take a subway to Imadegawa Station 今出川駅 or take a bus to Karasuma-Imadegawa stop 烏丸今出川. If you are staying at a hotel near Kyoto Station, the subway is your best bet. If your hotel is elsewhere, find the best bus connection (or bus plus subway connection) by referring to map 3. The 30-minute English-guided tour starts at 10 a.m. at Seishomon Gate. An afternoon English-guided tour starts at 2

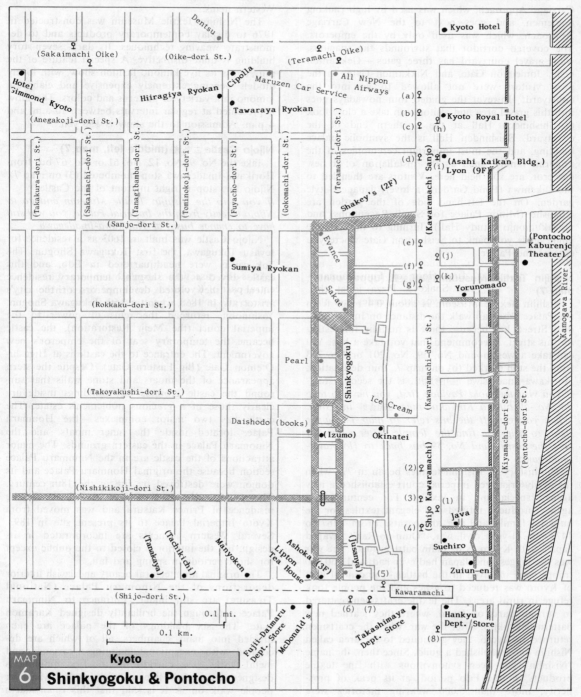

MAP
6

Kyoto
Shinkyogoku & Pontocho

p.m. To join the afternoon tour you have to arrive at the Household Agency's Office by 1:40 p.m. There is no afternoon tour on Saturday and no tours at all on Sunday. Admission is free.

Kyoto Imperial Palace was destroyed by fire many times, and the present buildings date from 1855. The original palace, built in 794 when the capital was moved to Kyoto, was located to the west of the present one, and was twice its size. The present location was selected in 1331 when the old palace was burned to the ground. The tour first visits the Carriage Approach, which was used by high ranking noblemen, and goes next to the New Carriage Approach, which was used only by the emperors. The covered corridor that surrounds the spacious, white-gravel courtyard has three gates — Gekkamon Gate, Jomeimon Gate, and Nikkamon Gate. In the past, visitors were not allowed to go into the courtyard. However the guided tour nowadays goes into this gravel area and visitors can take a close look at Shishinden Hall at the northern end of the courtyard. Shishinden Hall is the symbolic palace building, and the most important ceremonies of the imperial family, such as the installation of a new emperor, are still held here. Visitors are then led to the Oikeniwa (Pond Garden), a lovely Japanese-style garden. On the left-hand side of the garden are Kogosho (Minor Palace for Small Receptions) and Gogakumonjo (Study Hall). Turning to the left, the guide leads you back to Seishomon Gate where you entered the Palace.

Nishijin Textile Museum 西陣織会館 (upper center, map 7)

Nishijin Textile Museum is about 0.4 miles from the Palace. You can walk the distance on Imadegawa-dori Street, but because there is nothing interesting on this street, I recommend that you take a bus. You can take a west-bound No. 59, No. 201 or No. 203 from the stop marked (b) on map 7. Your destination, Horikawa-Imadegawa 堀川今出川, is the second stop. *If you visit the Gold Pavilion first, you have to take the No. 59 bus to Kinkakuji-mae 金閣寺前 bus stop. When you get off the bus refer to map 14 (upper right) to help you find the Temple. After your visit take the east-bound No. 59 bus back to Horikawa-Imadegawa.*

The history of Nishijin textiles began in 794 when the newly organized imperial court established a new agency specializing in textiles. For centuries the agency produced refined and elegant textiles for the imperial family and the aristocrats. From 1467 to 1477, an 11-year civil war, "Onin-no-Ran" ravaged Japan, with Kyoto as its main battleground. The war was the biggest one Japan had ever had, and 250,000 troops were involved in the battles. The central part of Kyoto was reduced to ashes and the people took refuge in rural areas. The textile craftsmen scattered to various parts of Japan, where they learned new patterns and skills. After the war, when the craftsmen returned to Kyoto, they gravitated to the area called Nishijin and established a guild. Since then, the name "Nishijin" has been synonymous with fine textile products. In the Edo period, at its peak of prosperity, more than 5,000 weaving factories were located in the Nishijin area. But the westernization that followed in the wake of the Meiji Restoration decreased the demand for traditional clothing, and the Nishijin textile industry suffered through a long stagnant period. It eventually revived with the "modern" popularity of Japanese kimono as a costume for formal occasions, and by producing "Western" items, such as ties, scarves and interior decorations. Radio City Music Hall's gigantic stage curtain is probably the most famous example of how Nishijin techniques can be beautifully adapted for Western items.

The Nishijin Textile Museum was constructed in 1976 to display contemporary products and to demonstrate weaving techniques. Its dark, seven-story building is quite distinctive. A special feature of the museum is its live kimono fashion show, with lovely models wearing extremely expensive and elaborate kimono in a variety of patterns and colors. The show is presented at regular intervals between 10 a.m. and 4 p.m. Admission to the show is 150 yen.

Nijojo Castle 二条城 (middle left, map 7)

Take the No. 9, No. 12, No. 61 or No. 67 bus from Horikawa-Imadegawa stop (numbered (3) on map 7). Nijojo bus stop is right in front of the Castle. *If you skip the Nishijin Textile Museum and go to Nijojo directly from the Imperial Palace, you will still have to change buses at Horikawa-Imadegawa.*

Nijojo Castle was built in 1603 as a residence for Ieyasu Tokugawa, the first Tokugawa Shogun. The Tokugawas were headquartered in Edo, and this castle served as the shoguns' temporary residence whenever they visited the emperors or the city's aristocrats. In 1868, when the 15th Tokugawa Shogun, Yoshinobu, returned the reins of power to the imperial court (the Meiji Restoration), the castle became the temporary seat of the emperor's new government. The entrance to the castle is at Higashi-Otemon Gate (Big Eastern Gate). Despite the stern appearance of the moats and stone walls that surround the castle grounds, the buildings inside are clearly those of a gracious noblemen's estate. The castle has two major complexes — the Honmaru Palace located inside the inner moats, and the Ninomaru Palace in the eastern grounds. The major attractions of the castle are in the Ninomaru Palace section because the original Honmaru Palace and its donjon were destroyed by fire in the 18th century. The present Honmaru Palace was built as the residence of Prince Katsura and was moved from Kyoto Imperial Palace to its present site in 1893. Several Western elements are incorporated in its design, but the interior is closed to the public except for short periods in spring and fall.

The original architectural beauty and lavish interior decorations of the Ninomaru Palace (National Treasure) are still intact. Entrance to Ninomaru Palace is through the brilliantly designed Karamon Gate. The six buildings of the palace are each divided into many chambers, all of which are decorated with exceptional paintings, carvings and metal works. The corridor of the first building is designed to squeak like a "nightingale" whenever people walk on it. It is said that this is an alarm device designed to prevent assassins from penetrating to the inner halls. Especially noteworthy are the paintings on the sliding screens in Ohiroma Hall. The hall was used for the meetings of shoguns and feudal lords. It's easy to recognize this hall because a number of dolls in formal costumes are arranged here to represent the scene when the 15th Tokugawa Shogun expressed his determination to surrender the reins of government to the Emperor. Ninomaru Garden, designed by Enshu, is, in its own right, as famous as the castle. Nijojo is open from 8:45 a.m. to 4 p.m. (Closed on Mondays. When Monday is a holiday, it's open on Monday and closed on Tuesday. Admission, covering both Ninomaru Palace and the Garden, is 450 yen.).

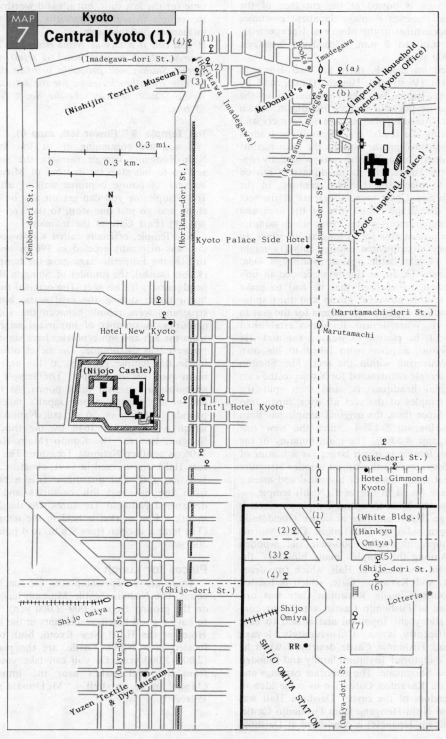

MAP 7 Kyoto

Central Kyoto (1)

Nishi-Honganji Temple and Costume Museum (middle center, map 8)

Take a south-bound No. 8 bus from the stop on the eastern side of Horikawa-dori Street, in front of Nijojo Castle. This is the only bus that goes directly to Nishi-Honganji 西本願寺 stop.

The Costume Museum 風俗博物館 is a small new establishment on the fifth floor of an office building. An English sign is posted at the entrance of the building. The museum displays Japanese costumes from pre-historic times to the Meiji era. Unexpectedly beautiful (9 a.m. to 5 p.m. Closed on Sundays. Admission 300 yen).

As pictured on map 8, there are two Honganji Temples, Nishi (West) and Higashi (East), side by side. Honganji Temple was the headquarters of the Jodo-Shinshu or Ikkoshu sect of Buddhism, which succeeded in spreading the religion to farmers and the poor during the feudal era. Because the leaders of this sect helped organize riots by the poor against the feudal lords, Jodo-Shinshu was constantly oppressed by the rulers and its headquarters moved from place to place. In the 15th century, in the central Japan Sea Coast area, adherents of the sect managed to defeat the feudal lord of the area and establish an autonomous government, which administered the Kanazawa area for as long as 100 years. In Osaka, the sect accumulated enough military might to wage an 11-year battle against Nobunaga Oda. When Hideyoshi Toyotomi finally succeeded in unifying the nation, he realized that he had to make concessions to this powerful group and thus sponsored construction of the headquarters for the sect in Kyoto in 1591. When Ieyasu Tokugawa established his government, he plotted to weaken the sect. He supported Kyojo, a priest who failed in his own political maneuvering within the sect. The Shogun had another temple constructed for Kyojo to the east of the original headquarters, and then split the subordinate temples of the sect all over Japan into two groups. Since then, the original temple has been called Nishi-Honganji 西本願寺 , and the new one Higashi-Honganji 東本願寺. The main building of the east (Higashi) temple is much larger (as a matter of fact this 1895 structure is the largest wooden structure in Kyoto), but many objects of historical and artistic significance are found in the west (Nishi) temple.

Entrance to the Nishi-Honganji Temple precincts is free of charge. Upon entering at either Goeidomon Gate (northern side) or Hondomon Gate, visitors encounter huge, impressive 300-year old wooden structures. Among the temple's many buildings, the most important are Daishoin Hall, which runs from east to west, and Karamon Gate, which is located along the southern walls. Karamon Gate was originally located at Fushimijo Castle, which was constructed by Hideyoshi Toyotomi and is said to have been magnificently lavish. Unfortunately, Ieyasu Tokugawa had Fushimijo Castle destroyed when he defeated the dictatorial Toyotomi family and founded the Tokugawa Shogunate. The elaborate carvings and decorations on Karamon Gate give us some idea of the lost splendors of the castle. Daishoin Hall was also moved to Nishi-Honganji from Fushimijo Castle. A guided tour (in Japanese) is conducted at Daishoin

Hall four times a day, at 10 a.m., 11 a.m., 1:30 p.m. and 2:30 p.m. (Morning tours only on Saturday). Permission to enter the Hall must be obtained at the temple office (indicated with a red star on map 8). Each of the many sections of Daishoin Hall has elegant paintings, carvings and other 16th century decorations. Two Noh stages and a small garden are attached to the Hall. You probably won't arrive in time for the last tour, but it's still worthwhile visiting the temple to see the grandeur of one of the most influential Buddhist sects.

If you call it a day at Nishi-Honganji Temple, find your way back to your hotel by referring to map 3. Kyoto Station will probably provide the best connection for other buses or for the subway. To get to Kyoto Station you can take the No. 9, No. 28 or No. 75 bus.

Toji Temple 東寺 (lower left, map 8)

If you are continuing on to Toji Temple, leave Nishi-Honganji Temple through the southern gate and go to bus stop (a) in front of Mitsubishi Bank. You can of course continue walking all the way to Toji Temple, or you can get on any bus that comes along and go just one stop, to the Toji Tomon stop 東寺東門 (East Gate of the temple).

Toji Temple, officially called Kyo-o-gokokuji Temple, was originally erected in 796 by imperial edict. In 818, the Emperor Saga gave the temple to Kukai (Kobo Daishi), the founder of Shingon Buddhism, as headquarters for his sect. The original buildings were burnt down during the civil wars, but the major structures were rebuilt between the 15th and 17th centuries. A number of important religious objects from the 8th and 9th centuries have survived and are preserved in the temple. The ticket office is located inside the temple grounds, at the entrance to the main part of the temple. The temple also has a spacious garden with three ponds. At the southern end of the garden stands Japan's tallest five-story pagoda (184 feet or 56 m. tall, National Treasure), which was built in 1644 by the third Tokugawa Shogun, Iemitsu. The Kondo (Main Hall), built in 1606, is another National Treasure. The Kodo (Lecture Hall), constructed in 1491, contains 21 statues of Buddha, gods and guardians; fifteen of these date from the 8th and 9th centuries and have been designated National Treasures. On the 21st of each month a flea market is held in the temple precincts (The temple is open from 9 a.m. to 4 p.m. Admission 300 yen).

Places for Lunch

There are no special places for lunch along this route. The Nishijin Textile Museum has a restaurant on the ground floor (1,000-2,000 yen). If you want to have a good lunch, restaurants in the International Hotel or the Hotel New Kyoto, both of which are located near Nijojo Castle, are the places to visit (2,000-3,000 yen). Or you can take your lunch out from the McDonald's near the Imperial Palace (Japan in a nutshell — "McDonald's near the Palace"!!)

Other places of interest if you are in Kyoto for an extended period

Locomotive Museum 梅小路蒸気汽関車館 (middle left, map 8) not only displays steam locomotives but also operates them three times a day, at 11 a.m., 1 p.m. and 3:30 p.m. (Open 9:30 a.m. to 4:30 p.m. Closed on Mondays. If Monday is a holiday, closed on Tuesday. Admission 200 yen).

Shimabara 島原 (middle left, map 8) is the district where the first authorized houses of prostitution were located during the Edo era. Since the outlawing of prostitution, the area has been desolate, and has completely lost the bustling atmosphere of the licensed pleasure quarters. **Daimon Gate,** the entrance to the area, and a few old buildings still stand quietly as reminders of bygone days.

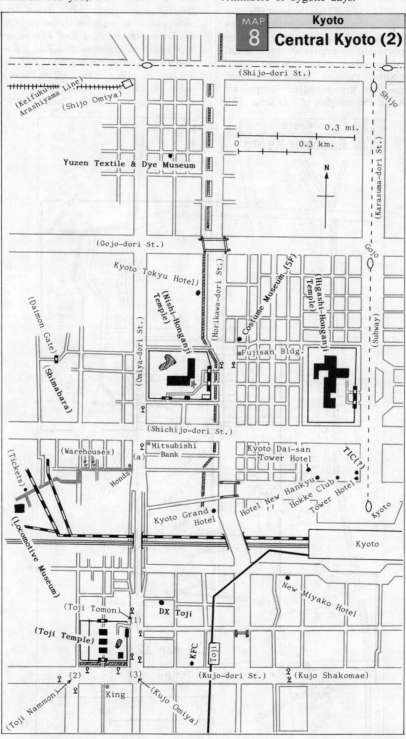

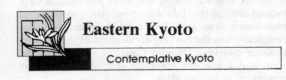

Eastern Kyoto

Contemplative Kyoto

Eastern Kyoto nestles against Higashiyama (Eastern Mountain). The area contains innumerable temples and shrines in quiet settings, and provides visitors with an ideal opportunity to appreciate the natural beauty and cultural splendors of this ancient capital city. The famous Silver Pavilion, Nanzenji Temple, Heian Jingu Shrine and Kiyomizudera Temple are just a few examples of the delights of this area. This

is the area I give top priority in Kyoto. Eastern Kyoto is introduced in two one-day itineraries.

If your time is limited and you want to see just the highlights of the area, follow the following modified itinerary (refer to map 9):

Start your tour at Silver Pavilion. After the visit, take a south-bound No. 5 bus to Kyoto Kaikan Bijutsukan-mae stop. Visit Heian Jingu Shrine, and then make a walking tour to Chion-in Temple, Maruyama-Koen Park and Kiyomizudera Temple. If you still have time take a bus from the Gojozaka stop to Higashiyama Shichijo, and visit Sanjusangen-do Hall (details of this walking tour are pictured on maps 10-12).

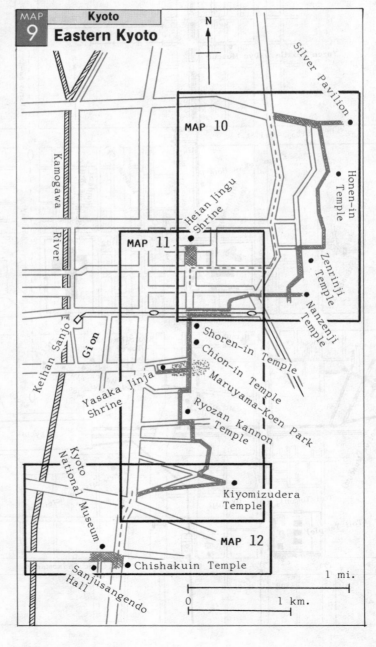

MAP 9   Kyoto   Eastern Kyoto

N

MAP 10

Silver Pavilion

Honen-in Temple

Kamogawa River

Heian Jingu Shrine

MAP 11

Zenrinji Temple

Nanzenji Temple

Keihan Sanjo

Gion

Shoren-in Temple

Chion-in Temple

Yasaka Jinja Shrine

Maruyama-Koen Park

Ryozan Kannon Temple

Kyoto National Museum

Kiyomizudera Temple

MAP 12

Chishakuin Temple

Sanjusangendo Hall

1 mi.

0   1 km.

Day 1
Northern Part of Eastern Kyoto

The first day itinerary starts at Heian Jingu Shrine. After this visit, take a bus to Silver Pavilion, and then walk along the narrow path to Maruyama-Koen Park, visiting Zenrinji, Nanzenji and Chion-in Temples on your way. The day ends at Maruyama-Koen Park.

Heian Jingu Shrine 平安神宮 (middle left, map 10)

Heian Jingu Shrine can be reached by either the No. 5 bus (Kyoto Kaikan Bijutsukan-mae 京都会館美術館前), or the No. 203 bus (Okazaki-michi stop 岡崎道). Find the best connection by referring to map 3. If you are staying at a hotel near Kyoto Station, simply take the No. 5 bus. Otherwise, Sanjo Keihan bus terminal should provide a good connection to the No. 5 bus.

Heian Jingu Shrine was built in 1895 to commemorate the 1,100th anniversary of the city of Kyoto, and dedicated to two famous emperors — Kammu, the founder of Kyoto, and Komei, the last emperor to live in the city. The Shrine consists of the East and West Honden (Main Halls), the Daigokuden (Great Hall of State), two pagodas, the Otemmon Gate (Main Gate), a spacious white-gravel front yard, and a garden. A huge torii gate stands to the south of the Shrine at the entrance to the broad main approach. The brightly colored vermilion-red buildings are reduced scale replicas of the first Imperial Palace. Though its historical value is low, the Shrine is a good place to understand what the 8th century capital was like and an ideal starting point for your exploration of this ancient imperial city. The garden at the rear of the Shrine is famous for its weeping cherries, maples, azaleas, irises and waterlilies. Each season has its own elegant beauty. The garden is a living relic of the brilliant days of the imperial and aristocratic families at the dawn of Japanese history. (The precincts are open throughout the day. The garden is open from 8:30 a.m. to 5 p.m. Until 4:30 p.m. in winter. Admission to the garden is 300 yen).

Silver Pavilion 銀閣寺 (upper right, map 10)

Take the No. 5 bus from either the stop marked (1) on the map, Kyoto Kaikan Bijutsukan-mae, or from the stop marked (3) on the map, Dobutsuen-mae, to Ginkakuji-michi stop 銀閣寺道 (the bus route is indicated by a broken red line).

Silver Pavilion, popularly called Ginkakuji Temple in Japanese and formally known as Jishoji Temple, was built in 1482 by Shogun Yoshimasa Ashikaga. As a result of the 11-year "Onin-no-Ran" civil war between the most powerful feudal lords (1467—1477), the Ashikaga Shogunate lost power, and Yoshimasa retired from the world of politics to spend his days in this exquisite country retreat indulging himself in wine, women and cultural activities. He intended that his villa be a counterpart to the famous Gold Pavilion, that his grandfather, Yoshimitsu, had built, and planned to have the entire structure

covered with silver foil. But he died before this was accomplished, and his grand residence was converted into a temple. Even without the glimmer of silver foil it is a magnificent structure. The Togudo Hall houses a statue of Yoshimasa dressed as a priest. A tiny tea room tucked into the northeastern corner of the Togudo is said to be the oldest tea ceremony room in Japan. The Butsuden Hall (Hall of Buddha) features an image of Buddha. The garden, with a pond, pine trees and carefully arranged "mountains" of sand, supposedly the work of Soami, is one of Kyoto's most attractive. The trees along the neatly maintained curved entrance path form a beautiful green screen (8:30 a.m. to 5 p.m. In winter 9 a.m. to 4:30 p.m. Admission 200 yen).

Ginkakuji Temple·the Silver Pavilion.

Path of Philosophy 哲学の道

The 0.75-mile (1.2 km.) path along the small creek from Ginkakuji Temple to Nyakuoji Jinja Shrine is called the Path of Philosophy. The path is lined with cherry, willow and maple trees and is completely traffic free. All through Japanese history famous priests and philosophers wandered along the quiet path, lost in contemplation. Today, the path still lives up to its name; it is a favorite haunt of teachers, students, an area especially conducive to quiet contemplation.

Honen-in Temple 法然院 (middle right, map 10)

Honen-in Temple is a short walk from the Path of Philosophy to the east. Coffee & Tea Lounge Pino is a good landmark for finding the street that leads to the temple. This small thatched temple was built in 1680 in commemoration of the priest Honen. Honen was one of the greatest priests in the history of Japanese Buddhism. He liberated the new religion from the narrow circle of the ruling class and propagated it to the general public, emphasizing the equality of all human beings in the eyes of Buddha. Jodo-Shinshu (remember Nishi-Honganji Temple?), the most influential people's religion of the feudal era, was established by Honen's disciple Shinran in the 13th century. Enter the temple grounds at the southern gate near the telephone box pictured on map 10, because the highlight of the temple is the approach to the main buildings. The narrow path, which is densely covered with old trees, is incredibly quiet. The sand piles on both sides of the path are arranged to reflect and complement the beauties of the seasons. Even though the interior of the temple is open only for limited periods in the spring and autumn, the atmosphere of the precincts and the garden make a visit to Honen-in well worth your while (free of charge).

Zenrinji Temple 禅林寺 (lower right, map 10)

Nyakuoji Jinja Shrine's 若王子神社 claim to fame is that the oldest willow tree in Kyoto is located in its precincts. If you are interested, the shrine is only a one minute walk from the path. I intentionally included many of the coffee shops along the path on the map not only as landmarks but also so that you'll be able to find a place to take a break if you get tired.

Zenrinji Temple was erected in 856 by the priest Shinsho. The temple is popularly known as Eikando 永観堂 to honor the memory of the 11th century priest Eikan, who tended to the physical as well as the spiritual needs of the people by involving himself in social activities such as founding a hospital in the temple precincts. The temple is famous for its unique image of Buddha looking back over his shoulder. One morning when Eikan was walking around reciting his prayers, as was his daily custom, Buddha came down from the altar and started praying with him. Thinking that he was dreaming, Eikan stopped praying and stood still. Buddha turned around to look at him and said, "Eikan, why did you stop?" In order to share that image of Buddha with others, Eikan had this statue made.

Though the original buildings were destroyed in the civil wars of the 15th century, many were reconstructed. The halls are connected by covered corridors. Even if all the sliding paper doors are closed, you can open them and enter the inside of the hall, to worship or just to look at the paintings on the walls. Just be sure to close the doors behind you. A Japanese sign asks visitors to "keep the doors closed so pigeons can't get in." The image of Buddha looking over his shoulder is in Amidado Hall at the southern end of the complex. You can only reach Amidado by climbing one of the staircases at the southern end of the complex. At the top of the opposite staircase is a pagoda where visitors can command a grand view of the city of Kyoto. The temple is also famous for its maple trees. The brilliance of their autumnal tints has always been a popular theme with Japanese poets (9 a.m. to 4 p.m. Admission 350 yen).

Nomura Museum 野村美術館 (lower right, map 10) (optional)

This museum was established recently to display the collection of Mr. Tokushichi Nomura, founder of one of Japan's biggest conglomerates (Nomura Securities, Daiwa Bank, etc.). The collection includes hanging scrolls, paintings, pottery and tea ceremony utensils (10 a.m. to 4:30 p.m. Closed on Mondays. Admission 500 yen).

Nanzenji Temple 南禅寺 (lower right, map 10)

Past the Nomura Museum, the road leads to the precincts of Nanzenji Temple, Kyoto's most important Zen temple. It was originally constructed as a villa for Emperor Kameyama in 1264. The original buildings were burnt down in the civil wars, and those standing today were constructed in the late 16th century. The temple's Chokushimon Gate, Sammon Gate, Hatto Hall and Hojo Hall are laid out in a straight line from west to east. These magnificent structures are surrounded by small minor temples. Entrance to the precincts is free of charge. Sammon Gate, built in 1628, is famous for the splendid view of Kyoto from its top floor (which is reached by a steep, narrow stairway). Unless you really enjoy climbing, it's better to spend your time and money on other facilities in the precincts (admission to Sammon Gate is 150 yen. Open from 9 a.m. to 5 p.m.). Hojo Hall (National Treasure) was moved here from Kyoto Imperial Palace in the early 17th century. Its chambers are divided by sliding doors covered with brilliant paintings of the Kano school. The garden attached to the hall is in typical Zen style, with stones, elaborately-shaped trees and sand. The stones and trees clustered in one area of the spacious garden are said to represent tigers crossing a stream (300 yen).

There are three more minor temples here with beautiful gardens, each worth visiting. Because your time will be limited you should select only one of them. **Nanzen-in Temple** 南禅院 is located at the southern end of the precincts. A small creek (actually run off from Lake Biwako) flows on an elevated brick waterway; this was a very unusual structure in the feudal era. The path to Nanzen-in Temple goes under this Roman-like structure. The garden is designed around a pond surrounded by wild trees from Higashiyama Mountain. Reflecting its beginnings as an imperial villa, the garden features many elegant maple trees and beautiful moss (150 yen). **Tenjuan Temple** 天寿庵 displays a picture of its garden at the entrance. Because my time was limited too I skipped this garden, but the picture made the garden look very attractive (300 yen). **Konchiin Temple** 金地院 was originally built as an independent temple in the northern part of Kyoto in the late 14th century. It was later moved here and became a satellite of the Nanzenji complex. The bonsai trees, rocks and sand of the garden represent deep mountains and an ocean with two islands. This typically Japanese use of limited space is considered one of the best works of Enshu (300 yen).

Places for Lunch

If you begin your tour at Heian Jingu Shrine at about 8 or 8:30 in the morning, it will be a little after noon by the time you arrive at Nanzenji Temple. If you want to have lunch before you visit Nanzenji Temple, **Okutan,** a famous restaurant that specializes in yodofu (bean curd dipped in boiling water), is your best choice. The Nanzenji area is famous for imaginative yodofu cuisine and Okutan is the oldest restaurant of its kind. Lunch is 2,500 yen. If you wait until after your visit to Nanzenji Temple, **Junsei,** located to the west of the temple, is another famous yudofu restaurant with similar prices. If you're willing to walk for yet another ten minutes, you can have a really authentic Japanese lunch at **Hyotei** (lower left, map 10, at the end of the approach of Nanzenji Temple). Though it has no English sign, this restaurant is housed in an easily recognizable traditional building and displays a distinctive sign shaped like a gourd. A full course dinner here costs more than 20,000 yen, but a special set menu lunch called "Shokado Bento" is only about 3,500 yen. Specify

"Shokado Bento" when you order. There are two more famous restaurants in the neighborhood, **Minokichi**, and another **Junsei**. Both have English signs and display color pictures of the dishes they serve. Japanese lunches range in price from 1,600 to 3,000 yen. If you are tired of walking by the time you get to Nanzenji Temple, have lunch in the area and take a taxi to Shoren-in Temple. There is no convenient bus service.

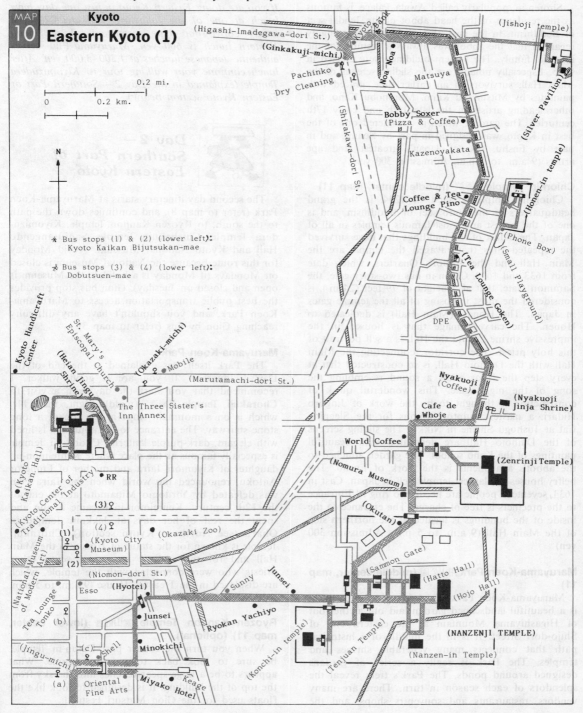

MAP 10
Kyoto
Eastern Kyoto (1)

Shoren-in Temple 青蓮院 (middle center, map 11)

If you are covering Eastern Kyoto in one day, you should visit Silver Pavilion first and then take the No. 5 bus to Heian Jingu Shrine. After visiting Heian Jingu you should walk south along the main approach until you reach Shoren-in Temple. Because of time limitations you should keep going straight, to Chion-in Temple (explained next), skipping Shoren-in. You'll stop for lunch at Maruyama-Koen Park (explained below) after your visit to Chion-in Temple.

Shoren-in, popularly called Awata Palace, is famous as the residence of the head abbot of the Tendai sect of Buddhism. In the past, this position was so highly regarded that the abbot was always a member of the imperial family. The present buildings were erected in 1895. Especially notable are the sliding screens of the Main Hall, survivors of an earlier time, graced with paintings by Mitsunobu Kano, Motonobu Kano, and other leading artists of the late 16th and early 17th centuries. The garden, which is considered one of the best in Kyoto, was designed in part by Soami, and in part by Enshu, two of Japan's greatest landscape artists (9 a.m. to 5 p.m. Admission 300 yen).

Chion-in Temple 知恩院 (middle center, map 11)

Chion-in Temple, erected in 1234, is the grand headquarters of the Jodo sect of Buddhism, and is one of the largest and most famous temples in all of Japan. The oldest of the buildings that have survived the repeated fires that ravaged the temple are the Main Hall and the Abbot's Quarters, which date from 1633 and 1639. Chion-in has two-story gate, the Sammon Gate, that at a height of 79 feet (24 m.), is considered the most imposing of all the temple gates in Japan. The Hondo (Main Hall) is dedicated to Honen. The carved image that is housed in the impressive shrine behind the Hall is a self portrait of this holy priest. The corridor, connecting the Main Hall with the Daihojo Hall, is so constructed that at every step the floor emits a sound resembling the song of the nightingale. This wonderful quirk of construction is thought to be the work of Jingoro Hidari, a master sculptor famous for the Sleeping Cat at Toshogu Shrine in Nikko. The sliding screens of the Daihojo Hall are decorated with beautiful paintings of the Kano school. The garden attached to the abbot's apartments is the work of Enshu. The belfry houses the largest temple bell in Japan. Cast in 1633, seventeen people are needed to ring it! Entrance to the precincts is free of charge. The entrance to the inside of the buildings is located at the northern side of the Main Hall (9 a.m. to 5 p.m. Admission 300 yen)

Maruyama-Koen Park 円山公園 (middle center, map 11)

Maruyama-Koen Park, Kyoto's main public park, is a beautiful landscaped garden laid out at the foot of Higashiyama Mountain at the eastern end of Shijo-dori Street. It is in the middle of a historical path that connects many venerable shrines and temples. The Park is really a series of gardens designed around ponds. The Park's trees reveal the splendors of each season in turn. There are many vendors, restaurants and souvenirs shops, and the

Park always has a gay festival atmosphere. This is the last stop on the first-day of the walking tour of Eastern Kyoto. Take your time and relax. Here you are very close to Gion, and can easily spend your evening there. **Yasaka Jinja Shrine** is on the way to Gion. This shrine was erected when an epidemic swept the city in 876, to honor the god able to cure diseases. The vermilion red shrine is famous as the host of Gion Matsuri Festival, Kyoto's biggest festival (held in July every year).

*If you are doing Eastern Kyoto in just one day, have lunch at one of the following: **Kaikatei** 開花亭, a handy coffee-shop type restaurant. A set menu Western lunch is 600 yen. **Maruyama** 円山 serves authentic Japanese lunches at 1,300 - 3,000 yen. After lunch continue your walking tour to Kiyomizudera Temple (explained in the Day 2 — Southern Part of Eastern Kyoto section below).*

Day 2 — Southern Part of Eastern Kyoto

The second day itinerary starts at Maruyama-Koen Park (refer to map 8), and continues down the path to the south, to Ryozen Kannon Temple, Kiyomizudera Temple, Chishakuin Temple, Sanjusangendo Hall and Kyoto National Museum. Avoid Monday for this route because the National Museum is closed on Mondays (if Monday is a holiday, the Museum is open and closed on Tuesday). Gion bus stop provides the best public transportation access to Maruyama-Koen Park, and you shouldn't have any difficulty reaching Gion by bus (refer to map 3).

Maruyama-Koen Park

The Park itself was explained at the end of the Day 1 itinerary. If you are a good walker, I recommend that you start the day with a visit to **Chorakuji Temple** 長楽寺 (middle right, map 11), which is on a mountain slope at the top of a long stone stairway. The entrance to the approach is lined with elegant, dark-purple lanterns. Chorakuji Temple is especially famous as the place where Kenreimon-in, daughter of Kiyomori Taira and mother of Emperor Antoku, renounced the world when the Taira clan was defeated by Yoritomo Minamoto at the end of the 12th century. Kenreimon-in became a nun and spent the rest of her days at Jakkoin Temple in Ohara (see Northern Kyoto section). Chorakuji Temple is known for the statue of Honen in the Main Hall and for the realistic statues of seven other priests who were connected with the temple, which are displayed in the Treasure House (9 a.m. to 5 p.m. Admission 300 yen).

Ryozen Kannon Temple 霊山観音 (lower center, map 11) (optional)

When you turn the corner past Daiun-in Temple, be sure to look back toward the temple. What appears to be a huge spear reaches into the sky from the top of the building. It is designed to look like the floats used for the Gion Matsuri Festival.

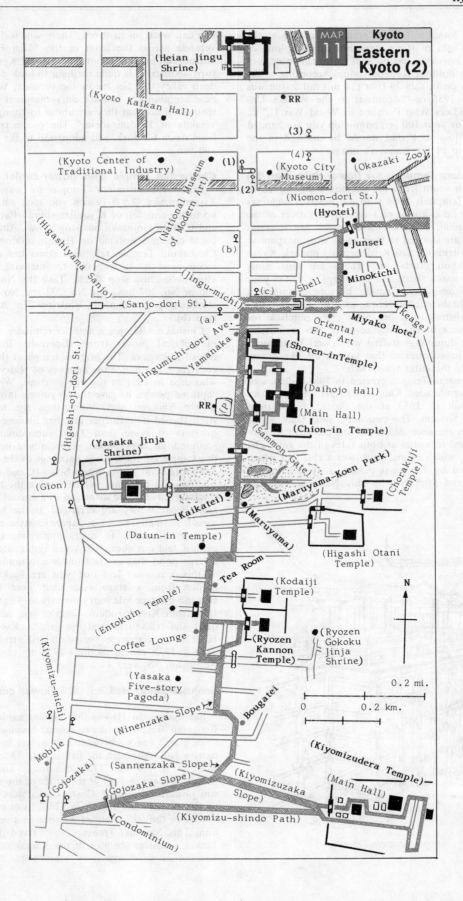

MAP 11 Kyoto Eastern Kyoto (2)

(Heian Jingu Shrine)

(Kyoto Kaikan Hall)

RR

(3)

(Kyoto Center of Traditional Industry)

(1)

(National Museum of Modern Art)

(4)

(Kyoto City Museum)

(Okazaki Zoo)

(2)

(Niomon-dori St.)

(Hyotei)

(b)

Junsei

(Higashiyama Sanjo)

Minokichi

(Jingu-michi)

(c)

Shell

(Sanjo-dori St.)

(a)

Oriental Fine Art

Miyako Hotel

(Keage)

(Jingumichi-dori Ave.)

Yamanaka

(Shoren-in Temple)

(Daihojo Hall)

RR

P

(Main Hall)

(Chion-in Temple)

(Higashi-oji-dori St.)

(Sammon Gate)

(Yasaka Jinja Shrine)

(Chorakuji Temple)

(Gion)

(Maruyama-Koen Park)

(Kaikatei)

(Maruyama)

(Daiun-in Temple)

(Higashi Otani Temple)

Tea Room

N

(Kodaiji Temple)

(Entokuin Temple)

Coffee Lounge

(Ryozen Kannon Temple)

(Ryozen Gokoku Jinja Shrine)

(Kiyomizu-michi)

(Yasaka Five-story Pagoda)

0.2 mi.

0   0.2 km.

(Ninenzaka Slope)

Bougatei

(Kiyomizudera Temple)

Mobile

(Sannenzaka Slope)

(Gojozaka)

(Gojozaka Slope)

(Kiyomizuzaka Slope)

(Main Hall)

(Condominium)

(Kiyomizu-shindo Path)

Ryozen Kannon Temple, which is located at the top of a flight of stone steps not quite as long as those of Chorakuji, has no real historical value, but features an outdoor Kannon statue. According to the inscription on it, this 79 foot (24 m.) tall statue was erected in 1955 in "Memorial to the World's Unknown Soldiers Who Perished in World War II." In exchange for your 100 yen admission you are handed a burning joss stick that should be inserted in the box in front of the Kannon's image.

Kiyomizudera Temple 清水寺 (lower right, map 11)

The path south from the Kannon image to Kiyomizudera Temple is lined with old wooden buildings and is a good example of a typical backstreet of the ancient capital. Most of these houses are souvenir shops that are stocked to their eaves with inexpensive traditional items such as Kiyomizuyaki pottery, Kyoto dolls, bamboo crafts, etc. There are also many traditional snack shops and tea shops here. On your way to Kiyomizudera Temple, be sure to sample a free Yatsuhashi cookie. These are the souvenir that Japanese visitors to Kyoto most often purchase for the folks back home. They come in two varieties — soft, sweet dumplings stuffed with sweet bean paste, or hard, curved cookies that taste a bit like ginger snaps. Only the latter travel well.

Kiyomizudera Temple, erected in 798, is dedicated to the Eleven-headed Kannon. The present structures were re-built in 1633 at the order of the third Tokugawa Shogun. The two-story West Gate serves as the main entrance. Statues of the guardian Kongo-Rikishi stand in niches at both sides of the gate. The Main Hall, which extends out over a cliff and which is supported by 139 giant pillars, is quite a unique structure, and probably the only National Treasure

Kiyomizudera Temple.

you can walk on in shoes. There is a wide, wooden veranda across the front of the Main Hall where visitors can enjoy a panoramic view of Kyoto and its surroundings. It is quite thrilling to look down at the deep valley that lies below the veranda. When Japanese are about to embark on some great adventure, they often say that they are about to "jump from the veranda of Kiyomizudera." The precincts are open from dawn till dusk, and admission to the veranda is 100 yen.

Chishakuin Temple 智積院 (lower center, map 12)

Leave Kiyomizudera Temple by way of either Kiyomizuzaka 清水坂 (which you took on your way up to the temple), or Kiyomizu-shindo Path 清水新道, and walk to Gojozaka bus stop 五条坂. Although you could continue walking on Higashi-oji-dori Street to Chishakuin Temple, this wide street has nothing to recommend it. It is better to just take a bus to Higashi-Shichijo stop 東七条. Take the No. 202, No. 206 or No. 207 bus. The No. 202 and No. 207 buses stop at stop (c) (map 12), while the No. 206 stops at stop (b).

Chishakuin Temple is another reminder of the shift of political power from Hideyoshi Toyotomi to Ieyasu Tokugawa. The original temple at this site was constructed to honor the memory of Hideyoshi's son, who died in 1591 at the age of three. When Ieyasu captured power, he gave this Toyotomi family temple to the Shingon sect. Since then the temple has strengthened its influence and has become the headquarters of more than 3,000 subordinate temples scattered all over Japan. Especially noteworthy at this temple are its brilliant paintings of the Hasegawa School (a rival of the Kano School), and its garden. The colorful paintings, which feature the beauties of the four seasons, are displayed in a special exhibition hall. Because they are arranged at the height they would normally be in a Japanese style room, you have to sit down to really appreciate them. The garden, laid out about 400 years ago, centers around a large pond that extends under a veranda. Because of this, you may feel that you are looking at the garden from a stage suspended over the pond. Because most people hurry directly to Sanjusangendo Hall from Kiyomizudera Temple, you can spend a quiet and relaxed time at the garden. Kondo (Main Hall) is an elaborate vermilion red structure (but only a 1975 reconstruction) (9 a.m. to 4:30 p.m. Admission 300 yen).

Sanjusangendo Hall 三十三間堂 (lower center, map 12)

Sanjusangendo Hall is the popular name given to Rengeoin Temple. It was so named because of the 33 ("sanjusan") spaces between the pillars in the long, narrow hall. Although the hall is only 33 feet (10 m.) wide, it is 394 feet (120 m.) long. The original temple, erected in 1164 at the order of the retired but still powerful Emperor Goshirakawa, was destroyed by fire in 1249 and rebuilt in 1266. Its chief image is a wooden thousand-handed Kannon in a seated position. This National Treasure was carved in 1254 by Tankei, a master sculptor of the Kamakura era. The Kannon is surrounded by statues of 28 faithful

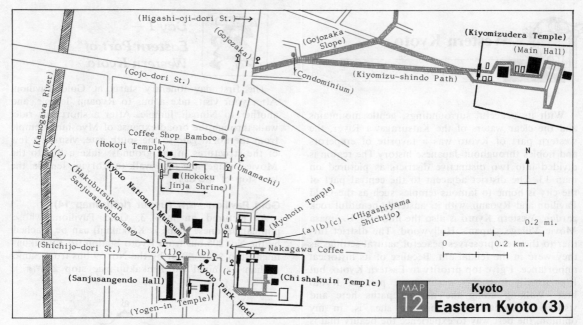

MAP 12 — Kyoto: **Eastern Kyoto (3)**

followers (National Treasures), and an additional one thousand and one smaller statues of the Kannon fill the remainder of the gallery. It is said that everyone can find at least one face like that of a friend (or sweetheart?) among these 1,001 images (8 a.m. to 4:40 p.m. Till 3:40 p.m. in winter. Admission 300 yen).

Kyoto National Museum 京都国立博物館 (middle center, map 12)

Kyoto National Museum was erected in 1879 by the Imperial Household Agency as a repository for precious art objects and other treasures. It is divided into three sections — history, fine arts, and handicrafts. Its 17 exhibit rooms house some 2,000 pieces of rare and valuable art, and historical and religious objects. Set aside as much time as possible for this museum (9 a.m. to 4 p.m. Closed on Mondays. Admission 250 yen).

Hokoji Temple and Hokoku Jinja Shrine (middle center, map 12) (optional)

After your visit to the National Museum (you will probably finish around 4 p.m.), you should consider visiting these two sites if your curiosity and energy are still intact.

Hokoji Temple 方広寺 (to the north of the Museum) was built at the order of Hideyoshi to house Japan's biggest image of Buddha. Larger even than that of Nara's Todaiji Temple (which is today Japan's biggest statue), the huge Buddha was recast three times before finally falling victim to fires and earthquakes. Only the old stone walls along the western side of the precincts remain to give us an idea of Hideyoshi's grand scheme for the temple complex. A large temple bell, cast at the order of Hideyori Toyotomi, Hideyoshi's successor, also stands in the temple grounds. The inscriptions on the bell say, "Peace for the Nation, and Prosperity for the People," 国家安康 but two of the Chinese characters used in the inscription are characters used in Ieyasu 家康 Tokugawa's name as well. On the inscription these two characters were split — unluckily — and another character interspersed. Ieyasu took this as an insult and claimed that the unlucky inscription illustrated Hideyori's desire to destroy Ieyasu's influence. For Ieyasu this constituted an excuse to commence hostilities, and the resulting battle at Osakajo Castle led to the ascendancy of the Tokugawas and the collapse of the Toyotomi family. A one hundred yen coin will purchase you the privilege of ringing the bell.

Hokoku Jinja Shrine 豊国神社 was built to honor Hideyoshi Toyotomi. Originally it was located on Higashiyama Mountain overlooking the city. Ieyasu destroyed the buildings after he ruined the Toyotomis. The shrine was reconstructed during the Meiji Era (after the fall of the Tokugawas) in the precincts of Hokoji Temple. The Treasure House of the shrine contains many objects related to Hideyoshi (9 a.m. to 4:30 p.m. Admission 300 yen). The displays are really not worth the 300 yen admission. Entrance to the grounds is free of charge.

Places for Lunch

You should have lunch either before or after your visit to Chishakuin Temple. Because there are no adequate restaurants within walking distance of Higashiyama Shichijo bus stop, the Kyoto Park Hotel is the logical selection. The main dining room and a Chinese restaurant are on the ground floor, a Japanese restaurant is in the basement, and there is a coffee shop on the second floor.

Western Kyoto

Poetic Kyoto

With its peaceful surroundings, gentle mountains and the clear waters of the Katsuragawa River, the western part of Kyoto was a favorite of emperors and nobles throughout Japanese history. The region is divided into two distinctive districts as pictured on map 13. The district adjacent to the central part of the city is home to famous temples such as the Gold Pavilion and Ryoanji, with its austerely beautiful rock garden. Western Kyoto is also the home of Uzumasa Movie Village, Japan's Hollywood. The district further to the west preserves peaceful natural settings as they were in the feudal era. Because of its historical importance, I give top priority to Eastern Kyoto, but I personally love this westernmost part of Kyoto best. Walking along the narrow paths here and visiting the area's many historic sites is, in my opinion, the best way to experience the beauty that is Kyoto.

Western Kyoto is introduced in two one-day itineraries.

If your time is limited and you want to cover the region in one day, combine the itineraries thusly: start your day in Western Kyoto at the Movie Village, but don't spend too much time there. Koryuji Temple is only a 5-minute walk from the Village. Take a train to Arashiyama and visit Tenryuji Temple and then walk to a couple of smaller temples along the natural path. The visit to Gold Pavilion should be incorporated into your tour of Central Kyoto as already explained in the Central Kyoto section.

Day 1 — Eastern Part of Western Kyoto

The first day itinerary starts at Gold Pavilion. After your visit, take a bus to Ryoanji Temple, and another to Ninnaji Temple. After a short bus ride, walk through the broad expanse of Myoshinji Temple from the north gate to the south gate, visiting a few of the structures in the grounds. Take a bus to the Movie Village, and then walk to Koryuji Temple, the last stop of the day.

Gold Pavilion 金閣寺 (upper right, map 14)

As pictured on map 3, Gold Pavilion (whose popular Japanese name is Kinkakuji) can be reached by the No. 205 bus from Kyoto Station (to Kinkakuji-michi stop 金閣寺道) or by the No. 59 bus from Sanjo Keihan Terminal (to Kinkakuji-mae stop 金閣寺前).

Kinkakuji Temple-the Gold Pavilion.

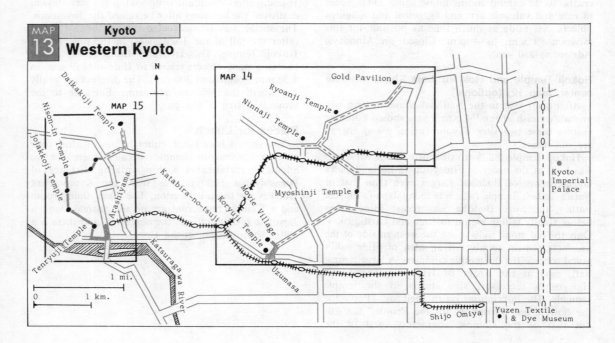

Horikawa-Imadegawa (upper left, map 3) provides a good connection to the No. 59 bus if you are staying at a hotel that isn't on the No. 205 or No. 59 route. Kinkakuji-michi stop is a 3-minute walk to the temple and Kinkakuji-mae stop is just in front of the entrance.

Gold Pavilion, formally Rokuonji Temple, was constructed in 1397 by the third Ashikaga Shogun, Yoshimitsu, who spent the latter part of his life here in retirement. His son, Yoshimochi, in accordance with the dictates of his father's will, had the villa converted to a Buddhist temple. The garden still reflects the beauty of the refined contemplative life of the Ashikagas, but most of the original buildings have been destroyed by repeated fires, including the tragic loss, by arson, in July 1950, of the precious Gold Pavilion itself. A new Gold Pavilion — an exact reproduction of the original — was erected on the same spot in October 1955. After walking through Chumon Gate, you will see two shimmering gold pavilions. One is the three-story golden building with a bronze phoenix on its roof. The other is its reflection in the calm, beautiful pond that lies in front of the Pavilion. The walls of the Pavilion are completely covered with gold foil. The Main Hall of the temple houses images of three Buddhist divinities - Kannon, Benten and Kokushi-Muso. In the tiny courtyard of the Main Hall is a 500-year old pine that generations of gardeners have trained into the shape of a sailing ship (9 a.m. to 5 p.m. Until 5:30 p.m. in summer. Admission 300 yen).

Domoto Museum 堂本美術館 (upper right, map 14) (optional)

If you enjoy contemporary art, you should visit Domoto Museum, which is located at Kinugasa 衣笠 bus stop. Take the No. 59 bus from Kinkakuji-mae. The modern three-story museum displays paintings, sculptures and other works of Insho Domoto (10 a.m. to 5 p.m. Admission 500 yen. Closed on Mondays.).

Ryoanji Temple 竜安寺 (upper center, map 14)

If you don't visit Domoto Museum, you should still take the No. 59 bus, but should stay on it to Ryoanji-mae stop 竜安寺前. Ryoanji Temple belongs to the Rinzai sect of Zen Buddhism, and was founded in 1473 by Katsumoto Hosokawa, a powerful Kyoto feudal lord, whose grave is in the temple grounds. It is famous for its rock garden. Consisting of only rocks and pebbles, it is regarded as the quintessential Zen garden. Some say that the 15 rocks arranged on the surface of white pebbles look like islands on a huge ocean, while other think that they look like tigers crossing a big river. The rocks are so arranged that visitors can only see 14 of them at once, no matter what the angle from which they view the garden (except perhaps from the air!) (8 a.m. to 5 p.m. Admission 300 yen).

Ninnaji Temple 仁和寺 (middle center, map 14)

Take the No. 59 bus three stops, from Ryoanji-mae stop to Omuro Ninnaji stop 御室仁和寺. Ninnaji Temple was formerly known as Omuro Palace. Emperor Koko, the Temple's first patron, ordered work on it begun in 886, but passed away before it was completed. His successor, Emperor Uda had the work completed two years later, and when he retired became the temple's first abbot. From then until the Meiji Restoration, the temple's abbot was always an imperial prince. Originally, there were more than 60 buildings scattered around the temple precincts, but frequent fires have reduced their number. The oldest buildings still standing date from the first half of the 17th century. The five-story pagoda, about 108 feet (33 m.) tall, was built in 1637. The Main Hall (National Treasure) at the northernmost end of the precincts was formerly the Main Ceremonial Hall of the Imperial Palace and was moved here in the early 17th century. The Main Hall contains a wooden image of Amitabha (National Treasure) as its chief object of worship. Admission to the temple grounds is 100 yen. It costs an additional 300 yen to see the interior of Goten Hall, the palace that the abbots used as their residence. The Treasure House is open to the public only for two weeks in the fall (9 a.m. to 4 p.m.).

Myoshinji Temple 妙心寺 (lower center, map 14; expanded map of the precincts is included at the lower right corner of the map)

You can easily walk the 0.5 mile (0.8 km.) distance from Ninnaji to Myoshinji, and frequent bus service is also available. Take the No. 8, No. 10 or No. 26 bus from the stop right in front of the South Gate of Ninnaji Temple (make sure to take one going east, from the northern side of the road).

Upon entering the precincts of Myoshinji Temple at the North Gate, you'll feel that you're walking along a stone path running between temple after temple. Myoshinji is one of the few temples that have enough of its original buildings intact to give you some idea of the magnificent scale of Japan's traditional temple architecture. It was founded in 1337 on the site of Emperor Hanazono's imperial villa. There are more than 40 minor buildings, and each has its own refined garden. Japan's oldest bell (National Treasure), cast in 698, hangs in a belfry near South Gate. Four of Myoshinji's buildings are open to the public:

Main Halls: You will see the entrance on your left

Rock garden at Ryoanji Temple.

just after passing under the elevated corridor between the main buildings. The main attraction of the Main Halls is the picture of a dragon painted on the ceiling of Hatto (Ceremonial) Hall. The painting is often described as "A Dragon Glaring in Eight Directions" because his eyes seem to stare at you no matter where you stop to look up at him (9 a.m. to 4 p.m. Admission 300 yen).

Taizoin Temple 退蔵院 , erected in 1404, is renowned for its landscaped garden, which represents a stream coursing down a mountain and forming a river. The grounds are quiet and really beautiful (9 a.m. to 5 p.m. Admission 300 yen).

Daishin-in 大心院 , erected in 1492, and **Keishun-in** 桂春院 , erected in 1632, also have famous gardens, but, due to time limitations, I did not visit them. Daishin-in is open from 9 a.m. to 4 p.m. (300 yen), and Keishun-in from 9 a.m. to 5 p.m. (400 yen).

Uzumasa Movie Village 太秦映画村 (lower left, map 14)

Take the No. 61, No. 62 or No. 63 bus (westbound) at Myoshinji-mae stop to Uzumasa Eigamura (Eigamura is "Movie Village" in Japanese). The official name of the bus stop is "Hachigaokacho," but "Uzumasa Eigamura" is used much more frequently.

Uzumasa Movie Village, owned by the Toei Movie Company, has large open-air sets that recreate the buildings, bridges and streets of feudal and modern Japan. There are also indoor studios and museums. You can watch as the cameras roll on famous movie stars dressed in period costumes. It takes one hour just to tour the facilities, but a thorough visit to this world through the looking glass will probably take two or three hours. The Village is closed on the 4th Tuesday, Wednesday and Thursday of July, and from December 21 to January 1. Admission is 1,000 yen. (9 a.m. to 5 p.m.; 9:30 a.m. to 4 p.m. in winter).

If you plan to see Western Kyoto in just one day, you should start your day at the Movie Village. The easiest transportation there is the Keifuku Arashiyama Line 京福嵐山線 *from Shijo Omiya Station* 四条大宮駅 *to Uzumasa* 太秦駅 *(11 minutes, 170 yen). As pictured on map 3, Shijo Omiya Station is also easily accessible from most parts of the city via the loop bus. The Movie Village is only a 5-minute walk from Uzumasa Station.*

Koryuji Temple 広隆寺 (lower left, map 14)

A huge wooden gate marks the entrance to the precincts of Koryuji Temple, which was founded in 622 by Kawakatsu Hata, one of Kyoto's most powerful aristocrats. It was designed as a memorial for Regent Shotoku, who promulgated Japan's first, "Seventeen-Article" Constitution. (You might see his portrait if you get one of the old, large 5,000 or 10,000 yen bills that are still in circulation). The newly constructed Reihoden Treasure House is home to more that 50 masterpieces of Asuka, Nara and Heian sculpture. The exquisite statues, all of which were originally objects of worship, reflect the artistic splendor of those ancient eras, and many of them are National Treasures. Perhaps the most famous of all is the Miroku-Bosatsu, which was selected as Japan's first National Treasure and well deserves this honor. Strong yet gentle, serene and compassionate, the enigmatic beauty of the face of this Buddha casts its spell over every visitor to the Treasure House. The Treasure House is open from 9 a.m. to 5 p.m. Admission is 300 yen. The Keiguin Hall (National Treasure) is an elegant octagonal structure located in the northwestern part of the temple precincts.

Uzumasa Movie Village.

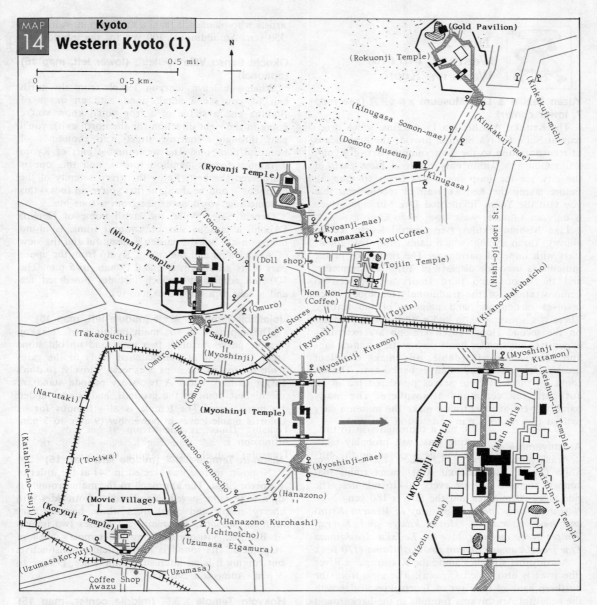

MAP 14 Kyoto
Western Kyoto (1)

If you are allocating two days for Western Kyoto, Koryuji will be the last stop on your first day tour. Take the Keifuku Arashiyama Line to Shijo Omiya, and then a bus to your hotel (refer to maps 7 and 3). *If you start your one day tour of Western Kyoto at the Movie Village, take a train from Uzumasa to Arashiyama (the last stop on the line) and continue your day in the westernmost part of Kyoto. The details are explained below.*

Places for Lunch

Yamazaki is located near Ryoanji-mae bus stop (upper center, map 14). Although it has no English sign, its plastic displays make it easy to recognize. Sandwiches are 500 yen, curry with pork cutlet is 850 yen, eel teriyaki ("unadon") is 1,200 yen.

Sakon is at Omuro Ninnaji bus stop (middle center, map 14). This restaurant has an English sign and serves a wide variety of set menu Japanese lunches at 1,600 yen to 2,800 yen.

The Movie Village has a huge restaurant that serves everything from noodles to fancy Japanese, Chinese and Western dishes. Both prices and quality are reasonable (800-2,000 yen).

If you are doing Western Kyoto in one day, have lunch after arriving at Arashiyama (explained below).

Day 2 — Western Part of Western Kyoto

Yuzen Textile & Dye Museum 友禅美術館 (see map 7, lower center)

The Keifuku Arashiyama Line trains, which originate at Shijo Omiya Station, provide the best means of transportation to the westernmost part of Kyoto. Shijo Omiya is within easy reach of most parts of the city via the loop line buses (refer to map 3). Before taking the Keifuku train, I recommend that you visit the Yuzen Textile and Dye Museum, which is only an 8-minute walk from Shijo Omiya.

Like Nishijin textiles (see Central Kyoto section above), Yuzen dyeing, which dates from 794, got its start with imperial patronage. The first floor of the museum is used for displays of Yuzen masterpieces, and the second and third floors are devoted to demonstrations of the traditional technique, which involves meticulous hand painting of the textiles. There is a souvenir shop and a do-it-yourself corner on the second floor. Yuzen kimono are extremely expensive, but smaller items such as ties, folding fans and scarves are affordable, and make excellent presents for friends and relatives back home. The tea room on the first floor serves powdered tea in an authentic tea ceremony atmosphere. The many bamboo trees at its entrance make the museum easy to find (9 a.m. to 5 p.m. Admission 300 yen).

Arashiyama 嵐山

Arashiyama Station is 4.5 miles (7.2 km.) from Shijo Omiya. The Keifuku Arashiyama trains that connect the two operate every 10-15 minutes. The ride takes 20 minutes and the fare is 180 yen.

If you are only spending one day in Western Kyoto and have visited the Movie Village and Koryuji Temple in the morning, take the Keifuku Arashiyama Line from Uzumasa Station to Arashiyama (170 yen).

Arashiyama stretches along the Katsuragawa River (the river is also called Oigawa). The view from the northern bank of the river of Togetsukyo Bridge with the beautiful Arashiyama foothills in the background is especially lovely. It is no wonder that throughout Japanese history, emperors, aristocrats and shoguns loved the area. Modern Japanese, too, are particularly fond of this area. You can rent a row boat for 900 yen per hour, or charter a small wooden boat (with a boatman) for 1,900 yen (for two) (about a 30-minute ride) at the pier pictured on map 15 (lower center, to the west of Togetsukyo Bridge).

Tenryuji Temple 天竜寺 (lower center, map 15)

Tenryuji Temple was founded in 1339 by Takauji, the first Ashikaga Shogun, in memory of Emperor Godaigo. The noted priest and landscape artist, Muso-Kokushi, was its first abbot. The temple was repeatedly ravaged by fire, and the present buildings date only from 1900, but the famous garden preserves the style of the 14th century original. Complementing its natural surroundings, the Tenryuji garden testifies to the great creative abilities of the Ashikaga era artists who planned it (8:30 a.m. to 5 p.m. Admission 350 yen. An additional 100 yen for the interior).

Okochi Sanso Villa 大河内山荘 (lower left, map 15) (optional)

When you leave Tenryuji Temple from the north exit (if you see a small pond with an image of Buddha and a statue of a frog you'll know you're going in the right direction for the north exit), you'll pass through a narrow street with thousands of beautiful bamboos. The westernmost part of Kyoto is famous for its bamboo forests, and this one is considered the best. Enjoy the green serenity of the bamboos — and be thankful that you're on foot — this is something you'd never see from a tour bus.

Okochi Sanso Villa, the lavish home of Denjiro Okochi, a famous star of samurai films, is of no interest itself, but the garden is beautiful and the view of Arashiyama and the city of Kyoto from the upper part of its grounds is splendid (9 a.m. to 5 p.m. The 700 yen admission — which includes powdered tea and a cake is a bit too expensive).

Jojakkoji Temple 常寂光寺 (middle left, map 15)

The approach to the main buildings of Jojakkoji Temple passes through two gates and up old stone steps. The view of the thatched roofs of the gates from the top of the steps is especially lovely, so don't forget to look back. A two-story pagoda stands at the highest point of the grounds, and is surrounded by many trees. The temple is also famous for its colorful maple leaves in November (9 a.m. to 5 p.m. Admission 200 yen).

Nison-in Temple 二尊院 (middle left, map 15)

Nison-in Temple was erected in 841 at the order of Emperor Saga. The approach to the main grounds is up a wide, stone-paved slope lined on both sides with cherry, maple and other trees whose beauties vary with the seasons. The main hall houses two images of Buddha. Visitors can ring the temple's "Bell of Happiness." Its sound is not particularly distinctive, but ringing it is an interesting experience. (9 a.m. to 5 p.m. Admission 200 yen).

Hokyoin Temple 宝筐院 (middle center, map 15) (optional)

Even few Japanese know about this temple. The tombs of two men, Yoshiakira Ashikaga and Masatsura Kusunoki, who were fierce rivals during Japan's medieval era, are located side by side in the precincts of Hokyoin Temple. Masatsura helped Emperor Godaigo regain power from the Kamakura Shogunate. Even though the Emperor triumphed in 1333 he was again soon supplanted, this time by the Ashikagas. Yoshiakira had great respect for his enemy Masatsura, and when he died in battle, Yoshiakira had this temple built to honor Masatsura's memory, and left instructions that he himself was to be buried next to Masatsura. The wooded precincts are extremely quiet and very peaceful (9 a.m. to 5 p.m. Admission 300 yen).

Seiryoji Temple 清涼寺 (middle center, map 15) (Optional)

This temple, popularly known as Saga-Shakado

嵯峨釈迦堂 (Saga Buddha Hall), was originally the villa of an imperial prince. It was converted to a temple to provide a home for a sandalwood image of Sakyamuni which had been imported from China. There are several buildings in the temple's spacious grounds, including Sutra Hall at the eastern end of the grounds, repository of thousands and thousands of sutras arranged on revolving shelves. Supposedly, if you spin the shelves once it has the same effect as reading the innumerable volumes of sutras contained on them. (It costs 100 yen per spin to try this

Readers' Digest approach to prayer.). Admission to the precincts is free of charge, but it costs 200 yen to enter the main hall and the garden attached to it (9:30 a.m. to 4:30 p.m.).

Those doing Western Kyoto in just one day will probably have to call it a day here. Take a bus back to the city from Saga-Shakado-mae stop. Make sure that you take the south-bound bus. You should go back to either Kyoto Station 京都駅 or Sanjo Keihan bus terminal 三条京阪バスターミナル, and then take a bus back to your hotel. The No. 28, No. 71, No. 72,

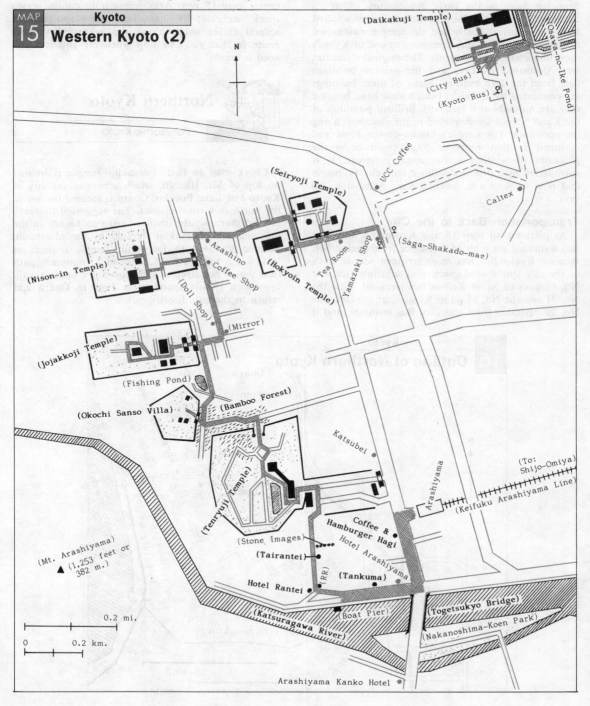

MAP
15

Kyoto
Western Kyoto (2)

(Daikakuji Temple)

(City Bus)

(Kyoto Bus)

(Seiryoji Temple)

UCC Coffee

Osawa-no-Ike Pond

(Saga-Shakado-mae)

Caltex

Azashino Coffee Shop

(Hokyoin Temple)

Tea Room

Yamazaki Shop

(Nison-in Temple)

(Doll Shop)

(Mirror)

(Jojakkoji Temple)

(Fishing Pond)

(Okochi Sanso Villa)

(Bamboo Forest)

Katsubei

Arashiyama

(To: Shijo-Omiya)

(Keifuku Arashiyama Line)

(Tenryuji Temple)

Coffee & Hamburger Hagi

Hotel Arashiyama

(Mt. Arashiyama)

▲ (1,253 feet or 382 m.)

(Stone Images)

(Tairantei)

(RR)

(Tankuma)

Hotel Rantei

0.2 mi.

0   0.2 km.

(Katsuragawa River)

(Boat Pier)

(Togetsukyo Bridge)

(Nakanoshima-Koen Park)

Arashiyama Kanko Hotel

No. 81 and No. 90 buses go to Kyoto Station (last stop for all the buses) and the No. 61 and No. 62 go to Sanjo Keihan bus terminal (the last stop).

Those who have a full day for the westernmost part of Kyoto should still have time to visit Daikakuji Temple. Take the north-bound No. 28, No. 61, No. 71, No. 81 or No. 91 bus at Saga-Shakado-mae (Daikakuji Temple is the last stop on all these lines).

Daikakuji Temple 大覚寺 (upper right, map 15)

Daikakuji Temple was originally built as a villa for Emperor Saga in the early 9th century. After its conversion to a temple, the abbots were selected from the imperial family and the temple maintained its high social status and reputation as one of Kyoto's most important establishments. The original structures were destroyed by fires and the present buildings date from the 16th century. Many of these buildings are connected by corridors (watch your head because they are only about 6 feet tall). Brilliant paintings of the Kano School are displayed in the chambers along the corridors. The temple's Osawa-no-Ike Pond was designed so that Emperor Saga could enjoy the pleasures of boating at his country retreat. It is surrounded by a promenade lined with cherry, maple and pine trees (9 a.m. to 4:30 p.m. Admission 300 yen).

Transportation Back to the City

As pictured on map 15, the Kyoto Bus and City Bus terminals are a bit of a distance from each other. Because Kyoto Bus has more frequent service back to the city you should check that schedule first. The No. 61 goes to Sanjo Keihan bus terminal while the No. 71 and the No. 81 go to Kyoto Station. Only the No. 28 operates from the City Bus terminal, and it goes back to Kyoto Station. The ride to either Kyoto Station or Sanjo Keihan terminal takes about 50 minutes.

Places for Lunch

There are number of famous restaurants near the Katsuragawa River. Drop in at **Tankuma, Hotel Rantei** or **Tairantei** (all are pictured on map 15, lower center) for an authentic Japanese lunch (2,000 - 4,000 yen). If you're in the mood for a Western lunch, **Coffee & Hamburger Hagi** (lower center, map 15, near Arashiyama train station) serves quick lunches at 600 - 1,000 yen. I have also pictured several coffee shops along the suggested walking route so that you can stop whenever you feel you need a break.

Northern Kyoto

Panoramic Kyoto

Check map 16 first. Enryakuji Temple is located on top of Mt. Hieizan, which separates the city of Kyoto and Lake Biwako. Ohara is located further to the north in a rural district. The suggested itinerary for Northern Kyoto involves visits to Ohara in the morning and Enryakuji Temple in the afternoon. Because the visit to Enryakuji Temple requires at least a 0.6 mile (1 km.) walk on a mountain path (one that is not steep), those who don't want to walk too much should spend more time in Ohara and return to the city directly.

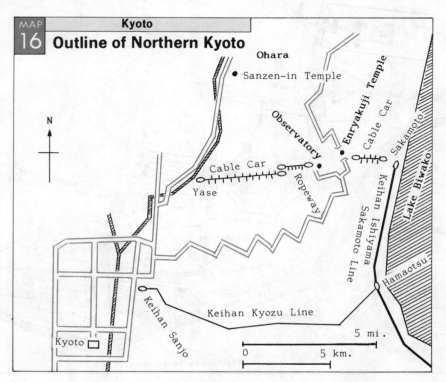

MAP 16 — Kyoto — **Outline of Northern Kyoto**

Suggested Itinerary

Transportation to Ohara from the City

As pictured on map 3, you can take either the No. 17 or No. 18 bus from Kyoto Station to Ohara. If it is easier for you to start from Sanjo Keihan bus terminal, take either the No. 16 or No. 17 bus. At Kyoto Station, the buses leave from stop D (pictured on map 2, upper left). From Sanjo Keihan terminal, catch your bus at the Kyoto Bus (5) stop (pictured on map 5, upper right). The trip from Kyoto Station takes about one hour (400 yen), and the trip from Sanjo Keihan to Ohara takes about 40 minutes.

Ohara 大原 (map 17)

Ohara, located in the quiet northern suburbs of Kyoto, is surrounded by mountains. Though the area is slowly modernizing, it still preserves much of the atmosphere of the ancient capital. Several destinations in this area are real gems. If you plan to visit Enryakuji Temple (and I recommend that you do), visit the temples on the eastern side of Ohara, skipping Jakkoin Temple, which is located on the western side. If you decide to skip Enryakuji Temple, you should be sure to include a visit to Jakkoin.

Sanzen-in Temple 三千院 (lower right, map 17)

The approach to Sanzen-in Temple is a gentle paved slope that runs alongside a small creek. Many souvenir shops and restaurants are, unfortunately, located here as well, cluttering up and commercializing this lovely natural setting. Sanzen-in Temple was originally located in Mt. Hieizan and was a branch

of Enryakuji Temple. The temple was moved to its present site in the 15th century. Traditionally, the abbots of the temple were selected from the imperial family. There are three buildings and beautiful gardens in the spacious precincts. The Main Hall houses an Amitabha trinity: the two disciples that flank Buddha are seated, which is quite unusual and make these goddesses seem very relaxed and merciful. The temple grounds and the approach have a reputation as one of Kyoto's best maple viewing locations in November (8:30 a.m. to 5 p.m. Until 4:30 p.m. in winter. Admission 400 yen).

Jikkoin Temple 実光院 (lower right, map 17)

Jikkoin Temple is only 0.1 miles north of Sanzen-in Temple, but because group tours only visit Sanzen-in and then rush off to Jakkoin Temple on the other side of Ohara, Jikkoin Temple and the other temples located north of Sanzen-in are never very crowded. Even though the adjacent Sanzen-in Temple was crowded with a lot of visitors when I arrived at Jikkoin, I was the only guest there for about 20 minutes. Unlike most temples, Jikkoin does not have a ticket office at its entrance. Upon entering the gate, you should ring the gong. The admission of 400 yen should be paid to the young lady who will lead you to a chamber overlooking a small garden. Powdered tea and a cake are served. Because the tea is served in a very casual manner, you can just relax and enjoy the delicate flavor of the tea and the view of the beautifully manicured garden, even if you don't know anything about the etiquette of tea ceremony. You can also take a walk in the garden. In this temple, I was especially impressed by the tiny bells in one corner of the visitors' chamber. Each bell has a distinctive but delicate tone; when the temple was a training center for new monks they were used

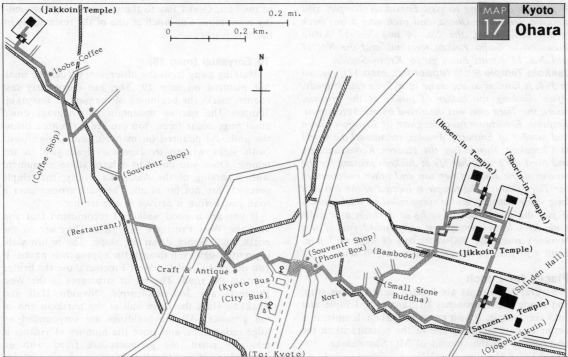

MAP 17 **Kyoto Ohara**

to help the novices learn their prayers (9 a.m. to 5 p.m.).

Shorin-in Temple 勝林院 (middle right, map 17)

The grounds of this temple are quite extensive. Even from the outside visitors can see a building that dates from 1013. Shorin-in Temple is famous as the place where the priest Honen debated and refuted the high ranking priests of other sects (9:30 a.m. to 5 p.m. Admission 100 yen).

Hosen-in Temple 宝泉院 (middle right, map 17)

Hosen-in Temple is famous for its 500-year old pine tree shaped like Mt. Fuji; this marvelous example of the gardener's art is just inside the entrance. As with Jikkoin Temple, there is no ticket window. This time you have to hit a wooden gong to inform the staff of your arrival. Again, you pay a 400-yen admission and are led to a chamber where tea and a cake are served in a casual manner. The room faces a beautiful bamboo forest and the pillars on that side of the room are arranged like an oversize frame so that the garden looks like a huge picture — and a very beautiful one at that (9 a.m. to 5 p.m.).

From Hosen-in Temple, walk down the rocky path along the small creek to the paved road, and then follow map 17.

To Go or Not To Go to Enryakuji

If you have decided to visit Enryakuji Temple, take a Kyoto Bus back to Yase-Yuenchi 八瀬遊園地 (Yase Playland), which you passed on your way to Ohara in the morning. Be careful because the Ohara bus stop for the Kyoto Bus, as pictured on map 16, is different from the stop for the City Bus. You can take any of the following Kyoto Buses: No. 11, No. 13, No. 14 No. 15, No. 16, No. 17 or No. 18.

If you are not going to visit Enryakuji Temple, visit Jakkoin Temple in Ohara, and then take a bus back to the city. Again, the No. 16 and No. 17 Kyoto Buses go to Sanjo Keihan terminal, and the No. 17 and No. 18 Kyoto Buses go to Kyoto Station.

Jakkoin Temple 寂光院 *(upper left, map 17), erected in 594, is famous as the scene of a Taira clan tragedy. After climbing the ladder of power at the imperial court, the Taira clan was destroyed by the Minamotos. Empress Kenreimon-in, a daughter of Kiyomori Taira and mother of Emperor Antoku, renounced the world at Chorakuji Temple (see the Eastern Kyoto section), and lived the rest of her life at Jakkoin praying for the repose of the souls of her son and other members of the Taira family. The temple is located at the top of a long stone stairway, and is surrounded by thick woods. If you are lucky enough to be at Jakkoin at a quiet time, its solemn atmosphere will remind you of this heroine's tragic life 800 years ago (8 a.m. to 5 p.m. Until 4:30 p.m. in winter. Admission 350 yen).*

Places for Lunch

Several restaurants are located near the bus stop, and along the approaches to Sanzen-in Temple and Jakkoin Temple. If you go to Enryakuji Temple, it is better to have lunch at one of the restaurants in the observatory on the summit of Mt. Shimeidake.

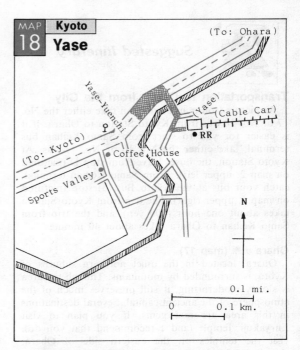

To Mt. Shimeidake 四明岳 (maps 18 & 19)

Yase cable car station is a few minutes walk from Yase-Yuenchi bus stop. The cable car operates every 30 minutes. The ride to Hiei Station takes nine minutes (500 yen). Transfer to the ropeway at Hiei for the trip to Sancho stop. The ropeway operates every 30 minutes and the ride takes three minutes (300 yen).

A revolving observatory is located on the top of Mt. Shimeidake (admission 300 yen). If the weather permits, you have a panoramic view of Lake Biwako to the east, Osaka Bay to the west and the surrounding mountains. Eat lunch at one of the restaurants in the observatory.

To Enryakuji (map 19)

Walking away from the observatory, find the small hut pictured on map 19. This hut (very dirty rest rooms) marks the beginning of the path to Enryakuji Temple. The narrow mountain path zigzags down amid huge cedar trees. You can see a ski area below the path. As pictured on map 19, several sign posts (with signs written in Japanese) lead you to the temple. Once you come to a large stone monument with a carving of the Amitabha trinity, the temple precincts are not far at all. The path crosses over a road just before it arrives at the temple.

If you are a good walker, I recommend that you visit the West Precincts 西塔 first. They are to the north, and further down the slope. The return walk is pretty tough even though the approach is paved. If you decide to visit the West Precincts, use the bridge to cross the road. The major structures in the West Precincts are Jodoin Temple, Ninaido Hall and Shakado Hall, the main hall at the northern end of the grounds. All the buildings are surrounded by huge cedar trees, and since the number of visitors is relatively small, the precincts are filled with an atmosphere of esoteric Buddhism.

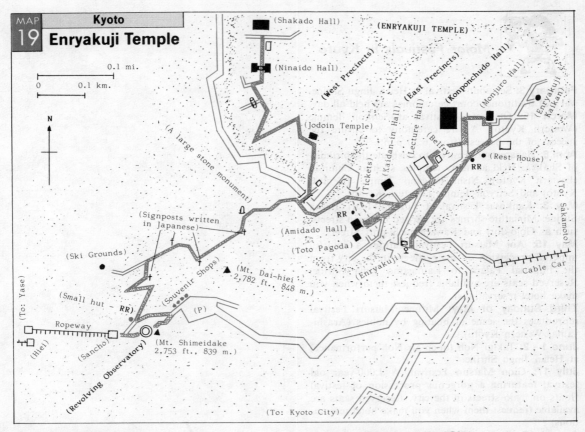

MAP 19 Kyoto Enryakuji Temple

(Shakado Hall)
(ENRYAKUJI TEMPLE)
(Ninaido Hall)
(West Precincts)
(East Precincts)
(Konponchudo Hall)
(Monjuro Hall)
(Enryakuji Kaikan)
(Jodoin Temple)
(Kaidan-in Hall)
(Lecture Hall)
(Belfry)
(Tickets)
(Rest House)
RR
0.1 mi.
0 0.1 km.
N
(A large stone monument)
(To: Sakamoto)
(Signposts written in Japanese)
RR
(Amidado Hall)
(Ski Grounds)
(Mt. Dai-hiei 2,782 ft., 848 m.)
(Toto Pagoda)
(Enryakuji)
Cable Car
(To: Yase)
(Small hut - RR)
(Souvenir Shops)
(P)
(Revolving Observatory)
(Mt. Shimeidake 2,753 ft., 839 m.)
Ropeway
(Hiei)
(Sancho)
(To: Kyoto City)

Enryakuji Temple 延暦寺

The East Precincts 東塔 are what most visitors see at Enryakuji Temple. Enryakuji was founded by the priest Saicho in 788. Enryakuji and Koyasan are the two giants of Japanese Buddhism and have played leading roles throughout their 1,200-year long history. Many new religious sects were established by priests who studied at Enryakuji Temple, including Honen and Shinran, the founder of the Jodo-Shinshu or Ikkoshu sect. At the peak of its prosperity, Enryakuji Temple contained 3,000 buildings in three major precincts and in the surrounding valleys. The temple even organized a private military force as big as that of a feudal lord. Because of this force, and because of the temple's influence in political matters, Nobunaga Oda attacked Enryakuji in 1571. Most of the buildings were burned to the ground and thousands of soldiers, priests and other residents of the temple grounds were killed in the battle. Most of the present structures were constructed in the middle of the 17th century.

The ticket office is located at the entrance to the East Precincts as pictured on map 19 (8:30 a.m. to 4:30 p.m. Admission 350 yen). Toto Pagoda is a recently completed gigantic two-story brilliant vermilion red structure. Konponchudo Hall 根本中堂 is the main hall of the temple. To get a good view of this huge hall, walk up the steep stone steps to Monjuro Hall, which used to be the main gate of the temple when the main approach was on the Lake Biwako side.

How to Return to the City

Take a bus back to the city. The No. 6 (going to Sanjo Keihan terminal), the No. 7 (to Kyoto Station via Sanjo Keihan) and the No. 51 (to Kyoto Station) buses all stop at the Enryakuji stop. Because each bus operates only every 2 - 3 hours, take whichever one comes first (there is at least one bus every hour). The ride to Kyoto Station takes about one hour (580 yen). Enryakuji is not the first stop for these buses, so make sure that the bus you get on is headed for Kyoto.

As indicated on map 16, there is another way to go back to Kyoto. Take a cable car to Sakamoto, and then walk for 15 minutes to Sakamoto Station on the Keihan Ishiyama Sakamoto Line. Then take a train to Hamaotsu Station, and transfer there to the Keihan Kyozu Line, which will take you to Keihan Sanjo Station (the same location as Sanjo Keihan bus terminal). I actually took this route, and even though the view of Lake Biwako from the cable car is fantastic, the rest of the connections are time consuming and the train rides boring, and I do not recommend this route for tourists.

Major Festivals in Kyoto

February 3: Setsubun Festival at Heian Jingu Shrine. Various traditional court ceremonies are held all day.

March 15: Otaimatsu Festival at Seiryoji Temple (Western Kyoto). A fire ceremony to ensure the success of the harvest (from 6:30 p.m.).

April 8: Hanamatsuri Festival to celebrate the birthday of Shakya. Held at many temples, such as Chion-in (Eastern Kyoto), Nishi-Honganji Temple (Central Kyoto) and Seiryoji Temple (Western Kyoto).

May 3: Kankosai Festival of Fushimi Inari Taisha Shrine. Miniature shrines are carried on main streets, such as Gojo-dori and Kawaramachi-dori Streets.

May 15: Aoi Matsuri Festival features a colorful imperial procession on main streets in the city from the Imperial Palace to Kamigamo Jinja Shrine. Reserved seats are available (request them when you make hotel reservations).

Third Sunday of May: Mifune Matsuri Festival reproduces the scene of boating by nobles (Arashiyama, Western Kyoto).

June 1 - 2: Takigi Noh (open-air Noh performance) at Heian Jingu Shrine.

July 17: Gion Matsuri Festival. A 1,000-year old festival featuring a gorgeous procession of festival floats on main streets in the city. Reserved seats are available (request them when you make hotel reservations).

August 16: Gozan Okuribi Festival or Bonfires on Five Mountains. Spectacular bonfires are lighted on the city's five mountains. The fires can be seen from downtown.

August 16: Manto Nagashi Festival. A number of paper lanterns with candles are floated on the river to send the spirits of ancestors back to Heaven (during the middle of August, they are supposed to visit us). The festival is held in the Arashiyama area (Western Kyoto).

Second Sunday of October: Jinkosai Festival features a procession of miniature shrines and festival floats on Nishi-oji-dori Street.

October 22: Jidai Matsuri Festival is a live reproduction of Japanese history. A huge procession featuring various costumes from olden times to the Meiji Restoration is held on main streets in the city. Reserved seats are available (request them when you make hotel reservations).

Second Sunday of November: Momiji Matsuri or Maple Viewing Festival. Traditional music and many dances and dramas are performed on boats in the Arashiyama area (Western Kyoto).

Gion Matsuri Festival in July.

Accommodations

HOTELS
First-class Hotels (20,000 yen and up for a twin room)

Miyako Hotel 都ホテル (middle right, map 20)
Address: Sanjo-Keage, Higashiyama-ku, Kyoto; Phone: (075) 771-7111. An internationally famous establishment with 480 rooms.

Kyoto Hotel 京都ホテル (middle center, map 20)
Address: Kawaramachi-Oike, Nakagyo-ku, Kyoto; Phone: (075) 211-5111. Another old establishment located in the downtown area (507 rooms).

Kyoto Tokyu Hotel 京都東急ホテル (lower left, map 20)
Address: Gojo-sagaru, Horikawadori, Shimogyo-ku, Kyoto; Phone: (075) 341-2411. A new deluxe property of the Tokyu Hotel Chain (437 rooms).

International Hotel Kyoto 京都国際ホテル (middle left, map 20)
Address: Nijo-sagaru, Aburakoji, Nakagyo-ku, Kyoto; Phone: (075) 222-1111. A deluxe property with a beautiful Japanese garden on the premises (332 rooms).

Hotel Fujita ホテル・フジタ (middle center, map 20)
Address: Nishizume, Nijo-Ohashi, Nakagyo-ku, Kyoto; Phone: (075) 222-1511. A sister property of the International Hotel. Overlooking the Kamogawa River (195 rooms).

Kyoto Grand Hotel 京都グランドホテル (lower left, map 20)
Address: Horikawa-Shiokoji, Shimogyo-ku, Kyoto; Phone: (075) 341-2311. A deluxe property in a slightly inconvenient location (578 rooms).

Standard Hotels (14,000 - 20,000 yen for a twin room)

Kyoto Royal Hotel 京都ロイヤルホテル (middle center, map 20)
Address: Kawaramachi, Sanjo, Nakagyo-ku, Kyoto; Phone: (075) 223-1234. Best location in the heart of downtown (395 rooms).

New Miyako Hotel ニューミヤコホテル (lower left, map 20)
Address: Nishi-Kujoincho, Minami-ku, Kyoto; Phone: (075) 661-7111. A sister property of the Miyako Hotel. A bit inconvenient for sightseeing (714 rooms).

Hotel New Hankyu Kyoto 京都新阪急ホテル (lower left, map 20)
Address: Shiokoji-Shinmachi, Shimogyo-ku, Kyoto; Phone: (075) 343-5300. A new high-standard hotel near Kyoto Station (320 rooms).

Kyoto Century Hotel 京都センチュリーホテル (lower center, map 20)
Address: Shiokoji-sagaru, Higashino-Toindori, Shimogyo-ku, Kyoto; Phone: (075) 351-0111. A standard city hotel near Kyoto Station with 243 rooms.

Kyoto Park Hotel 京都パークホテル (lower center, map 20)
Address: 644-2, Sanjusangendo-Mawarimachi, Higashiyama-ku, Kyoto; Phone: (075) 541-6301. Famous for the Japanese garden in the grounds (307 rooms).

Hotel Gimmond Kyoto ホテル・ギンモンド京都 (middle center, map 20)
Address: Takakura-kado, Oikedori, Nakagyo-ku, Kyoto; Phone: (075) 221-4111. A cozy 142-room small hotel.

Kyoto Palaceside Hotel 京都パレスサイドホテル (upper center, map 20)
Address: Shimodachiuri-agaru, Karasumadori, Kamigyo-ku, Kyoto; Phone: (075) 431-8171. In a quiet location near Kyoto Imperial Palace (120 rooms).

Holiday Inn Kyoto ホリデーイン京都 (upper right, map 20)
Address: 36, Nishi-Hirakicho, Takano, Sakyo-ku, Kyoto; Phone: (075) 721-3131. A resort-type city hotel. A little isolated from the heart of the city (270 rooms).

Hotel New Kyoto ホテル・ニュー京都 (middle left, map 20)
Address: Horikawa-Marutamachi, Kamigyo-ku, Kyoto; Phone: (075) 801-2111. A deluxe business hotel with 242 rooms.

Kyoto Tower Hotel 京都タワーホテル (lower center, map 20)
Address: Karasuma-Shichijo-sagaru, Shimogyo-ku, Kyoto; Phone: (075) 361-3211. In the Kyoto Tower Building in front of Kyoto Station (148 rooms).

Business Hotels (less than 14,000 yen for a twin room)

Kyoto Dai-ni Tower Hotel 京都第二タワーホテル (lower center, map 20)
Address: Higashino-Toindori-Shichijo-sagaru, Shimogyo-ku, Kyoto; Phone: (075) 361-3261. An economy version of Kyoto Tower Hotel with 306 rooms.

Kyoto Dai-san Tower Hotel 京都第三タワーホテル (lower left, map 20)
Address: Shinmachidori-Shichijo-sagaru, Shimo-gyo-ku, Kyoto; Phone: (075) 343-3111. A third property in the Kyoto Tower Hotel Group with 122 rooms.

Hokke Club Kyoto 法華クラブ京都 (lower left, map 20)
Address: Shiokojidori-Muromachi-Higashi-iru, Shimogyo-ku, Kyoto; Phone: (075) 361-1251. A typical economical business hotel with 138 rooms.

RYOKANS
First-class Ryokans (20,000 yen and up per person with two meals)

Tawaraya Ryokan 俵屋旅館 (middle center, map 20)
 Address: Fuyacho-Anegakoji-agaru, Nakagyo-ku, Kyoto; Phone: (075) 211-5566. 19 rooms.

Hiiragiya Ryokan 柊屋旅館 (middle center, map 20)
 Address: Fuyacho-Anegakoji-agaru, Nakagyo-ku, Kyoto; Phone: (075) 211-1136. 33 rooms.

These two ryokans represent authentic Japanese-style VIP treatment. They offer deluxe facilities, provide superior service and are extremely expensive. The average rate is around 40,000 - 45,000 yen per person.

Yachiyo 八千代 (middle right, map 20)
 Address: 34, Nanzenji-Fukuchicho, Sakyo-ku, Kyoto; Phone: (075) 771-4148. 26 rooms.

Seikoro 晴鴨楼 (lower center, map 20)
 Address: Tonyamachidori-Gojo-sagaru, Higashi-yama-ku, Kyoto; Phone: (075) 561-0771. 24 rooms.

Sumiya Ryokan 炭屋旅館 (middle center, map 20)
 Address: Fuyachodori-Sanjo-sagaru, Nakagyo-ku, Kyoto; Phone: (075) 221-2188. 26 rooms.

Kaneiwaro Bekkan 金岩楼別館 (lower center, map 20)
 Address: Kiyamachidori-Matsubara-sagaru, Shimo-gyo-ku, Kyoto; Phone: (075) 351-5010. 23 rooms.

The above five are all authentic Japanese ryokans. Expensive but worth it for travelers eager to experience Japan's aristocratic life style.

Standard Ryokans (12,000 - 20,000 yen per person with two meals)

Yoshiima Ryokan 吉今旅館 (middle center, map 20)
 Address: Yamato-oji-Higashi-iru, Shinmonzen, Higashiyama-ku, Kyoto; Phone: (075) 561-2620. On a quiet, historical street in Gion (19 rooms).

Hiiragiya Bekkan 柊屋別館 (middle center, map 20)
 Address: Gokocho-Nijo-sagaru, Nakagyo-ku, Kyoto; Phone: (075) 231-0157. The economy version of Hiiragiya Ryokan (14 rooms).

Inexpensive Ryokans (less than 12,000 yen per person with two meals)

Hiraiwa Ryokan 平岩旅館 (lower center, map 20)
 Address: 314, Hayaocho, Kaminoguchi-agaru, Ninomiyadori, Shimogyo-ku, Kyoto; Phone: (075) 351-6748. A small 16-room minshuku-style inn.

Ryokan Kyoka 旅館京花 (lower center, map 20) (10 rooms)
 Address: Higashino-Toin-Higashi-iru, Shimo-Juzuyamachidori, Shimogyo-ku, Kyoto; Phone: (075) 371-2709.

Matsubaya Ryokan 松葉屋旅館 (lower center, map 20) (11 rooms)
 Address: Higashino-Toin-Nishi-iru, Kami-Juzuya-machi-dori, Shimogyo-ku, Kyoto; Phone: (075) 351-3727.

Shichijoso 七条荘 (lower center, map 20) (10 rooms)
 Address: Higashi-Futasujime-Minami-iru, Shichijo-Ohashi, Higashiyama-ku, Kyoto; Phone: (075) 541-7803.

Ryokan Hinomoto 旅館ひのもと (middle center, map 20) (6 rooms)
 Address: 375, Kotakecho, Kawaramachi-Matsubara-agaru, Shimogyo-ku, Kyoto; Phone: (075) 351-4563.

Mishima Shrine 宿坊三島神社 (lower right, map 20)
 Address: 539, Kamiumamachi, Higashi-oji-Higashi-iru, Higashiyama-ku, Kyoto; Phone: (075) 551-0033. A small 9-room lodging attached to a real shrine.

Gion Umemura ぎおん梅村 (middle center, map 20)
 Address: 102, Hakata, Shijo-Yamato-oji-sagaru, Higashiyama-ku, Kyoto; Phone: (075) 525-0156. A small 11-room property owned by a former Sumo wrestler.

Three Sisters' Inn 洛東荘 (middle right, map 20)
 Address: 81, Higashi-Furukawa, Okazaki, Sakyo-ku, Kyoto; Phone: (075) 761-6336. Rooms with private bath are available in the Annex.

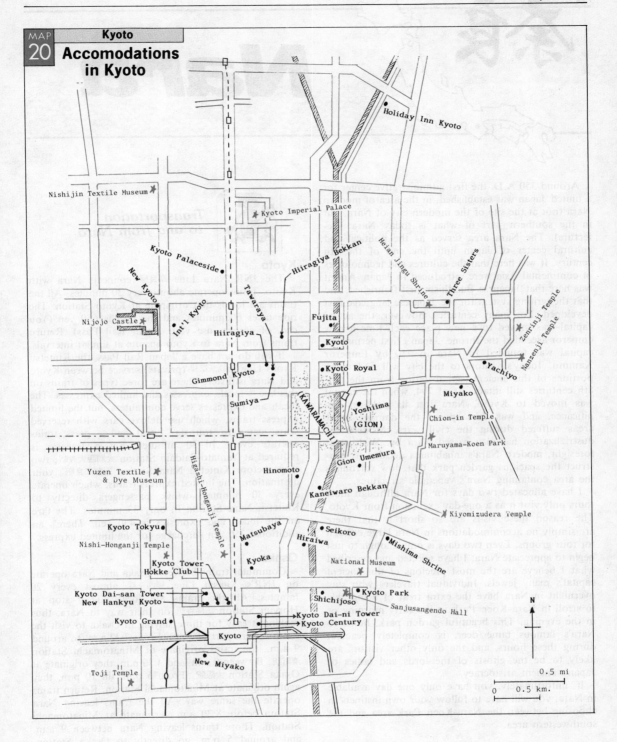

MAP
20

Kyoto
Accomodations
in Kyoto

Holiday Inn Kyoto

Nishijin Textile Museum

Kyoto Imperial Palace

Kyoto Palaceside

New Kyoto

Tawaraya

Hiiragiya Bekkan

Heian Jingu Shrine

Three Sisters

Zenrinji Temple

Nanzenji Temple

Int'l Kyoto

Nijojo Castle

Hiiragiya

Fujita

Kyoto

Yachiyo

Kyoto Royal

Gimmond Kyoto

Sumiya

Miyako

Chion-in Temple

Yoshiima
(GION)

(KAWARAMACHI)

Maruyama-Koen Park

Yuzen Textile
& Dye Museum

Hinomoto

Gion Umemura

Higashi-Honganji Temple

Kaneiwaro Bekkan

Kiyomizudera Temple

Kyoto Tokyu

Nishi-Honganji Temple

Matsubaya

Seikoro

Hiraiwa

Mishima Shrine

Kyoka

National Museum

Kyoto Tower
Hokke Club

Kyoto Dai-san Tower
New Hankyu Kyoto

Kyoto Park

Shichijoso

Sanjusangendo Hall

Kyoto Grand

Kyoto Dai-ni Tower
Kyoto Century

Kyoto

New Miyako

Toji Temple

N

0.5 mi

0   0.5 km.

Nara

Around 350 A.D. the first administrative center for a united Japan was established, in the area of modern Nara (not at the site of the modern city of Nara, but in the southern part of what is today Nara Prefecture). The Nara area served as the political and cultural center of Japan until the end of the 8th century. It was here that the cultures and technologies of continental Asia were introduced to Japan. And it was here that Japanese Buddhism first flourished, and that the writing system for the Japanese language first developed. For many centuries, however, the actual capital was moved to a new place each time a new emperor ascended the throne. Japan's first permanent capital was founded in Nara in 710 by Emperor Kammu. Today's visitors to the city will find many portions of this ancient capital dating from the 6th-8th centuries still intact. As of 794, when the capital was moved to Kyoto, Nara lost its political significance, and was thus spared the damage other areas suffered during the civil wars. Modern industrialization has also passed Nara by. With great foresight, modern Nara's inhabitants decided to construct the spacious garden park that now surrounds the area containing Nara's venerable structures.

I have allocated two days for Nara although most tours only visit it as a one-day excursion from Kyoto. The reason these visits are so short is that there are simply no accommodations in Nara large enough for tour groups. Even two days is only enough to just begin to appreciate Nara; I have selected and described what I believe are the most precious of this ancient capital's many jewels. Individual travelers who stay overnight in Nara have the extra treat of being able to stroll in Nara-Koen Park in the early morning or in the evening. This beautiful garden park, home to Nara's famous tame deer, is completely peaceful during these hours, and the only other visitors are likely to be the ghosts of the lords and ladies of Japan's ancient aristocracy.

If, unfortunately, you have only one day available in Nara, you will have to follow your own instincts in choosing between the Nara-Koen Park area and the southwestern area.

Transportation to and from Nara

Kyoto

The JNR Nara Line 奈良線 connects Nara with Kyoto. Trains operate about every 30 minutes. All the trains are locals that originate at Kyoto Station. The ride takes 60 minutes and the fare is 660 yen (You can, of course, use your Japan Rail Pass). Return trains from Nara to Kyoto operate at similar intervals.

If you do not have a Japan Rail Pass, the Kintetsu Kyoto Line 近鉄京都線 (private) service between Kyoto and Nara is faster. There are three types of trains on this line — locals, expresses and limited expresses. The locals and expresses serve commuters, but the limited express trains, which use deluxe cars with reserved seats, cater to tourists. Local and express trains operate every 10-30 minutes, but a transfer is required at Yamato-Saidaiji Station 大和西大寺駅, two stops before Kintetsu Nara Station 近鉄奈良駅, your destination. The limited express trains, which operate every 30 minutes, whisk passengers directly to Kintetsu Nara Station in only 33 minutes. The fare on the locals and expresses is 430 yen. There's an additional 350 yen surcharge for the limited express.

Osaka

Commuter trains between Osaka and Nara operate on JNR's Kansai Line 関西本線 almost every 20 minutes. All the trains are locals. They stop at Horyuji Station 法隆寺駅 on their way to Nara, thus making it easy for those staying in Osaka to visit the southwestern part of Nara. From 7:32 a.m. to around 9 a.m., the trains originate at Minatomachi Station 湊町駅. Between 9 a.m. and 4:30 p.m. they originate at Osaka Station 大阪駅. From 5 p.m. till 10 p.m. they again originate at Minatomachi Station. Return trains operate the same way. All the trains leaving Nara Station before 8:30 a.m. terminate at Minatomachi Station. Those trains leaving Nara between 9 a.m. and around 5 p.m. go directly to Osaka Station. After 5 p.m. all trains again terminate at Minatomachi Station. Because Minatomachi Station is within walking distance of the Midosuji Subway Line's Namba Station 難波駅, which serves Osaka Station (Umeda subway stop), the connection between them is quite easy (Refer to the Osaka Chapter for the locations of the stations). The ride between Minatomachi and Nara takes about 45 minutes, and the ride between Osaka and Nara takes about 50 minutes. The fare to Nara is 510 yen from Minatomachi, and 640 yen from Osaka.

The private Kintetsu Railways also operates a Kintetsu Nara Line 近鉄奈良線 between Kintetsu Namba Station 近鉄難波駅 in Osaka and Kintetsu Nara Station 近鉄奈良駅. As is the case with the Kintetsu trains from Kyoto, there are three types of trains: locals, expresses, and limited expresses. The limited express has deluxe cars with all reserved seating, and operates once every hour. The ride takes 31 minutes, and the fare is 760 yen (410 yen basic fare plus a 350 yen special charge). The express and local trains operate frequently, and take 10-20 minutes longer than the limited expresses (the fare is 410 yen).

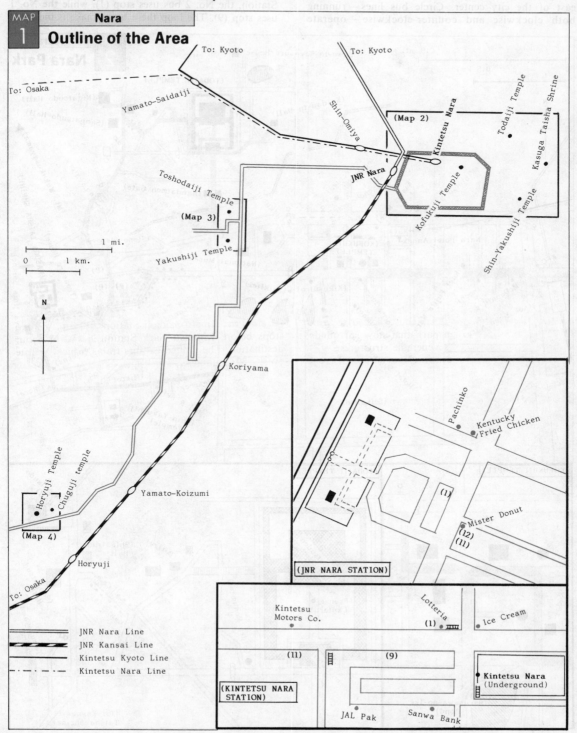

MAP 1

Nara

Outline of the Area

JNR Nara Line
JNR Kansai Line
Kintetsu Kyoto Line
Kintetsu Nara Line

Itinerary 1
The Nara-Koen Park
Area

As shown on map 1, famous sites such as Todaiji Temple and Kasuga Taisha Shrine are located to the east of the city center. Circle bus lines — running both clockwise and counter-clockwise — operate

frequently and are quite convenient for tourists. Recorded English announcements herald the next stop. The buses operate on a 110-yen flat fare system (pay upon boarding). The clockwise loop bus is Number 2, while the counter-clockwise loop is No. 1. At JNR Nara Sation, the No. 2 bus (clockwise) uses bus stop (1) (refer to map 1), and the No. 1 bus (counter-clockwise) uses stop (11). At Kintetsu Nara Station, the No. 2 bus uses stop (1), while the No. 1 uses stop (9). The loop these buses make is indicated

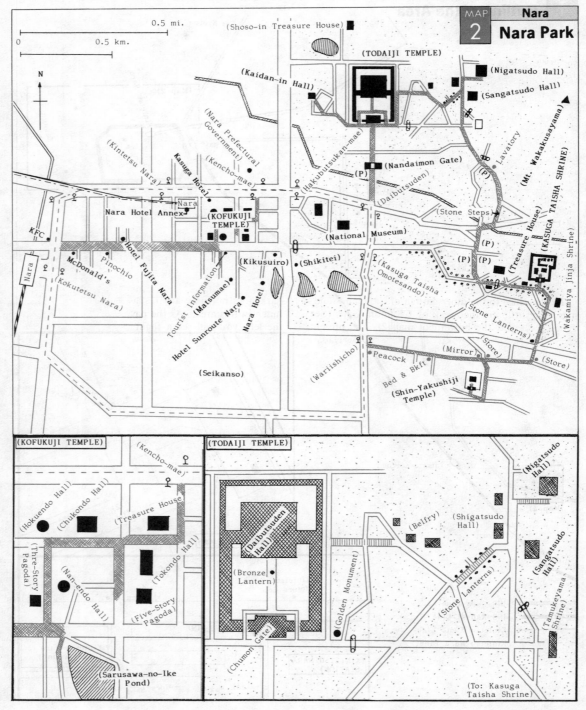

on map 1 with shaded red; on map 2 the bus loop is indicated with a red dotted line, and the names of major bus stops are also shown.

Todaiji Temple 東大寺 (upper center, map 2; detailed map at lower right on the same page)

Take the No. 2 bus to Daibutsuden stop (middle right, map 2). Todaiji Temple was originally constructed at the order of Emperor Shomu in 752. Though most tourists see only the statue of the Great Buddha in the main builiding, the wide temple precincts contain a number of buildings and sculptures of great historical and cultural significance. **Nandaimon Gate** 南大門 (National Treasure) is the main entrance to the temple. The Gate, reconstructed in 1199, is supported by 19 pillars, and is a good example of the Chinese architectural technology the Japanese imported in the 12th century. There are two 26-foot tall statues of guardians in niches on both sides of the gate. These two National Treasures, carved in 1203 by Unkei and Kaikei, are representative of the high artistic achievements of the Kamakura era.

Before entering the main building, visit **Kaidan-in Hall** 戒壇院 located to its west. In the medieval era Kaidan-in was the most important ceremonial Buddhist hall in all of Japan, and was the site of ordinations of new priests. The small building, reconstructed in 1732 after a fire, is particularly famous for the exquisite clay images of the Four Heavenly Guardians (National Treasures) that were produced in the 7th century and that stand at the four corners of the hall (8 a.m. to 4:30 p.m. Admission 200 yen).

The entrance to the inner garden of the main buildings is a little to the west of Chumon Gate (See detailed inset at the bottom of map 2). The present huge **Daibutsuden Hall** 大仏殿 (Hall of the Great Buddha, National Treasure) was constructed in 1708 after repeated fires. The Hall, 187 feet (57 m.) wide, 164 feet (50 m.) deep, and 157 feet (48 m.) tall, is the largest wooden structure in the world. However, the original, built in 752, was 1.5 times larger than the present Hall. In front of the Hall stands a 15-foot (4.5 m.) tall octagonal bronze lantern (National Treasure) which is noteworthy for its fine carvings of Heavenly Maidens. The image of the Great Buddha in the Daibutsuden Hall is the holiest object of Todaiji Temple. Completed in 752, the original was damaged several times by fire and earthquake. The present 53-foot (16 m.) tall statue was repaired quite extensively in 1692 (7:30 a.m. to 5:30 p.m. Admission 200 yen).

To the east of the main buildings, atop a flight of stone steps, there are several structures including the old Bath House and belfry (National Treasure). Further to the west in an elevated location are **Nigatsudo Hall** 二月堂 (February Hall), **Sangatsudo Hall** 三月堂 (March Hall), and **Shigatsudo Hall** 四月堂 (April Hall). The view of the city of Nara from the corridor of Nigatsudo Hall is not to be missed. Nigatsudo is also famous as the home of an elaborate fire festival held in early March. Sangatsudo Hall, built in the middle of the 8th century, is the oldest building in the Todaiji complex. It contains more than 10 statues produced in the 8th century (National Treasures) (8 a.m. to 5:30 p.m. Admission to Sangatsudo Hall is 200 yen).

Kasuga Taisha Shrine 春日大社 (middle right, map 2)

Passing Tamukeyama Jinja Shrine 手向山神社, walk to the south skirting the western foot of Mt. Wakakusayama 若草山 (1,115 feet, or 342 m.). The right side of the street is lined with souvenir shops and restaurants. Because the southern part of Nara-Koen Park does not have any restaurants, you should have lunch in this area. As the paved street curves toward the left, you will see a flight of stone steps on your right. Take this short cut down to the small stream at the bottom, and walk across Kasuga Taisha Shrine's wide parking lot —this will take only a minute. **The Treasure House** 春日大社宝物殿 of the Shrine, located at the southern end of the parking lot, is housed in a modern two-story concrete building. It displays the Shrine's treasures, which include Noh masks and equipment for Shinto ceremonies (Optional. 8:30 a.m. to 4:30 p.m. Admission 200 yen).

To the south of the Treasure House stands a torii gate, the formal entrance to Kasuga Taisha Shrine (As a matter of fact, this is the second of the Shrine's torii gates. The first is located far to the west, near the National Museum). Both sides of the approach to the Shrine are lined with stone lanterns of various sizes and shapes. Altogether there are about 3,000 lanterns along the approach. Twice a year, in early February and in the middle of August, all of them are lighted, creating a dreamy, yet solemn world. The small building located just in front of the torii gate is Kurumayadori House, where nobles' carriages were stored when they visited the Shrine. Through the torii gate, you come first to Tochakuden (Arrival Hall), then to Minamimon Gate, entrance to the main buildings of Kasuga Taisha Shrine. Covered red and green corridors extend in two different directions from the gate, and surround the major buildings of the Shrine. The Shrine was originally erected in 710, and its buildings were reconstructed periodically ac-

Todaiji Temple's Great Buddha.

cording to Shinto tradition, which requires that places of worship be pulled down and then completely rebuilt at regular intervals (usually every 20 years). The spacious grounds of the Shrine are inside Minamimon Gate. Several of the natural wood buildings, including Heiden Hall (Offering Hall) and Naoraiden (Entertainment Hall), are used for various Shinto ceremonies. Behind Chumon Gate (Middle Gate) are four Honden Halls (Main Shrines), each in the same architectural style and each a National Treasure. They were last rebuilt in 1893, supposedly for the 56th time (8:30 a.m. to 4 p.m. Admission 500 yen).

Shin-Yakushiji Temple (lower right, map 2), or Nara National Museum (middle center, map 2)

You may not have enough time to cover both of these. If you would like to see relics of the past in their original setting, you should visit Shin-Yakushiji Temple. If you are interested in seeing a greater number of ancient objects, you should go to Nara National Museum. If it is Monday you have no choice, because the Museum is closed. If you are lucky enough to be in Nara at the end of October and beginning of November, you should definitely visit the Museum because that is the one time of the year that the treasures of Todaiji Temple (kept in Shosoin House) are displayed.

Shin-Yakushiji Temple 新薬師寺

After you pass Wakamiya Jinja Shrine 若宮神社, the narrow path enters a refreshing and romantic thick forest. Crossing a wider street, you'll come to a T-shaped intersection, where you should turn right (Refer to map 2). The traffic mirror and the small store are good landmarks to help you find the street that leads to Shin-Yakushiji Temple.

Shin-Yakushiji Temple was originally erected in the middle of the 8th century at the order of Empress Komyo, as a thanks offering for the recovery of Emperor Shomu from a serious disease. Only the original Dining Hall (the present Main Hall, National Treasure) has been preserved; the other buildings were destroyed by fire and typhoon and were reconstructed after the 13th century. At the center of the dark Main Hall sits the image of Yakushi-Nyorai (God of Medicine, National Treasure), which is surrounded by clay images of Twelve Divine Generals. Eleven of the 12 originals remain, and are National Treasures. They are especially famous for their powerful, dynamic expressions (8:30 a.m. to 5:30 p.m. Admission 300 yen).

Your next destination is Kofukuji Temple (middle center, map 2). Walk west to Wariishicho bus stop, and take the north-bound No. 1 bus to Kencho-mae stop 県庁前.

Nara National Museum 奈良国立博物館

If you're going to the Museum you should go back to Kasuga Taisha Shrine's torii gate and walk further to the west, past the stone lanterns and the spacious grass fields of Nara-Koen Park.

The Museum consists of two buildings. The Main Hall, patterned on a traditional Japanese architectural style, has a display of Buddhist images that illustrates how ideas of divine beings changed over the centuries. The Western-style annex displays archeological relics, most of which were found in old tombs (9 a.m. to 4:30 p.m. Admission 250 yen. Closed on Mondays).

The next and the last visit of the day is Kofukuji Temple, which is just across the wide street.

Kofukuji Temple 興福寺 (middle center, map 2; detailed map at lower left on the same page)

Kofukuji Temple was constructed in the early 700's by Fuhito Fujiwara, a leading aristocrat of the time. Patronized by emperors, the temple has enjoyed incomparable prosperity throughout its history. The precincts were once filled with 175 buildings, all of which were destroyed by fire. The present buildings, much smaller in scale than the originals, were built after the 13th century. The five-story pagoda (National Treasure) is the second highest pagoda (164 feet or 50 m.) in Japan (the tallest is the Toji Temple's pagoda in Kyoto). The present pagoda was built in 1426 as an exact replica of the 730 original. The Tokondo Hall (National Treasure) was rebuilt in 1415 from the plans of the 726 original. The Treasure House is a concrete building that houses more than 20 statues that are National Treasures along with many other fine objets d'art of the temple. Hokuendo and Nan-endo Halls are octagonal buildings constructed in the 13th and 18th centuries respectively. The three-story pagoda (National Treasure) was erected in 1143. Because of its graceful shape many consider it one of the best in Japan (Entrance to the precincts is free of charge. Admission to the Treasure House is 400 yen. Open 9 a.m. to 5 p.m.).

Sarusawa-no-Ike Pond 猿沢池

Before walking back to either the JNR Nara or Kintetsu Nara Station, visit this pond south of Kofukuji Temple. With the five-story pagoda in the background the pond is an especially lovely, not-to-be-missed camera shot.

Itinerary 2
The Southwestern Part
of Nara

As shown on map 1, four major temples, Toshodaiji Temple, Yakushiji Temple, Chuguji Temple and Horyuji Temple, are located in this area. The No. 52 bus conveniently connects these four historical sites, originating at Kintetsu Nara Station, and stopping at the JNR Station, Toshodaiji Temple, Yakushiji Temple and Horyuji Temple (last stop). The bus then turns around and follows the same route in reverse back to the Kintetsu station. The No. 63 bus also provides service to Toshodaiji Temple. At Kintetsu Nara Station, both of these buses use stop (11) (lower right, map 1) and at JNR Nara Station they use stop (12) (middle right, map 1). The ride to Toshodaiji Temple, your first stop of the day, takes 17 minutes and the fare is 160 yen. (The buses have recorded English announcements). Take a numbered ticket upon boarding and put the fare and your ticket in the box near the driver when you get off.

Toshodaiji Temple 唐招提寺 (middle center, map 3)

The No. 52 bus stop is on the main street, only 0.2 miles (0.3 km.) from the South Gate of Toshodaiji Temple. The No. 63 bus stops right in front of the Gate.

Toshodaiji Temple was erected by the Chinese priest Ganjin in 759, who visited Japan at the invitation of Emperor Shomu. Ganjin was 66 when he finally arrived in Japan, twelve years after the invitation was issued. His attempts to reach Japan from the continent were thwarted by political interference by Chinese officials, five shipwrecks, and various diseases, one of which left him blind. Despite these difficulties Ganjin fulfilled the imperial commission and supervised the construction of this magnificent temple.

Toshodaiji Temple, unlike most other temples, has suffered no fires or other accidents; its original buildings still stand. Kondo Hall (Main Hall, National Treasure) contains a 10-foot tall image of Sakya (National Treasure) as its main object of worship. The image of Sakya is flanked by statues of his disciples, and all of them are protected by the Four Heavenly Generals (National Treasures) whose statues stand in the four corners of the Hall. The eight pillars at the front of Kondo Hall are entastic (i.e., they balloon almost imperceptibly). This borrowing from Greek architecture testifies to the fact that cultural exchange via the "Silk Road" had an impact even in Nara as early as the 8th century. Behind Kondo Hall is Kodo Hall (Lecture Hall, National Treasure) which was moved from Nara Imperial Palace in celebration of Ganjin's completion of the temple. Since Nara Imperial Palace was completely destroyed in a later era, this Kodo Hall is the only relic we have today of palace architecture of the Nara era. A graceful atmosphere pervades the precincts. (8:30 a.m. to 4 p.m. Admission 300 yen). The Treasure House is open to the public from March 20 to May 19 in the spring, and from September 15 to November 5 in the fall (200 yen).

Yakushiji Temple 薬師寺 (lower center, map 3)

The street connecting Toshodaiji and Yakushiji Temples is popularly called the "Path of History" because emperors and nobles used this path when they visited these two important temples.

Yakushiji Temple was originally erected in the Asuka district (further to the south) by Emperor Temmu in 680, and was moved to its present location in 718. The gorgeous buildings of Yakushiji were called "Heavenly Palace," and the temple enjoyed the patronage of successive emperors. Unfortunately, all of the buildings except East Tower, a three-story

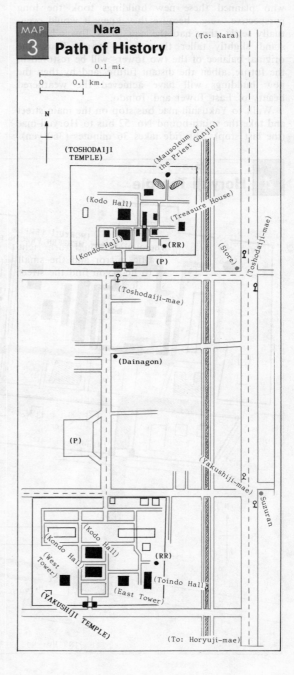

pagoda constructed in 730, were destroyed by fires and earthquakes. The 112-foot (34 m.) tall East Tower pagoda looks like it has six stories because of the three decorative roofs placed between the real ones. The balanced beauty of East Tower has been described as "frozen music." Toindo Hall was built in the Kamakura Era (the 13th century) and houses a Kannon statue crafted in the 7th century (National Treasure). Kondo Hall was rebuilt in 1976, and a reconstruction of West Tower was completed in 1981, as part of a very controversial project. These two replicas of the originals are painted vermilion red and seem glaringly out of place set as they are against the subdued elegance of the other buildings. But those who planned these new buildings took the long perspective — e.g., because they knew it would eventually settle, they had the new West Tower built to stand slightly taller than East Tower. Thus, the original balance of the two towers will be restored in the future, albeit the distant future, and by then the new buildings will have achieved the weathered beauty of East Tower and Toindo.

Walk to Yakushiji-mae bus stop on the main street and take the south-bound No. 52 bus to Horyuji-mae (the last stop). The ride takes 36 minutes (360 yen).

Ashura - a guardian of Buddhism.

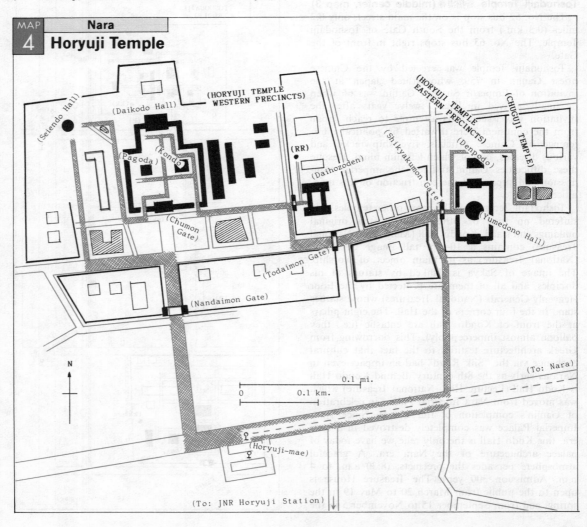

Horyuji Temple 法隆寺 (map 4)

If you travel to Nara from Osaka, Horyuji should be your first destination in Nara. Horyuji train station is located to the south of the Temple (outside map 4). It is about a 15-minute walk. If you start at Horyuji, Chuguji Temple should be your next destination, and you should then take the No. 52 bus to Yakushiji-mae, so that you can continue your day with visits to Yakushiji and Toshodaiji Temples. You should then take either the No. 52 or No. 63 bus to JNR Nara Station and take the train back to Osaka.

Because of its isolated location, foreign tourists often skip Horyuji. This is a mistake. In light of its historical importance and the number of treasures exhibited there, Horyuji Temple should be given great, if not top, priority in the Nara area.

Pine trees flank the main approach to the temple which was originally erected in 607 by Prince Shotoku, the promulgator of the first Japanese constitution. The original structures were destroyed by fire in 670, but the present buildings of the Western Precincts were reconstructed immediately, at the end of the 7th century. They are possibly the oldest wooden structures in the world. The buildings in the Eastern Precincts were built sometime later, around 739. All the buildings of Horyuji are National Treasures. If time permits, visit the octagonal **Seiendo Hall** 西円堂 (upper left, map 4), which houses many important images and statues. On both sides of Chumon Gate are images of Deva Kings which were sculpted in 711. Inside the Gate is the main part of Horyuji Temple. At your right is Kondo Hall (Main Hall). At your left is a five-story pagoda (112 feet, or 34 m. tall), with roofs that decrease in size toward the top; the pagoda projects an ethereal yet stable image. Inside the pagoda are 95 images clustered in four groups. The varied faces of these images reflect the artistic realism of the era. There are several other old buildings to the east of the corridors. At the eastern end of the Western Precincts is **Daihozoden** 大宝蔵殿 (Great Treasure House). This concrete building preserves hundreds of temple treasures, including images, statues, carvings and metalwork from the 7th and 8th centuries. If you also find time to visit the Gallery of Horyuji Treasures at Tokyo National Museum, you will have seen the most splendid art works of ancient times that Japan has to offer. Leave the Western Precincts through Todaimon Gate and walk east to the end of the wide lane, where Shikyakumon Gate (a typical four-legged gate), the entrance to the Eastern Precincts of Horyuji Temple, is located. The main hall of this part of Horyuji is **Yumedono Hall** 夢殿 (National Treasure), an octagonal building constructed in 739. Yumedono Hall is surrounded by covered corridors. Dempodo Mansion, located to the north of the corridors, is representative of mansion architecture for the nobles of the 8th century (National Treasure). Horyuji Temple is open to the public from 8 a.m. to 5 p.m. (till 4:30 p.m. in winter). Admission is 400 yen.

Chuguji Temple 中宮寺

Chuguji Temple is adjacent to the northeastern corner of the Eastern Precincts of Horyuji Temple. It has the quiet neatness of a nunnery, and is especially famous for its wooden statue of Miroku-Bosatsu (National Treasure), whose soft and tender features have been pronounced the consummate expression of mercy. It is said that her face changes delicately with changes in temperature or humidity (9 a.m. to 4:15 p.m. Until 3:45 p.m. in winter. Admission 300 yen).

Back to Nara City

Take the north-bound No. 52 bus from Horyuji-mae stop to either JNR Nara 奈良駅 or Kintetsu Nara Station 近鉄奈良駅. The ride takes 51 minutes to the former and 54 minutes to the latter. The fare is 480 yen. If you have a Japan Rail Pass, you can walk south from Horyuji-mae bus stop for about 10 minutes, to JNR Horyuji Station 法隆寺駅. From there you can catch the JNR Kansai Line to Nara. Trains run every 30 minutes, and the ride takes only 12 minutes. The fare, for those who don't have Rail Passes, is 180 yen.

Places for Lunch

Dainagon Restaurant (middle center, map 3) is located between Toshodaiji and Yakushiji. Katsudon (fried pork cutlet on a bowl of rice) is 700 yen and curry rice is 500 yen. There are also several restaurants near Horyuji-mae bus stop and along the main approach to Horyuji Temple, which serve similar simple lunches.

Good-Will Guides in Nara

Nara has two organizations that provide foreign tourists with free guides. The main purposes of both organizations are to promote international friendship and to give the volunteers opportunities to speak with native speakers of English.

Nara Student Guide was established with the support of the municipal government. Advance reservations can be made at (0742) 26-4753 (10 a.m. to 4 p.m.).

Nara YMCA suggests at least a one-day advance reservation at (0742) 44-2207.

Major Festivals in Nara

January 15: Grass Burning Festival at Mt. Wakakusayama in Nara-Koen Park. Fires are set at 6 p.m. Todaiji and Kofukuji Temples, silhouetted against the fire, create a spectacular image.

February 2 or 3 (on the day of Bean Scattering Festival): Mantoro Festival at Kasuga Taisha Shrine. About 3,000 lanterns are lit and create a magical, solemn atmosphere.

March 1-14: Shunie Festival at Nigatsudo Hall of Todaiji Temple. A fire festival every night, with the biggest one on the 12th.

May 2: Shomu-Tenno-sai (Festival for Emperor Shomu) at Todaiji Temple. The festival is designed to honor the founder of the Temple of the Great Buddha. A colorful parade in traditional costumes is held in the afternoon.

May 11-12: Takigi Noh (Open-air performances of Noh) at Kofukuji Temple. Firelight Noh performances by masters of Japan's four major Noh schools (from 4 p.m.).

August 14-15: Mantoro Festival at Kasuga Taisha Shrine. The second time during the year that the lanterns are lit.

August 15: Daimonji-Okuribi Festival or Great Bonfire Festival. A spectacular bonfire in the shape of the character for "big" is lighted at 8 p.m. on Mt. Koenzan, not far from the city.

September 15: Shiba-Noh. A firelight Noh performance on the grass meadow of Nara-Koen Park (from 5:30 p.m.).

December 17: Kasuga-Wakamiya-Onmatsuri (Great Festival of Wakamiya Jinja Shrine). A large procession with all participants dressed in traditional costumes.

Accommodations

HOTELS

First-class Hotels (20,000 yen and up for a twin room)

Hotel Fujita Nara ホテル・フジタ奈良 (middle left, map 2)
 Address: 47-1, Sanjomachi, Nara; Phone: (0742) 23-8111. A recently opened modern hotel with 120 rooms.

Nara Hotel 奈良ホテル (middle center, map 2)
 Address: Nara-Koen-nai, Nara; Phone: (0742) 26-3300. A 70-year old establishment. Sixty-seven Western-style rooms are contained in an authentic Japanese-style structure.

Standard Hotel (14,000 - 20,000 yen for a twin room; Higher rates are applicable on weekends)

Nara Hotel Annex 奈良ホテル別館 (middle center, map 2)
 Address: Nara-Kintetsu Bldg., 6F, Nara; Phone: (0742) 26-3101. A "standard" version of Nara Hotel. Thirty-four rooms located on the 6th through 8th floors of Kintetsu Nara Station.

Business Hotel (less than 14,000 yen for a twin room)

Hotel Sunroute Nara ホテル・サンルート奈良 (middle center, map 2)
 Address: 1110, Takahatacho, Nara; Phone: (0742) 22-5151. A convenient location for sightseeing in Nara-Koen Park (95 rooms).

RYOKANS

First-class Ryokans (20,000 yen and up per person with two meals)

Kikusuiro 菊水楼 (middle center, map 2)
 Address: 1130, Takahata Bodaimachi, Nara; Phone: (0742) 23-2001. The most deluxe property in Nara. Famous for its interior decorations and for its garden (17 rooms).

Shikitei 四季亭 (middle center, map 2)
 Address: 1163, Takahatacho, Nara; Phone: (0742) 22-5531. Another authentic ryokan located in Nara-Koen Park (18 rooms).

Standard Ryokan (12,000 - 20,000 yen per person with two meals)

Kasuga Hotel 春日ホテル (middle center, map 2)
 Address: 40, Noboriojimachi, Nara; Phone: (0742) 22-4031. A modern ryokan with 20 Japanese rooms, 7 Western rooms and 16 combination suites.

Inexpensive Ryokans (less than 12,000 yen per person with two meals)

Seikanso 静観荘 (lower center, map 2)
 Address: 29, Higashi-Kitsujicho, Nara; Phone: (0742) 22-2670. A small family operated property (12 rooms).

Matsumae 松前 (middle center, map 2)
 Address: 28-1, Higashi-Terabayashicho, Nara; Phone: (0742) 22-3686. A small, 12-room ryokan near Kofukuji Temple.

大阪 Osaka

At the dawn of Japanese history, when Japan was divided into many small "nations," powerful clans were based in the Osaka area; it was these fiefdoms that later formed the core of the unified nation. Osaka was once the capital of Japan for a short period in the 7th century, but when a permanent capital was established first in Nara, and then in Kyoto, Osaka disappeared from the political scene. Osaka's modern prosperity as a merchant city began at the end of the 16th century when Hideyoshi Toyotomi built Japan's largest castle here. During the Edo period (1603—1868), Osaka prospered as a distribution center. The local fuedal lords sent the products of their territories, mainly rice, to Osaka, where the merchants arranged distribution to Edo and other large cities. The city was administered directly by the Tokugawa Shogunate, and was called the "Kitchen of Japan." Although its population of 2,548,000 makes it the country's third largest city (Yokohama is marginally larger), Osaka, a confident, bustling industrial and commercial center, is clearly Japan's "Second City."

Outline of the City

The city of Osaka has 26 wards and is spread over a wide area, but all the main municipal and business areas are clustered inside and immediately outside the JNR Osaka Kanjo (Loop) Line. As pictured in the upper right corner of map 2, the area of central Osaka is about half the size of the central area of Tokyo. There are two major shopping and eating districts in Osaka. One is called "Kita" (North) (but is located to the south of Osaka Station, at middle center, map 1); it is an area of newly constructed modern buildings and extensive underground shopping centers. The other is called both "Minami" (South) and "Shinsaibashi," and is located right in the center of the JNR loop (lower center, map 1). Shinsaibashi is a fashionable shopping quarter, while Minami is famous for its inexpensive eating and drinking facilities and theaters. Public institutions such as Osaka City Hall, the Prefectural Library, the Bank of Japan, Osaka Festival Hall and Toyo Toji Museum (Oriental Pottery Museum) are located on Nakanoshima island. Major business offices are located in the Osaka Station area and along the Midosuji subway line (indicated with red double dotted lines on map 1). Osaka's two major historical sites are Osakajo Castle (middle right, map 1) and Shitennoji Temple (lower right, map 1). Osaka International Fair Grounds, where most large trade shows are held, are located just outside the JNR loop (lower left, map 1).

Transportation

Transportation to and from Osaka

Osaka is connected with other major cities, such as Tokyo, Nagoya, Hiroshima and Fukuoka, by the Shinkansen. The Shinkansen Station in Osaka is called Shin-Osaka 新大阪駅 (New Osaka) and is located about 2 miles (3 km.) to the north of Osaka Station 大阪駅 (upper center, map 2). Details on the Shinkansen are in the Transportation within Japan Chapter.

As outlined in the Kansai Chapter above, JNR commuter trains and private railways conveniently connect Osaka with Kyoto, Kobe, Nara and Koyasan, major places of interest in the Kansai region, as follows:

Between Osaka and Kyoto

The JNR's blue colored commuter train, the Tokaido-Sanyo Line 東海道・山陽本線, which runs between Kyoto and Nishi-Akashi, stops at Shin-Osaka and Osaka Stations. Trains operate every five to 15 minutes. Some trains terminate at intermediate stations (If that happens, just take the next train in the same direction). The fare between Kyoto and Osaka is 560 yen one way.

The Hankyu Kyoto Line 阪急京都駅 (private) operates three types of commuter trains—a limited express, an express and a local—between Kawaramachi 河原町 in Kyoto and Umeda 阪急梅田 in Osaka. The exact location of Kawaramachi Station is on Kyoto maps 4 and 6, and that of Umeda Station is on Osaka map 5. Each type of train operates every 15-40 minutes. The ride takes 38 minutes on a limited express, 44 minutes on an express, and 72 minutes on a local. The fare is 300 yen for all three.

Those with Japan Rail Passes can use the Shinkansen even for the short distance between Kyoto and Osaka. Regular travelers shouldn't take the Shinkansen because the short trip costs 1,310 yen. The Shinkansens operate every five to 15 minutes, and the ride between Kyoto and Shin-Osaka takes only 17 minutes.

Between Osaka and Nara

Refer to the Nara Chapter above.

Between Osaka and Kobe

Refer to the Kobe and Mt. Rokkosan Chapter below.

Between Osaka and Koyasan

Refer to the Koyasan Chapter below.

Transportation in Osaka
Subways

I have selected five of Osaka's lines (the sixth is of no use for tourists), and indicated them with red lines on map 2. You will probably use only the **Midosuji** subway line 地下鉄御堂筋線 (indicated with double dotted lines), which connects Shin-Osaka Station, Umeda Station (near JNR's Osaka Station), Shinsaibashi, Namba and Tennoji, Osaka's most important stations, all of which are pictured on map 2. The

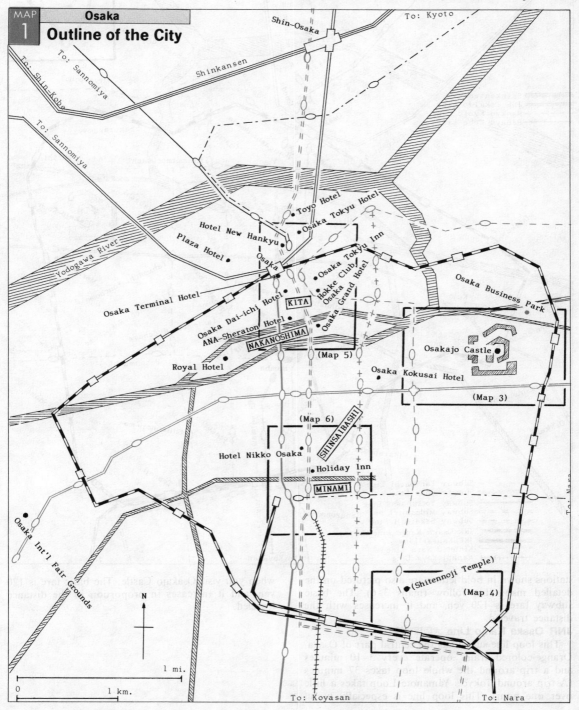

MAP 1

Osaka
Outline of the City

To: Kyoto

Shin-Osaka

To: Sannomiya

To: Shin-Kobe

To: Sannomiya

Shinkansen

Toyo Hotel

Osaka Tokyu Hotel

Hotel New Hankyu

Osaka Tokyu Inn

Plaza Hotel

Osaka

Yodogawa River

Osaka Business Park

Osaka Terminal Hotel

Osaka Tokyu Club

Osaka Dai-ichi Hotel

KITA

Hokke Club

Osaka Grand Hotel

ANA-Sheraton Hotel

NAKANOSHIMA

(Map 5)

Osakajo Castle

Royal Hotel

Osaka Kokusai Hotel

(Map 3)

(Map 6)

SHINSAIBASHI

Hotel Nikko Osaka

Holiday Inn

MINAMI

(Shitennoji Temple)

(Map 4)

Osaka Int'l Fair Grounds

N

To: Nara

1 mi.

0   1 km.

To: Koyasan   To: Nara

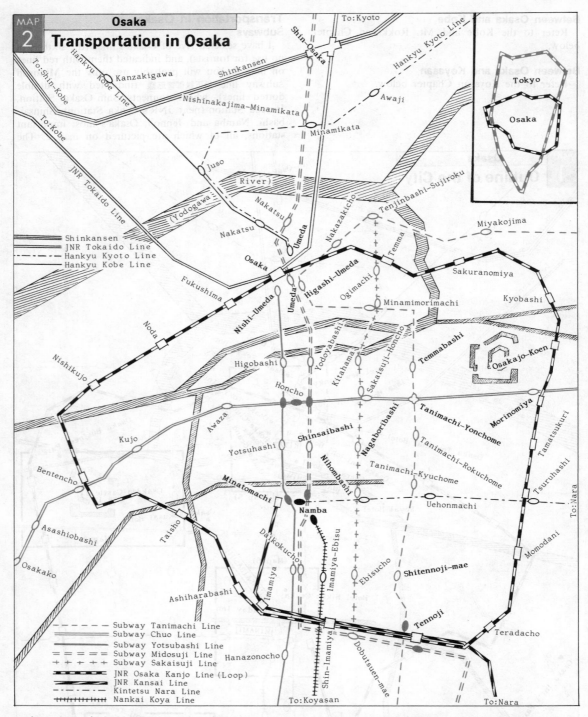

MAP 2 Osaka
Transportation in Osaka

Legend (map):
- Shinkansen
- JNR Tokaido Line
- Hankyu Kyoto Line
- Hankyu Kobe Line

- Subway Tanimachi Line
- Subway Chuo Line
- Subway Yotsubashi Line
- Subway Midosuji Line
- Subway Sakaisuji Line
- JNR Osaka Kanjo Line (Loop)
- JNR Kansai Line
- Kintetsu Nara Line
- Nankai Koya Line

stations shown in bold letters are also pictured on the detailed maps that follow (maps 3-6). The basic subway fare is 120 yen, and it increases with the distance traveled.

JNR Osaka Kanjo Line 大阪環状線

This loop line surrounds the central part of Osaka. Orange-colored trains operate every 3-10 minutes and a trip around the whole loop takes 37 minutes (A trip around Tokyo's Yamanote Loop takes a little over one hour). This loop line is especially useful when you visit Osakajo Castle. The basic fare is 120 yen, and it increases in proportion to the distance traveled.

Places of Interest

If you are a tourist traveling in Japan for just two to three weeks, a half-day is a reasonable amount of time to allocate for sightseeing in Osaka. If you spend a half-day in Osaka, I recommend that you visit Osakajo Castle in the afternoon and spend the evening in the Shinsaibashi and Minami area. If you are staying for several days in Osaka on business or for some other reason, you may be able to cover the other areas introduced in this chapter.

Osakajo Castle 大阪城 (map 3)

Take the JNR Osaka Kanjo (Loop) Line to Morinomiya Station 森ノ宮駅, or the Tanimachi subway line to Temmabashi Station 天満橋駅, or the Chuo subway line to Tanimachi-Yonchome Station 谷町四丁目駅. Otemon Gate (middle center, map 3) is the main entrance to the Castle and a 10-15 minute walk from any of the above stations.

Osakajo Castle was built in 1585 at the order of Hideyoshi Toyotomi. Even though the modern reconstruction is on a smaller scale than the grand original, the Castle still symbolizes the power Hideyoshi gained by means of his victories over the other feudal lords during the civil wars. After the death of Hideyoshi in 1598, Ieyasu Tokugawa seized political power. With the establishment of the Tokugawa Shogunate in Edo (modern Tokyo), the Toyotomi family realm was reduced to just the immediate Osaka area. Underground movements, however, worked to overthrow the Tokugawas and restore the Toyotomis. To crush these would-be rebels, Ieyasu's troops opened fire on Osakajo Castle

in 1614. The Toyotomis and their allies were destroyed in the battle, and the Castle was burned down in 1615.

The present donjon (130 feet or 40 m. tall), reconstructed in 1931, is a replica of the original. The top of the five-roofed eight-story donjon commands an extensive view of the city and its vicinity. Especially fascinating are the Castle's huge rock walls. At the order of the Tokugawa government the feudal lords of western Japan donated them when the Castle was repaired after the 1615 war. Hokoku Jinja Shrine, which is dedicated to the Toyotomi family, was moved to its present location in 1903 to honor the founder of the Castle. The donjon is open to the public from 9 a.m. to 4:30 p.m. Admission is 300 yen.

Osakajo Castle.

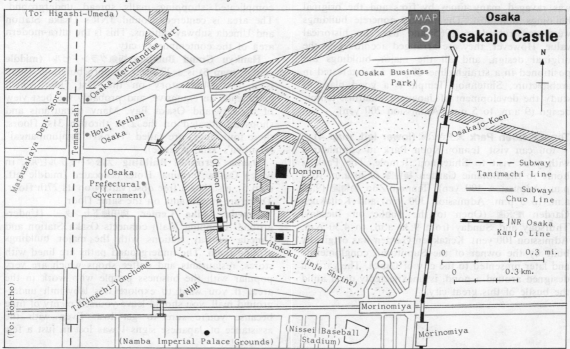

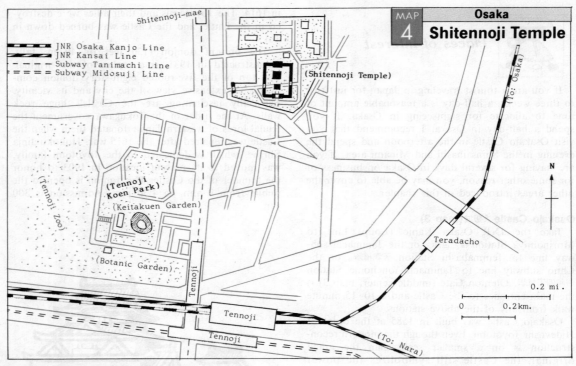

MAP
4

Osaka
Shitennoji Temple

JNR Osaka Kanjo Line
JNR Kansai Line
Subway Tanimachi Line
Subway Midosuji Line

Shitennoji-mae

(Shitennoji Temple)

(Tennoji Koen Park)

(Keitakuen Garden)

(Tennoji Zoo)

(Botanic Garden)

Tennoji

Tennoji

Tennoji

Teradacho

(To: Osaka)

(To: Nara)

N

0.2 mi.

0   0.2km.

Shitennoji Temple 四天王寺 (map 4)

Shitennoji Temple is a five minute walk from Shitennoji-mae Station 四天王寺前駅 on the Tanimachi subway line, and a 15 minute walk from the Tennoji Station 天王寺駅 of either the JNR Osaka Kanjo (Loop) Line or the Midosuji subway line.

Shitennoji Temple was originally erected in 593 at the order of Prince Shotoku, who later, in 607, had Horyuji Temple in Nara built. Shitennoji is known as the birthplace of Japanese Buddhism. The Temple was ravaged many times by fires and the original buildings were lost. The present concrete buildings were constructed in 1965 and have no historical value. However, they are arranged according to the original design, and all the major buildings are positioned in a straight line. If you are interested in architecture, Shitennoji Temple is a good place to study the development of Japanese Buddhist temple design (9 a.m. to 5 p.m. Admission 200 yen).

Tennoji-Koen Park 天王寺公園 (lower left, map 4)

You can visit Tennoji-Koen Park in conjunction with your visit to Shitennoji Temple. The Park is home to the Botanic Garden 植物園 (9:30 a.m. to 5 p.m. Admission 100 yen), Tennoji Zoo 動物園 (9:30 a.m. to 5 p.m. Admission 300 yen) and Keitakuen Garden 慶沢園 (Open to the public on Tuesday, Thursday and Sunday from 9:30 a.m. to 4:30 p.m. Admission 100 yen). Keitakuen Garden was originally built by the owner of the Sumitomo conglomerate and later presented to the city of Osaka. The garden, designed around a pond, is unexpectedly quiet amid the bustle of this great city.

Kita and Nakanoshima

The northern part of the city, called "Kita," has tall concrete buildings rising into the sky, and complicated shopping malls spread underground. The area is centered around JNR's Osaka Station and Umeda subway stations. This is the ultra-modern area of the contemporary city.

Hankyu Grand Building 阪急グランドビル **(middle center, map 5)** is a 32-story modern building. There is a free observatory on the 31st floor which commands an extensive, and probably the best view of the city and Osaka Bay. Many restaurants and shops are located on the 27th through 31st floors; these four floors are called "Hankyu Sanjunibangai" (Hankyu's 32nd Avenue).

Osaka Terminal Building 大阪ターミナルビル , in which Osaka Terminal Hotel is located (middle left, map 5), also has a free observatory on its 27th floor. There are restaurants on the same floor.

Umeda Chika Center 梅田地下センター (Underground Shopping Mall) connects Osaka Station and Umeda subway stations with the major buildings around them. The underground paths are lined with stores, restaurants and coffee shops which are very popular with the business people who work in the area. If you want to explore this labyrinth underground mall, you should leave yourself plenty of time because you're sure to get lost. Even with the assistance of Japanese signs I was lost in just a few minutes!

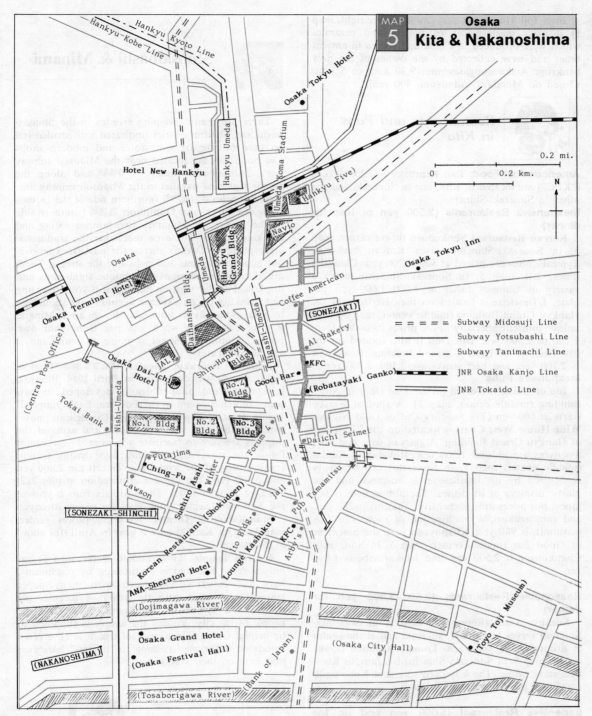

MAP
5

Osaka
Kita & Nakanoshima

0.2 mi.

0   0.2 km.

N

Hankyu Kyoto Line

Hankyu-Kobe Line

Osaka Tokyu Hotel

Hotel New Hankyu

Hankyu Umeda

Umeda Koma Stadium

Hankyu Five)

Navio

Hankyu Grand Bldg.

Osaka

Osaka Tokyu Inn

Osaka Terminal Hotel

Umeda

Daihanshin Bldg.

Coffee American

(SONEZAKI)

Al Bakery

(Central Post Office)

Higashi-Umeda

JAL

Osaka Dai-ichi Hotel

Shin-Hankyu Bldg.

KFC

No. 4 Bldg.

Good Bar

(Robatayaki Ganko)

Tokai Bank

Nishi-Umeda

No. 1 Bldg.

No. 2 Bldg.

No. 3 Bldg.

Forum 4

Daiichi Seimei

Futajima

Ching-Fu

Wihler

Lawson

Suehiro Asahi

Korean Restaurant (Shokudoen)

Jail

(SONEZAKI-SHINCHI)

Ito Bldg.

Lounge Kashuku

KFC

Arby's

Pub Tamamitsu

ANA-Sheraton Hotel

(Dojimagawa River)

(NAKANOSHIMA)

Osaka Grand Hotel

(Osaka Festival Hall)

(Bank of Japan)

(Osaka City Hall)

(Toyo Toji Museum)

(Tosaborigawa River)

===== Subway Midosuji Line

──── Subway Yotsubashi Line

----- Subway Tanimachi Line

▬▬▬ JNR Osaka Kanjo Line

════ JNR Tokaido Line

There are four new office buildings south of Osaka Station. They are numbered No. 1 through No. 4. The 32nd through 34th floors of **No. 3 Building** 駅前第3ビル house restaurants that command a good view of the city.

There are two eating and drinking districts in Kita. **Sonezaki** 曽根崎 (southeast of Osaka Station) still contains a number of inexpensive eating and drinking establishments as well as many obscure cabarets. An arcade runs through the center of Sonezaki. **Sonezaki-**

Shinchi 曽根崎新地 (south of Osaka Station) has many first-class (and generally expensive) bars and restaurants. You will find business people drinking with their colleagues in the Sonezaki district, while business people entertaining guests on expense accounts can be found in the Sonezaki-Shinchi district.

Osaka Festival Hall 大阪フェスティバル・ホール **(lower left, map 5)** is the most prestigious concert hall in Osaka. Many concerts by both Japanese and foreign artists are held here year round.

Toyo Toji Museum 東洋陶磁美術館 **(lower right, map 5)** displays masterpieces of pottery and ceramics which were produced in China and Korea in ancient times and were collected by the owner of the now bankrupt Ataka conglomerate (9:30 a.m. to 5 p.m. Closed on Mondays. Admission 300 yen).

Restaurants and Pubs in Kita

American Fast Food: Two Kentucky Fried Chickens ("KFC") are located in Kita, one in Sonezaki and the other in Sonezaki-Shinchi.

Inexpensive Restaurants (2,500 yen or less for dinner)

Korean Restaurant Shokudoen (lower center, map 5, in Sonezaki-Shinchi) serves Korean barbecue. Typical dishes are priced at 800-1,200 yen. **Ching-Fu** (lower left, map 5, in Sonezaki-Shinchi) serves a variety of Chinese dishes at 1,000-1,600 yen per plate. **L'Omelette** is located on the 31st floor of the Hankyu Grand Building (middle center, map 5). This unique omelette specialty house prices its dishes from 1,200 to 2,000 yen. **Din Don** is also located on the 31st floor of the Hankyu Grand Building. Roast beef is 2,100 yen, and beef steaks are 2,100-3,700 yen.

Inexpensive Pubs

Top of Osaka is located on the 33rd floor of No. 3 Building (middle center, map 5). A shot of whisky starts at 600 yen (Try Suntory Old or Gold Nikka). **Wine House West Coast** is located on the 27th floor of Hankyu Grand Building. A glass of wine and hors d'oeuvres are around 1,500 yen. **Robatayaki Ganko** (middle center, map 5, in Sonezaki) can be easily recognized by its Japanese style entrance and the plastic displays of its dishes. The atmosphere is not fancy, but prices are inexpensive. Yakitori is 280 yen, and robatazukuri, a combination of sliced raw fish (sashimi), is 980 yen. **Kitanoyado** is in the basement of Good Bar (middle center, map 5, in Sonezaki). Chankonabe is 2,500 yen, and Ishikarinabe is 1,800 yen.

Reasonable Restaurants (2,500-5,000 yen for dinner)

Suehiro Asahi (lower left, map 5, in Sonezaki-Shinchi) serves beef steak, sukiyaki and shabu-shabu at around 3,500 yen each. **Lounge Kashuku** (lower center, map 5, in Sonezaki-Shinchi) is a famous Kobe beef steak house. The 4,500 yen succulent Kobe steak meal is a good buy.

Expensive Restaurant (5,000 yen and up for dinner)

Kawakyu, located on the 33rd floor of No. 3 Building (middle center, map 5), is an authentic Japanese restaurant. Full course Japanese Kaiseki meals start at 7,000 yen.

Shinsaibashi & Minami

There are many shopping arcades in the Shinsaibashi and Minami district (indicated with shaded red on map 6). Department stores and modern shops and boutiques are located near the Midosuji subway line's Shinsaibashi Station 心斎橋駅 and along the arcade that runs parallel to the Midosuji subway line.

Soemoncho 宗右衛門町 (northern side of the Dotonborigawa River) and **Dotonbori** 道頓堀 (southern side of the River) are Minami's two famous eating and drinking streets. The area maintains the traditional atmosphere of Osaka's mercantile past. Inexpensive, but good restaurants and pubs line the streets. There are glittering neon signs and unique signboards and displays. Popular wisdom holds that if you are eating and drinking on an expense account you should go to Kita, especially its Sonezaki-Shinchi area. Minami is your destination when you pay from your own pocket. Dotonbori Street is home to many movie and stage theaters.

National Bunraku Theater 国立文楽劇場 (middle right, map 6) was completed in April 1984. Bunraku is a traditional puppet drama developed to new peaks of achievement in the Edo era. Each puppet is manipulated by three puppeteers. The delicate movements of the eyes, mouths, fingers and arms of the puppets are sure to fascinate you even if you cannot follow the story exactly. The plays usually feature tragic stories of the feudal era. Tickets are 2,800 yen and 3,500 yen. You can get information at (06) 212-1122, or at your hotel. There are six runs a year at the National Theater; each lasts for about 20 days.

Shin-Kabukiza Theater 新歌舞伎座 **(lower center, map 6)** stages Kabuki once a year in April (for about a 25-day run).

Hozenji Temple 法善寺 **(middle center, map 6)** has only a small hall and is surrounded by restaurants, bars and cabarets. Decorated with many paper lanterns and filled with the smell of incense, the temple is a symbol of traditional Osaka and the people of the city. Visiting the temple is supposed to be helpful to those in pursuit of true love (I've often wondered if the men rushing to "hostess" bars ever stop here on their way!).

Bunraku performance.

Restaurants and Pubs in Minami

American Fast Food: Three McDonald's are located on the long shopping arcade (upper center, middle center, and lower center, map 6). There are also two Shakey's (upper center, in the shopping arcade, and middle center, on Dotonbori, map 6), and Kentucky Fried Chicken ("KFC", middle center, map 6, on Dotonbori).

Inexpensive Restaurants (2,500 yen or less for dinner)

Chugoku Daihanten (upper center, map 6, in the shopping arcade) has 200 different Chinese dishes (500-1,200 yen). **Korean Restaurant Shokudoen** (middle center, map 6, on Soemoncho) serves Korean

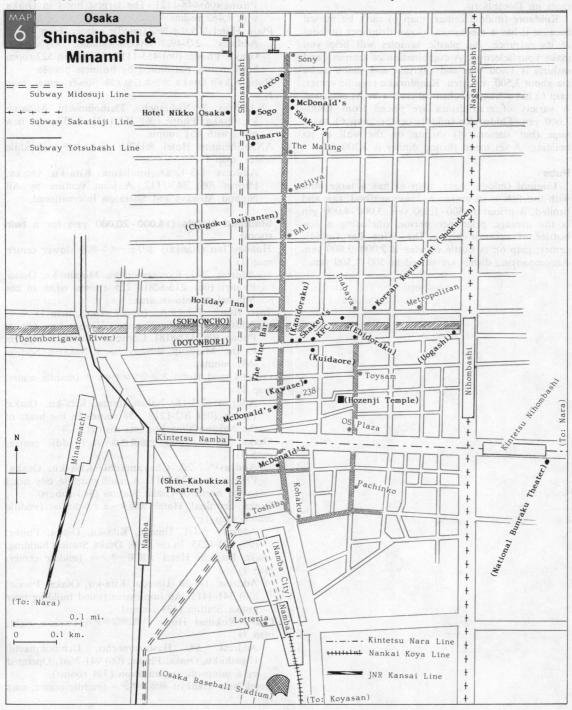

MAP 6

Osaka

Shinsaibashi & Minami

--- Subway Midosuji Line

+-+- Subway Sakaisuji Line

=== Subway Yotsubashi Line

Shinsaibashi

Parco

Sony

McDonald's

Hotel Nikko Osaka

Sogo

Shakey's

Daimaru

The Maling

Meijiya

(Chugoku Daihanten)

BAL

Inabaya

Korean Restaurant (Shokudoen)

Metropolitan

Holiday Inn

(Kanidoraku)

Shakey's

(SOEMONCHO)

(DOTONBORI)

KFC

(Ebidoraku)

(Uogashi)

Nihombashi

(Dotonborigawa River)

The Wine Bar

(Kuidaore)

Toysam

(Kawase)

238

■(Hozenji Temple)

McDonald's

OS Plaza

Kintetsu Namba

Kintetsu Nihonbashi

(To: Nara)

N

McDonald's

Namba

Kohaku

Pachinko

(National Bunraku Theater)

(Shin-Kabukiza Theater)

Minatomachi

Namba

Toshiba

(Namba City)

(To: Nara)

0.1 mi.

0   0.1 km.

Lotteria

Namba

-·-·- Kintetsu Nara Line

++++ Nankai Koya Line

▬▬ JNR Kansai Line

(Osaka Baseball Stadium)

(To: Koyasan)

barbecue at 600-950 yen per dish. **Moti** (on the third floor of Shakey's, middle center, map 6, on Dotonbori) is an Indian restaurant. Most meals are around 1,000 yen. **Kawase** (middle center, map 6) has a sign that says "Int'l Goodwill Shop" in its show window. Naniwa Teishoku (a combination of tempura and sashimi) is 2,500 yen.

Reasonable Restaurants

The following are the three most famous restaurants on Dotonbori:

Kuidaore (middle center, map 6) can't be missed because it has a mechanical clown drummer in front of its entrance. Big plastic samples will help you make your selection. A combination of tempura and sashimi is 1,600 yen, and sukiyaki and shabu-shabu are about 3,500 yen each. **Kanidoraku** (middle center, map 6) has a huge mechanical crab over its entrance. A variety of crab dishes are priced from 1,600-3,600 yen. **Ebidoraku** (middle center, map 6) has a huge (but stationary!) shrimp on the wall of its building. A set menu shrimp dinner is 3,200 yen.

Pubs

Uogashi (middle right, map 6) has a large tank with live fish at its entrance. Fresh seafood, raw and broiled, is priced at 500-1,500 yen. 3,000-4,000 yen is the average price per person (including a few bottles of sake or beer.) **The Wine Bar** (middle center, map 6): A bottle of wine is 2,000-3,000 yen. Accompanying dishes are priced at 500-1,500 yen.

Accommodations

First-class Hotels (20,000 yen and up for a twin room)

Royal Hotel ロイヤルホテル (middle center, map 1)
    Address: 5-3-68, Nakanoshima, Kita-ku, Osaka; Phone:(06)448-1121. The largest hotel in Osaka with 1,462 rooms.
Plaza Hotel プラザホテル (middle cemter, map 1)
    Address: 2-2-49, Oyodo-Minami, Oyodo-ku, Osaka; Phone: (06) 453-1111. A modern 527-room hotel mainly patronized by business people.
Hotel Nikko Osaka ホテル日航大阪 (lower center, map 1)
    Address: 7, Nishinocho, Daihojimachi, Minami-ku, Osaka; Phone (06) 252-1121. A 32-story new hotel with 651 rooms.
ANA-Sheraton Hotel 全日空シェラトンホテル (middle center, map 1)
    Address: 1-3-1, Dojimahama, Kita-ku, Osaka; Phone: (06) 347-1112. A joint venture by All Nippon Airways and Sheraton International.

Standard Hotels (14,000-20,000 yen for a twin room)

Holiday Inn (Nankai) ホリデーイン南海 (lower center, map 1)
    Address: 28-1, Kyuzaemoncho, Minami-ku, Osaka; Phone: (06) 213-8281. 225 rooms right in the Minami downtown area.
Toyo Hotel 東洋ホテル (upper center, map 1)
    Address: 3-16-19, Toyosaki, Oyodo-ku, Osaka; Phone: (06) 372-8181. Convenient location adjacent to the Midosuji subway line's Nakatsu Station (641 rooms).
Osaka Grand Hotel 大阪グランドホテル (middle center, map 1)
    Address: 2-3-18, Nakanoshima, Kita-ku, Osaka; Phone: (06) 202-1212. 358 rooms in the heart of the Nakanoshima business district.
Osaka Tokyu Hotel 大阪東急ホテル (middle center, map 1)
    Address: 7-20, Chayamachi, Kita-ku, Osaka; Phone: (06) 373-2411. A multi-purpose city hotel to the north of Osaka Station (340 rooms).
Osaka Terminal Hotel 大阪ターミナルホテル (middle center, map 1)
    Address: 3-1-1, Umeda, Kita-ku, Osaka; Phone: (06) 344-1235. In the JNR Osaka Station building.
Osaka Dai-ichi Hotel 大阪第一ホテル (middle center, map 1)
    Address: 1-9-20, Umeda, Kita-ku, Osaka; Phone: (06) 341-4411. An impressive round building near Osaka Station (428 rooms).
Osaka Kokusai Hotel 大阪国際ホテル (middle right, map 1)
    Address: 58, Hashizumecho, Uchihonmachi, Higashi-ku, Osaka; Phone: (06) 941-2661. Operated by a nonprofit organization (394 rooms).
Hotel New Hankyu 新阪急ホテル (middle center, map 1)

Address: 1-1-35, Shibata, Kita-ku, Osaka; Phone: (06) 372-5101. A high-class business hotel with 1,029 rooms.

Business Hotels (less than 14,000 yen for a twin room)

Osaka Tokyu Inn 大阪東急イン (middle center, map 2)

Address: 2-1, Doyamacho, Kita-ku, Osaka; Phone: (06) 315-0109. A functional hotel in a convenient location (402 rooms).

Hokke Club Osaka 法華クラブ大阪 (middle center, map 2)

Address: 12-19, Toganocho, Kita-ku, Osaka; Phone: (06) 313-3171. The Osaka branch of a nationwide business hotel chain (254 rooms).

高野山

Koyasan

Koyasan is a 3.5 mile (5.6 km.) long and 1.4 mile (2.2 km.) wide tableland hid amid 3,000 foot (900 m.) mountains. It is inhabited by 7,000 people, and the area has the usual facilities of a modern town including schools, banks and amusement places, but this temple town also has its own character and atmosphere. All accommodations available here are in temples, and they serve only special vegetarian food, reflecting the traditional diet of the priests. There are about 120 temples scattered throughout the area. They are surrounded by magnificent forests. To enter Koyasan is to enter a mysterious world of Buddhism. Ever since Kukai (Kobo Daishi), founder of the Shingon sect, opened a temple here in 816, Koyasan has prospered as the capital of Japanese Buddhism. The more than 100,000 monuments commemorating the giants of Japanese history that line the approach to Okunoin Cemetery testify to the respect that Koyasan has received for the past 12 centuries.

Koyasan is an ideal one-night-two-days destination from Kyoto or Osaka. Though it is possible to make a one-day excursion here from Osaka, I don't recommend it because your day will be too rushed, and because the overnight stay at a temple accommodation is one of the major reasons for a visit to Koyasan.

Transportation

Between Osaka and Gokurakubashi (Refer to Kansai Map 1 in the Kansai Area Inter-City Transportation Chapter above)

From Osaka

The Nankai Koya Line 南海高野線 (private) operates a direct train from Osaka's Namba Station 難波駅 to Gokurakubashi 極楽橋 via Hashimoto. Nankai's Namba Station is pictured on Osaka Map 6 (lower center) and can be reached easily by the Midosuji subway line. There are three limited express trains from Namba Station every day. Additional limited express trains operate in spring and fall.

Namba (Osaka) to Gokurakubashi

Train Name	Lv. Namba	Ar. Gokurakubashi
Koya	9:20 a.m.	10:36 a.m.
Koya	9:50 a.m.	11:07 a.m.
Koya	1:20 p.m.	2:36 p.m.

The limited express trains use deluxe cars and have only reserved seats. The basic fare from Namba to Gokurakubashi is 700 yen. The limited express surcharge is 700 yen.

In addition to the limited expresses, commuter-type express trains operate about once every 30 minutes from early in the morning till late at night. The ride from Namba to Gokurakubashi takes one hour and 40 minutes, and the fare is 700 yen (No surcharge is added). Because the express trains take only 20 minutes longer than limited expresses and because the fare is one-half, it might be wise to take an express unless you are adamant about a deluxe reserved seat.

Return to Osaka

The schedule of the limited express trains on the Nankai Koya Line is as follows:

Gokurakubashi to Namba (Osaka)

Train Name	Lv. Gokurakubashi	Ar. Namba
Koya	11:37 a.m.	12:54 p.m.
Koya	3:35 p.m.	4:52 p.m.
Koya	4:20 p.m.	5:37 p.m.

As explained above, many express trains are also available for the return trip to Osaka.

Between Kyoto and Gokurakubashi (Refer to Kansai Map 1 in the Kansai Area Inter-City Transportation Chapter)

From Kyoto

There are two methods of transportation from Kyoto to Koyasan. If you don't have a Japan Rail Pass, I recommend that you go to Osaka's Namba Station and use the Nankai Koya Line (see the above). As for the access to Namba Station from Kyoto refer to the transportation section of the Osaka chapter.

Japan Rail Pass holders should combine three JNR trains and one private line as follows: (1) Kyoto to Nara on the JNR Nara Line; (2) Nara to Takada on the JNR Sakurai Line; and (3) Takada to Hashimoto on the JNR Wakayama Line.

At Hashimoto Station you transfer to the Nankai Koya Line (private) for Gokurakubashi. The train operates frequently and the ride from Hashimoto to Gokurakubashi takes about 45 minutes (260 yen).

Convenient JNR train connections are as follows:

Return to Kyoto/Nara

The same routes as the above can be used for the return trip. The JNR train connections from Hashimoto to Kyoto via Takada and Nara are listed below:

Kyoto to Hashimoto

Lv. Kyoto	Ar. Nara	Lv. Nara	Ar. Takada	Lv. Takada	Ar. Hashimoto
8:10 a.m.	9:18 a.m.	9:52 a.m.	10:38 a.m.	10:57 a.m.	11:51 a.m.
10:26 a.m.	11:29 a.m.	11:55 a.m.	12:46 p.m.	12:50 p.m.	1:46 p.m.

Hashimoto to Kyoto

Lv. Hashimoto	Ar. Takada	Lv. Takada	Ar. Nara	Lv. Nara	Ar. Kyoto
2:34 p.m.	3:25 p.m.	3:30 p.m.	4:14 p.m.	4:41 p.m.	5:51 p.m.
5:41 p.m.	6:37 p.m.	7:03 p.m.	7:53 p.m.	8:15 p.m.	9:15 p.m.

The fare is 1,000 yen from Hashimoto to Nara and 1,700 yen to Kyoto. All the stations where you have to transfer are pretty small, so you shouldn't have any trouble.

Cable Car between Gokurakubashi and Koyasan (Refer to Kansai Map 1 in the Kansai Area Inter-City Transportation Chapter above)

A cable car operates every 20-30 minutes from Gokurakubashi Station, connecting with the arriving Nankai trains. The ride takes five minutes, and the fare is 300 yen. The cable car climbs up a steep mountain slope; it is unbelievable that there is such a wide tableland at the top of such a precipitous mountain.

Bus Service between Koyasan Cable Car Station and Okunoin-mae via Ichinohashi-guichi

Several bus routes originate at Koyasan cable car station. The most important one, which connects Koyasan Station with Okunoin-mae 奥の院前, is indicated with a red dotted line on Koyasan Map 1. The bus operates every 20-30 minutes, connecting with the arriving cable cars. About half the buses go all the way to Okunoin-mae. The other half, however, terminate at Ichinohashi stop 一の橋 (middle right, map 1, near Seijoshin-in Temple). Take either bus. Major bus stop names are indicated on map 1. The fare from Koyasan cable car station is 260 yen to Ichinohashi and 320 yen to Okunoin-mae.
Plenty of taxis are also available in Koyasan.

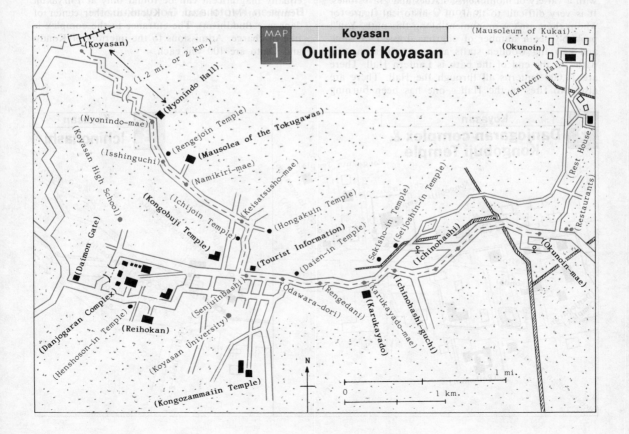

Places of Interest

Koyasan can be divided into two sections: the western part contains the temple precincts where many grand structures and the Reihokan Treasure House are located; the eastern part is a cemetery where more than 100,000 tombs of historic figures and the mausoleum of Kukai, the founder of Koyasan, are located. This area is shaded with cedar trees hundreds of years old. Visit one half in the afternoon of the day you arrive and the other half the following morning. If you are taking a late afternoon train back to Osaka or Kyoto, you may be able to squeeze in everything I will introduce below. If your time is limited, skip the places marked optional.

Okunoin 奥の院 (upper right, map 1)

The stone-paved main approach to Okunoin begins at Ichinohashi, but there is a shortcut to Okunoin from Okunoin-mae bus stop that bypasses some of the approach. You can start your walking tour at either Ichinohashi (see map 3) or Okunoin-mae, depending on where your bus leaves you off. On your way back to the bus, be sure to take the path you didn't use on your way in so that you can cover all the major parts of the cemetery area. The 1.3 mile (2 km.) long main approach is lined on both sides with a variety of monuments, statues and gravestones. It is very difficult to think of a historical figure for whom there isn't a monument along this path. You'll probably see a number of pilgrims dressed in white and carrying wooden staffs as you walk along the path. At the end of the path is Lantern Hall. There are 11,000 lanterns all through the Hall. There are also two fires in the Hall—one has been burning since 1016 and the other since 1088. The mausoleum of Kukai is in back of Lantern Hall. The entire area is densely wooded: the huge trees prevent any sunshine from breaking through. The mysterious atmosphere is enhanced by the pervasive smell of incense. A visit here will help you understand why Koyasan has been so important to Japanese Buddhism.

Kongobuji Temple 金剛峯寺 (middle center, map 1, or upper right, map 2)

Kongobuji Temple is the headquarters of the Shingon sect of Buddhism, the Japanese form of Buddhism most akin to the Buddhism of Tibet. The temple was erected in 1592 at the order of Hideyoshi Toyotomi as a family temple for his mother, and later became Koyasan's main temple. The chambers of the main building are separated by sliding doors decorated with brilliant pictures by artists of the Kano school (8 a.m. to 5 p.m. Admission 300 yen).

Danjogaran Complex 壇上伽藍 (middle left, map 1, or middle left, map 2)

The Danjogaran Complex consists of more than 15 halls, and the sight of these magnificent buildings never fails to impress visitors. The complex has suffered repeated fires, but the oldest building dates from 1198. The two most important buildings are Kondo and Daito. Kondo is the main hall of the complex, and Daito is a gigantic pagoda. Though Daito dates only from 1937, it is a very impressive two-story vermilion red structure (A two-story pagoda equally magnificent can be found only at Enryakuji Temple on Mt. Hieizan in Kyoto, another center of Japanese Buddhism). The entrance to the complex is free of charge. Admissions to the interiors of Kondo and Daito are 100 yen each.

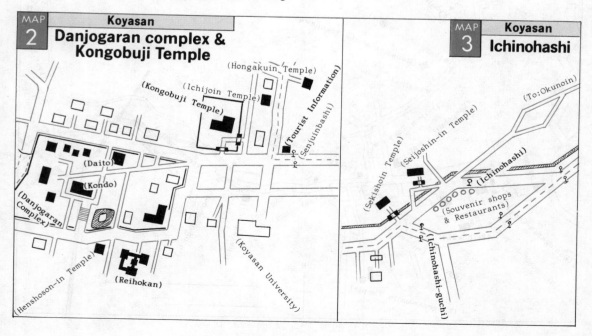

Reihokan Treasure House 霊宝館 (lower left, map 1, or lower center, map 2)

Koyasan's proud artistic achievements are displayed here. Reihokan preserves about 5,000 treasures of Koyasan, 180 of which have been designated National Treasures and Important Cultural Properties. The exhibits are changed periodically (9 a.m. to 4 p.m., till 5 p.m. in summer. Admission 300 yen).

Kongozammaiin Temple 金剛三昧院 (lower center, map 1) (optional)

Kongozammaiin Temple dates from 1211 and was erected to commemorate Yoritomo Minamoto, the founder of the Kamakura Shogunate, Japan's first military government, which was established in 1192. The two-story pagoda, built in 1223, is a National Treasure. Kyakuden Hall (Guest Hall) is famous for the gorgeous pictures on its sliding screens.

Mausolea of the Tokugawas 徳川家霊台 (upper left, map 1) (optional)

Mausolea of the first and the second Tokugawa Shoguns are located here. As is the case with many of the shrines, monuments and mausolea related to the Tokugawas, these buildings feature brilliant gold and silver ornamentation (9 a.m. to 5 p.m. Admission 100 yen).

Daimon Gate 大門 (middle left, map 1) (optional)

In olden times, the main entrance to Koyasan was through Daimon Gate. This huge structure, which was under repair when I visited Koyasan, is located in the westernmost part of the tableland and comands a fine view of the surrounding mountains and valleys.

Accommodations

As mentioned before, the only accommodations available in Koyasan are in temples. Fifty-three out of the 120 temples in the area have lodgings. The facilities are basically the same as a regular Japanese-style inn — tatami mats on the floors, futon matresses instead of beds, public baths, etc. The greatest differences are that the kitchens prepare the same vegetarian dishes for guests that are served to the priests and that these accommodations are imbued with the solemn atmosphere of the temple precincts. The rates are 8,000 - 12,000 yen per person (including two meals and tax and service charge). Each temple has 30 - 50 rooms.

(a) Sekisho-in Temple 赤松院 (middle right, map 1, or middle left, map 3).

(b) Seijoshin-in Temple 清浄心院 (middle right, map 1, or middle left, map 3).

(c) Daien-in Temple 大円院 (middle center, map 1).

(d) Kongozammaiin Temple 金剛三昧院 (lower center, map 1).

(e) Henshoson-in Temple 遍照尊院 (lower left, map 1).

(f) Ichijoin Temple 一乗院 (middle center, map 1, or upper right, map 2).

(g) Hongakuin Temple 本覚院 (middle center, map 1, or upper right, map 2).

(h) Rengejoin Temple 蓮華定院 (upper left, map 1).

神戸 六甲山 Kobe & Mt. Rokkosan

Because the early development of Japan took place in the western part of the archipelago where the calm Inland Sea was the main transportation route, Kobe has been a prosperous port town since the pre-historic period. The early port was called Muko-no-Minato, and was located in what is now the western part of the city. Kobe's prosperity was enhanced during the Edo era when nearby Osaka was used by the Tokugawa Shogunate as its national distribution center.

The area was opened to foreign traders in 1868, at the end of the nation's long period of isolation, but because the government did not want to open the prosperous main port to foreigners, only a smaller area to the northeast of the main port was made available to them. The development of international trade which followed led to the expansion of this new port, and the center of Kobe eventually shifted to this area. Because Kobe has had a large foreign population for more than one hundred years, it has the cosmopolitan atmosphere of an international city. Kobe beef is a famous specialty of the city, and Kobe's sophisticated restaurants feature all sorts of international dishes, making the city a gourmets' paradise. The city's population is 1,346,000.

Mt. Rokkosan consists of several peaks at altitudes of 2,300 - 2,600 feet (700 - 800 m.). Many recreational facilities are located on the gentle slopes of the mountains, including golf courses, a botanic garden and athletic fields. Mt. Rokkosan is famous for its splendid "million dollar" glittering nighttime view of the city and the port.

Outline of the Area

Kobe, sandwiched between the sea on the south and Mt. Rokkosan on the north, is quite long from northeast to southwest (refer to map 1). The area around Sannomiya Station, rather than Kobe Station, is the center of the city.

Port Island, a large man-made island, was constructed several years ago to expand port facilities, especially container facilities, and to provide convenient residential and recreational areas for the people of Kobe.

Mountain top observatories are located to the northeast of the city, and can be reached easily by bus, cable car and ropeway.

Transportation

Transportation to and from Kobe

Kobe is served by the Shinkansen and can be reached easily from other major cities. The Shinkansen station is called Shin-Kobe (New Kobe) 新神戸駅 and is located about 1 mile to the north of Sannomiya Station 三ノ宮駅. Except when visiting Kobe from Osaka, the Shinkansen is the most convenient method of transportation even though you need to take a short taxi ride between Sannomiya and Shin-Kobe. For information on the Shinkansen, refer to Chapter "Transportation within Japan".

Transportation between Kobe and Osaka

JNR and two private railways operate parallel commuter lines between Sannomiya and Osaka. To avoid confusion, I have introduced only the JNR Tokaido-Sanyo Line and the Hankyu Kobe Line.

The JNR's blue colored Tokaido-Sanyo commuter trains 東海道・山陽本線 operate between Kyoto and Nishi-Akashi, stopping at Osaka and Sannomiya Stations (Refer to Kansai Map 1 in the Kansai Area Inter-City Transportation Chapter above). The ride between Osaka and Sannomiya takes 35 minutes, and the fare is 510 yen.

The Hankyu Kobe Line 阪急神戸線 (private) operates three types of trains — a limited express, an express and a local — between Umeda (near the JNR Osaka Station) and Sannomiya. The ride takes 28 minutes on the limited express, 39 minutes on the express and 51 minutes on the local. Each type of train operates about once every 10 minutes. The fare is the same for all the trains (230 yen).

The best connections for visits to Mt. Rokkosan are available at the Hankyu Kobe Line's Rokko Station. The limited express skips this station, so you'll have to take either an express or a local train.

Transportation between Kobe and Osaka Airport

A shuttle bus operates between Osaka Airport and Sannomiya Station three times an hour, from 6:10 a.m. to 8:10 p.m. The bus stop is located near the JNR and Hankyu Sannomiya Stations (The stop is pictured at the upper right of map 2). The fare is 600 yen, and the ride takes about 40 minutes.

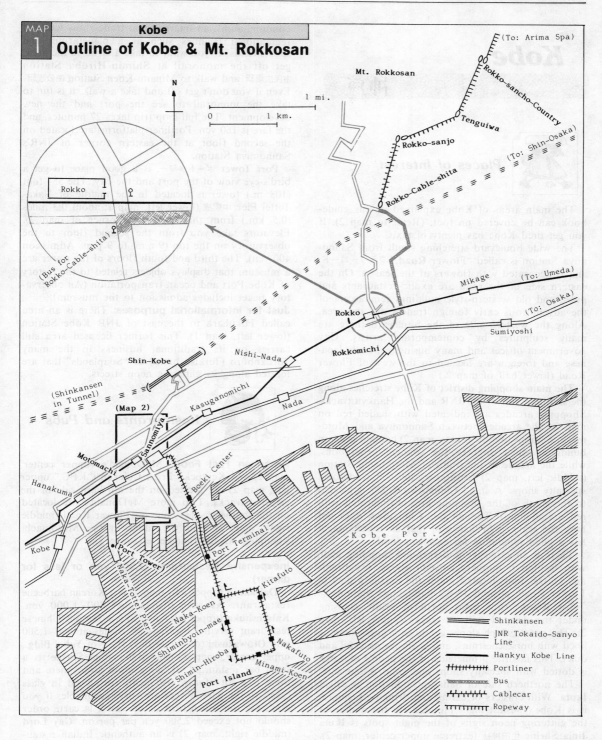

MAP
1

Kobe
Outline of Kobe & Mt. Rokkosan

N

1 mi.

0   1 km.

Mt. Rokkosan

(To: Arima Spa)

Rokko-sancho-Country

Tenguiwa

Rokko-sanjo

(To: Shin-Osaka)

Rokko-Cable-shita

Rokko-Cable-shita

Rokko

Mikage   (To: Umeda)

(Bus for
Rokko-Cable-shita)

(To: Osaka)

Sumiyoshi

Nishi-Nada

Rokkomichi

(Shinkansen
in Tunnel)

Shin-Kobe

Kasuganomichi

Nada

(Map 2)

Sannomiya

Motomachi

Boeki Center

Hanakuma

Kobe Port

Kobe

Port Tower

Port Terminal

Naka-Koen   Kitafuto

Shiminbyoin-mae

Shimin-Hiroba   Nakafuto

Minami-Koen

Port Island

	Shinkansen
	JNR Tokaido–Sanyo Line
	Hankyu Kobe Line
	Portliner
	Bus
	Cablecar
	Ropeway

Kobe

神戸

Places of Interest

The main areas of Kobe explained in this guidebook can be covered on foot. (Refer to map 2). If you get tired Kobe has plenty of taxis.

The wide boulevard stretching south from Sannomiya Station is called **"Flower Road,"** フラワーロード and is decorated with flowers of the season. On the eastern side of the road are exotic restaurants and pubs, and old western-style buildings reminiscent of the adventurous early foreign traders dot the area. Along the western side of the boulevard there are many sculptures by contemporary artists. City government offices and many businesses, both Japanese and foreign, are located to the west of Flower Road (lower half of map 2.)

The main shopping district of Kobe stretches along the southern side of the JNR and the Hankyu tracks. Shopping arcades are indicated with shaded red on map 2. The arcades between Sannomiya and Motomachi Stations (middle center, map 2) contain modern buildings which cater to the younger generations, while the arcade to the south of Motomachi Station (middle left, map 2) features established traditional specialty shops. A small **Chinatown** 南京町 is located to the south of the shopping arcade (indicated with red dotted lines). Though this Chinatown does not have the scale or brilliance of that of Yokohama, it has a good reputation for excellent food.

There is an extensive **underground shopping mall**, with fashion boutiques, souvenir shops, restaurants and coffee shops located under the northern part of Flower Road, around JNR's Sannomiya Station.

Tor Road runs from north to south, crossing under the elevated railroad tracks (upper left, map 2). The street, which slopes gently as it goes north, is lined with horse chestnuts, and is always peaceful and quiet. This favorite promenade of the people of Kobe is dotted with specialty shops and good restaurants.

The northern side of Sannomiya Station is called **Ikuta**. With clusters of eating and drinking facilities, it is Kobe's busiest night life area. In the middle of the glittering neon signs of the night spots is **Ikuta Jinja Shrine** 生田神社 (extreme upper center, map 2). The woods behind the vermilion red shrine were once quite extensive, and were the subject of a famous poem in olden times.

Port Island ポートアイランド (lower center, map 1) is connected with Sannomiya Station by automatic monorails called Portliners ポートライナー. The monorail makes a counter clockwise loop and stops at eight stations. The island features large container terminals for international ocean freight, a number of condominiums, an international trade show hall and recreational facilities such as a planetarium and sports fields. If you want to take a stroll in the area, get off the monorail at Shimin-Hiroba Station 市民広場駅 and walk to Minami-Koen Station 南公園駅. Even if you don't get off and take a walk, it is fun to take the monorail to see the port and the new development. The full loop trip takes 27 minutes, and the fare is 160 yen. Portliner platforms are located on the second floor at the eastern corner of JNR's Sannomiya Station.

Port Tower ポートタワー is a good place to get a bird's-eye view of the port and the city. The 354 foot (108 m.) tower is located in the middle of Naka-Tottei Pier 中突堤 (lower left, map 1; about 0.3 miles (0.5 km.) from the lower left corner of map 2). Elevators take you from the second floor to the observatory on the top (9 a.m. to 9 p.m. Admission 400 yen). The third and fouth floors of the tower are a museum that displays objects related to the history of Kobe Port and ocean transportation (An observatory ticket includes admission to the museum).

Just for informational purposes: There is an area called Fukuhara to the east of JNR Kobe Station (lower left, map 1). This former licensed area still carries on its traditional business in the many Torukoburo (Turkish baths) or "Soaplands" that are located along its glittering neon streets.

Restaurants and Pubs

American Fast Food: McDonald's (upper center, map 2) and Kentucky Fried Chicken ("KFC," upper left, map 2) are located on the northern side of the railroad tracks. Two more McDonald's are located on the southern side — one on Flower Road (middle right, map 2), and the other in the Motomachi Shopping Arcade (middle left, map 2).

Inexpensive Restaurants (2,500 yen or less for dinner)

Dairakuen (upper left, map 2) is a Korean barbecue restaurant. Average dishes cost 800-1,000 yen. **Kaisenshuka** (upper left, map 2) is a famous Chinese restaurant serving a variety of dishes at 800-1,500 yen. **Otowazushi** (on the ground floor of **Yubel Bldg.**, upper center, map 2, near Ikuta Jinja Shrine) is a sushi bar restaurant. It has a good atmosphere and there is a lot of raw fish neatly displayed in glass cases on the bars. Prices are very reasonable. If you don't eat too much toro or uni, an a la carte order should not exceed 2,500 yen per person. **Gay Lord** (middle right, map 2) is an authentic Indian restaurant. Curries are priced at 1,200-1,500 yen. **Steak House Volks** (middle center, map 2) has a 2,500 yen set menu steak dinner.

All the restaurants in **Chinatown** (middle left, map 2) are reasonably priced. Prices start at around 800 yen.

Reasonable Restaurants (2,500-5,000 yen for dinner)

Akanoren (middle center, map 2) can be recognized by its Japanese style entrance. **Sanmarino's** English sign will be a good landmark. This Japanese restaurant serves set menu authentic Japanese meals at 2,000-3,000 yen. **Matsusaka** (next to Akanoren above) is a steak house. Many handicrafts and ukiyoe (woodblock prints) are on display in the restaurant. A steak dinner starts at 3,800 yen. Sukiyaki and shabu-shabu are also served in a tatami room on the third floor (around 4,000 yen). **Steak Land Kobe** (upper center, map 2) is another famous steak house. Prices range from 2,600 to 3,800 yen.

Expensive Restaurants (5,000 yen and up for dinner)

Both **Misono** (upper center, map 2) and **Rengatei** (upper left, map 2) are typical Kobe steak restaurants. A steak dinner at Misono starts at 6,800 yen, while one at Rengatei will cost you at least 7,300 yen. You won't have any complaints about the quality, but portions are rather smallish.

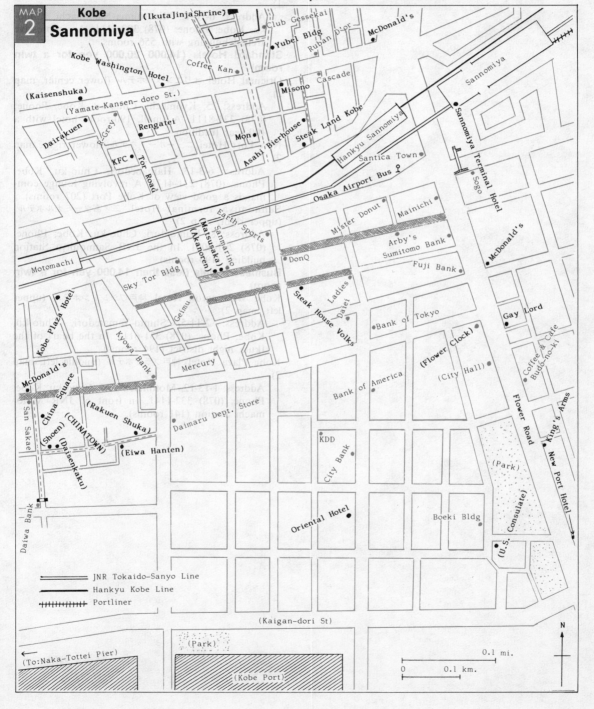

MAP 2 Kobe Sannomiya

Pubs

Asahi Bierhouse (upper center, map 2) is a typical beer hall for white collar workers. Foods to accompany the drinks are priced at 600-1,000 yen. **King's Arms** (lower right, map 2), an English-style pub restaurant, is very popular with Kobe's foreign residents.

Accommodations

HOTELS

First-class Hotel (20,000 yen and up for a twin room)

Kobe Portopia Hotel 神戸ポートピアホテル (near Shimin-Hiroba Station on Port Island, refer to map 1)

> Address: 6-10-1, Minatojima-Nakamachi, Chuo-ku, Kobe; Phone: (078) 302-1111. An impressive arched building with 556 rooms.

Standard Hotels (14,000-20,000 yen for a twin room)

Oriental Hotel オリエンタルホテル (lower center, map 2)

> Address: 25, Kyomachi, Chuo-ku, Kobe; Phone: (078) 331-8111. A small, 190-room hotel with a 100-year tradition.

New Port Hotel ニューポートホテル (lower right, map 2)

> Address: 6-3-13, Hamabedori, Chuo-ku, Kobe; Phone: (078) 231-4171. A revolving lounge commands a good view of Kobe Port (207 rooms).

Sannomiya Terminal Hotel 三ノ宮ターミナルホテル (upper right, map 2)

> Address: 8, Kumoidori, Chuo-ku, Kobe; Phone: (078) 291-0001. In the JNR Sannomiya Station building (190 rooms).

Business Hotels (less than 14,000 yen for a twin room)

Kobe Washington Hotel 神戸ワシントンホテル (upper left, map 2)

> Address: 2-11-5, Shimo-Yamatedori, Chuo-ku, Kobe; Phone: (078) 331-6111. In the heart of the Ikuta night district (194 rooms).

Kobe Plaza Hotel 神戸プラザホテル (middle left, map 2)

> Address: 1-13-12, Motomachidori, Chuo-ku, Kobe; Phone: (078) 332-1141. In front of JNR Motomachi Station (141 rooms).

Mt. Rokkosan
六甲山

If you are tired of the bustling city life of Osaka or Kobe, Mt. Rokkosan is the ideal place to take a breather, relax, and enjoy nature. The mountain top commands a grand view of the city of Kobe and its port. A half-day excursion from either Osaka or Kobe is a great way to visit the area. If you stay on the mountain until early evening, you can also enjoy the glittering night view of Kobe Port.

Transportaion

The No. 16 bus travels to Rokko-Cable-shita Station 六甲ケーブル下駅 via the Hankyu Kobe Line's Rokko Station 六甲駅 and the JNR Tokaido-Sanyo Line's Rokkomichi Station 六甲道駅 (Refer to map 1). The stop for the No. 16 bus at Hankyu's Rokko Station is on the southern side of the station across the railroad tracks (pictured at upper left, map 1). The bus operates every 10 minutes and the fare is a 140 yen flat rate (Pay when you get off).

The cable car ascends the steep mountain slope between Rokko-Cable-shita and Rokko-sanjo 六甲山上 every 20 minutes, from 7 a.m. to 10 p.m. The ride takes 10 minutes and the fare is 480 yen.

A ropeway operates between Rokko-sanjo and Rokko-sancho-Country 六甲山頂カンツリー via the intermediate stop of Tenguiwa 天狗岩, every 7 - 13 minutes, from 9 a.m. to 8:40 p.m. in summer (and every 20 minutes from 9:20 a.m. to 6 p.m. the rest of the year). The ride to Rokko-sancho-Country takes 12 minutes, and the fare is 650 yen one way and 1,170 yen round trip.

Attractions

The Rokko-sanjo Station area commands a panoramic view of Kobe. From the ropeway itself you have an even wider view of the city. Rokko-sancho-Country is the highest point of the ropeway. There is a revolving observatory near the station (9 a.m. to 10 p.m. in summer. Till 4:40 p.m. in other seasons. Admission 200 yen). The beautiful settings of the mountain area are relaxing and refreshing. The area also has several fashionable restaurants. Rokko Country House (Playland) is within walking distance of the station (9 a.m. to 5 p.m. Admission 300 yen).

Central Japan

As pictured on map 1, Japan has many mountains that top 10,000 feet (3,000 m.). This rugged topography and the severe winter weather of the mountains have isolated Central Japan from the industrial development that seems to have reached every area along the Pacific coast. As a result, many traditional buildings and handicrafts have been preserved in this area, especially in Takayama. The beautiful scenery of the Japan Alps is another attraction of the area.

During the Edo period, Kanazawa was the home of Japan's second most powerful feudal family, the Maedas. (The most powerful was, of course, the Tokugawas). To avoid confrontations with the Tokugawas, the Maedas stressed cultural activities rather than military affairs. Kutani pottery, Kaga Yuzen dyeing and other crafts were developed to high standards here and they still flourish today. Though Kanazawa has developed into a modern city, many historical and cultural sites are still preserved to testify to the areas' unique historical background.

Two more important places of interest are located between Kanazawa and Kyoto. Cape Tojimbo is on the beautiful, rugged Japan Sea coast, and Eiheiji Temple, headquarters of the Soto sect of Buddhism, is still a prosperous training center for Zen priests.

Central Japan is presented here as a four-night, five-day itinerary, starting from Kyoto, with two nights each in Kanazawa and Takayama. If you skip Cape Tojimbo and Eiheiji Temple, a three-night, four-day itinerary is possible. I will introduce the area in clockwise order. If you start your trip from Tokyo, you should follow the same route in counterclockwise order. I definitely recommend that you travel light on this route, and suggest that you consider making this tour as an excursion from Kyoto. If you visit this area on the way to or from Tokyo or Kyoto, you should consider arranging a separate baggage transfer. If you still want to carry your big bags with you, it is better to skip Eiheiji Temple and Cape Tojimbo.

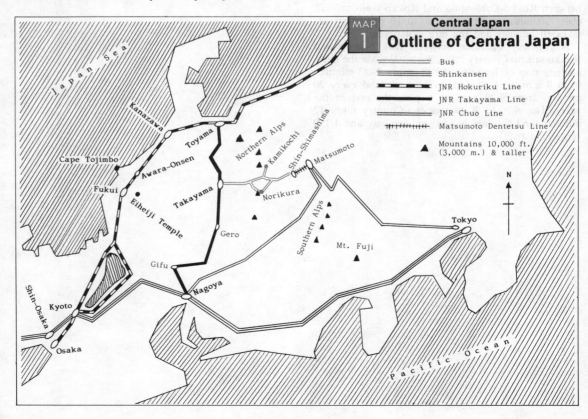

MAP 1	Central Japan
	Outline of Central Japan

Bus
Shinkansen
JNR Hokuriku Line
JNR Takayama Line
JNR Chuo Line
Matsumoto Dentetsu Line
▲ Mountains 10,000 ft. (3,000 m.) & taller

Transportation

Here, I will outline inter-city transportation, i.e., between Kyoto and Kanazawa, Kanazawa and Takayama, and Takayama and Nagoya. City transportation is explained in each of the sections that follow.

Between Kyoto and Kanazawa via Fukui and Awara-Onsen (140 miles, or 225 km.)

The JNR Hokuriku Line 北陸本線 originates at Osaka and runs northeast via Kyoto, Fukui 福井, Awara-Onsen 芦原温泉, Kanazawa 金沢, etc. Some trains terminate at Kanazawa, but many operate further northeast along the Japan Sea coast. Service in the opposite direction is the same — some trains originate at Kanazawa, but most come from the cities northeast of Kanazawa. When the Hokuriku Line trains skirt Lake Biwako, some go via the eastern side of the Lake, and some via the western side. Both routes give passengers a good view of the Lake.

Assuming that some of you may begin or end your trips to Central Japan in Osaka, it too is included in the timetables that follow.

The Raicho train has 12 cars, and most are arranged as follows: one Green Car (first class, reserved seats), six ordinary cars with reserved seats (one of them is a no smoking car), and three ordinary cars with nonreserved seats (one of them is a no smoking car). The ride between Kyoto and Kanazawa costs 6,100 yen, including a limited express surcharge. The Green Car (first class) is an additional 4,200 yen.

Kyoto to Kanazawa

Train Name	Lv. Osaka	Ar. Kyoto	Ar. Fukui	Ar. Awara-Onsen	Ar. Kanazawa
Raicho-1	7:05 a.m.	7:38 a.m.	9:17 a.m.	9:30 a.m.	10:11 a.m.
Raicho-3	7:35 a.m.	8:08 a.m.	9:46 a.m.	9:59 a.m.	10:41 a.m.
Raicho-5	8:05 a.m.	8:38 a.m.	10:11 a.m.	10:24 a.m.	11:04 a.m.
Raicho-7	9:05 a.m.	9:38 a.m.	11:18 a.m.	11:31 a.m.	12:13 p.m.
Raicho-9	10:05 a.m.	10:38 a.m.	12:16 p.m.	12:29 p.m.	1:11 p.m.
Raicho-11	11:05 a.m.	11:38 a.m.	1:16 p.m.	1:29 p.m.	2:11 p.m.
Raicho-13	11:35 a.m.	12:08 p.m.	1:46 p.m.	1:59 p.m.	2:41 p.m.
Raicho-15	12:05 p.m.	12:38 p.m.	2:16 p.m.	2:29 p.m.	3:11 p.m.
Raicho-17	1:05 p.m.	1:38 p.m.	3:16 p.m.	3:29 p.m.	4:11 p.m.
Raicho-21	2:05 p.m.	2:38 p.m.	4:16 p.m.	4:29 p.m.	5:11 p.m.
Raicho-25	3:05 p.m.	3:38 p.m.	5:16 p.m.	5:29 p.m.	6:11 p.m.
Raicho-27	4:05 p.m.	4:38 p.m.	6:16 p.m.	6:29 p.m.	7:11 p.m.

In addition to the above, several other trains are also available from Fukui or Awara-Onsen to Kanazawa

Kanazawa to Kyoto

Train Name	Lv. Kanazawa	Ar. Awara-Onsen	Ar. Fukui	Ar. Kyoto	Ar. Osaka
Raicho-4	7:38 a.m.	8:21 a.m.	8:35 a.m.	10:20 a.m.	10:52 a.m.
Raicho-6	8:12 a.m.	8:53 a.m.	9:05 a.m.	10:45 a.m.	11:17 a.m.
Raicho-8	9:12 a.m.	9:54 a.m.	10:06 a.m.	11:50 a.m.	12:22 p.m.
Raicho-10	10:12 a.m.	10:54 a.m.	11:06 a.m.	12:50 p.m.	1:22 a.m.
Raicho-12	11:12 a.m.	11:54 a.m.	12:06 p.m.	1:50 p.m.	2:22 p.m.
Raicho-14	12:12 p.m.	12:54 p.m.	1:06 p.m.	2:50 p.m.	3:22 p.m.
Raicho-18	1:02 p.m.	1:44 p.m.	1:56 p.m.	3:40 p.m.	4:12 p.m.
Raicho-20	1:42 p.m.	2:24 p.m.	2:36 p.m.	4:20 p.m.	4:52 p.m.
Raicho-22	2:42 p.m.	3:24 p.m.	3:36 p.m.	5:20 p.m.	5:52 p.m.
Raicho-24	3:42 p.m.	4:24 p.m.	4:36 p.m.	6:20 p.m.	6:52 p.m.
Raicho-26	4:12 p.m.	4:54 p.m.	5:06 p.m.	6:50 p.m.	7:22 p.m.
Raicho-28	5:12 p.m.	5:54 p.m.	6:06 p.m.	7:50 p.m.	8:22 p.m.

In addition to the above, several other trains from Kanazawa to Awara-Onsen or Fukui are also available.

Between Kanazawa and Takayama via Toyama (93 miles, or 149 km.)

When you travel from Kanazawa to Takayama, you need to transfer at Toyama Station. Kanazawa 金沢 and Toyama 富山 are linked by the JNR Hokuriku Line 北陸本線 and the JNR Takayama Line 高山本線 runs between Toyama and Takayama 高山. The ride between Kanazawa and Takayama costs 2,200-4,400 yen depending on the types of trains used. I have listed the most convenient train connections for the both directions.

Kanazawa to Toyama, and then to Takayama

Train Name	Lv. Kanazawa	Ar. Toyama	Train Name	Lv. Toyama	Ar. Takayama
Hokuetsu-5	8:38 a.m.	9:24 a.m.	Norikura-6	9:33 a.m.	11:11 a.m.
(local)	8:47 a.m.	9:49 a.m.	(local)	10:23 p.m.	12:41 p.m.
(local)	11:31 a.m.	12:32 p.m.	(local)	1:02 p.m.	3:53 p.m.
Raicho-7	12:15 p.m.	1:00 p.m.	Norikura-8	1:46 p.m.	3:37 p.m.

Takayama to Toyama, and then to Kanazawa

Train Name	Lv. Takayama	Ar. Toyama	Train Name	Lv. Toyama	Ar. Kanazawa
(local)	7:46 a.m.	10:16 a.m.	Raicho-12	10:25 a.m.	11:10 a.m.
(local)	10:07 a.m.	12:06 p.m.	Raicho-18	12:15 p.m.	1:00 p.m.
Norikura-1	11:54 a.m.	1:26 p.m.	Shirasagi-8	1:33 p.m.	2:18 p.m.
	1:12 p.m.	3:21 p.m.	Shirasagi-10	3:33 p.m.	4:18 p.m.
Kita-Alps	1:59 p.m.	3:38 p.m.	Raicho-28	4:23 p.m.	5:10 p.m.
(local)	3:57 p.m.	6:07 p.m.	Raicho-36	6:25 p.m.	7:10 p.m.

Between Takayama and Nagoya (104 miles, or 167 km.)

The ride costs 5,300 yen on Hidas (limited expresses) and 3,900 yen on Norikuras (expresses). The Green Car is an additional 2,900 yen.

Takayama to Nagoya

Train Name	Lv. Takayama	Ar. Nagoya
Hida-2	8:31 a.m.	11:28 a.m.
Norikura-4	9:44 a.m.	1:00 p.m.
Norikura-6	11:17 a.m.	2:32 p.m.
Hida-4	1:24 p.m.	4:27 p.m.
Hida-6	2:32 p.m.	5:37 p.m.
Norikura-8	3:46 p.m.	6:58 p.m.
Hida-8	5:05 p.m.	7:57 p.m.

Nagoya to Takayama

Train Name	Lv. Nagoya	Ar. Takayama
Norikura-1	8:30 a.m.	11:50 a.m.
Hida-1	9:23 a.m.	12:20 p.m.
Hida-3	10:39 a.m.	1:42 p.m.
Hide-5	12:43 p.m.	3:39 p.m.
Norikura-3	1:33 p.m.	4:57 p.m.
Norikura-5	2:33 p.m.	6:13 p.m.
Norikura-7	3:24 p.m.	6:35 p.m.

Eiheiji Temple & Cape Tojimbo
永平寺, 東尋坊

If you want to visit both the Temple and the Cape on your way to Kanazawa, take the Raicho-5 at the latest from Kyoto or Osaka. Get off the train at Fukui Station and transfer to the Keifuku Echizen Line 京福越前線 for Eiheiji 永平寺 (lower right, map 2). When you finish your visit to Eiheiji Temple, take a direct bus to Cape Tojimbo 東尋坊 (upper left, map 2). After enjoying the view of the Japan Sea, and, if possible, a sightseeing boat ride, take a bus to Awara-Onsen Station 芦原温泉駅 to catch a train to Kanazawa. If you cannot take an early morning train, you'll have to forego either Eiheiji or Tojimbo. I recommend that if you can only visit one you choose the Cape because this is the only place along this route where you can see the beautiful coast of the Japan Sea. If this is the case you should take a train to Awara-Onsen Station, and then a bus to Tojimbo. If you are more interested in the Temple, get off the train at Fukui and make the trip to and from Eiheiji on the Keifuku Echizen Line.
If you travel the Central Japan route in reverse, from Kanazawa to Kyoto/Osaka, visit Cape Tojimbo first. Then take a bus to Eiheiji Temple. After the visit to the temple, take the Keifuku Echizen Line to Fukui Station and catch the train to Kyoto/Osaka.

Eiheiji Temple 永平寺

As pictured on map 2, the Keifuku Railways (private) operates two lines from Fukui Station. One line runs to the north to Mikuniko Station near Cape Tojimbo. The other, the Keifuku Echizen Line, provides service to Eiheiji Station. The Keifuku Lines leave Fukui Station from either track No. 7 or No. 8 (Refer to map 3). The following is the schedule of the trains between Fukui and Eiheiji Stations (The one-way fare is 690 yen):
Be careful at Fukui Station. A second branch of the Keifuku Echizen Line also originates there, but it branches off at Higashi-Furuichi Station and provides service further to the east. Use conversation Card 3

at Fukui Station to make sure you get on an Eiheiji-bound train.

Fukui to Eiheiji		Eiheiji to Fukui	
Lv. Fukui	Ar. Eiheiji	Lv. Eiheiji	Ar. Fukui
9:35 a.m.	10:11 a.m.	11:15 a.m.	11:51 a.m.
10:35 a.m.	11:11 a.m.	12:15 p.m.	12:51 p.m.
11:35 a.m.	12:11 p.m.	1:15 p.m.	2:15 p.m.
12:35 p.m.	1:11 p.m.	2:15 p.m.	2:51 p.m.
1:35 p.m.	2:11 p.m.	3:15 p.m.	3:51 p.m.

Eiheiji Temple is just a 10-minute walk from the train station. The approach to the temple is lined with souvenir shops and restaurants (Refer to map 4).

Eiheiji Temple is one of the two principal temples of the Soto sect of Zen Buddhism (The other is Sojiji Temple in Tsurumi—see the Kamakura and Yokohama Chapter above.). The Temple is located deep in the mountains about 10 miles (16 km.) east of Fukui. It was founded in 1244 as a Zen monastery. The temple grounds occupy 3,600 sq. ft. and contain about 70 buildings. Two hundred monks live there, devoting themselves to Zen training. Eiheiji Temple accepts visitors as worshippers but not as mere tourists. This, according to the official explanation, is to maintain the temple's strict atmosphere. They do, however, collect an admission fee. Visitors, including

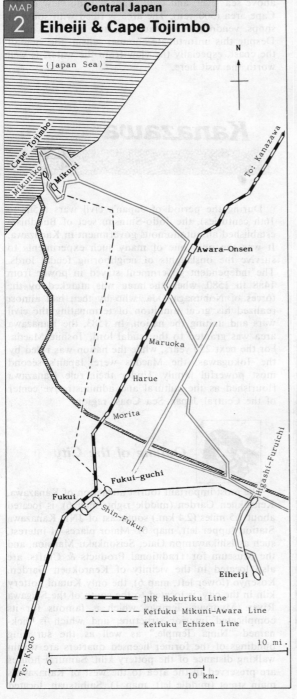

MAP 2
Central Japan
Eiheiji & Cape Tojimbo

(Japan Sea)

N

Cape Tojimbo

Mikuniko

Mikuni

To: Kanazawa

Awara-Onsen

Maruoka

Harue

Morita

Higashi-Furuichi

Fukui-guchi

Fukui

Shin-Fukui

Eiheiji

To: Kyoto

▬▬▬ JNR Hokuriku Line
▬ ▬ ▬ Keifuku Mikuni-Awara Line
━━━━━ Keifuku Echizen Line

10 mi.

0   10 km.

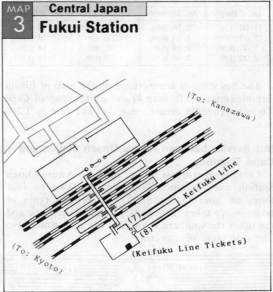

MAP 3
Central Japan
Fukui Station

(To: Kanazawa)

Keifuku Line

(7)
(8)

(To: Kyoto)

(Keifuku Line Tickets)

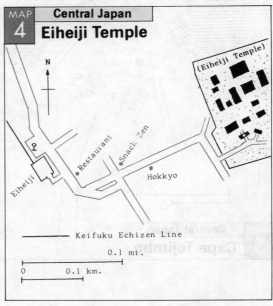

MAP 4
Central Japan
Eiheiji Temple

N

(Eiheiji Temple)

Eiheiji

Restaurant

Snack Zen

Hokkyo

━━━━━ Keifuku Echizen Line

0.1 mi.

0   0.1 km.

foreigners, are first guided to a reception hall for a 15-minute long (and rather tedious) explanation by one of the monks, of the temple's history and facilities. The talk and the warnings about behaving properly in the temple are only in Japanese, but an English brochure is given to foreigners. All the buildings of the temple are connected by covered corridors. (The snow is quite deep here in winter). Visiting this temple is the best way to understand how Zen training is conducted. The temple is open to the public from 5 a.m. to 5 p.m. Admission is 300 yen. (The tickets are sold in vending machines!).

Eiheiji Temple to Cape Tojimbo (map 2)

There are only four buses a day each way between Eiheiji Station and Cape Tojimbo as follows:

Eiheiji to Cape Tojimbo   Cape Tojimbo to Eiheiji

Lv. Eiheiji	Ar. Tojimbo	Lv. Tojimbo	Ar. Eiheiji
11:00 a.m.	12:14 p.m.	10:00 a.m.	11:14 a.m.
12:00 noon	1:14 p.m.	11:00 a.m.	12:14 p.m.
1:00 p.m.	2:14 p.m.	12:00 noon	1:14 p.m.
2:00 p.m.	3:14 p.m.	1:00 p.m.	2:14 p.m.

The bus stations are pictured on the map of Eiheiji Temple (middle left, map 4) and on the map of Cape Tojimbo (middle center, map 5). The fare is 1,200 yen.

Bus Service between Awara-Onsen Station and Cape Tojimbo

There is shuttle bus service between Awara-Onsen Station and Tojimbo. Buses operate two to four times an hour (570 yen). There are two types of buses — one takes the northern road to the Cape and the other the southern road. You can take either one. The ride takes 40 minutes.

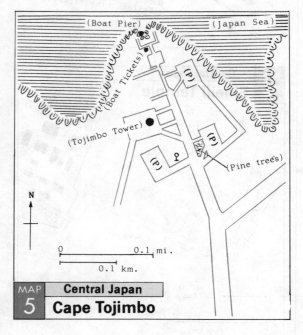

(Boat Pier)   (Japan Sea)

(Boat Tickets)

(Tojimbo Tower)

(P)

(P)   (P)

(Pine trees)

N

0   0.1 mi.
0.1 km.

MAP 5   **Central Japan**
Cape Tojimbo

Cape Tojimbo (map 5)

The dark greyish andesite of the cape looks like pillars. A 164-foot (50 m.) tall cliff supported by these pillars extends along the Japan Sea coast creating a beautiful, rugged coastline. A 30-minute sightseeing boat operates frequently from the tip of the Cape. The view of the cliff from the water is much more impressive than what you'll see staying on land. The ride costs 780 yen. If your time is limited, take the elevator to the top of Tojimbo Tower. The observatory is located 328 feet (100 m.) above sea level, and commands a wide view of the Cape area (500 yen). The area is filled with souvenir shops, vendors and restaurants, and is a little noisy. Despite this unfortunate commercialism, the view of the coast, especially the view from the water, is well worth the visit here.

Kanazawa
金沢

During the period of Japan's civil wars (15th to 16th centuries), the Jodo-Shinshu sect of Buddhism established an autonomous government in Kanazawa. It was the only one of many such experiments to survive the onslaughts of neighboring feudal lords. The independent government stayed in power from 1488 to 1580, when the area was attacked by the forces of Nobunaga Oda, who by then had almost realized his great ambition of terminating the civil wars and uniting the nation. In 1583, the Kanazawa area was granted to the feudal lord, Toshiie Maeda. For the next 250 years, while the nation was ruled by the Tokugawas, the Maedas were Japan's second most powerful family. Under their rule Kanazawa flourished as the cultural and administrative center of the Central Japan Sea Coast region.

Outline of the City

The most important tourist attraction of Kanazawa, Kenrokuen Garden (middle right, map 6), is located about 1.5 miles (2.4 km.) southeast of JNR Kanazawa Station (upper left, map 6). Major places of interest, such as Ishikawamon Gate, Seisonkaku Mansion, and the Museum for Traditional Products & Crafts, are also located in the vicinity of Kenrokuen Garden. Kosenyo (lower left, map 6), the only Kutani pottery kiln in the city, is located to the south of the Saigawa River. Myoryuji Temple, which is famous for its complicated interior structure, and which is nick-named "Ninja Temple," as well as the surviving buildings of the former licensed quarters are within walking distance of the pottery kiln. Samurai houses are preserved in the area to the west of Kanazawa's main street (middle left, map 1). Saihitsuan, located in the same area, is a small Kaga Yuzen Dyeing factory. Oyama Jinja Shrine (middle center, map 6) is also within walking distance. Kanazawa's downtown stretches north to south along the main street (between Musashigatsuji bus stop and Katamachi bus stop). Most shops are between Musashigatsuji and Minamicho, while business offices are between Minamicho and Korimbo, and eating and drinking places between Korimbo and Katamachi. Government offices are to the east of Korimbo.

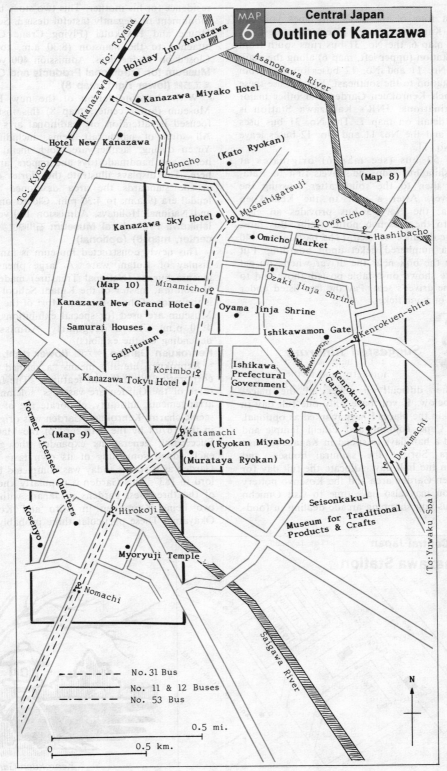

MAP 6

Central Japan
Outline of Kanazawa

To: Toyama

Kanazawa

To: Kyoto

Holiday Inn Kanazawa

Asanogawa River

Kanazawa Miyako Hotel

Hotel New Kanazawa

Honcho

(Kato Ryokan)

(Map 8)

Kanazawa Sky Hotel

Musashigatsuji

Owaricho

Hashibacho

Omicho Market

Ozaki Jinja Shrine

(Map 10) Minamicho

Kanazawa New Grand Hotel

Oyama Jinja Shrine

Kenrokuen-shita

Samurai Houses

Ishikawamon Gate

Saihitsuan

Korimbo

Ishikawa Prefectural Government

Kenrokuen Garden

Kanazawa Tokyu Hotel

(Map 9)

Katamachi

(Ryokan Miyabo)

(Murataya Ryokan)

Dewamachi

Seisonkaku

Museum for Traditional Products & Crafts

(To: Yuwaku Spa)

Former Licensed Quarters

Hirokoji

Kosenyo

Myoryuji Temple

Nomachi

Saigawa River

- - - - - No. 31 Bus
———— No. 11 & 12 Buses
-·-·-·- No. 53 Bus

0.5 mi.

0   0.5 km.

N

Transportation in Kanazawa

Using just four of the city's bus lines you can easily cover Kanazawa's major places of interest. As pictured on map 6, the No. 31 bus runs south from Kanazawa Station (upper left, map 6) along the main street. The No. 11 and No. 12 buses operate from Kanazawa Station to the southeast. You can use these buses to reach Kenrokuen Garden and other major tourist destinations. JNR's Kanazawa Station is pictured in detail on map 7. The No. 31 bus uses stop No. 8, and the No. 11 and No. 12 buses leave from stop No. 11.

The No. 53 bus (see map 6) originates at Kenrokuen-shita bus stop and travels first to Kata-machi, and then to the south after crossing the Saigawa River. After a visit to the Kenrokuen Garden area, the No. 53 bus provides an easy connection to the Kosenyo pottery kiln. Bus fares vary with the distance traveled. (The base fare is 140 yen). Take a numbered ticket upon boarding. Put your fare in the box near the driver when you get off. Fares are shown on a table posted above and to the left of the driver's seat. Pay the fare listed under the number of your ticket.

Suggested Itinerary

It is rather difficult to cover all the places introduced below. If you have only one full day in Kanazawa, skip the places I have marked as optional. If you skip Cape Tojimbo and Eiheiji Temple and have one and a half days to spend in Kanazawa, visit Oyama Jinja Shrine, the samurai houses, and Saihitsuan on the half day. Allocate the full day for the Kenrokuen Garden area and the Kosenyo pottery kiln area. You may also have time to visit Omicho Market, a bustling shopping arcade dealing in food-stuffs.

Seisonkaku　成巽閣 (lower right, map 8)

Take No. 11 or No. 12 bus to Dewamachi 出羽町 stop. Seisonkaku is a one-minute walk from this stop (lower right, map 8). Seisonkaku was constructed in 1863 by the 13th lord of the Maeda family as a residence for his mother. This two-story building is a monument of elegantly tasteful design. Seikoken Tea House and Hikakutei (Flying Crane Garden) are attached to the mansion (8:30 a.m. to 4:30 p.m. Closed on Wednesdays. Admission 400 yen).

Museum for Traditional Products and Crafts 伝統産業工芸館 (lower right, map 8)

With the completion of the new Prefectural Museum (lower center, map 8) this institution has focused its attention on traditional arts and crafts. All sorts of handicraft items, including pottery, Yuzen dyeing, lacquerware, gold, metal and wood items, and handmade toys and papers, are displayed here. The displays illustrate the glories of the high artistic standards the area developed during the feudal era (9 a.m. to 4:30 p.m. Closed on Thursdays and National Holidays. Admission 100 yen).

Ishikawa Prefectural Museum 石川県立美術館 (lower center, map 8) (optional)

This newly constructed museum is famous for its display of Kutani ware. A large pheasant-shaped incense burner (National Treasure) made by Ninsei Nonomura, master of the Kutani School of pottery, is the pride of the collection. Most of the halls of the Museum are used for special exhibitions (9 a.m. to 4:30 p.m. Closed irregularly. Admission varies depending on the exhibits).

Kenrokuen Garden 兼六園 (lower right, map 8)

Kenrokuen literally means "a refined garden incorporating six different features." The famous features of the Garden are vastness, solemnity, precise arrangements, antiquity, elaborate use of water, and scenic charm. Kenrokuen Garden was originally built in the 1670's by the fifth lord of the Maeda family. Succeeding generations expanded the garden and each added something of its own taste to it. The Garden as it stands today was completed by the 12th lord in 1837. This Garden is popularly known as one of the three best gardens in Japan, with the other two being Kairakuen in Mito and Korakuen in Okayama. These particular three probably made the

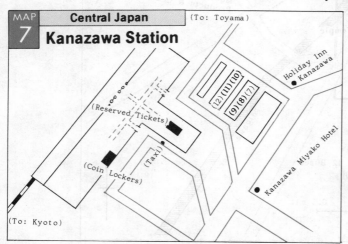

MAP 7　**Central Japan**　(To: Toyama)
Kanazawa Station

(Reserved Tickets)
(Coin Lockers)
(Taxi)
Holiday Inn Kanazawa
Kanazawa Miyako Hotel
(12)(11)(10)
(9)(8)(7)
(To: Kyoto)

Kenrokuen Garden.

list because each was owned by an influential feudal lord. Though I have my doubts about the other two, I certainly agree that Kenrokuen belongs on the list. From the top parts of the Garden, visitors can command a good view of the city, and can even see the Japan Sea in the distance (6:30 a.m. to 6 p.m.; 8 a.m. to 4:30 p.m. in winter. Admission 100 yen).

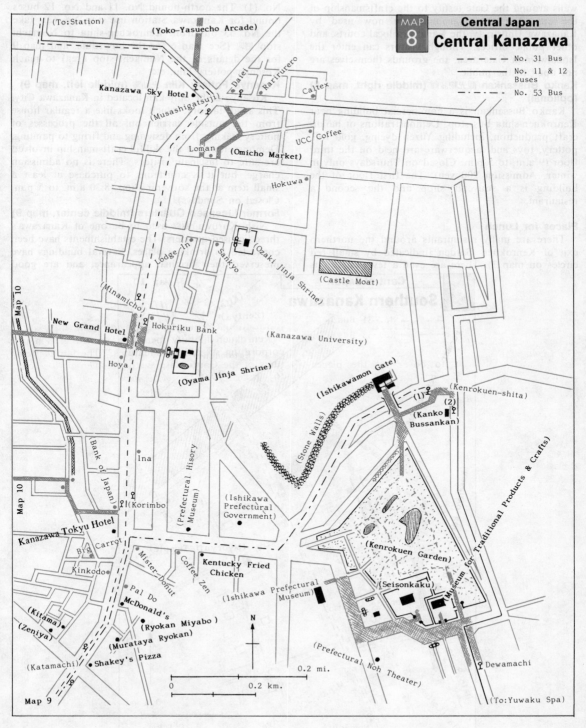

MAP 8 — **Central Japan — Central Kanazawa**

- – – – No. 31 Bus
- ———— No. 11 & 12 Buses
- ———— No. 53 Bus

Ishikawamon Gate 石川門 (middle center, map 8)

Ishikawamon Gate was the southern entrance to Kanazawajo Castle. The entire compound was burned down in 1881 and only a few structures, including the Gate, survived the fire. The magnificence of the Gate gives modern visitors some idea of the power of the Maeda family, and the beautifully arranged stone walls around the Gate testify to the craftsmanship of the era. The castle grounds are now used by Kanazawa University, the Kanazawa local courts, and other public offices. Though visitors can enter the Ishikawamon Gate area, the grounds themselves are not open to the public.

Kanko Bussankan 観光物産館 (middle right, map 8) (optional)

Kanko Bussankan is a commercial building near Kenrokuen-shita bus stop. Demonstrations of handicraft production, including Yuzen dyeing, gold foil, pottery, toys and lacquerware are held on the third floor (9 a.m. to 5 p.m. Closed on Thursdays only in winter. Admission 200 yen). The first floor of the building is a souvenir shop and the second a restaurant.

Places for Lunch

There are many restaurants around the northern exit of Kenrokuen Garden (indicated by small red circles on map 3). There are even a few restaurants located in the Garden. (They are usually very crowded). The second floor of Kanko Bussankan serves reasonably-priced meals.

Kenrokuen-shita bus stops 兼六園下 (middle right, map 8)

The west-bound No. 53 bus originates at bus stop No. (1). The north-bound No. 11 and No. 12 buses bound for Kanazawa Station use stop No. (2). Take the No. 53 bus from Kenrokuen-shita to Nomachi stop 野町 (See map 6 for the bus route, and map 9 for the details of the Nomachi stop area) to reach Kosenyo pottery kiln, etc.

Kosenyo Pottery Kiln 光仙窯 (middle left, map 9)

Kosenyo is the only kiln located in Kanazawa City. This small factory, which looks like a regular house from the outside carries out all the processes of pottery making, from designing and firing to painting. Demonstrations of the skillful craftsmanship involved are sure to fascinate visitors. There is no admission charge, but it is courteous to purchase at least a small item at the souvenir shop (8:30 a.m. to 5 p.m. Closed on Sundays).

Former Licensed Quarters (middle center, map 9)

Nishi-Kuruwa 西廓 used to be one of Kanazawa's three licensed quarters. The establishments have been converted to drinking places. Several buildings have preserved their original appearance, and are good

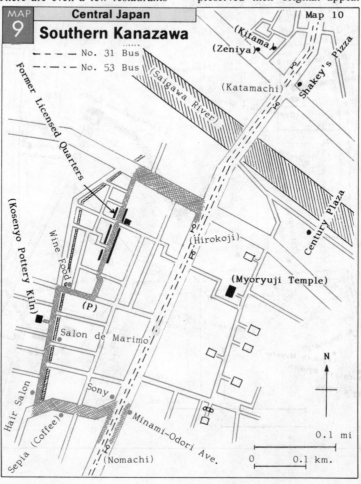

subjects for photographers. A gatehouse used as a checkpoint to keep the girls from escaping from the district has also been preserved. (Indicated on map 9 with a black rectangle).

Myoryuji Temple 妙立寺 (middle right, map 9) (optional)

A number of temples are located on the southern side of the Saigawa River. Among them is Myoryuji Temple. Because of its complicated structure, with 29 staircases and 21 secret chambers, the Temple is popularly known as Ninja-dera, or Temple for Secret Agents. Guided tours are organized from time to time so that visitors don't get lost in this tricky temple. Travelers who only have limited time should skip Myoryuji because advance reservations are required. If you have time to make a visit here, ask your hotel to make a reservation for you at (0762) 41-2877.

Hirokoji to Korimbo by Bus (or on Foot)

Take a north-bound No. 31 bus from Hirokoji 広小路 stop to Korimbo 香林坊 (the second stop) (Refer to map 9 and map 10). The samurai houses are only a few minutes walk from the bus stop.

Saihitsuan and Samurai Houses (middle left, map 10)

The Nagamachi district was inhabited by high ranking samurais during the Edo era. Several samurai houses 武家屋敷 and tile-roofed mud walls along the narrow street have been preserved. Saihitsuan 彩筆庵, one of these houses, has been converted to a small Kaga Yuzen dye works. Kanazawa is proud of the high artistic standards of Kaga Yuzen dyeing, which is comparable to the fine work done in Kyoto. The delicate hand-painting process is demonstrated here (9 a.m. to 4 p.m. Admission 500 yen). Nomura's House 野村家, which was actually moved here from another part of the city, provides visitors a chance to see the interior of the house of a high-ranking samurai. A small but authentic Japanese-style garden is attached to the house, and armor and other samurai utensils are displayed in its various rooms (9 a.m. to 5 p.m Admission 300 yen. Optional).

Oyama Jinja Shrine 尾山神社 (upper right, map 10, or middle left, map 8)

As indicated with the shaded red, Oyama Jinja Shrine will probably be the last visit of your full-day sightseeing in Kanazawa. The Shrine was erected in 1873 in memory of Toshiie Maeda, the first lord of the Maeda family. The Shrine's three-story Shimmon Gate is famous for its colorful stained glass windows on the third level; this is a very unusual structure for Japan. The shrine's garden skillfully combines a pond, rocks, islets and bridges. Entrance to the shrine grounds is free of charge.

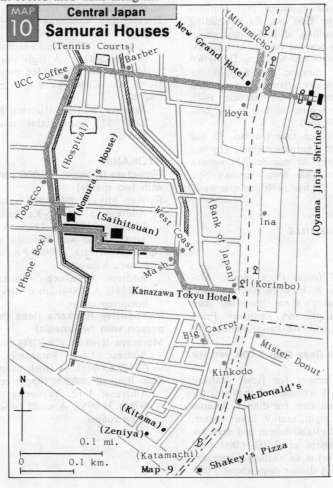

MAP 10 **Central Japan**
Samurai Houses

(Tennis Courts)
Barber
New Grand Hotel
(Minamicho)
UCC Coffee
(Hospital)
(Nomura's House)
Hoya
Tobacco
(Saihitsuan)
West Coast
(Bank of Japan)
Oyama Jinja Shrine
Ina
(Phone Box)
Mash
(Korimbo)
Kanazawa Tokyu Hotel
Big Carrot
Mister Donut
Kinkodo
McDonald's
(Kitama)
(Zeniya)
(Katamachi)
Shakey's Pizza
N
0.1 mi.
0 0.1 km.
Map 9

Other Places of Interest if You are in Kanazawa for an Extended Period

Omicho Market 近江町市場 **(upper center, map 8)** is the kitchen of Kanazawa. About 200 small shops, most of which handle foodstuffs, cluster under narrow covered alleys. Visitors are amazed at the variety of seafood and the reasonable prices. Having grown up in the Tokyo area, I always envy people living in the local cities like Kanazawa whenever I visit this kind of bustling market.

Ozaki Jinja Shrine 尾崎神社 **(middle center, map 8)** is often described as Kanazawa's version of the famous Toshogu Shrine in Nikko. Actually, to demonstrate their loyalty to the Tokugawa Shogunate, local lords all over Japan had Toshogu-type shrines built and dedicated to Ieyasu Tokugawa. Ozaki Jinja Shrine is one of them. The Shrine has deteriorated and does not retain its original magnificence.

Yoko-Yasuecho Arcade 横安江町アーケード **(upper left, map 8)** is lined with many modern stores. Several shops dealing in Buddhist altars are scattered among them. The arcade can be an alternative destination, especially if you happen to get caught in a rain storm.

Edo-mura Village 江戸村 (41 minutes by bus from Kanazawa Station)

If you are staying in Kanazawa for more than one and a half days, you should consider a visit to Edo-mura Village, an open-air museum that features about 20 buildings of the Edo era. Each building represents the typical dwelling of a different social class of the era. You can see the homes of farmers, merchants, craftsmen, priests and warriors. **Dampuen** 檀風苑, another open-air museum that displays the tools and products of various craftsmen, is connected to Edo-mura by frequent mini-bus service. Both facilities are open from 8 a.m. to 6 p.m. A joint admission ticket costs 700 yen.

To reach Edo-mura Village, take the No. 12 bus from Kanazawa Station or Kenrokuen-shita. The bus operates about once every 30 minutes. Edo-mura Village is a few minutes walk from Yuwaku Spa 湯湧温泉, the last stop on the line (470 yen one way).

Restaurants

American Fast Food: I found three shops — McDonald's (lower left, map 8, between Korimbo and Katamachi bus stops), Shakey's Pizza (lower left, map 8, at Katamachi bus stop), and Kentucky Fried Chicken (lower center, near Ishikawa Prefectural Government).

Reasonable Restaurants (less than 5,000 yen for dinner)

Because Kanazawa is famous for fresh seafood caught in the Japan Sea, I recommend that you try an authentic Japanese restaurant for dinner. **Kitama** (lower left, map 8; upper right, map 9; lower center, map 10) is a 122-year old establishment and serves a variety of set menu dinners at 3,500-4,000 yen. **Zeniya** (near Kitama above) is an authentic counter-style Japanese restaurant. A dinner costs about 5,000 yen.

Century Plaza (middle right, map 9) is a modern restaurant overlooking the Saigawa River. **Jimbei,** located on the first floor, serves traditional Japanese dinners starting at 3,000 yen.

Accommodations

HOTELS
Standard Hotels (14,000-20,000 yen for a twin room)

Kanazawa New Grand Hotel 金沢ニューグランドホテル (middle center, map 6)
> Address: 1-50, Takaokamachi, Kanazawa; Phone: (0762) 33-1311. 190 high standard rooms located in the city center.

Kanazawa Miyako Hotel 金沢都ホテル (upper left, map 6)
> Address: 6-10, Konohanacho, Kanazawa; Phone: (0762) 31-2202. 92 modern rooms conveniently located near Kanazawa Station.

Kanazawa Sky Hotel 金沢スカイホテル (upper center, map 6)
> Address: 15-1, Musashimachi, Kanazawa; Phone: (0762) 33-2233. Right on the busy Musashigatsuji intersection (133 rooms).

Holiday Inn Kanazawa ホリデーイン金沢 (upper left, map 6)
> Address: 1-10, Horikawacho, Kanazawa; Phone: (0762) 23-1111. A high standard version of the Holiday Inn Chain (169 rooms).

Hotel New Kanazawa ホテル・ニュー金沢 (upper left, map 6)
> Address: 2-14-10, Honcho, Kanazawa; (0762) 23-2255. 117 comfortable rooms near Kanazawa Station.

RYOKANS
First-class Ryokans (20,000 yen and up per person with two meals)

Ryokan Miyabo 旅館みやぼ (middle center, map 6)
> Address: 3, Shimo-Kakinokibatake, Kanazawa; Phone: (0762) 31-4228. A 39-room authentic Japanese inn with beautiful gardens.

Hakuunro Hotel 白雲楼ホテル (Yuwaku Spa, near Edo-maru Village)
> Address: Yuwakucho, Kanazawa; Phone: (0762) 35-1111. A 100-room deluxe property in a quiet hotspring resort.

Inexpensive Ryokans (less than 12,000 yen per person with two meals)

Murataya Ryokan 村田屋旅館 (middle center, map 6)
> Address: 1-5-2, Katamachi, Kanazawa; Phone: (0762) 63-0455. A small property with 12 rooms.

Kato Ryokan 加藤旅館 (upper center, map 1)
> Address: 4-12, Yasuecho, Kanazawa; Phone: (0768) 21-0952. A small family-operated inn with seven rooms.

Takayama

高山

Takayama Valley is located at the western foot of the Japan Alps. The Alps in this area consist of a number of 10,000-foot (3,000 m.) tall mountains, and are called the roof of Japan. After Hideyoshi Toyotomi unified Japan after almost 250 years of civil war, the feudal lord Nagachika Kanamori was assigned to govern the Takayama area in 1586. During the next 100 years, the Kanamori family successfully encouraged the development of agriculture and handicrafts and made Takayama one of the most prosperous local cities in Japan. In 1692, defeated in a political struggle with the Tokugawa Shogunate, the Kanamori family was exiled to a northern area of Japan, and Takayama fell under the direct control of the Tokugawa Shogunate. Since the Shogunate's principal interest in this prosperous area was in collecting taxes, economic activities were even further encouraged. Protected. by the power of the Shogunate, Takayama merchants and craftsmen expanded their activities into the territories of other feudal lords, and underwrote cultural activities at home with the profits they made elsewhere. The elaborate floats still used in Takayama Festivals testify to the economic prosperity and high cultural standards achieved by the people of Takayama.

As you approach Takayama from the direction of either the Pacific Ocean or the Japan Sea, the train goes along a narrow, beautiful river basin surrounded by mountains. The train ride is enjoyable in all seasons, but especially wonderful in winter, when the mountains are covered with snow. Though your activities will be restricted by the snow and the severe winter cold, the winter train ride is recommended as a detour on your way to Kyoto from Tokyo or on your way back to Tokyo from Kyoto. It is amazing that a city as lovely as Takayama was built in such an isolated mountain valley.

Transportation in Takayama

Buses are the only means of public transportation in Takayama City. Taxis are also plentiful. Since major places of interest are located in a comparatively narrow area, you won't even have to use the buses except to visit Hida-no-sato Village (Details are introduced in the first day itinerary). Just for your information, I have also pictured a circle bus line that loops around the downtown part of Takayama (map 12), which is introduced in the second day itinerary.

Outline of Takayama

The main part of the city is to the east of the JNR Takayama Line tracks. In addition to business and governmental offices, there are a number of places of historical interest in this part of the city. The area to the west of the railroad tracks is mountainous and less developed. Hida-no-sato Village (an open-air museum) and Hida Minzokukan (Hida Folklore Museum) are here. They are perched on mountain sides and surrounded by thick forests.

Suggested Itinerary

One and a half days are ideal for a visit to Takayama: a half day for Western Takayama, and a full day for Eastern Takayama. This is how I will present the itineraries. If you can allocate only one day for Takayama, skip the places I have marked optional.

Afternoon of the First Day
Takayama Station to Hida-no-sato by Bus

As indicated with a red dotted line on map 11, there is circle line bus service from Takayama Station to Hida-no-sato and Minzokukan-mae. The bus leaves from bus stop No. 4 at Takayama Station three times an hour. (Take a numbered ticket upon boarding, and pay when you get off, 160 yen).

On your way to Hida-no-sato you will see a huge golden temple building (probably the biggest structure in Takayama), which is the newly constructed headquarters of the Mahikari religious group. It is a bit disappointing to see a glaringly modern building like this in the quiet surroundings of a mountain village.

Hida-no-sato Village 飛騨の里 **(lower left, map 11)**

Hida-no-sato Village is Takayama's version of Williamsburg, Virginia. Old farm houses, which were destined to be destroyed for the construction of dams or because their owners planned to move to larger cities, have been moved here and preserved as living museums. They illustrate the life style of farmers and craftsmen of the Takayama area. More than 30 buildings are situated on a hillside around a small pond. Many of them are also used for demonstrating the production processes of handicrafts such as lacquerware, carving, dyeing, woodenware, and handmade paper. The village is located in an elevated area and provides visitors with a good view of the city, with the Japan Alps rising in the background. The Village is open from 8:30 a.m. to 5 p.m. The 300 yen admission ticket also entitles you to entrance to Hida Minzokukan. (Hold on to your ticket until you get there!).

Hida-no-sato Village to Hida Minzokukan on foot

Although you can take a bus to Hida Minzokukan you should walk if you are able to do so. The walk itself is a trip through a living museum presentation of the traditional Takayama area. The descending road is dotted with old houses most of which are now souvenir shops or restaurants. Especially noteworthy are **Gokura** 郷倉 and **Hida Goten** 飛騨御殿. Neither of them have English signs, but you will have no difficulty recognizing them. Gokura is an antique shop, in a big old converted warehouse. Because it handles comparatively large-sized antiques, most of them won't be suitable for souvenirs, but the shop itself is like a museum. Hida Goten is the biggest wooden structure in Takayama. It was originally constructed as a rich farmer's house and was moved here for preservation. Its complicated roof and beautiful wall designs are very impressive. Happyaku-Yacho is adjacent to Hida Goten. This commercial establishment contains several replicas of old houses of the Edo era. The 500-yen admission is too expensive for what it has to offer, and you should skip it.

Hida Minzokukan 飛騨民俗館 (Folklore Museum) (middle center, map 11)

Hida Minzokukan consists of four buildings. Wakayama House was built in 1751 and transferred to this site in 1959. It is a good example of the "Gasshozukuri" architectural style — with a steep roof shaped like hands joined together in prayer. You can step inside to see the interior and its antique furniture

and handicraft items. A grain storehouse and an old one-story house are other examples of the everyday environment of the people of the Edo era. The Mountain Museum exhibits materials collected in the Japan Alps by the Hida Mountaineering Club, but the arrangement of the displays unfortunately lacks a focus.

You can take the circle bus back to Takayama Station. End of the first day itinerary.

Second Day Itinerary

There is another circle bus line in Eastern Takayama. (Its route is indicated with a red dotted line on map 12). If you follow my suggested itinerary, you won't have to use it, but you might want to take the bus from Takayama Jinya (lower center, map 12), back to Takayama Station at the end of the itinerary if you are tired.

If you have only one day in Takayama, you should take the bus from the station to Kusakabe Mingeikan-mae (upper right, map 12). The bus leaves from stop No. 2 at Takayama Station every 10-15 minutes. (Take a numbered ticket upon boarding, and pay when you get off. 100 yen).

Kokubunji Temple 国分寺 (middle left, map 12, optional)

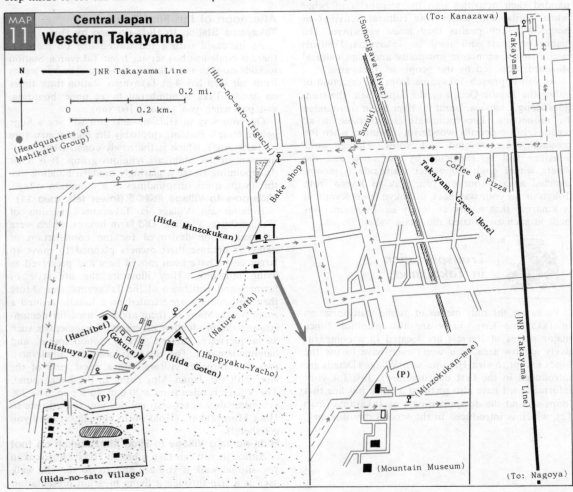

MAP 11 Central Japan
Western Takayama

N

JNR Takayama Line

0.2 mi.

0   0.2 km.

(Headquarters of Mahikari Group)

(Hida-no-sato-Iriguchi)

(Hida-no-sato-Iriguchi)

(Sunorigawa River)

Suzuki

(To: Kanazawa)

Takayama

Bake shop

Coffee & Pizza

Takayama Green Hotel

(Hida Minzokukan)

(Nature Path)

(Hachibei)

(Gokura)

(Hishuya)

UCC

(Happyaku-Yacho)

(Hida Goten)

(P)

(Minzokukan-mae)

(P)

(JNR Takayama Line)

(Mountain Museum)

(Hida-no-sato Village)

(To: Nagoya)

Kokubunji Temple was originally erected at the order of Emperor Shomu in 746. (Kokubunji Temples were built all over Japan at that time as subordinate branch temples of Nara's Todaiji Temple, or Temple of the Great Buddha). The original buildings were burnt down during the civil wars. The present Main Hall was built in 1615 by the Kanamori family. The three-story pagoda, built in 1807, is the only one of this type in the Takayama area. A huge gingko tree in the precincts is 1,200 years old, and has been designated a Natural Monument. The entrance to the temple grounds is free of charge.

Shunkei Kaikan 春慶会館 **(upper center, map 12, optional)**

Shunkei Kaikan, a white warehouse-like building, exhibits exquisite lacquerware of the Shunkei School. The Shunkei School, established in Takayama at the beginning of the 17th century, is famous for its

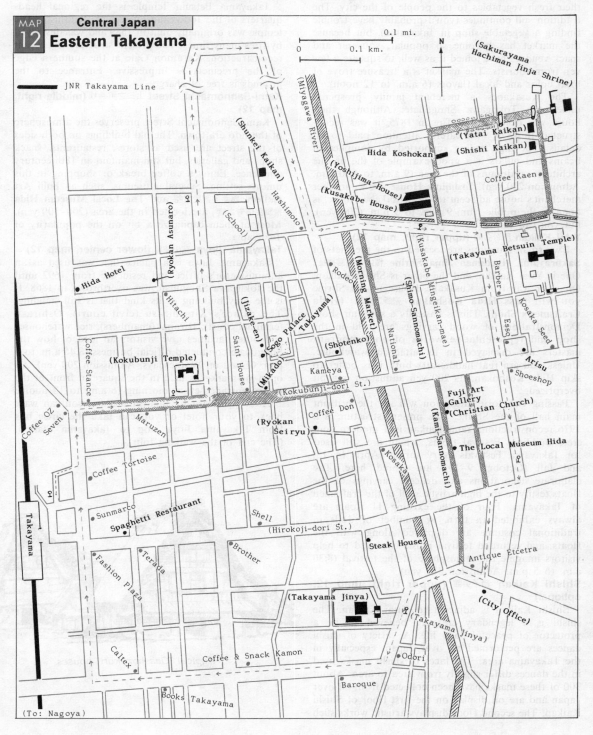

MAP 12

Central Japan

Eastern Takayama

—— JNR Takayama Line

0.1 mi.

0   0.1 km.

N

(Sakurayama Hachiman Jinja Shrine)

(Miyagawa River)

(Shunkei Kaikan)

Hashimoto

(Yatai Kaikan)

Hida Koshokan

(Shishi Kaikan)

(Yoshijima House)

Coffee Kaen

(Kusakabe House)

(School)

(Ryokan Asunaro)

Hida Hotel

Hitachi

(Jizake-en)

(Kusakabe Mingeikan-mae)

(Takayama Betsuin Temple)

Morning Market)

Rodeo

Takayama

Barber

Esso

Kosaka Seed

(Shimo-Sannomachi)

National

Coffee Stance

Saint House

(Mikado)

Sogo Palace

(Shotenko)

(Kokubunji Temple)

Kameya

Arisu

Shoeshop

Coffee OZ

Seven

Maruzen

(Kokubunji-dori St.)

Coffee Don

Fuji Art Gallery

(Christian Church)

(Kami-Sannomachi)

(Ryokan Seiryu)

Coffee Tortoise

The Local Museum Hida

Kosaka

Sunmarco

Spaghetti Restaurant

Shell

(Hirokoji-dori St.)

Takayama

Brother

Steak House

Antique Etcetra

Fashion Plaza

Terada

(Takayama Jinya)

(City Office)

(Takayama Jinya)

Caltex

Coffee & Snack Kamon

Odori

Baroque

Books Takayama

(To: Nagoya)

technique of making use of the natural beauty of the grains of the woods. (8:30 a.m. to 5 p.m. Admission 200 yen).

Kusakabe House 日下部民芸館 (upper right, map 12)

On your way from Shunkei Kaikan to Kusakabe House you will cross the Miyagawa River. Along the eastern bank of the river an **open-air market** 朝市 is held in the morning. The market was originally organized by farmers in the Takayama vicinity to sell their fresh vegetables to the people of the city. The tradition still continues (you'd probably have trouble finding a vegetable shop in Takayama), but because the market has become so popular, souvenir and snack vendors have joined it as well, to squeeze a few yen from tourists. The market is a treasure trove of local color and local flavors (6 a.m. to 12 noon).

The Kusakabes, a merchant family, prospered under the Tokugawa Shogunate. Although their house was destroyed by fire in 1875, it was reconstructed in 1879 with careful attention paid to all details. The high ceiling supported by complicated beams and pillars is a good example of the unique architectural designs of the area (9 a.m. to 4:30 p.m. Admission 200 yen). **Yoshijima House** 吉島家, another merchant's house adjacent to the Kusakabe House, is open to the public from 9 a.m. to 5 p.m. (200 yen), but you can skip it.

Yatai Kaikan 屋台会館 (upper right, map 12)

Two small museums are located in the precincts of **Sakurayama Hachiman Jinja Shrine** 桜山八幡宮神社. One is Yatai Kaikan, and the other is Shishi Kaikan. On your way from Kusakabe House to the Shrine you will pass **Hida Koshokan** 飛騨工匠館 (**Hida Craftsmen's Shop**). This is basically a souvenir shop. Demonstrations of wood carvings are held in the shop and representative works of contemporary masters are displayed in its attached warehouse. Unless you are real handicrafts buff, it is better to skip Hida Koshokan; its 200 yen admission is a bit overpriced.

Passing two torii gates, you will see the brilliant main hall of the Shrine. The present structure is a 1976 reconstruction. Yatai Kaikan is a modern concrete building. Festival floats, which are still used for Takayama Festivals every spring (April 14-15) and fall (October 9-10), are stored here. The elaborate decorations and delicate carvings of the floats testify to the high artistic skill of the craftsmen of Takayama. Four of the existing 11 floats are always exhibited in turn. A number of dolls in traditional costume are displayed along with the floats, and recorded festival music is played to help visitors imagine the atmosphere of the festival (8:30 a.m. to 5 p.m. Admission 380 yen).

Shishi Kaikan 獅子会館 (upper right, map 12, optional)

Shishi Kaikan is adjacent to Yatai Kaikan. The shishi is a legendary creature believed to be a protector of peaceful daily life. A variety of shishi dances are performed all over Japan, especially in the Takayama area. The faces of shishi masks used in the dances differ slightly from area to area. About 300 of these masks have been collected from all over Japan and are on display on the first floor of Shishi Kaikan. The second floor displays artistic works such

as hanging scrolls and folding screens. A short demonstration of the traditional puppet show which is performed on the floats during Takayama Festivals, is given here every 10 minutes. Because the stage is in the dining room the atmosphere is a bit strange, but the complicated movements of the puppets are fascinating. (9 a.m. to 4:30 p.m. Admission 400 yen).

Takayama Betsuin Temple 高山別院 (middle right, map 12, optional)

Takayama Betsuin Temple is the regional headquarters of the Jodo-Shinshu sect of Buddhism. The temple was originally built in 1589 and was destroyed by fires many times. The present structure is a recent reconstruction. Karamon Gate at the southern edge of the precincts is impressive. Entrance to the grounds is free of charge.

Kami-Sannomachi Street 上三之町通り (middle right, map 12)

Kami-Sannomachi Street preserves the atmosphere of the Edo era town. The old buildings on both sides of the street are used as stores, restaurants, snack shops and galleries, but still maintain an 18th century ambience. Enjoy a coffee break or shopping in this unique setting. Several museums, such as **Fujii Art Gallery** 藤井美術民芸館 and **The Local Museum Hida** 飛騨民俗考古館, are located in the area (200-300 yen). Most of them capitalize a bit on the popularity of Takayama.

Takayama Jinya 高山陣屋 (lower center, map 12)

Takayama Jinya is a palace that was used as an administrator's office and residence from 1692 until the Tokugawa Shogunate was overthrown in 1868. It is the only building of its kind that is still standing. The palace's Kitashirasu (civil court), Oshirasu (criminal court), Hiroma (chambers), rice warehouses and other facilities give visitors an idea of how the Shogunate conducted official business (8:45 a.m. to 5 p.m. Closed on Wednesdays. Admission 200 yen). **An open-air market** is held in the square in front of the palace entrance every morning (6 a.m. to 12 noon).

After your visit to Takayama Jinya you can walk back to your hotel or you can take the circle bus from Takayama Jinya stop to Takayama Station. (The end of the walking tour).

Typical "Gasshozukuri" houses.

Shopping

Many souvenir shops are located around the tourist attractions. If you want to combine an evening stroll and shopping, Kokubunji-dori 国分寺通り Street (middle center, map 12) has many shops handling handicraft items. (These shops close around 8 p.m.).

Restaurants and a Pub

American Fast Food: There are still no such establishments in Takayama.

Inexpensive Restaurants (2,500 yen or less for dinner)

Spaghetti Restaurant (lower left, map 12) serves a variety of spaghetti dishes at 650-1,000 yen. **Mikado** (middle center, map 12; located at the corner, no English sign): Pork cutlet is 1,000 yen, and tempura 1,100 yen. A special set menu dinner ("Sansai Teishoku," or assorted mountain vegetables) is 2,500 yen and includes one small bottle of sake. **Shotenko** (middle center, map 12) is a Chinese restaurant. Typical dishes cost 600-1,000 yen. **Steak House** (lower center, map 12) serves a 2,000 yen steak dinner. (Don't expect too much).

Pub

Jizake-en (middle center, map 12) is a Japanese style pub. Thirteen different brands of sake brewed in the Takayama area are available here. Chankonabe (1,700 yen) is a good accompaniment for the sake. The sake barrels piled at the entrance are a good landmark and make this pub easy to find.

Accommodations

HOTELS
Standard Hotels (14,000-20,000 yen for a twin room)

Takayama Green Hotel 高山グリーンホテル (middle right, map 11)

> Address: 2-180, Nishino-Isshikicho, Takayama; Phone: (0577) 33-5500. The largest accommodation in Takayama, with 122 Western and 62 Japanese rooms.

Hida Hotel ひだホテル (upper left, map 12)

> Address: 2-60, Hanaokacho, Takayama; Phone: (0577) 33-4600. A small, 41-room hotel. A new annex will be completed in 1985.

RYOKANS
First-class Ryokan (20,000 yen and up per person with two meals)

Hishuya 飛州屋 (lower left, map 11)

> Address: 2581, Kami-Okamotocho, Takayama; Phone (0577) 33-4001. Sixteen quiet rooms close to Hida-no-sato Village. The best ryokan in Takayama.

Standard Ryokans (12,000-20,000 yen per person with two meals)

Sogo Palace Takayama ホテル・ソーゴパレス高山 (middle center, map 12)

> Address: 54, Suehirocho, Takayama; Phone: (0577) 33-5000. Conveniently located in the heart of the city (33 rooms).

Ryokan Asunaro 旅館あすなろ (upper left, map 12)

> Address: 2-96-2, Hatsudacho, Takayama; Phone: (0577) 33-5551. Also conveniently located for city sightseeing (30 rooms).

Ryokan Seiryu 旅館清龍 (middle center, map 12)

> Address: 6, Hanakawacho, Takayama; Phone: (0577) 32-0448. A 25-room standard property in the middle of downtown.

Inexpensive Ryokan (less than 12,000 yen per person with two meals)

Hachibei 八兵衛 (lower left, map 11)

> Address: 2561, Kami-Okamotocho, Takayama; Phone: (0577) 33-0573. A minshuku with a small garden.

Crossing the Japan Alps
日本アルプス

Takayama to Matsumoto (Map 13)

After the spring thaw, as an alternative to taking the train from Takayama to Nagoya, you can cross the Japan Alps by bus. The buses usually operate from the middle of May to the beginning of October, depending on the snow conditions. If you plan to travel from Takayama to Matsumoto in one day, take the bus from Takayama Station (lower left, map 13) to Norikura 乗鞍 (lower center, map 13), and then transfer to another bus at Norikura for the trip to Shin-Shimashima 新島々 (middle right, map 13). Shin-Shimashima and Matsumoto 松本 are connected by the Matsumoto Dentetsu Line 松本電鉄. (If you hire a car from Takayama to Matsumoto, it costs about 30,000 yen - 40,000 yen.).

The bus between Takayama and Norikura operates three times a day as follows (seven times a day in July and August). The fare is 2,150 yen. At Norikura you'll enjoy a great view of the 10,000 foot mountains of the Japan Alps. You can also take a walk to some of the nearby peaks as you wait for a connecting bus.

Takayama to Norikura		Norikura to Takayama	
Lv. Takayama	Ar. Norikura	Lv. Norikura	Ar. Takayama
8:20 a.m.	9:55 a.m.	10:50 a.m.	12:20 p.m.
9:30 a.m.	11:05 a.m.	12:10 p.m.	1:40 p.m.
12:30 a.m.	2:05 p.m.	3:00 p.m.	4:30 p.m.

The bus between Norikura and Shin-Shimashima also operates three times a day (seven times a day in July and August). The fare is 2,550 yen. Norikura bus terminal is located at an altitude of 8,957 feet (2,730 m.), just 971 feet (296 m.) below the summit of Mt. Norikuradake.

Norikura to Shin-Shimashima		Shin-Shimashima to Norikura	
Lv. Norikura	Ar. Shin-Shimashima	Lv. Shin-Shimashima	Ar. Norikura
10:40 a.m.	12:13 p.m.	7:10 a.m.	9:00 a.m.
1:25 p.m.	3:15 p.m.	9:20 a.m.	11:10 a.m.
3:00 p.m.	4:50 p.m.	12:10 p.m.	2:00 p.m.

The train between Shin-Shimashima and Matsumoto operates about once every hour. The ride takes 30 minutes, and the fare is 530 yen.

Kamikochi 上高地 *(upper center, map 13)*

If you have extra time for this area, you should consider a visit to Kamikochi. If you decide to do so, take a bus to Kamikochi from Norikura rather than a bus to Shin-Shimashima. This bus operates three times a day (six times a day in summer), and the fare is 2,350 yen.

Norikura bus terminal and the Japan Alps.

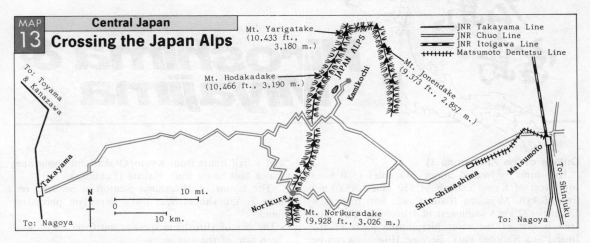

MAP
13
Central Japan
Crossing the Japan Alps

Mt. Yarigatake
(10,433 ft.,
3,180 m.)

Mt. Hodakadake
(10,466 ft., 3,190 m.)

Mt. Jonendake
(9,373 ft., 2,857 m.)

Kamikochi

To: Toyama
& Kanazawa

Takayama

To: Nagoya

Norikura

Mt. Norikuradake
(9,928 ft., 3,026 m.)

Shin-Shimashima

Matsumoto

To: Shinjuku

To: Nagoya

———— JNR Takayama Line
———— JNR Chuo Line
–·–·– JNR Itoigawa Line
+++++ Matsumoto Dentetsu Line

JAPAN ALPS

N

10 mi.

0

10 km.

Norikura to Kamikochi		Kamikochi to Norikura	
Lv. Norikura	Ar. Kamikochi	Lv. Kamikochi	Ar. Norikura
10:40 a.m.	12:35 a.m.	9:20 a.m.	11:20 a.m.
1:30 p.m.	3:25 p.m.	10:00 a.m.	12:00 noon
2:15 p.m.	4:10 p.m.	11:40 a.m.	1:40 p.m.

Kamikochi is at an altitude of 4,900 feet (1,500 m.) in a valley surrounded by the Japan Alps. It has some of the most picturesque mountain scenery in Japan. There are several ryokans in the valley, but they are very crowded. Make reservations as far in advance as possible. In Kamikochi you can enjoy a stroll along the Azusagawa River and Taishoike Pond as well as the beautiful view of the rugged mountains.

Kamikochi is one of the most popular mountaineers' entry ways to the Japan Alps. The hikers who also love this area dress just as casually as the mountaineers. This is a good chance for you to get out your jeans and casual shirts and sweaters. Don't take a fancy suitcase to this area or you'll just be embarrassed.

The bus between Kamikochi and Shin-Shimashima operates about once every hour (some of them go beyond Shin-Shimashima to Matsumoto), and the ride to Shin-Shimashima takes 75 minutes and costs 1,650 yen.

Accommodations in Kamikochi

Standard Ryokans (14,000 - 20,000 yen per person with two meals)
Shirakabaso 白樺荘
   Address: 4468, Kamikochi, Azumimura, Nagano Pref.; Phone: (026395) 2131. (58 rooms).
Nishiitoya 西糸屋
   Address: 4469-1, Kamikochi, Azumimura, Nagano Pref.; Phone: (026395) 2206. (30 rooms).
Gosenjaku Ryokan 五千尺旅館
   Address: 4468, Kamikochi, Azumimura, Nagano Pref.; Phone: (026395) 2111 (31 rooms).

Matsumoto to Tokyo or Nagoya
The JNR Chuo Line 中央本線 provides service between Matsumoto and Tokyo (Shinjuku Station 新宿駅), and between Matsumoto and Nagoya 名古屋.

Trains on both routes operate about once an hour. The ride from Matsumoto to Nagoya takes about two hours and 20 minutes, and the ride between Matsumoto and Tokyo's Shinjuku Station takes about three hours and 20 minutes. Trains consist of one Green Car (reserved seat first class), four to five ordinary reserved cars, and three to four ordinary nonreserved cars.

If you leave Takayama in the morning, it is not difficult to catch a late afternoon train to Shinjuku or Nagoya. (If you are spending time in Kamikochi, you can easily catch a train at Matsumoto even if you leave Kamikochi after noon).

Matsumoto
If you have a few hours in Matsumoto, visit Matsumotojo Castle 松本城 . *The Castle is located about one mile northeast of Matsumoto Station. The donjon (National Treasure) was completed at the end of the 16th century, and is the oldest donjon in Japan (8:30 a.m. to 5 p.m. Admission 200 yen). The castle grounds also contain a Folklore Museum housed in a modern building. The Museum displays about 60,000 artistic and archaeological objects of the area. (9 a.m. to 4:30 p.m. Admission 150 yen).*

Accommodations in Matsumoto

Business Hotels (less than 14,000 yen for a twin room)
Matsumoto Tokyu Inn 松本東急イン
   Address: 1-2-37, Fukashi, Matsumoto; Phone: (0263) 36-0109. A two minute walk from Matsumoto Station (99 rooms).
Hotel Sunroute Matsumoto ホテル・サンルート松本
   Address: 1-1, Agata, Matsumoto; Phone: (0263) 33-3131. A 10-minute walk from Matsumoto Station (90 rooms).

広島、
宮島

Hiroshima & Miyajima

Outline of the Area (map 1)

Hiroshima is located about 240 miles (380 km.) southwest of Kyoto and about 550 miles (895 km.) from Tokyo. Miyajima Island (lower left, map 1) is 13 miles (22 km.) southwest of Hiroshima City. The area is one of the most picturesque parts of the Inland Sea National Park. Because Hiroshima can be reached easily by Shinkansen, the area can be incorporated into almost every itinerary, especially for those on their way to or from Kyushu. A two-night stay in the area is ideal, but even a one-night, two-day visit as an excursion from Kyoto provides you with a good opportunity to enjoy the area's peaceful marine scenery and gives you enough time to visit the historic sites and Peace Memorial Park.

Transportation to and from Hiroshima

The Shinkansen is the most convenient way to travel to Hiroshima. Details on the Shinkansen can be found in Chapter "Transportation within Japan." It takes about five and a half hours to reach Hiroshima from Tokyo by Shinkansen, about two

and a half hours from Kyoto/Osaka, and about one and a half hours from Hakata (Fukuoka).

The layout of Hiroshima Station is pictured on map 2. You should bear three important points in mind:

- The city of Hiroshima spreads out from the southern side of the station;
- The Shinkansen platforms are located on the northernmost side of the station. (They are so inconveniently placed merely because they were constructed much later than the regular tracks and platforms); and
- The city's streetcar terminal ("Hiroshima-ekimae") is in front of the southern side of the station.

Suggested Itinerary

If you are making an excursion here from Kyoto or Osaka, take a morning Shinkansen, and arrive in Hiroshima before noon. The afternoon of the first day should be spent in the city of Hiroshima. The second day should be allocated to a visit to Miyajima. You can take a late afternoon Shinkansen back to

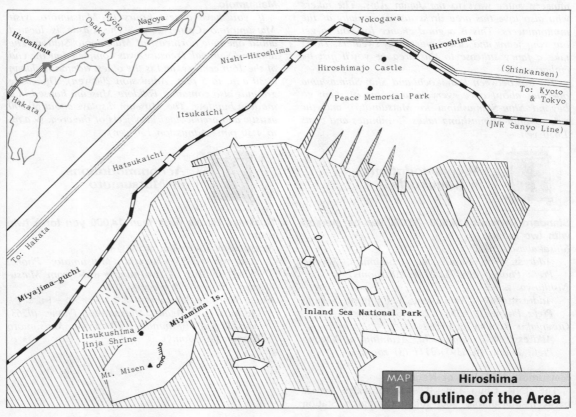

| MAP 1 | Hiroshima Outline of the Area |

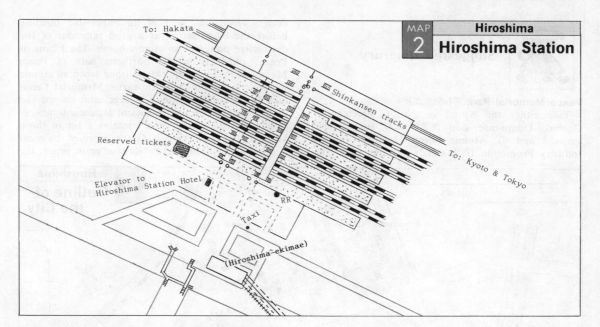

MAP 2 Hiroshima
Hiroshima Station

Kyoto/Osaka. If you can allocate one more day for the area, spend the second night in either Hiroshima or Miyajima (Miyajima is a good place to stay at a Japanese ryokan), and take a half-day cruise to Setoda on the third day. You can take a Shinkansen back to Kyoto/Osaka from Mihara Station (Details are explained below).

If you plan to visit this area on your way to Kyushu, you should allocate two nights for Hiroshima/Miyajima, and the full second day in Miyajima. On the third day take a morning Shinkansen to Hakata, and transfer there to another JNR train for your destination. You can reach Kumamoto or Nagasaki by early afternoon.

Hiroshima

広島

This city got its name when the feudal lord Terumoto Mori built a castle here at the end of the 16th century and named it "Hiroshima"-jo (Broad Island Castle). The Mori family was followed by the Fukushima family, and then the Asanos, who, by encouraging industry, laid the foundation for the development of the castle town. During the Sino-Japanese War (1894-1895), imperial headquarters were set up in Hiroshimajo Castle, and the city was a bustling land and sea transportation center. On August 6, 1945, at 8:15 a.m., Hiroshima was atom-bombed. The city was completely flattened in an instant, and more than 200,000 lives lost. Two years later the citizens of Hiroshima held their first Peace Festival. Its theme was: "No more Hiroshimas." It has since become an annual event to promote world peace. Now the city, with a population of 870,000, serves as the administrative, educational and communications center of the Chugoku district.

Outline of the City

There are four major places of interest in Hiroshima — Peace Memorial Park (middle left, map 3); Hiroshimajo Castle (upper center, map 3); Shukkeien Garden (upper center, map 3, to the east of the Castle); and Hijiyama-Koen Park (lower right, map 3). The downtown section of the city is on the southern side of Route 54. (Shopping arcades are indicated with shaded red). Many drinking spots and obscure cabarets are located around the eastern end of the shopping arcades. Hiroshima Prefectural Government and other governmental offices are located on the northern side of Route 54. These places and JNR Hiroshima Station are conveniently connected by several streetcars as explained next.

Transportation in Hiroshima

Hiroshima has eight streetcar lines. I have pictured five of them, which can be used by tourists conveniently and easily. All the stops these five lines make are pictured on map 3. The No. 1, No. 2, No. 5 and No. 6 streetcars charge a 110-yen flat fare regardless of the distance you ride. The No. 9 streetcar, which makes only five stops, charges a 90-yen flat rate. No transfer tickets are available. You have to pay for each ride separately.

If you are planning to take a half-day cruise from Hiroshima to Setoda, or a sunset cruise in Hiroshima harbor (explained below), you can take either the No. 5 or No. 1 streetcar to Ujina Port 宇品港 *(the last stop on both lines). The pier for the cruise ships is a one-minute walk from Ujina.*

Suggested Itinerary

Peace Memorial Park 平和記念公園

Take either the No. 2 or No. 6 streetcar to Genbaku-Domu-mae stop 原爆ドーム前 (upper left, maps 3 and 4). **Atomic Bomb Dome** (Ruins of Industry Promotion Hall) stands near the stop. The

dome, which was part of an impressive building before the blast, serves as a grim reminder of the destructive power of an atomic bomb. **The Flame of Peace**, which is in the northern part of Peace Memorial Park, will be extinguished when all atomic weapons disappear from the earth. **Memorial Cenotaph for A-Bomb Victims** is a large vault shaped like the clay figurines found in ancient Japanese tombs. A stone chest under the vault contains a list of those killed by the atomic bomb. On the front of the chest is an epitaph in Japanese: "Repose ye in peace, for

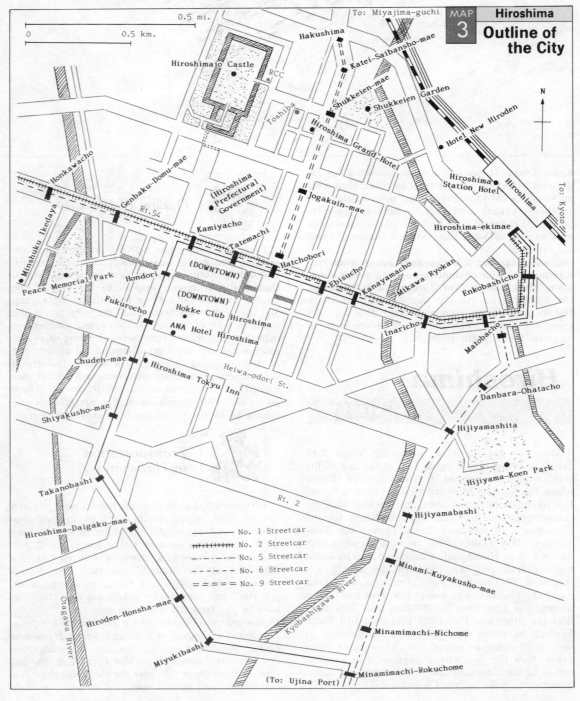

the error shall not be repeated." The cenotaph was designed by Dr. Kenzo Tange, the world renowned architect, so that those standing in front of it can see the Flame of Peace and the Atomic Bomb Dome beyond it. **Peace Memorial Museum** displays objects and photographs that illustrate the devastation caused by the atomic bomb (9 a.m. to 6 p.m. Till 5 p.m. in winter. Admission 50 yen). Every adult should visit the Museum in order to understand the era in which we live. Even though viewing the displays is an uncomfortable experience, it is one that should not be avoided. On the second floor of the adjacent Peace Memorial Hall, documentary films on the A-bomb are shown from time to time, one in English and the other in Japanese.

Hiroshimajo Castle 広島城 (upper center, map 3)

The Castle is about 0.5 miles (0.8 km.) from Peace Memorial Park and your two legs are the best means of transportation there. Hiroshimajo Castle was originally constructed in 1589 by Terumoto Mori. The donjon was registered as a National Treasure until 1945, when the bomb explosion destroyed the entire castle. The five-story donjon was reconstructed for the Hiroshima Rehabilitation Exposition in 1958. The interior is a local museum. From the top, there is a panoramic view of the entire city. Entrance to the castle grounds is free of charge. The donjon is open to the public from 9 a.m. to 5 p.m. (till 4:30 p.m. in winter). Admission is 200 yen.

Shukkeien Garden 縮景園 (upper center, map 3)

Leave the castle grounds through the eastern exit, and walk 0.4 miles (0.6 km.) further east to Shukkeien Garden. The English signs for RCC and Toshiba are good landmarks.

Shukkeien Garden was designed in 1620 by the feudal lord Nagaakira Asano. It is situated on the Kyobashigawa River, from which water is drawn to make streams and ponds within the garden grounds. The Garden's islets and bridges, colorful carp, fantastically-shaped pine trees and the surrounding woods combine to give it special beauty (9 a.m. to 6 p.m. Till 5 p.m. in winter. Admission 150 yen).

Hijiyama-Koen Park 比治山公園 (lower right, map 3)

Unless you are in Hiroshima during cherry blossom season, you should skip this park. It is located on a small hill and there's good view of the city from the top.

Restaurants and a Pub Downtown

American Fast Food: McDonald's is located on the main shopping arcade (middle center, map 4).

Inexpensive Restaurants (2,500 yen or less for dinner)

New Tokyo is a restaurant building (middle right, map 4). The building does not have an English sign, but you can easily recognize it because it is located at an intersection, and because it has plastic displays of the dishes it serves. **Kurama** (B1) serves shabu-shabu at 2,500 yen. **Bon** is located on the third floor. Beef stew is 1,350 yen, and steak 1,500 yen to 2,700 yen. **Tsukumo** (4F) serves set menu tempura at 1,200 yen.

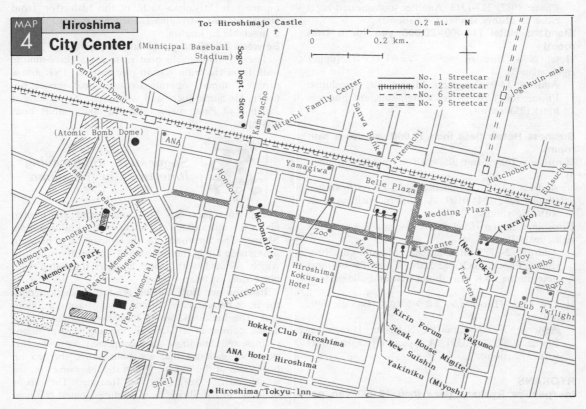

MAP 4

Hiroshima City Center (Municipal Baseball Stadium)

To: Hiroshimajo Castle

0.2 mi.
0.2 km.

— No. 1 Streetcar
||||||| No. 2 Streetcar
---- No. 6 Streetcar
==== No. 9 Streetcar

Genbaku-Domu-mae
(Atomic Bomb Dome)
ANA
Flame of Peace
(Memorial Cenotaph)
Peace Memorial Park
(Peace Memorial Hall)
(Peace Memorial Museum)
Sogo Dept. Store
Kamiyacho
Hitachi Family Center
Hondori
Yamagiwa
McDonald's
Zoo
Narumi
Hiroshima Kokusai Hotel
Fukurocho
Sanwa Bank
Tatemachi
Belle Plaza
Wedding Plaza
Levante
Hatchobori
Ebisucho
(Yaraiko)
(New Tokyo)
Joy
Jumbo
Roro
Trebien
Pub Twilight
Jogakuin-mae
Kirin Forum
Steak House Mimitei
New Suishin
Yakiniku (Miyoshi)
Yakumo
Hokke Club Hiroshima
ANA Hotel Hiroshima
Shell
Hiroshima Tokyu-Inn

Yaraiko (middle right, map 4) is a Chinese restaurant. Most of the dishes are priced from 600-1,200 yen. **Yakiniku Miyoshi** (middle center, map 4) is a Korean-style barbecue restaurant. Its dishes are priced from 700-1,100 yen.

Moderate Restaurants

New Suishin (middle center, map 4) is a French restaurant, which serves a set menu dinner at 2,000-4,000 yen. **Yagumo** (lower right, map 4) is a Japanese restaurant specializing in seafood. Various nabe dishes range from 3,500 to 4,500 yen. **Steak House Mimitei** (middle center, map 4) specializes in steak and serves a set menu steak dinner at 5,000 yen.

Pub

Kirin Forum is a Kirin beer (Japan's most popular brand) hall (middle center, map 4).

Accommodations

HOTELS

First-class Hotels (20,000 yen and up for a twin room)

ANA Hotel Hiroshima 広島全日空ホテル (middle left, map 3)

> Address: 7-20, Nakamachi, Naka-ku, Hiroshima; Phone: (082) 241-1111. A new high-class hotel with 431 rooms.

Hiroshima Grand Hotel 広島グランドホテル (upper center, map 3)

> Address: 4-4, Hatchobori, Naka-ku, Hiroshima; Phone: (082) 227-1313. Another sophisticated hotel close to historical sites (397 rooms).

Standard Hotel (14,000-20,000 yen for a twin room)

Hotel New Hiroden ホテル・ニューヒロデン (upper right, map 3)

> Address: 14-9, Osugacho, Minami-ku, Hiroshima; Phone: (082) 263-3456. A high standard business hotel (353 rooms).

Business Hotels (less than 14,000 yen for a twin room)

Hiroshima Tokyu Inn 広島東急イン (middle left, map 3)

> Address: 3-17, Komachi, Naka-ku, Hiroshima; Phone: (082) 244-0109. A modern business hotel with 286 rooms.

Hiroshima Station Hotel 広島ステーションホテル (upper right, map 3)

> Address: 2-37, Matsubaracho, Minami-ku, Hiroshima; Phone: (082) 262-3201. A no-frills business hotel in the JNR Hiroshima Station building (137 rooms).

Hokke Club Hiroshima 法華クラブ広島 (middle left, map 3)

> Address: 7-7, Nakamachi, Naka-ku, Hiroshima; Phone: (082) 248-3371. A typical efficiency hotel with 372 rooms.

RYOKANS

Inexpensive Ryokans (less than 12,000 yen per

person with two meals)

Mikawa Ryokan 三河旅館 (middle right, map 2)

> Address: 9-6, Kyobashicho, Minami-ku, Hiroshima; Phone: (082) 261-2719. A small, 13-room property (A seven minute walk from Hiroshima Station).

Minshuku Ikedaya 民宿池田屋 (middle left, map 2)

> Address: 6-36, Dobashicho, Naka-ku, Hiroshima; Phone: (082) 231-3329. A small, family-operated inn near the Peace Memorial Park (16 rooms).

Miyajima 宮島

Miyajima, also called Itsukushima, is an island about 19 miles (30 km.) in circumference. It is famous for its shrine built on supports that extend into the sea, and is also noted for its cherry blossoms at the beginning of April and its autumn tints in November. Tame deer wander about the island.

Transportation to and from Hiroshima

Between Hiroshima and Miyajima-guchi

Commuter trains on the JNR Sanyo Line 山陽本線 operate about every 15-30 minutes, and connect Hiroshima and Miyajima-guchi 宮島口. As pictured on map 1, Miyajima-guchi is the fifth stop from Hiroshima. At Miyajima-guchi train station, there is a timetable in English.

Between Miyajima-guchi and Miyajima

The Miyajima-guchi boat piers are a three-minute walk from the train station (see map 5). JNR and a private company operate frequent boat service between Miyajima-guchi and Miyajima. If you have a Japan Rail Pass, make sure you take a JNR boat 国鉄連絡船.

Suggested Sightseeing Itinerary in Miyajima

The boat piers on Miyajima Island are located about 0.5 miles (0.8 km.) north of Itsukushima Jinja Shrine. The approach to the Shrine is a pleasant promenade along the Inland Sea, the southern half of which is lined with stone lanterns (indicated with black dots on map 6).

Itsukushima Jinja Shrine 厳島神社 is dedicated to the three daughters of Susano-o-no-Mikoto, a Shinto god. The buildings, which have been rebuilt several times, consist of a Main Shrine and several minor shrines and buildings — all connected by wide corridors or galleries that are built above the sea on both sides of the Shrine. When the tide comes in, the whole edifice seems to be floating. The major buildings of the Shrine have been designated National

Treasures. A vermilion torii gate rises of the sea about 525 feet (160 m.) from the shore. This 53-foot (16 m.) tall torii gate, the largest in Japan, was erected in 1875, and is a symbol of the island. Itsukushima Jinja Shrine is open to the public from 6:30 a.m. to 6 p.m. Admission is 200 yen.

Itsukushima Jinja Shrine Treasure House 厳島神社宝物館 (lower left, map 6) is just across the street from the exit of the Shrine. This modern structure contains nearly 4,000 objects, more than 130 of which have been designated National Treasures or Important Cultural Properties (9 a.m. to 5 p.m. Admission 250 yen).

Momijidani-Koen Park 紅葉谷公園 **and Mt. Misen** 弥山. Follow the red arrows on map 6 to Momijidani-Koen Park, Maple Valley Park, a quiet retreat on a hillside amid groves of maple trees. A free mini-bus operates between the two stops pictured on map 6 (The bus route is indicated with a red broken line) every 20 minutes, but because it's so lovely you should consider walking through the Park to the

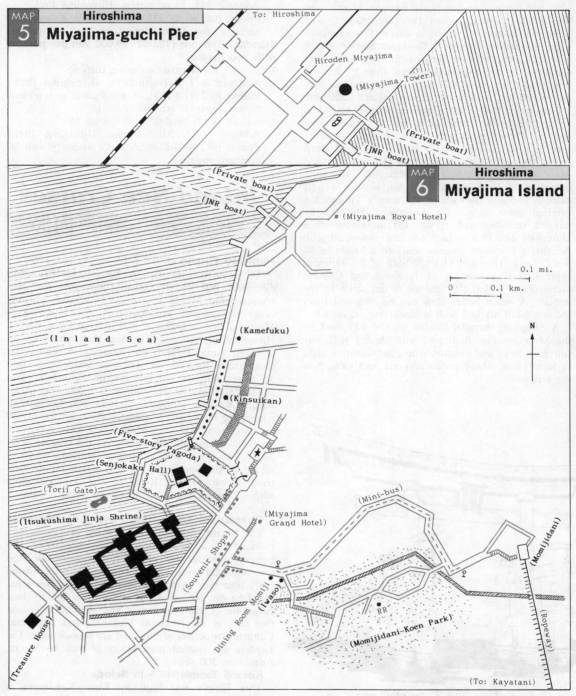

MAP 5

Hiroshima
Miyajima-guchi Pier

To: Hiroshima

Hiroden Miyajima

(Miyajima Tower)

(Private boat)

(JNR boat)

(Private boat)

(JNR boat)

MAP 6

Hiroshima
Miyajima Island

• (Miyajima Royal Hotel)

0.1 mi.

0   0.1 km.

N

(Inland Sea)

• (Kamefuku)

• (Kinsuikan)

(Five-story Pagoda)

(Senjokaku Hall)

(Torii Gate)

(Itsukushima Jinja Shrine)

(Souvenir Shops)

(Mini-bus)

(Miyajima Grand Hotel)

(Momijidani)

Dining Room Momiji

(Iwaso)

RR

(Momijidani-Koen Park)

(Ropeway)

(Treasure House)

(To: Kayatani)

ropeway station pictured at the lower right of map 6. The ropeways take visitors almost to the top of Mt. Misen. The first ropeway, a small six-passenger car, connects Momijidani Station with Kayatani Station. The cars operate every 30 seconds. A larger gondola, with a capacity of 26, operates every 15 minutes from Kayatani to Shishiiwa. The real summit of Mt. Misen (1,739 feet, or 530 m.) is a 15-20 minute walk from Shishiiwa Station. From the gondola, and, of course, from Shishiiwa, visitors have a splendid view of Inland Sea National Park and its innumerable islets and the picturesque boats. Many wild monkeys live on Mt. Misen. When they are playing near Shishiiwa, visitors are asked to check their handbags in complimentary lockers in Shishiiwa Station. There is no danger to visitors, but the monkeys are rather naughty. The two ropeways operate from 8 a.m. to 5 p.m. (From 8 a.m. to 4:20 p.m. in winter). One way fare is 800 yen, and round trip tickets are 1,300 yen.

Senjokaku Hall 千畳閣 (lower left, map 6). When you return to the shrine area, visit Senjokaku Hall and the **Five-story Pagoda** 五重塔. These two structures are located on a hill, atop a flight of steep steps. Senjokaku Hall, or the Hall of One Thousand Mats, is an old building that Hideyoshi Toyotomi dedicated to Itsukushima Jinja Shrine in 1587. (It actually contains only about 450 mats!). Though the original plans called for Senjokaku Hall to be painted vermilion red, it was left unpainted when Hideyoshi died (9 a.m. to 5 p.m. Admission 50 yen). Nearby, a five-story pagoda soars to a height of 90 feet (27 m.). Thatched with the bark of the Japanese cypress, it is a mixture of Japanese and Chinese architectural styles. (Its interior is not open to the public). A much better view can be obtained from the small hill marked with a black star on map 6.

A Shopping Arcade, located on the way back to the Miyajima Pier (indicated with shaded red), has souvenir shops and vendors who give visitors a taste of local color. Many restaurants are also located in the arcade.

Itsukushima Jinja Shrine's torii gate.

Accommodations

There are no Western-style hotels in Miyajima.
RYOKANS
First-class Ryokan (20,000 yen and up per person with two meals)
Iwaso 岩惣 (lower center, map 6)
  Address: 345, Miyajimacho, Hiroshima Pref.;
  Phone: (08294) 4-2233. An authentic, deluxe property in quiet Momijidani-Koen Park (45 rooms).
Standard Ryokans (12,000-20,000 yen per person with two meals)
Kamefuku かめ福 (middle center, map 6)
  Address: 849, Miyajimacho, Hiroshima Pref.;
  Phone: (08294) 4-2111. A good place to sample a typical Japanese inn (44 rooms).
Kinsuikan 錦水館 (middle center, map 6)
  Address: 1133, Miyajimacho, Hiroshima Pref.;
  Phone: (08294) 4-2133. A small property with 26 standard rooms.

Inland Sea Cruises

瀬戸内海

Half-Day Cruise STSライン
As pictured on map 7, Setonaikai Steamship Company 瀬戸内海汽船 (private) operates half day cruises, from March 1 through November 30. Advance reservations are required. The boat leaves Miyajima Pier at 8:40 a.m. and stops at Ujina Port in Hiroshima at 9:10 a.m. The boat then makes a stop at Omishima Island so passengers can visit Oyamazumi Jinja Shrine. The boat arrives at Setoda 瀬戸田 at 1:05 p.m. The fare for the cruise boat from either Miyajima or Hiroshima is 6,200 yen. After visiting Kosanji Temple in Setoda you can take a connecting ferry, which operates about once every 30 minutes, from Setoda to Mihara 三原 (The ferry ride takes 25-50 minutes depending on the type of boat. 560-1,230 yen.). JNR's Mihara Station, which is served by the Shinkansen, is only a five-minute walk from Mihara Port. (Refer to the Transportation within Japan Chapter for the Shinkansen schedule.)

Oyamazumi Jinja Shrine 大山祇神社 on Omishima
The Shrine, originally constructed in 719, is surrounded by a thick forest of camphor trees. The present buildings are 1427 reconstructions. Because several feudal lords dedicated treasures to the Shrine every time they won a battle in the Inland Sea area, the Treasure House of the Shrine has Japan's best collection of samurai armor and swords. It is said that 80% of the National Treasures and Important Cultural Properties of this kind are housed here. The displays are rotated periodically (8 a.m. to 5 p.m. Admission 500 yen)
Kosanji Temple 耕三寺 in Setoda
This Temple was built by Kozo Kanamoto, a

successful businessman born in Setoda, and dedicated to his mother. It took 30 years to complete the entire complex. All the buildings are modeled on famous structures all over Japan, and the Temple itself is a museum of replicas of National Treasures. The replicas include copies of Yomeimon Gate of Toshogu Shrine in Nikko; Silver Pavilion in Kyoto; Yumedono Octagonal Hall of Horyuji Temple in Nara; Five-story Pagoda of Murooji Temple in Nara; Phoenix Hall of Byodoin Temple in Kyoto, etc.

Sunset Cruise　サンセット・クルーズ

Setonaikai Steamship Co. recently introduced a new sunset harbor cruise. It leaves from Hiroshima's Ujina Port at 6:30 p.m. every evening and returns at 8:50 p.m. If you don't have time for the half-day cruise you might enjoy this trip around the harbor. The marine scenery is especially beautiful in the sunset glow. The fare is 2,000 yen.

Onomichi

尾道

If after the half-day Inland Sea cruise you want to spend one more night in the area, I recommend that you visit Onomichi.

Setoda to Onomichi

From Setoda take a boat to Onomichi instead of to Mihara. The boat to Onomichi is operated by the Setonaikai Steamship Co. (the same company that operates the half-day Inland Sea Cruise), and makes about six trips a day, leaving Setoda about once every 90 minutes. Because the boat has only reserved seats, make reservations for this trip when you make your arrangements for the half-day cruise. The ride takes 35 minutes and the fare is 1,400 yen. Onomichi train station is only a four-minute walk from the boat pier.

Places of Interest

The city of Onomichi hugs the coast of the Inland Sea. Steep hills rise on the northern side of the city. Though modernization has altered the face of the downtown area, the city still has many traditional districts along its hilly, narrow streets. Onomichi is especially famous for its panoramic view of the Inland Sea National Park from Senkoji-Koen Park 千光寺公園, which can be reached by ropeway. The Park is famous for its 9,000 cherry trees and is absolutely spectacular when they are in bloom in early April. The ropeway runs every 15 minutes from 9 a.m. to 5:15 p.m. (200 yen); the station is only about 0.5 miles (0.8 km.) from the train station. Because Onomichi is a small town you shouldn't have any difficulties locating the ropeway. Onomichi's beautiful marine scenery and its exotic, historic port town atmosphere have attracted a number of poets and novelists as well as tourists. Many poems on this lovely town have been engraved on large stones in Senkoji-Koen Park. There are also many old temples in the city. Especially famous among them are Senkoji Temple (in the Park), and Jodoji Temple.

Onomichi to Fukuyama

You can take the JNR Sanyo Line's 山陽本線 local train from Onomichi to Fukuyama 福山, and then transfer to the Shinkansen. The local train operates about once every 20 minutes, and the trip from Onomichi to Fukuyama, the third stop, takes 20 minutes. Refer to Chapter "Transportation within Japan" for the Shinkansen schedule.

Accommodations in Onomichi

First-class Ryokans (20,000 yen and up per person with two meals)

Nishiyama Bekkan 西山別館
　Address: 678-1, Yamanami-machi, Onomichi; Phone: (0848) 37-3145. An authentic 17-room ryokan overlooking the Inland Sea (10 minutes by car from Onomichi Station).

Takemuraya 竹村家
　Address: 3-14-1, Kubo, Onomichi; Phone: (0848) 37-1112. Another renowned ryokan located in the downtown area (10 rooms; five minutes by car from Onomichi Station).

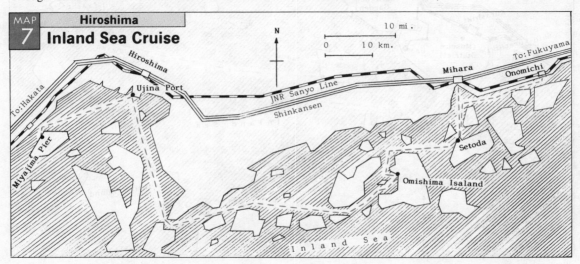

MAP 7　**Hiroshima**
Inland Sea Cruise

Kurashiki, Okayama & Himeji
倉敷, 岡山, 姫路

Along the Inland Sea between Hiroshima and Kyoto/Osaka there are several other places of interest. For those who have extra days in the area, I will outline three cities below — Kurashiki (middle left, map 8), Okayama (middle left) and Himeji (upper right).

Transportation

Kurashiki, Okayama and Himeji are all located on the Shinkansen and are conveniently connected with other major cities.

In Kurashiki, the Shinkansen station, Shin-Kurashiki 新倉敷駅, is about six miles (10 km.) west of the city center. Kurashiki Station 倉敷駅, the city's main station, is served by the JNR Sanyo Line 山陽本線, but not by the Shinkansen. In addition, about half of the Shinkansen trains skip Shin-Kurashiki.

Therefore, when you travel to Kurashiki on the Shinkansen, it is more convenient to get off at Okayama Station 岡山駅 and transfer there to a local train on the JNR Sanyo Line. The Sanyo Line connects Okayama, Kurashiki and Shin-Kurashiki Stations. The trains operate about every 20-30 minutes. The ride between Okayama and Kurashiki takes 17 minutes; the extra journey between Kurashiki and Shin-Kurashiki takes 9 minutes.

In Okayama and Himeji, the Shinkansen stations are located in the city centers.

Kurashiki

In the feudal era, Kurashiki was a prosperous port town that handled the distribution of the rice and cotton produced in the region. Several old warehouses have been preserved and converted to museums. New museums have also been constructed in the same historical district, making Kurashiki a cultural center. The museums are clustered along a small canal (0.3 miles or 0.5 km. long) lined on the both sides with willow trees. The canal is 0.5 miles (0.8 km.) south of Kurashiki Station and can be reached easily on foot. Because most of the museums are closed on Mondays, don't plan a visit to Kurashiki for a Monday.

Ohara Museum 大原美術館 consists of several buildings featuring a variety of art works. The Museum is

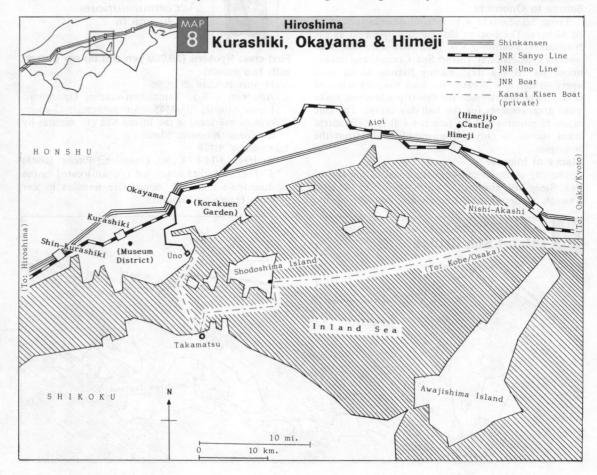

especially famous for its collection of Western art. The exhibits include works of El Greco, Gauguin, Picasso, Renoir, etc. They are housed in the main building which was designed to look like a Greek pantheon. The annex building displays contemporary paintings by both Western and Japanese artists. Four other smaller buildings feature ceramics, wood-block prints, textiles and Oriental antiquities. (9 a.m. to 4:30 p.m. Admission 300 yen for the main and annex buildings. An additional 100 yen for the four smaller halls.) **Kurashiki Folkcraft Museum** 倉敷民芸館 is housed in an old rice warehouse built in the Edo era. Folk art items from all parts of Japan are displayed here (9 a.m. to 4 p.m. Admission 300 yen). **Kurashiki Archaeological Museum** 倉敷考古館 is in another converted warehouse. About 1,500 historical objects unearthed in the area are arranged and displayed chronologically (9 a.m. to 4:30 p.m. Admission 300 yen). **Japan Folk-Toy Museum** 日本郷土玩具館 displays 5,000 folk-toys from around the world (8 a.m. to 5 p.m. Admission 200 yen). **Kojima Torajiro Memorial Museum** 児島虎次郎館 (about 60 paintings of the local artist Torajiro Kojima), **Kurabo Memorial Hall** 倉紡記念館 (objects related to the development of weaving in Japan) and **Kurashiki Museum** 倉敷美術館 (Egyptian, Greek and Persian sculptures, etc) are also located in the same district.

Accommodations
HOTELS
Standard Hotels (12,000 - 20,000 yen for a twin room)
Kurashiki Kokusai Hotel 倉敷国際ホテル
    Address: 1-1-44, Chuo, Kurashiki; Phone: (0864) 22-5141. A small, 70-room hotel located in the museum district.
Kurashiki Terminal Hotel 倉敷ターミナルホテル
    Address: 7-2-901, Achi-Itchome, Kurashiki; Phone: (0864) 26-1111. A 212-room high standard business hotel right in front of Kurashiki Station.
Kurashiki Ivy Square 倉敷アイビースクエア
    Address: 7-2, Honcho, Kurashiki; Phone: (0864) 22-0011. A small, 157 room hotel constructed on the grounds of a former textile factory.

RYOKANS
First-class Ryokans (more than 20,000 yen per person with two meals)
Ryokan Kurashiki 旅館くらしき
    Address: 4-1, Honcho, Kurashiki; Phone: (0864) 22-0730. An authentic Japanese inn located on the canal in the museum district (20 rooms).
Ryokan Tsurukata 旅館鶴形
    Address: 1-3-15, Chuo, Kurashiki; Phone: (0864) 24-1635. Another authentic ryokan. Some of the guest rooms are in a converted warehouse (13 rooms).

Okayama

Two legacies of the feudal era, Korakuen Garden and Okayamajo Castle, are the major tourist attractions in Okayama. **Korakuen Garden** 後楽園 is located on a small sand bar in the Asahikawa River one mile (1.6 km.) to the east of Okayama Station. The Garden was laid out at the beginning of the 18th century at the order of Tsunamasa Ikeda, a feudal lord. Its spacious grounds feature ponds, mounds, elaborate wooden huts, cherry, maple, and plum trees and tea bushes that reflect the changes of the seasons. The Garden is open from 8:30 a.m. to 5:30 p.m. (9 a.m. to 4:30 p.m. in winter) and admission is 150 yen. **Okayamajo Castle** 岡山城 is a few minutes walk to the south from Korakuen. The six-story donjon is a 1966 reconstruction, but the turrets and stone walls are 1573 originals. There are observatories on the 5th and 6th floors. The lower floors house a local museum (9 a.m. to 5 p.m. Admission 150 yen).

Accommodations
HOTELS
Standard Hotels (14,000 - 20,000 yen for a twin room)
Okayama Royal Hotel 岡山ロイヤルホテル
    Address: 2-4, Ezucho, Okayama; Phone: (0862) 54-1155. A modern 192-room hotel a three minute taxi ride from Okayama Station.
Okayama Tokyu Hotel 岡山東急ホテル
    Address: 3-2-16, Otomo, Okayama; Phone: (0862) 33-2411. A new 240-room hotel a five minute taxi ride from Okayama Station.
Okayama Plaza Hotel 岡山プラザホテル
    Address: 2-3-12, Ichihama, Okayama; Phone: (0862) 72-1201. In a quiet location near Korakuen Garden (83 rooms).
Okayama Terminal Hotel 岡山ターミナルホテル
    Address: 1-5, Ekimotomachi, Okayama; Phone: (0862) 33-3131. In the Okayama Station building (213 rooms).
Business Hotel (less than 14,000 yen for a twin room)
Hotel Sunroute Okayama ホテル・サンルート岡山
    Address: 1-3-12, Shimoishii, Okayama; Phone: (0862) 32-2345. A 123-room hotel a seven minute walk from Okayama Station.

Himeji

Himeji was a prosperous castle city in the feudal era. Himejijo Castle 姫路城, in an extensive compound of about 80 buildings, was built in 1601 at the order of the feudal lord, Terumasa Ikeda. Though Himeji was devastated during World War II, the Castle survived. Because of its magnificent scale and gracious design the castle is often called "White Heron Castle" and is considered by many the most beautiful castle in Japan. The donjon and the main buildings are National Treasures (9 a.m. to 4 p.m. Till 3:30 p.m. in winter. Admission 200 yen). The Castle is only 0.6 miles (1 km.) north of Himeji Station. Except for the castle, the city has been completely modernized. Even if you don't stop in Himeji, you can catch a glimpse of the castle from the train.

九州

Kyushu

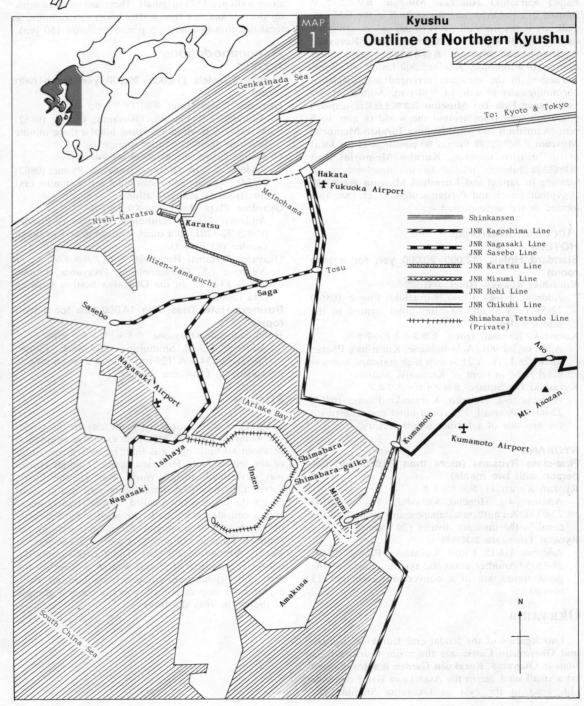

MAP 1

Kyushu

Outline of Northern Kyushu

Genkainada Sea

To: Kyoto & Tokyo

Hakata
✝ Fukuoka Airport

Meinohama

Nishi-Karatsu
Karatsu

Tosu

Hizen-Yamaguchi

Saga

Sasebo

Nagasaki Airport ✈

(Ariake Bay)

Aso

Mt. Asozan ▲

Kumamoto

Kumamoto Airport ✝

	Shinkansen
	JNR Kagoshima Line
	JNR Nagasaki Line
	JNR Sasebo Line
	JNR Karatsu Line
	JNR Misumi Line
	JNR Hohi Line
	JNR Chikuhi Line
	Shimabara Tetsudo Line (Private)

Isahaya

Shimabara

Nagasaki

Unzen

Shimabara-gaiko

Misumi

Amakusa

South China Sea

N

Kyushu, the third largest of Japan's islands, is at the southwestern end of the archipelago. In the chapter that follows I will introduce only the western half of the island because this area contains the most interesting natural, historical and cultural attractions.

Many readers have probably heard of Beppu, a famous hotspring resort on the eastern coast of Kyushu, but because this book is written with independent travelers in mind, I have omitted it. Beppu is enjoyable if you are traveling in a large group, but not much fun if you're traveling on your own. The main attractions in Beppu are the large hotspring baths that are attached to most of the area's accommodations. Like many insular peoples, the Japanese have a great deal of curiosity about foreigners, especially Westerners. In Beppu, your most overwhelming experience is likely to be as an object of curiosity at the baths. If you are with a large tour, the group will probably overwhelm the Japanese gawkers, but if you are alone you are likely to be a bit uncomfortable.

The southern part of Kyushu, especially Kagoshima, also contains great tourist attractions including Mt. Sakurajima, Kirishima National Park, Ibusuki hotspring resort and historical relics of one of the nation's most influential feudal cities. However, because your time in Japan is sure to be limited, and because of the many other places you should not miss, I have also omitted — in this case, very reluctantly — Southern Kyushu. I hope to be able to include it in future editions.

Transportation

CONNECTIONS WITH OTHER CITIES
By Train
The most inexpensive way to get to Kyushu, especially for those traveling with Japan Rail Passes, is to take a Shinkansen to Hakata (upper center, map 1). The trip to Hakata takes about seven hours from Tokyo, about four hours from Kyoto/Osaka, and about two hours from Hiroshima. Refer to the Transportation within Japan Chapter for details on the Shinkansen.
By Air
Tokyo: There are about 20 flights daily each way between Haneda Airport (Tokyo) and Fukuoka Airport; about five flights daily each way between Haneda and Nagasaki; and about five flights daily each way between Haneda and Kumamoto. One-way fare from Tokyo to Fukuoka is 27,100 yen, to Nagasaki 31,100 yen, and to Kumamoto 29,200 yen.
Osaka: There are about eight flights daily each way between Osaka and Fukuoka; four between Osaka and Nagasaki; and five between Osaka and Kumamoto. One-way fare from Osaka to Fukuoka is 15,400 yen, to Nagasaki 19,000 yen, and to Kumamoto 16,900 yen.

Fukuoka Airport is only a 15-minute bus ride from Hakata Station (220 yen), but the airports in Nagasaki and Kumamoto are rather far from the centers of the cities (see map 1). The bus ride from

Nagasaki Airport to Nagasaki Station takes 65 minutes (1,050 yen), and the ride from Kumamoto Airport to Kumamoto Station takes 54 minutes (600 yen).

For access to Haneda Airport from Tokyo, and for access to Osaka Airport from Kyoto/Osaka, refer to Chapter "Airport Transportation."

KYUSHU'S TRANSPORTATION NETWORK
As with the other areas of Japan, convenient and punctual train and boat service is available between the major cities of Kyushu. Here, I will outline long distance transportation (in the order suggested in the itineraries that follow). City transportation, such as streetcars, subways and buses is introduced in each city section.

Between Hakata and Kumamoto (74 miles or 118.4 km.)
The JNR Kagoshima Line's 鹿児島本線 limited expresses connect these two cities. The trains usually consist of seven cars — one Green Car (first class, reserved seats), two ordinary-class reserved-seat cars and four ordinary-class nonreserved-seat cars. One of the four nonreserved-seat cars is a non-smoking car. The fare is 3,400 yen for ordinary-class, and 6,200 yen for the Green Cars, which include the limited express surcharge. Most trains continue beyond Kumamoto and terminate further south. The following are the major trains between Hakata and Kumamoto:

Hakata to Kumamoto

Train Name	Lv. Hakata	Ar. Kumamoto
Ariake-1	7:00 a.m.	8:28 a.m.
Ariake-3	8:06 a.m.	9:43 a.m.
Ariake-5	8:52 a.m.	10:33 a.m.
Ariake-7	9:53 a.m.	11:24 a.m.
Ariake-9	10:52 a.m.	12:33 p.m.
Ariake-11	11:52 a.m.	1:27 p.m.
Ariake-13	12:52 p.m.	2:21 p.m.
Ariake-15	1:52 p.m.	3:27 p.m.
Ariake-17	2:52 p.m.	4:27 p.m.
Ariake-19	3:52 p.m.	5:32 p.m.
Ariake-21	4:52 p.m.	6:27 p.m.
Ariake-23	5:52 p.m.	7:26 p.m.
Ariake-25	6:52 p.m.	8:31 p.m.
Ariake-27	7:52 p.m.	9:31 p.m.
Ariake-29	8:52 p.m.	10:31 p.m.

Kumamoto to Hakata

Train Name	Lv. Kumamoto	Ar. Hakata
Ariake-2	6:42 a.m.	8:24 a.m.
Ariake-4	7:42 a.m.	9:24 a.m.
Ariake-6	8:42 a.m.	10:24 a.m.
Ariake-8	9:47 a.m.	11:24 a.m.
Ariake-10	10:53 a.m.	12:24 p.m.
Ariake-12	11:47 a.m.	1:24 p.m.
Ariake-14	12:48 p.m.	2:24 p.m.
Ariake-16	1:42 p.m.	3:24 p.m.
Ariake-18	2:47 p.m.	4:24 p.m.
Ariake-20	3:42 p.m.	5:24 p.m.
Ariake-22	4:46 p.m.	6:32 p.m.
Ariake-24	5:53 p.m.	7:32 p.m.
Ariake-26	6:42 p.m.	8:24 p.m.
Ariake-28	7:58 p.m.	9:24 p.m.
Ariake-30	9:18 p.m.	10:54 p.m.

Between Kumamoto and Aso (31 miles or 49.9 km)

The JNR Hohi Line 豊肥本線 links Kumamoto and Mt. Asozan National Park. If you have a Japan Rail Pass, you should use this line when you make a day trip to Mt. Asozan. From Aso Station 阿蘇駅 you have to take a short bus ride to the mountain. (Direct bus service from Kumamoto to the mountain is also available. These buses are explained in the section on Mt. Asozan.). Express and local trains operate between Kumamoto and Aso Stations. One-way fare on the local is 740 yen, and on the express 1,240 yen. The following are the major trains between Kumamoto and Aso (all seats nonreserved):

Kumamoto to Aso

Train Name	Lv. Kumamoto	Ar. Aso
"Donko" (local)	7:34 a.m.	9:08 a.m.
Hinoyama-1	9:49 a.m.	10:54 a.m.
"Donko" (local)	10:18 a.m.	11:48 a.m.
Hinoyama-3	12:00 noon	1:04 p.m.
"Donko" (local)	1:17 p.m.	2:47 a.m.
Hinoyama-5	2:02 p.m.	3:14 p.m.

Aso to Kumamoto

Train Name	Lv. Aso	Ar. Kumamoto
Hinoyama-2	10:29 a.m.	11:34 a.m.
"Donko" (local)	11:39 a.m.	1:06 p.m.
Hinoyama-4	1:45 p.m.	2:43 p.m.
"Donko" (local)	2:20 p.m.	3:38 p.m.
"Donko" (local)	3:37 p.m.	4:56 p.m.
"Donko" (local)	4:34 p.m.	6:07 p.m.
Hinoyama-6	5:22 p.m.	6:24 p.m.
"Donko" (local)	6:03 p.m.	7:22 p.m.

Between Kumamoto and Misumi (23 miles or 36.5 km.)

The JNR Misumi Line 三角線 connects Kumamoto and Misumi 三角. From there you take a boat to Shimabara-gaiko. All trains except for one express are locals. Only nonreserved seats are available on the locals. One-way fare is 590 yen on the local, and 1,090 yen on the express. The following are the major trains between Kumamoto and Misumi:

Kumamoto to Misumi

Train Name	Lv. Kumamoto	Ar. Misumi
"Donko" (local)	7:28 a.m.	8:16 a.m.
"Donko" (local)	8:21 a.m.	9:15 a.m.
"Donko" (local)	9:48 a.m.	10:38 a.m.
"Donko" (local)	10:19 a.m.	11:15 a.m.
"Donko" (local)	11:50 a.m.	12:41 p.m.
"Donko" (local)	1:14 p.m.	2:05 p.m.
Hinoyama-4	2:52 p.m.	3:30 p.m.

Misumi to Kumamoto

Train Name	Lv. Misumi	Ar. Kumamoto
Hinoyama-2	11:20 a.m.	11:56 a.m.
"Donko" (local)	12:47 p.m.	1:41 p.m.
"Donko" (local)	2:17 p.m.	3:11 p.m.
"Donko" (local)	3:43 p.m.	4:36 p.m.
"Donko" (local)	4:23 p.m.	5:17 p.m.
"Donko" (local)	6:20 p.m.	7:14 p.m.
"Donko" (local)	8:06 p.m.	9:00 p.m.

Between Misumi and Shimabara-gaiko 島原外港

The boat ride across Ariake Bay is one of the highlights of the trip between Kumamoto and Nagasaki. The boat is operated by Kyushu Shosen 九州商船, a private company. The Japan Rail Pass cannot be used for this cruise. The fare is 810 yen for second class and 1,620 yen for first class. Second class is comfortable, and I don't think there's any reason to have to take first class, but if you buy a second class ticket and decide you want to upgrade it, you can do so even after boarding the boat.

Misumi to Shimabara-gaiko

Lv. Misumi	Ar. Shimabara-gaiko
8:50 a.m.	9:50 a.m.
9:40 a.m.	10:40 a.m.
10:25 a.m.	11:25 a.m.
11:30 a.m.	12:30 p.m.
12:35 p.m.	1:35 p.m.
1:20 p.m.	2:20 p.m.
2:20 p.m.	3:20 p.m.
3:10 p.m.	4:10 p.m.
4:00 p.m.	5:00 p.m.

Shimabara-gaiko to Misumi

Lv. Shimabara-gaiko	Ar. Misumi
12:00 noon	1:00 p.m.
12:55 p.m.	1:55 p.m.
1:50 p.m.	2:50 p.m.
2:40 p.m.	3:40 p.m.
3:35 p.m.	4:35 p.m.
4:25 p.m.	5:25 p.m.
5:15 p.m.	6:15 p.m.
6:15 p.m.	7:15 p.m.

Between Shimabara-gaiko and Isahaya (27 miles or 43.2 km.)

The Shimabara Tetsudo Line 島原鉄道 (private) links Shimabara-gaiko with Isahaya 諫早. Shimabara, a castle town, is the second stop from Shimabara-gaiko. You can stop over at Shimabara 島原 if you have a through ticket to Isahaya (980 yen). All the trains are local and have only nonreserved seats.

Shimabara-gaiko to Isahaya

Lv. Shimabra-gaiko	Ar. Shimabara	Ar. Isahaya
10:34 a.m.	10:44 a.m.	11:46 a.m.
11:34 a.m.	11:50 a.m.	1:01 p.m.
12:55 p.m.	1:05 p.m.	2:03 p.m.
1:49 p.m.	2:00 p.m.	2:59 p.m.
2:32 p.m.	2:44 p.m.	3:32 p.m.
3:45 p.m.	3:53 p.m.	4:55 p.m.
5:01 p.m.	5:11 p.m.	6:01 p.m.
5:58 p.m.	6:08 p.m.	7:19 p.m.

Isahaya to Shimabara-gaiko

Lv. Isahaya	Ar. Shimabara	Ar. Shimabara-gaiko
8:40 a.m.	9:45 a.m.	10:00 a.m.
10:22 a.m.	11:24 a.m.	11:34 a.m.
11:10 a.m.	12:14 p.m.	12:22 p.m.
12:18 p.m.	1:06 p.m.	1:15 p.m.
1:15 p.m.	2:21 p.m.	2:32 p.m.
2:15 p.m.	3:15 p.m.	3:24 p.m.
3:11 p.m.	4:17 p.m.	4:25 p.m.
4:24 p.m.	5:30 p.m.	5:38 p.m.

Between Nagasaki and Hakata via Isahaya and Saga

(Nagasaki to Isahaya — 16 miles or 24.9 km.; Nagasaki to Saga — 63 miles or 100.3 km.; Nagasaki to Hakata — 96 miles or 153.9 km.)

If you follow my suggested itinerary, you'll take this Nagasaki Line 長崎本線 twice. First from Isahaya to Nagasaki 長崎 when you travel from Kumamoto to Nagasaki, and then from Nagasaki to either Saga 佐賀 or Hakata 博多. (If you have time, you should visit Karatsu via Saga. If your time is limited, you should take this line from Nagasaki to Hakata and transfer there to the Shinkansen.). The following is the schedule of the limited expresses between Hakata and Nagasaki (I have also listed some local trains for the short trip between Nagasaki and Isahaya):

For the trip between Isahaya and Nagasaki those who don't have Rail Passes will save money by using the "Donko" (local). The fare for the "Kamome" limited express between Isahaya and Nagasaki is

1,560 yen, but drops to 360 yen on the local. The local trip takes about an hour, while the limited express covers the distance in about 20 minutes. If you're traveling at lunch time, you might want to consider buying a box lunch ("bento") in the station and eating it on the local.

The limited express fare from Nagasaki to Hakata is 4,300 yen, and 3,400 yen to Saga. If you follow my suggested itinerary in reverse, please take note of the following: from Hakata, the "Kamome" limited express combines cars going to Sasebo with cars bound for Nagasaki. At Hizen-Yamaguchi Station, the cars bound for Sasebo are separated from the "Kamome" (see map 1) and become the Sasebo-bound "Midori." Cars from No. 1 through No. 8 are "Kamome" and those from No. 9 to No. 12 are "Midori." Make sure that you are on a Nagasaki-bound car! Cars No. 1, 2 and 3 are ordinary-class reserved seat cars, No. 4 is a Green Car (first class, reserved), and Nos. 5, 6, 7 and 8 are ordinary-class nonreserved-seat cars (No. 8 is non-smoking).

Hakata to Nagasaki via Saga and Isahaya

Train Name	Lv. Hakata	Ar. Saga	Ar. Isahaya	Ar. Nagasaki
Kamome-5	10:01 a.m.	10:42 a.m.	12:00 p.m.	12:24 p.m.
Kamome-7	10:44 a.m.	11:27 a.m.	12:46 p.m.	1:08 p.m.
Kamome-9	11:44 a.m.	12:27 p.m.	1:44 p.m.	2:06 p.m.
"Donko" (local)	—	—	2:24 p.m.	3:14 p.m.
Kamome-11	12:44 p.m.	1:25 p.m.	2:42 p.m.	3:04 p.m.
Kamome-13	1:44 p.m.	2:27 p.m.	3:42 p.m.	4:06 p.m.
Kamome-15	2:44 p.m.	3:25 p.m.	4:35 p.m.	5:01 p.m.
"Donko" (local)	—	—	5:15 p.m.	6:17 p.m.
"Donko" (local)	—	—	5:53 p.m.	6:26 p.m.
Kamome-17	3:44 p.m.	4:25 p.m.	5:48 p.m.	6:10 p.m.
"Donko" (local)	—	—	6:06 p.m.	6:59 p.m.
"Donko" (local)	—	—	7:02 p.m.	7:36 p.m.
Kamome-19	4:44 p.m.	5:27 p.m.	6:53 p.m.	7:15 p.m.
Kamome-21	5:44 p.m.	6:27 p.m.	7:44 p.m.	8:05 p.m.

Nagasaki to Hakata via Isahaya and Saga

Train Name	Lv. Nagasaki	Ar. Isahaya	Ar. Saga	Ar. Hakata
Kamome-2	7:07 a.m.	7:27 a.m.	8:48 a.m.	9:32 a.m.
"Donko"(local)	7:17 a.m.	7:47 a.m.	—	—
Kamome-4	8:15 a.m.	8:35 a.m.	9:48 a.m.	10:32 a.m.
Kamome-6	9:08 a.m.	9:30 a.m.	10:53 a.m.	11:36 a.m.
"Donko" (local)	9:16 a.m.	10:08 a.m.	—	—
Kamome-8	10:02 a.m.	10:23 a.m.	11:48 a.m.	12:32 p.m.
Kamome-10	11:08 a.m.	11:32 a.m.	12:50 p.m.	1:32 p.m.
Kamome-12	12:03 p.m.	12:25 p.m.	1:50 p.m.	2:32 p.m.
Kamome-14	1:02 p.m.	1:24 p.m.	2:48 p.m.	3:32 p.m.
Kamome-16	2:00 p.m.	2:22 p.m.	3:50 p.m.	4:32 p.m.
Kamome-18	2:58 p.m.	3:20 p.m.	4:48 p.m.	5:32 p.m.
Kamome-20	4:01 p.m.	4:20 p.m.	5:49 p.m.	6:32 p.m.
Kamome-22	5:02 p.m.	5:22 p.m.	6:50 p.m.	7:32 p.m.

Between Saga and Karatsu (29 miles or 46.7 km.)

As pictured on map I, the JNR Karatsu Line 唐津線 connects Saga and Karatsu 唐津. All the trains on this line are locals and have only nonreserved seats. The fare is 740 yen one way.

Saga to Karatsu		Karatsu to Saga	
Lv. Saga	Ar. Karatsu	Lv. Karatsu	Ar. Saga
9:36 a.m.	10:48 a.m.	8:26 a.m.	9:42 a.m.
11:01 a.m.	12:10 p.m.	10:06 a.m.	11:16 a.m.
12:47 p.m.	1:56 p.m.	12:54 p.m.	2:08 p.m.
2:33 p.m.	3:49 p.m.	2:17 p.m.	3:25 p.m.
3:44 p.m.	4:56 p.m.	4:15 p.m.	5:24 p.m.
5:05 p.m.	6:15 p.m.	6:17 p.m.	7:34 p.m.

Between Karatsu and Hakata (27 miles or 42.6 km. to Meinohama plus 6 miles or 9.5 km. to Hakata)

The JNR Chikuhi Line 筑肥線 operates between Nishi-Karatsu and Meinohama via Karatsu. All the trains, however, run on the city subway tracks once the train enters Hakata. Trains bound for Karatsu also originate at Hakata Station. The fare on the JNR portion is 660 yen, and the subway portion is 180 yen. If you have a Japan Rail Pass, you are required to pay for the subway. All the trains are local and have only nonreserved seats.

Karatsu to Hakata

Lv. Karatsu	Ar. Meinohama	Ar. Hakata
8:12 a.m.	9:18 a.m.	9:40 a.m.
9:43 a.m.	10:38 a.m.	11:00 a.m.
10:36 a.m.	11:28 a.m.	11:55 a.m.
11:47 a.m.	12:38 p.m.	1:00 p.m.
12:43 p.m.	1:36 p.m.	1:58 p.m.
2:46 p.m.	3:41 p.m.	4:03 p.m.
3:29 p.m.	4:22 p.m.	4:44 p.m.
4:12 p.m.	5:05 p.m.	5:27 p.m.
4:42 p.m.	5:34 p.m.	5:57 p.m.
5:39 p.m.	6:35 p.m.	6:57 p.m.
6:21 p.m.	7:14 p.m.	7:36 p.m.
7:08 p.m.	8:02 p.m.	8:24 p.m.

Hakata to Karatsu

Lv. Hakata	Ar. Meinohama	Ar. Karatsu
8:00 a.m.	8:19 a.m.	9:14 a.m.
9:00 a.m.	9:19 a.m.	10:14 a.m.
9:44 a.m.	10:03 a.m.	11:07 a.m.
11:05 a.m.	11:24 a.m.	12:28 p.m.
11:59 a.m.	12:18 p.m.	1:14 p.m.
1:04 p.m.	1:23 p.m.	2:16 p.m.
2:02 p.m.	2:21 p.m.	3:17 p.m.
2:48 p.m.	3:07 p.m.	4:02 p.m.
4:07 p.m.	4:26 p.m.	5:23 p.m.
4:48 p.m.	5:07 p.m.	6:10 p.m.
5:30 p.m.	5:49 p.m.	6:54 p.m.
6:00 p.m.	6:19 p.m.	7:18 p.m.

How to Arrange Your Itinerary for Kyushu

A visit to Kyushu requires at least three nights if you're starting from Kyoto/Osaka, and four nights if you're starting from Tokyo (three nights if you fly from Tokyo).

If you have only three nights

1st Day: Arrive in Kumamoto before 3 p.m. and you will have time to visit Kumamotojo Castle. If it is summer time, you may be able to visit Suizenji-Koen Park as well.

2nd Day: An enjoyable full-day trip from Kumamoto to Nagasaki via Shimabara.

3rd Day: Sightseeing in Nagasaki.

4th Day: Return to Kyoto/Osaka or Tokyo via Hakata.

If you have one additional day

Your second day should be spent in a full-day excursion to Mt. Asozan and you should spend one more night in Kumamoto. The 2nd and 3rd days above will be your 3rd and 4th days.

If you have two additional days

1st Day: Arrive in Kumamoto and visit Kumamotojo Castle (plus Suizenji-Koen Park if possible).

2nd Day: A full-day excursion to Mt. Asozan from Kumamoto.

3rd Day: Travel from Kumamoto to Nagasaki via Shimabara.

4th Day: Full day in Nagasaki.

5th Day: Nagasaki to Karatsu via Saga. You can stay over night in Karatsu or Fukuoka.

6th Day: Return to Kyoto/Osaka or Tokyo.

If you have three additional days

Allocate an additional day for Nagasaki.

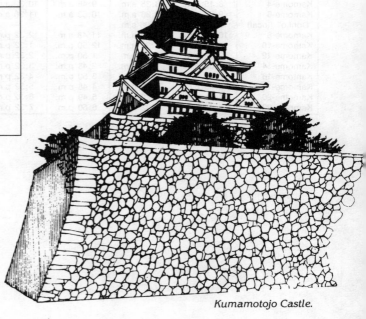

Kumamotojo Castle.

Kumamoto 熊本

Kumamoto's prosperity began when Kiyomasa Kato, one of the most influential of Hideyoshi Toyotomi's generals, had a magnificent castle built here in 1601. The city was later granted by the Tokugawa Shogunate to the feudal lord Tadatoshi Hosokawa. Throughout the Edo era, Kumamoto prospered under the reign of successive generations of the Hosokawa family. After the Meiji Restoration, when Japan moved toward modernization and democratization, samurai warriors who resisted the new order fought their last battle in Kumamoto.

Kumamoto is often called the "forested city." The many trees in every neighborhood of this lovely city help create and maintain its fresh and pleasant atmosphere.

Transportation in Kumamoto

Streetcars are the most convenient public transportation. As pictured on map 2, there are two streetcar lines — No. 2 and No. 3. The route number is posted on the front of the car. The No. 2 line, which is indicated with a solid line on map 2, operates every 5-6 minutes. The No. 3 line, which is indicated with a broken line on map 2, operates every 15 to 30 minutes. Take a numbered ticket when you enter the streetcars. The fare is displayed on signs above and to the left of the driver's seat. When you get off pay the exact amount shown under the number corresponding to your ticket. Fares start at 110 yen.

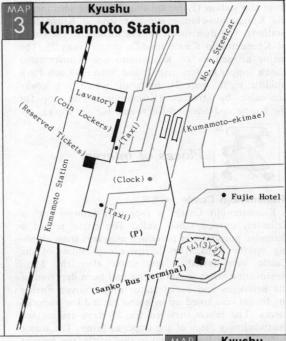

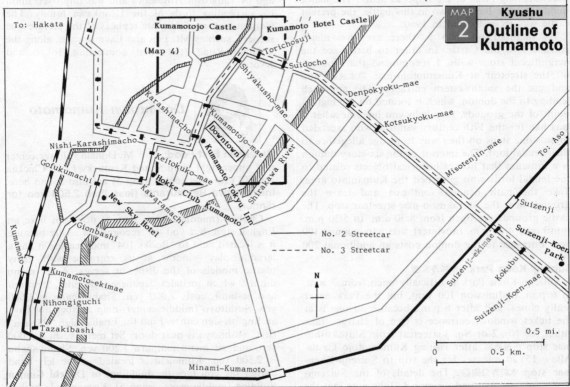

Outline of the City

JNR's Kumamoto Station is rather isolated from the city's downtown, but thanks to the No. 2 streetcar, it is quite easy to reach the downtown area from the station (Refer to map 3 for the location of the Kumamoto-ekimae streetcar stop at Kumamoto Station). The downtown area is located to the south of Kumamotojo Castle (middle center, map 2). The major attractions of Kumamoto are Kumamotojo Castle (upper center, map 2) and Suizenji-Koen Park (middle right, map 2), both of which are easily accessible by streetcar (Kumamotojo-mae stop for the Castle and Suizenji-Koen-mae for the Park).

Places of Interest

Kumamotojo Castle   熊本城

Kumamotojo Castle is especially famous for its delicately curved stone walls. The curve served a defensive purpose and prevented attackers from climbing up the walls. The defensive capabilities of the Castle were tested a few years after the Meiji Restoration when samurai who had been deprived of the privileges and social status they enjoyed during the feudal era, holed up in it and battled the imperial forces. The rebels survived for 55 days against the overwhelming force of the imperial army. The major buildings were burnt down in this battle; the present castle was reconstructed in 1960.

As pictured on map 5, there are two major entrances to the Castle. In order to better see the magnificent stone-walls, I recommend that you get off the streetcar at Kumamotojo-mae 熊本城前 stop and use the southwestern entrance. The approach leading to the donjon, which is located on the highest point of the grounds, may help you imagine what it was like for the 17th century samurai who ascended these stone steps on their way to pledge allegiance to their feudal lord. The interior of the six-story donjon is a museum that houses historical objects related to the feudal lords who governed the Kumamoto area. Take the path headed southeast and leave the grounds near the Shiyakusho-mae streetcar stop. The castle grounds are open from 8:30 a.m. to 5:30 p.m. (until only 4:30 p.m. in winter), and admission is 100 yen. Entrance to the donjon costs an additional 200 yen.

Suizenji-Koen Park   水前寺公園

Suizenji-Koen Park is officially open from 7 a.m. to 6 p.m. (Admission 100 yen), but the Park never really closes, and after 6 p.m., because no one is at the ticket window, entrance is free of charge. Take either the No. 2 or No. 3 streetcar from Shiyakusho-mae stop 市役所前 after visiting Kumamotojo Castle. Allow 15-20 minutes for the trip to Suizenji-Koen-mae stop 水前寺公園前. The details of the Suizenji-Koen area are pictured on map 4. Take note that the

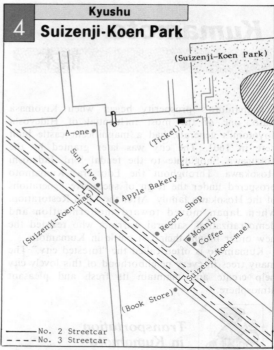

Kyushu

4 Suizenji-Koen Park

(Suizenji-Koen Park)

A-one
Sun Live
(Ticket)
Suizenji-Koen-mae
Apple Bakery
Record Shop
Moanin Coffee
Suizenji-Koen-mae
(Suizenji-Koen-mae)
(Book Store)

——— No. 2 Streetcar
- - - - No. 3 Streetcar

stops for the west-bound streetcar and the east-bound streetcar are about 0.1 miles away from each other. (When I first visited the Park about 10 years ago, it was in the evening and quite dark. On my way back downtown, I couldn't find the stop for the east bound streetcar, and ended up hailing a taxi).

Suizenji-Koen Park was established over 300 years ago by Tadatoshi Hosokawa and was improved upon by succeeding lords of the Hosokawa family. The Garden features miniature replicas of the picturesque scenery, such as Mt. Fuji and Lake Biwako, along the Tokaido Road (the road connecting Tokyo and Kyoto).

Downtown Kumamoto

American Fast Food: Two McDonald's (lower center and upper right, map 5) and Kentucky Fried Chicken ("KFC") (middle center, map 5) are also found here.
Inexpensive Restaurants (less than 2,500 yen for dinner)

Chohan (middle center, map 5) does not have an English sign, but you can recognize it easily because it is located next to "Books 104" and because it has a large display window at its entrance with many plastic models of the dishes it serves. A set menu dinner, which includes Japanese-style pilaf, tempura and sashimi, costs 2,000 yen. Shabu-shabu is 1,600 yen. **Sushitoyo** (middle center, map 5) does not have an English sign either. Find the English sign "Papaya" first. Sushitoyo is next door. Set menu sushi is 2,000 yen, and set menu tempura 1,200 yen. Shabu-shabu is 2,500 yen. **Kumaichi** is located in the left hand corner (as you face the building) of **Daiichi Ginnan Building** (middle center, map 5). Korean-style barbe-

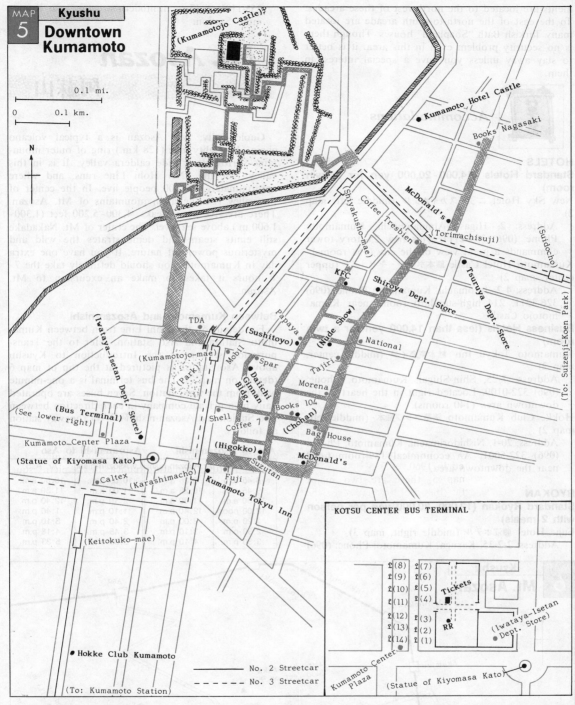

MAP 5 Kyushu **Downtown Kumamoto**

(Kumamotojo Castle)?

0.1 mi.
0   0.1 km.

N

Kumamoto Hotel Castle

Books Nagasaki

McDonald's

Coffee Tresbien

(Shiyakusho-mae)

(Torimachisuji)

(Suidocho)

(To: Suizenji-Koen Park)

Tsuruya Dept. Store

Tsuruya Dept. Store

KFC

Shiroya Dept. Store

Papaya

(Nude Show)

TDA

(Sushitoyo)

National

Tajiri

Mobil

Spar

Daiichi
Ginnan
Bldg.

Morena

Books 104

(Iwataya-Isetan Dept. Store)

(Kumamotojo-mae)

(Park)

Shell

Coffee 7

(Chohan)

Bag House

(Bus Terminal)
(See lower right)

(Higokko)

McDonald's

Kumamoto Center Plaza

(Statue of Kiyomasa Kato)

Caltex

(Karashimacho)

Fuji

Suzutan

Kumamoto Tokyu Inn

(Keitokuko-mae)

Hokke Club Kumamoto

No. 2 Streetcar
No. 3 Streetcar

(To: Kumamoto Station)

KOTSU CENTER BUS TERMINAL

£(8)	£(7)
£(9)	£(6)
£(10)	£(5)
£(11)	£(4)
£(12)	£(3)
£(13)	£(2)
£(14)	£(1)

Tickets

RR

(Iwataya-Isetan Dept. Store)

Kumamoto Center Plaza

(Statue of Kiyomasa Kato)

cue is 2,080 yen. **Wakaba** (5F of Daiichi Ginnan Building) serves a tempura dinner at 1,800 yen and a Japanese-style set menu dinner at 2,500 yen.

Inexpensive Pub

Higokko (lower center, map 5) is a robatayaki pub. It does not have an English sign, but displays a number of red paper lanterns at its entrance.

Department Stores Downtown

From northeast to southwest, Tsuruya Department Store (middle right), Shiroya Department Store (middle center) and Iwataya-Isetan Department Store (lower left) are located downtown.

Tips for Strolling in the Downtown Area

The wide street indicated with shaded red on the map and home of two McDonald's, is an arcade. The short horizontal street on the lower side of map 5, between Kumamoto Tokyu Inn and McDonald's is also an arcade. Most drinking and eating establishments are located to the northwest of these arcades. To the east of the north-to-south arcade are located many Turkish Bath "Soapland" houses. Though there is no security problem even in this area, it is better to stay away unless you have a special interest in them.

Accommodations

HOTELS
Standard Hotels (14,000 - 20,000 yen for a twin room)
New Sky Hotel ニュースカイホテル (middle left, map 2)
   Address: 2, Higashi-Amidajimachi, Kumamoto; Phone: (096) 354-2111. This new 25-story tower commands a great view of the city (358 rooms).
Kumamoto Hotel Castle 熊本ホテル・キャッスル (upper center, map 2)
   Address: 4-2, Jotomachi, Kumamoto; Phone: (096) 326-3311. 214 high-standard rooms near Kumamotojo Castle.
Business Hotels (less than 14,000 yen for a twin room)
Kumamoto Tokyu Inn 熊本東急イン (middle center, map 2)
   Address: 7-25, Shin-Shigai, Kumamoto; Phone: (096) 322-0109. Located right in the heart of the downtown area (140 rooms).
Hokke Club Kumamoto 法華クラブ熊本 (middle left, map 2)
   Address: 20-1, Nishidorimachi, Kumamoto; Phone: (096) 322-5001. An economical 139-room hotel near the downtown area.

RYOKAN
Standard Ryokan (12,000 - 20,000 yen per person with 2 meals)
Fujie Hotel 藤江ホテル (middle right, map 3)
   Address: 2-2-35, Kasuga, Kumamoto; Phone: (096)

353-1101. A 47-room modern structure near Kumamoto Station.

Mt. Asozan

阿蘇山

Geologically, Mt. Asozan is a typical volcano chain. An eighty-mile (128 km.) ring of outer mountains surrounds a wide caldera valley. It is in this valley that the JNR Hohi Line runs, and where approximately 100,000 people live. In the center of the valley rise the main mountains of Mt. Asozan. There are five main peaks, 4,300 - 5,200 feet (1,300 - 1,600 m.) above sea level. The crater of Mt. Nakadake still emits steam and demonstrates the wild and mysterious powers of nature. If you have one extra day in Kumamoto, you should definitely take the 7 - 8 hours it takes to make an excursion to Mt. Asozan.

Between Kumamoto and Asozan-nishi
For details on the Hohi Line train between Kumamoto Station and Aso Station, refer to the Transportation section of the Introduction to Kyushu above. Aso Station is pictured at the top of map 6 (details on map 7). The bus terminal is a one-minute walk from the train station. Seven buses are operated daily by a private company in each direction between Aso Station and Asozan-nishi 阿蘇山西 ropeway station as follows:

Aso to Asozan-nishi		Asozan-nishi to Aso	
Lv. Aso	Ar. Asozan-nishi	Lv. Asozan-nishi	Ar. Aso
8:45 a.m.	9:25 a.m.	10:00 a.m.	10:30 a.m.
9:45 a.m.	10:25 a.m.	11:00 a.m.	11:30 a.m.
10:50 a.m.	11:30 a.m.	12:10 p.m.	12:40 p.m.
12:00 noon	12:40 p.m.	1:10 p.m.	1:40 p.m.
1:20 p.m.	2:00 p.m.	2:40 p.m.	3:10 p.m.
2:30 p.m.	3:10 p.m.	3:45 p.m.	4:18 p.m.
3:30 p.m.	4:10 p.m.	5:00 p.m.	5:33 p.m.

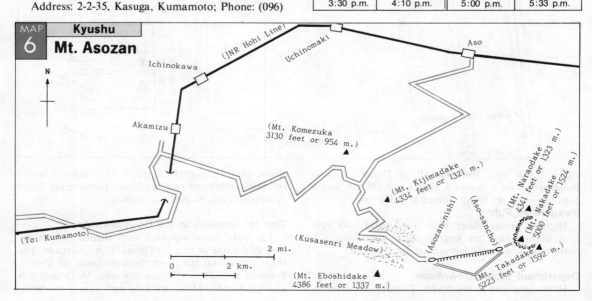

MAP 6 Kyushu **Mt. Asozan**

(JNR Hohi Line)
Uchinomaki
Aso
N
Ichinokawa
Akamizu
(Mt. Komezuka 3130 feet or 954 m.) ▲
(Mt. Naraodake 4341 feet or 1323 m.) ▲
(Mt. Kijimadake 4334 feet or 1321 m.) ▲
(Mt. Nakadake 5000 feet or 1524 m.) ▲
(Asozan-nishi)
(Aso-sancho)
(To: Kumamoto)
(Kusasenri Meadow)
(Mt. Takadake 5223 feet or 1592 m.) ▲
(Mt. Eboshidake 4386 feet or 1337 m.) ▲
2 mi.
0   2 km.

You can purchase a bus ticket at the ticket office in the terminal building; the one-way fare is 490 yen.

The road leading to Asozan-nishi ropeway station is a well-maintained toll road that zigzags up the mountain slope. The valley between the inner (main) mountains and outer mountains falls away under your eyes. Along the way the bus passes a distinctive mountain shaped like an inverted bowl of rice (called "Komezuka", or rice mound) and a spacious, picturesque meadow (called "Kusasenri" or 2,500-mile meadow). The bus usually makes a short stop at Kusasenri to allow passengers time to get off the bus and enjoy the scenery (and to provide the professional cameramen waiting there with opportunities to take the passengers' photos).

If you don't have a Japan Rail Pass, another option is to take a direct bus from Kumamoto to Asozan-nishi. There are two terminals in Kumamoto: one is the Sanko Bus Terminal 産交バスターミナル *near Kumamoto Station (map 3); and the other is in the Kotsu Center Bus Terminal* 熊本交通センター *near downtown (middle left, map 5, and on the detailed map at lower right on the same page). Four buses operate daily in each direction as follows:*

Kumamoto to Asozan-nishi

Lv. Sanko Terminal	Ar. Kotsu Center	Ar. Asozan-nishi
8:21 a.m.	8:30 a.m.	10:22 a.m.
9:31 a.m.	9:40 a.m.	11:32 a.m.
11:21 a.m.	11:31 a.m.	1:22 p.m.
1:51 p.m.	2:00 p.m.	3:52 p.m.

Asozan-nishi to Kumamoto

Lv. Asozan-nishi	Ar. Kotsu Center	Ar. Sanko Terminal
11:15 a.m.	12:36 p.m.	12:45 p.m.
12:40 p.m.	2:01 p.m.	2:10 p.m.
2:20 p.m.	3:41 p.m.	3:50 p.m.
4:50 p.m.	6:11 p.m.	6:20 p.m.

The one-way fare from Kumamoto to Asozan-nishi is 1,450 yen, but the fare for the return trip is only 1,200 yen.

Between Asozan-nishi and Aso-sancho 阿蘇山頂 (Top of Mt. Nakadake)

Aso-sanjo Jinja Shrine is adjacent to the ropeway station. There are many restaurants and souvenir shops in and around the ropeway station (see map 8). You should have lunch at one of these shops either before or after your visit to the summit. There are no adequate restaurants at the top of the mountain.

The 0.56-mile (0.9 km.) long ropeway operates every 8 minutes and takes visitors to the top of Mt. Nakadake 中岳 in only 4 minutes. The one-way fare is 400 yen (no discount for round trip). From the ropeway you can see a pleasant walking path on the lava slope. If the weather permits, and if you are a good walker, it is enjoyable to take the path on your way back to Asozan-nishi bus terminal.

The crater of Mt. Nakadake is 0.7 miles (1.1 km.) wide from north to south, 0.25 miles (0.4 km.) long from east to west and about 330 feet (100 m.) deep. Steam billows forth from the bottom of the crater, and the pedestrian paths along its edge are dotted with shelters (Refer to map 9).

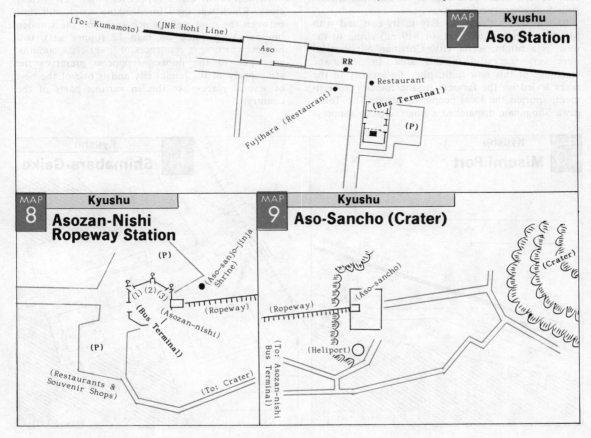

Shimabara
島原

The route from Kumamoto to Nagasaki features the beautiful natural scenery of Unzen-Amakusa National Park and the historical relics of Shimabara. This full-day trip is also an enjoyable sightseeing event in itself.

Transportation

All the schedules — trains between Kumamoto and Misumi, boats between Misumi and Shimabara-gaiko, trains between Shimabara-gaiko and Isahaya via Shimabara, and trains between Isahaya and Nagasaki — are explained in the Transportation section of the Introduction to Kyushu above. Misumi Station and Misumi Boat Pier are pictured on map 10, and the boat pier and train station at Shimabara-gaiko are pictured on map 11.

Places of Interest

Shimabara Station has both a check room and coin lockers. Leave your bags at the station and start your Shimabara walking tour.

Shimabara, with Ariake Bay to its east and with Mt. Mayuyama (2,687 feet, or 819 m.) rising to the west, is a bright, scenic city. Christian missionaries were very successful in this area. In 1638, the teachings of this new faith, plus the severity of the taxes levied on the farmers by the military government, spurred the local people to revolt. The Tokugawa Shogunate dispatched a huge force to suppress the rebellion, and, after three months of severe battles, 37,000 rebels were massacred. Amid the peaceful atmosphere of Shimabara today, it is difficult to imagine the bloody tragedy of the Christians and the farmers 350 years ago.

Shimabarajo Castle 島原城 is located at the end of the main street that begins at the train station. It was originally built in 1625, and the donjon was reconstructed in 1964. The entrance to the castle grounds is on the western side. The grounds are open from 8 a.m. to 6 p.m. (till 5 p.m. in winter), and admission is 10 yen (yes, ten yen!).

There is a great view of Ariake Bay from the top of the donjon. The six-story donjon is also a museum which displays Christian objects on the second floor, samurai weapons and armor on the third, and pottery on the fourth. Especially noteworthy is the collection of Christian objects. They are classified according to the eras when Christianity was introduced in Japan and when it was prohibited by the military government. (The 200 yen admission to the donjon includes admission to Seibo Memorial Museum 西望美術館). The eastern turret houses the Seibo Museum, which displays the works of Seibo Kitamura, a famous sculptor born in the area. The Peace Statue in Nagasaki's Peace Park is the work of Seibo. The western turret is used for display of a collection of kokeshi wooden dolls that include samples of this popular folkcraft item from all parts of Japan.

Samurai Houses 武家屋敷 still stand in Teppocho, northwest of the Castle (upper left, map 12). A clear creek, which was used for drinking water, still runs between the mud walls which surround the wooden houses. As pictured on map 12 (upper left), two houses, which were residences of lower-class samurai, are open to the public. Teppocho preserves the atmosphere of the feudal city and is one of the best of several places like this in various parts of the country.

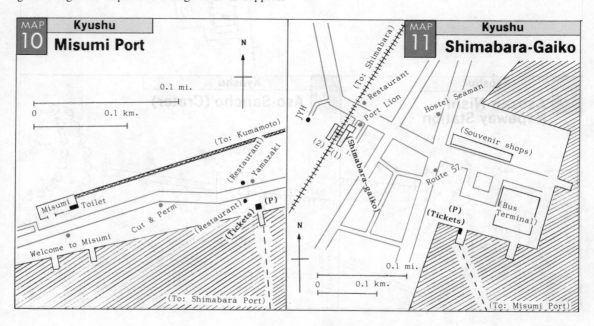

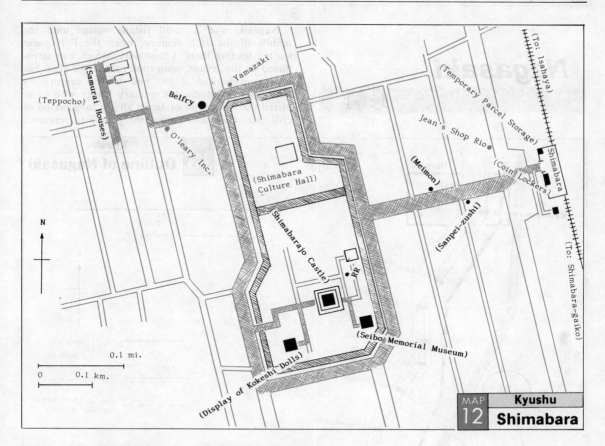

(Teppocho)

(Samurai Houses)

Yamazaki

Belfry

O'leary Inc.

(Shimabara Culture Hall)

Shimabarajo Castle

RR

(Display of Kokeshi Dolls)

(Seibo Memorial Museum)

N

0.1 mi.

0   0.1 km.

(Temporary Parcel Storage)

(To: Isahaya)

Jean's Shop Rio

(Meimon)

(Coin Lockers)

Shimabara

(Sanpei-zushi)

(To: Shimabara-gaiko)

| MAP | Kyushu |
| 12 | **Shimabara** |

After visiting the Castle and samurai houses, take a north-bound train to Isahaya from Shimabara Station.

Instead of visiting Shimabara, many tourists take a bus from Shimabara-gaiko to Nagasaki via **Unzen Spa.** *There is no denying that the volcanic "hells" at Unzen Spa are very impressive, but they are not peculiar to this area. Considering the historical role of Shimabara, and the historical and cultural relics preserved there, I am in favor of Shimabara, and have chosen to introduce it in this itinerary. If you are more interested in nature, you can take a bus from the bus terminal at Shimabara Port (lower right, map 11) to Unzen-Koen* 雲仙公園 *(they operate about once an hour). Another bus operates from Unzen-Koen to Nagasaki Station* 長崎駅 *at similar intervals.*

Places for Lunch

You should eat lunch at either Shimabara-gaiko or Shimabara City. There are no fancy restaurants in the area. Many of the souvenir shops around the port also operate no-frills restaurants. In Shimabara City, I could find only two restaurants — **Sanpei-Zushi,** a sushi bar, and **Meimon,** which serves Japanized western food such as pork cutlets. The prices range from 600 - 1,000 yen (both middle right, map 12).

Nagasaki

長崎

Nagasaki was a small fishing village until the middle of the 16th century, when the Portuguese started trading there. Christianity, which was introduced by the Jesuits, soon took root in the area, but it was prohibited at the end of the century by Hideyoshi Toyotomi, the military leader who completed the unification of Japan after a long period of civil war. Hideyoshi forced the people to renounce

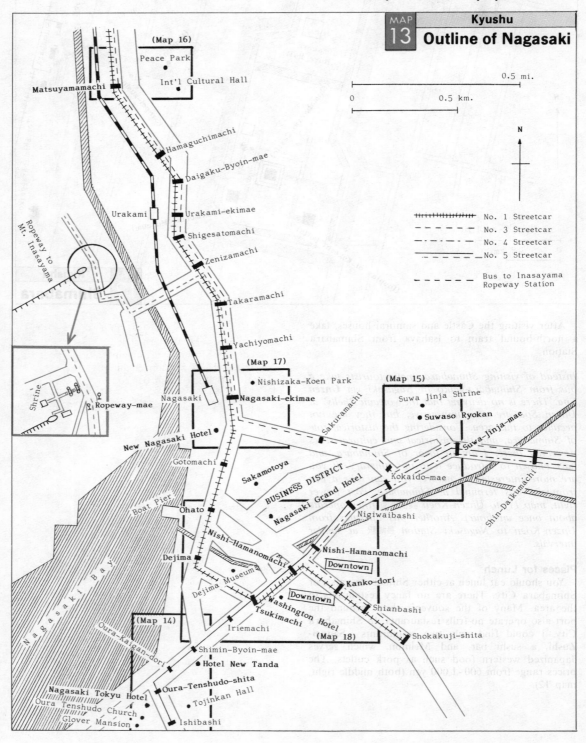

MAP 13 — **Kyushu** — **Outline of Nagasaki**

their religion. Twenty-six faithful Christians refused to do so, and were executed in 1597 at what is now Nishizaka-Koen Park. All of these martyrs were named saints by the Pope in 1862.

In 1639, the Tokugawa Shogunate adopted isolationism as a national policy and closed all Japanese ports except Nagasaki to foreign traders. The Tokugawas wanted to shut out the Christian influence of the European traders, and, at the same time, wanted to monopolize foreign trade, keeping all the profits for themselves. Only Dutch and Chinese traders who did not have any connections with Christian missionaries were allowed to continue trading at Nagasaki. Thus, during the nation's long period of isolation, Nagasaki became the eyes through which Japan watched the changes of the world. Until the middle of the 19th century when this isolationist policy was finally terminated, all modern ideas, science and technology were introduced into Japan through Nagasaki.

In the modern era, Nagasaki prospered as a port city, and became a shipbuilding center. An atomic bomb was exploded over Nagasaki on August 9, 1945, three days after the explosion at Hiroshima. The city was rebuilt and rehabilitated rapidly, and today, with a population of 447,000, Nagasaki is the center of Western Kyushu.

Outline of the City

Even though there are many shopping, eating and drinking places in its vicinity, JNR's Nagasaki Station (middle center, map 13) is rather isolated from downtown (lower center, map 13). The majority of the city's night spots and shopping centers are in the southern part of the city. Local government offices and business properties are located between downtown and Nagasaki Station. Most of the cultural and historical relics of Nagasaki are also located in the southern part of the city. The northern part of the city contains A-bomb related sites and monuments. Mt. Inasayama, the best place to view the whole city, is located to the west of Nagasaki Station.

Transportation in Nagasaki

Most places of interest, night life and shopping centers are conveniently connected by streetcars. The city's four different streetcar lines are pictured on map 13. All streetcars charge a flat 100-yen fare regardless of the distance traveled. Pay when you get off. A one-day pass, which allows unlimited rides on the four lines, can be purchased at major hotels (not on the streetcars) for 500 yen.

Places of Interest

My suggested Kyushu itinerary provides for only one full day of sightseeing in Nagasaki, even though I suggest that you stay in Nagasaki for two nights. (You will arrive in Nagasaki from Kumamoto late in the afternoon of the first day and leave Nagasaki for either Hakata or Karatsu the morning of the third day). However, because two one-day itineraries are ideal for Nagasaki, I have introduced Nagasaki that way, and have, of course, suggested how you can select major sites to reduce what I have written to a one-day itinerary.

DAY 1 ITINERARY
Oura Tenshudo Church 大浦天主堂 **(lower center, map 14)**

Take the No. 5 streetcar to Oura-Tenshudo-shita stop 大浦天主堂下, and walk past the Nagasaki Tokyu Hotel to the church. Oura Tenshudo Church is a wooden Gothic-style building constructed in 1864 to honor the 26 martyrs of Nagasaki. The Church features impressive stained glass windows, and has been designated a National Treasure (8 a.m. to 6 p.m. Admission 200 yen).

Glover Mansion グラバー邸 **(lower left, map 14)**

Glover Mansion is the oldest Western style building in Japan. The mansion is famous as the scene of Puccini's opera "Madam Butterfly." On the grounds of the Glover Mansion is a living museum which consists of several Western style buildings which were moved here from their original locations around Nagasaki. They are on a hillside equipped with escalators that ease your trip to the top. Probably the best way to appreciate the museum is to take the escalators to the top, and then walk down, visiting the various houses located on the hillside. You can have a good view of the port of Nagasaki from the grounds (8:30 a.m. to 5·p.m. Admission 600 yen).

Jurokubankan Mansion 十六番館 **(lower left, map 14)** (for a two-day itinerary only)

Jurokubankan, another Western style building located right outside the exit of the Glover Mansion grounds, is a museum of historical and cultural objects that illustrate early Western and Christian influence in Japan (8:30 a.m. to 5 p.m. Admission 400 yen).

To Ishibashi Streetcar Stop

A narrow street that runs east from Jurokubankan Mansion (indicated with shaded red on map 14) leads to the square in front of Oura Tenshudo Church. Instead of returning along the same street which you took on your way to the Church, take the narrow path stretching to the southeast (which is also indicated with shaded red on map 14). The path travels down a hillside on which are clustered a number of small houses typical of Nagasaki.

If you are spending only one day in Nagasaki, take the No. 5 streetcar from Ishibashi to Tsukimachi 築町 *(lower center, map 18) and visit the Dejima Museum.*

Tojinkan Hall and Hollander Slope (middle right, map 14)

Tojinkan Hall 唐人館 was built in 1893 by the Chinese residents of Nagasaki and was dedicated to Confucius. The present building was reconstructed after World War II. The Hall contains Chinese arts and crafts, as well as a restaurant and many souvenir shops (8:30 a.m. to 5:30 p.m. Admission 400 yen).

Hollander Slope オランダ坂 runs up the hillside (indicated with shaded red). The path was so named because Dutch traders often took walks here. It was probably a favorite with them because of the marvelous view. Take the No. 5 streetcar from Shimin-Byoin-mae stop to Tsukimachi (lower center, map 18), or you can continue to walk to Dejima Museum (0.4 miles or 0.6 km.).

Dejima Museum 出島 (middle left, map 18)

The site of the Dejima Museum was the only place foreigners were allowed to live and trade for more than 200 years. The original Dutch traders' residence still stands here. There are also miniature replicas of the secluded trading houses, which were completed in 1957 (9 a.m. to 5 p.m. Closed on Mondays. Admission free).

If you have only one day to spend in Nagasaki, take the north-bound No. 1 streetcar from Dejima to Matsuyamamachi to visit Peace Park (refer to maps 13 and 16) (details on Peace Park appear below).

Nagasaki was the eyes of Japan during the more than 200 year long isolation.

Suwa Jinja Shrine 諏訪神社

Returning to the Tsukimachi stop, take the east-bound No. 5 streetcar to Suwa-Jinja-mae 諏訪神社前 (see map 15).

Suwa Jinja Shrine was constructed at the order of the feudal government to promote Shintoism and to help wipe out Christian influence in the area. Slowly, it became very popular with the people of Nagasaki. A 277-step stone stairway leads to the wooded precincts and the magnificent shrine buildings. The shrine is famous as the home of Okunchi Festival, which is held each year from October 7-9. The precincts are open year round for worshippers and visitors (No admission charge).

When you finish at Suwa Jinja, it may be around 3 or 4 p.m. Take the west-bound No. 4 or No. 5 streetcar to Nigiwaibashi stop 賑橋 (or you can walk the distance of about 0.4 miles or 0.6 km.). Then enjoy a stroll across Meganebashi Bridge 眼鏡橋 (Eyeglasses Bridge) and around the downtown area (Refer to map 18. Nigiwaibashi stop and Meganebashi Bridge are pictured at the upper right of the map.) Details of the downtown area are explained later.

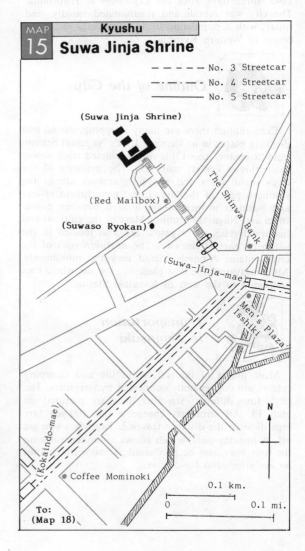

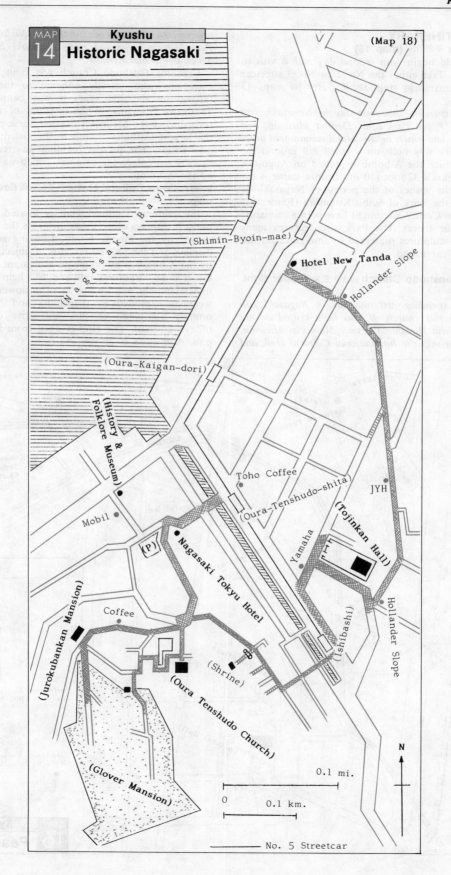

MAP
14

Kyushu
Historic Nagasaki

(Map 18)

(Nagasaki Bay)

(Shimin-Byoin-mae)

● Hotel New Tanda

Hollander Slope

(Oura-Kaigan-dori)

(History & Folklore Museum) ●

Toho Coffee ●

(Oura-Tenshudo-shita)

JYH

Mobil ●

Yamaha ●

(Tojinkan Hall)

(P)

Nagasaki Tokyu Hotel

(Jurokubankan Mansion) ■

Coffee ●

(Ishibashi)

Hollander Slope

(Shrine)

(Oura Tenshudo Church)

(Glover Mansion)

N

0.1 mi.

0   0.1 km.

— No. 5 Streetcar

DAY 2 ITINERARY
Peace Park 平和公園 (map 16)

You should begin your second day with a visit to Peace Park. Take either the No. 1 or No. 3 streetcar to Matsuyamamachi stop 松山町 (refer to maps 13 and 16).

If you are spending just one day in Nagasaki, you should visit Peace Park after Dejima Museum, and then have a late lunch in the Matsuyamamachi area.

Peace Park was built on a small hill around the spot over which the A-bomb exploded on August 9, 1945. The Park's 32-foot (10 m.) bronze statue is the symbol of the wishes of the people of Nagasaki for peace. It is the work of Seibo Kitamura (Remember Shimabarajo Castle? You might have seen a miniature of this statue there). The Park also features many statues and sculptures presented by foreign countries. It is open year round.

Urakami Tenshudo Church 浦上天主堂 (upper right, map 16)

If you are spending just one day in Nagasaki you should skip this church. If you have visited or are planning to visit Hiroshima's Peace Memorial Museum, you can also skip the International Cultural Hall, and proceed to the next destination—Nishizaka-Koen Park, which is located near Nagasaki Station and which is explained below.

Urakami Tenshudo Church was built by faithful Christians who secretly adhered to their religion throughout the 200 years it was banned by the Tokugawa Shoguns. When freedom of religion returned after the Meiji Restoration, these people built the largest Catholic church in the Orient with their own hands. The present building was reconstructed in 1959 to replace the original, which was destroyed by the A-bomb.

International Cultural Hall 国際文化会館 (lower center, map 16)

International Cultural Hall is located in a quiet park. It displays objects that illustrate the devastation caused by the atomic bomb. Looking at the panel displays and the twisted remains of objects destroyed by the A-bomb is by no means a pleasant experience, but it is an important one and will help you better understand the era we live in (The power of atomic weapons exploded in Hiroshima and Nagasaki is nothing compared to the destructive capacity of today's arsenal). The Hall is open from 9 a.m. to 5 p.m. Admission is 50 yen.

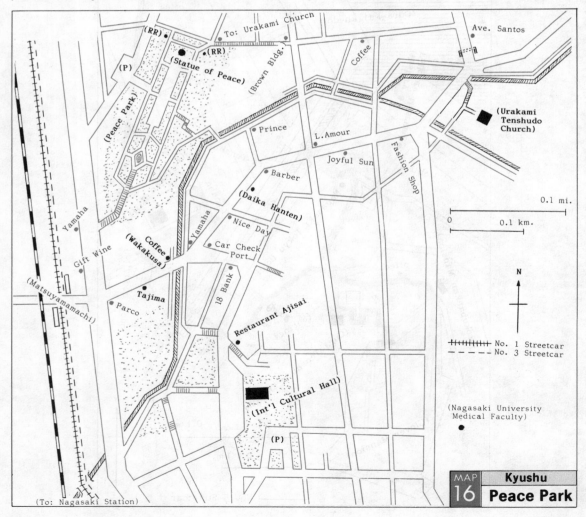

MAP 16 Kyushu Peace Park

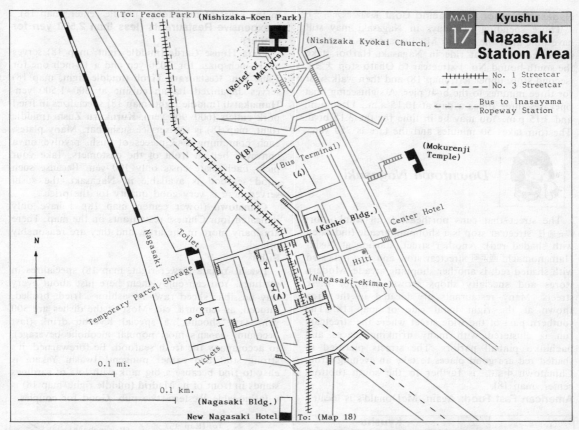

MAP 17 Kyushu

Nagasaki Station Area

++++++++ No. 1 Streetcar
– – – – – No. 3 Streetcar
– – – – – Bus to Inasayama Ropeway Station

(To: Peace Park) **(Nishizaka-Koen Park)**

(Nishizaka Kyokai Church)

(Relief of 26 Martyrs)

(Mokurenji Temple)

(Bus Terminal) **(4)**

(Kanko Bldg.) Center Hotel

Hilti

Nagasaki Toilet

(Nagasaki-ekimae) **(A)**

Temporary Parcel Storage

N

Tickets

0.1 mi.

0.1 km.

(Nagasaki Bldg.)

New Nagasaki Hotel To: (Map 18)

Nishizaka-Koen Park 西坂公園 (map 17)

Take the south-bound No. 1 or No. 3 streetcar from Matsuyamamachi stop to Nagasaki-ekimae 長崎駅前. Nishizaka-Koen is on a small hill northeast of Nagasaki Station. The twenty-six faithful Christians who defied the government mandate to renounce their religion were executed here in 1597. A bronze monument honoring the martyrs was completed in 1962. The Park's museum features objects related to Christianity in Japan. (Museum is open from 9 a.m. to 5 p.m. Admission 200 yen).

Monument of the twenty-six martyrs.

Mt. Inasayama 稲佐山 (middle left, map 13)

The bus to Inasayama Ropeway Station uses bus stop (A), which is located under the huge pedestrian bridge in front of Nagasaki Station (middle center, map 17). Take the north-bound No. 3 bus. Take a numbered ticket upon entering the bus. The fare is shown on the board above and to the left of the driver's seat. Pay the fare shown on the chart under the number corresponding to the number on your ticket. Ropeway-mae stop ロープウェー前 is your destination. The ride takes about five minutes.

The ropeway station is on a hillside (see the detailed map on map 13). It operates every 20 minutes from 9 a.m. to 5 p.m. (till 10 p.m. in summer). The one-way fare is 340 yen. The top of Mt. Inasayama (1,089 feet, or 332 m., a five-minute walk from the ropeway station) has a fantastic view of the city of Nagasaki; the summit also commands a beautiful view of Saikai National Park.

To Nagasaki Station

For the return trip from Ropeway-mae stop to Nagasaki Station, you have to take a different bus because most buses in Nagasaki operate as one-way loops. You should take the south-bound No. 30 or No. 40 bus. Nagasaki-ekimae 長崎駅前 bus stop is pictured on map 17 (stop(B)).

Those spending only one day in Nagasaki will run out of time at Mt. Inasayama. Take the south-bound No. 1 streetcar to Kanko-dori stop 観光通り downtown (middle center, map 18) and enjoy an evening stroll and dining out.

Nagasaki Harbor Sightseeing Boat 長崎港観光ボート

Those spending two days in Nagasaki may still have time after the visit to Mt. Inasayama. If you are interested in a boat ride in Nagasaki Harbor, take the south-bound No. 1 streetcar to Ohato stop 大波止 (second stop, upper left, map 18) and then walk west for three minutes to the boat pier. A sightseeing boat operates three times a day at 10:15 a.m., 11:40 a.m. and 3:15 p.m. You may be in time for the 3:15 boat. The tour takes 50 minutes and the fare is 750 yen.

Downtown Nagasaki

The street that runs northeast from Kanko-dori 観光通り streetcar stop is a shopping arcade (indicated with shaded red). Another street, starting at Nishi-Hamanomachi 西浜町 streetcar stop, and also indicated with shaded red, is another shopping arcade. Modern stores and specialty shops crowd both of these streets. Many restaurants are located in the area shown at the right hand side of map 18. The southern part of the wide street where the streetcars run is clustered with many drinking places and pachinko pinball parlors. The streets pictured in shaded red are good places to take an evening stroll. Chinatown 中華街 is further to the south (bottom center, map 18).

American Fast Food: Again, McDonald's is located in the heart of downtown (middle center, map 18).

Inexpensive Restaurants (less than 2,500 yen for dinner)

Pizza House Garde (middle right, map 18) serves an 11-inch pizza for 1,050 yen and a 13-inch one for 1,400 yen. **Restaurant Tivoli** (middle right, map 18) serves Japanized Italian cuisine at 800-1,500 yen. **Hamakatsu** (middle right, map 18) specializes in fried pork cutlets (600-900 yen). **Kurukuru Zushi** (middle right, map 18) is self-service sushi bar. Many plates, each containing 2-3 pieces of sushi revolve on a conveyor belt in front of the customers. Take your pick. Each plate costs only 100 yen. Because such good seafood is available in Nagasaki, the sushi served here is very good quality for the price.

Chinatown (lower center, map 18): I have only indicated four Chinese restaurants on the map. There are many more in the area, and they are reasonably priced.

Pubs

Iwashi Yakata (lower right, map 18) specializes in sardines. You can enjoy them here just about every way possible: sliced raw -as sashimi-, fried, broiled, minced, as tempura, etc. Most of the dishes are 300 yen. Try "shochu," a special Kyushu drink (fast becoming Japan's most popular alcoholic beverage), to accompany the fresh seafood. Be forewarned: it's strong stuff and rather pungent! Iwashi Yakata is easy to find because a big tank with lots of sardines stands in front of it. **Madrid** (middle right, map 18) is a fashionable Western-style pub. Good for couples.

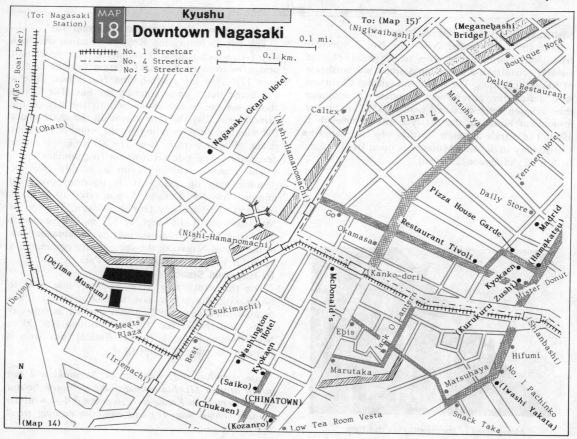

MAP 18 — Kyushu — Downtown Nagasaki

(To: Nagasaki Station)
To: (Map 15) (Nigiwaibashi)
(Meganebashi Bridge)

0.1 mi.

- No. 1 Streetcar
- No. 4 Streetcar
- No. 5 Streetcar

0   0.1 km.

(To: Boat Pier)

(Ohato)

Nagasaki Grand Hotel
(Nishi-Hamanomachi)
Caltex
Plaza L
Matsuhaya
Boutique Nora
Delica Restaurant
Ten-nen Hotel
Daily Store
Pizza House Garde
Madrid
Go
Okamasa
Restaurant Tivoli
Hamakatsu
Kyokaen
Mister Donut
Kanko-dori
Kurukuru Zushi
Shianbashi
(Dejima)
(Dejima Museum)
(Tsukimachi)
McDonald's
Epis
Jack O'Lantern
Hifumi
Meats Plaza
Best
Washington Hotel
Kyokaen
Marutaka
Matsuhaya
No. 1 Pachinko
(Iriemachi)
(Saiko)
(CHINATOWN)
Snack Taka
(Iwashi Yakata)
(Chukaen)
(Kozanro)
Low Tea Room Vesta

N

(Map 14)

Accommodations

HOTELS

First-class Hotel (20,000 yen and up for a twin room)

Nagasaki Tokyu Hotel 長崎東急ホテル (lower left, map 13)

Address: 1-18, Minami-Yamatemachi, Nagasaki; Phone: (0958) 25-1501. A 225-room modern hotel in the historic area.

Standard Hotels (14,000 - 20,000 yen for a twin room)

Hotel New Tanda ホテル・ニュータンダ (lower left, map 13)

Address: 2-24, Tokiwamachi, Nagasaki; Phone: (0958) 27-6121. Another modern hotel at a convenient location (161 rooms).

Nagasaki Grand Hotel 長崎グランドホテル (middle center, map 13)

Address: 5-3, Manzaimachi, Nagasaki; Phone: (0958) 23-1234. A small, 126-room hotel near the business district.

New Nagasaki Hotel ニュー長崎ホテル (middle left, map 13)

Address: 14-5, Daikokumachi, Nagasaki; Phone: (0958) 26-6161. A 60-room modern hotel near Nagasaki Station.

Business Hotel (less than 14,000 yen for a twin)

(Nagasaki) Washington Hotel 長崎ワシントンホテル (lower center, map 13)

Address: 9-1, Shinchimachi, Nagasaki; Phone: (0958) 28-1211. A recently opened high-class business hotel in the downtown area (177 rooms).

RYOKANS

First-class Ryokans (20,000 yen and up per person with two meals)

Sakamotoya 坂本屋 (middle center, map 13)

Address: 2-13, Kanayamachi, Nagasaki; Phone: (0958) 26-8211. A small, 20-room property in a convenient location.

Karatsu 唐津

If you leave Nagasaki early in the morning, you will arrive in Karatsu around noon (Transfer at Saga—Refer to the Transportation section in the Introduction to Kyushu above). After sightseeing in Karatsu you can stay there or move on to Hakata to take a look at the night face of Kyushu's largest city. There are a number of pottery kilns in Karatsu. Visit the information office in Karatsu Station to check on which kiln is open to the public for the day.

Suggested Itinerary

Kinshoji Temple 近松寺 (middle left, map 20) (optional)

This is the family temple of the Ogasawaras, feudal lords who governed the area during the Edo era. The temple is famous as the burial place of Monzaemon Chikamatsu. Chikamatsu wrote joruri—the chanted dramatic stories from which the modern Bunraku puppet plays developed. He was extremely prolific and wrote more than 51 plays. He has been called the father of Japanese drama. The temple also has a small museum that displays the family treasures of the Ogasawaras (Admission free).

Hikiyama Tenjijo Hall 曳山展示場 (middle center, map 20)

Karatsu Kunchi Festival (November 2-4) is famous for its colorful festival floats. Fifteen districts of the city have their own floats, each designed in a distinctive shape, such as a samurai helmet, a dragon, a fish, etc. These really impressive floats are displayed in Hikiyama Tenjijo Hall. Magnificently finished with gold and silver foil and lacquer, they testify to the high artistic standards of the area (9 a.m. to 5 p.m. Admission 200 yen).

Karatsujo Castle 唐津城 (upper center, map 19 or upper right, map 20)

Karatsujo Castle stands on a small hill facing the Genkainada Sea. Because of its white walls and its ideal location right on the water, the castle is popularly known as Maizurujo or Flying Crane Castle. The present building is a 1966 reconstruction. The view from the castle grounds of the sea, the city and Rainbow Pine Beach to the east is well worth the effort of climbing the long stone stairway.

Pottery Kiln via Niji-no-Matsubara (Rainbow Pine Beach)

Kyozan Kiln 鏡山窯 (upper right, map 19) is usually open to the public. Take a taxi at the exit of Karatsujo Castle (there are always many waiting there) to Kyozan Kiln. The taxi will pass through a dense pine forest along the sea. This pine forest is 0.4 miles (0.6 km.) wide and 3.1 miles (5 km.) long. Most of the pine trees are over 350 years old. This is the most beautiful forest of its kind in all of Japan.

Karatsu pottery is characterized by its plain dark brown glaze. Simple, and austerely beautiful, it is often used for tea ceremony. If you are unfamiliar with the process of pottery making, you will be impressed with the skillful handiwork of the craftsmen.

To Niji-no-Matsubara Station or to your hotel in Karatsu

If you are staying in Hakata (Fukuoka), take a taxi to the closest station (the station closest to Kyozan Kiln is Niji-no-Matsubara Station 虹ノ松原駅). The JNR Chikuhi Line operates almost every hour (see the Transportation section in the Introduction to Kyushu above).

If you are staying in Karatsu, I strongly recommend that you stay at Karatsu Seaside Hotel, which stands right on Rainbow Pine Beach.

Accommodations

Standard Hotel (14,000-20,000 yen for a twin room)

Karatsu Seaside Hotel 唐津シーサイドホテル (upper center, map 19)

Address: 4-182, Higashi-Karatsu, Karatsu; Phone: (0955) 73-5185. A 52-room resort hotel on the beautiful beach. 26 rooms are Japanese style.

Tea Ceremony

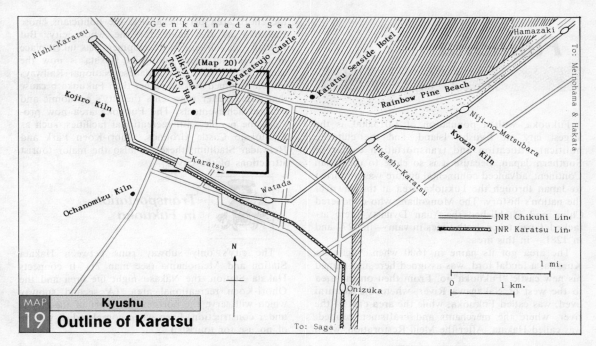

(Map 20)

MAP 19

Kyushu

Outline of Karatsu

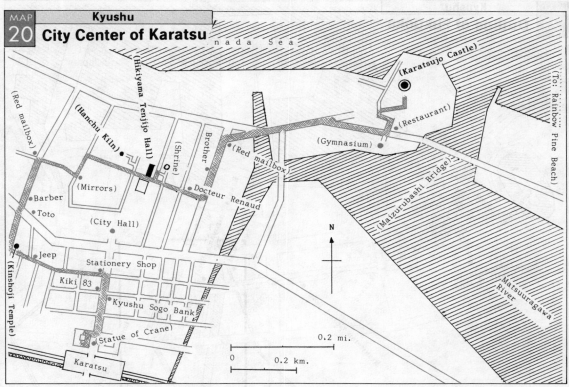

MAP 20

Kyushu

City Center of Karatsu

Fukuoka

福岡

Fukuoka, with a population of 1,015,000, is the largest city on Kyushu Island, and the cultural, political, education and transportation center of Southern Japan. Because it is so close to the Asian Continent, advanced continental culture was imported to Japan through the Fukuoka area at the dawn of the nation's history. The Mongolians who conquered China and established the Yuan Dynasty there attacked Japan twice, both times in vain — in 1274 and in 1281 — in this area.

The area got its name in 1600 when Nagamasa Kuroda, a feudal lord, was assigned here and named his new castle "Fukuoka"-jo. From then on the area to the west of Nakagawa River, where the samurai lived, was called Fukuoka, while the area east of the river, where the merchants and craftsmen resided, was called Hakata. After the Meiji Restoration, when the entire area became a city, the politicians chose Fukuoka as the name for the whole city. But virtually all subsequent development has taken place in the Hakata area, and thus Hakata is now the center of the city. The Japanese National Railways station is named Hakata rather than Fukuoka because that name better represents the city's economic and cultural achievements. The Fukuoka area now provides the people with recreational facilities, such as Fukuokajo Castle Grounds, Ohori-Koen Park and Heiwadai Stadium; these are also the major tourist attractions of the city.

Transportation in Fukuoka

The city's only subway runs between Hakata Station and Meinohama (see map 21). It connects Hakata Station, the Nakasu night life area and the Ohori-Koen recreational area. (A second subway which will serve the northeastern part of the city is under construction. Even when completed, it will be of no use for tourists.)

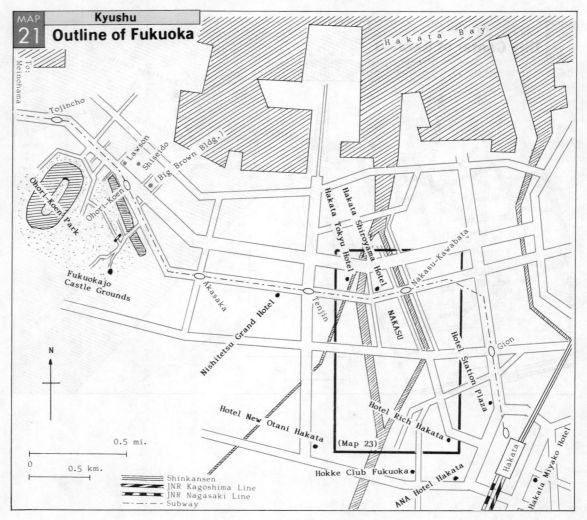

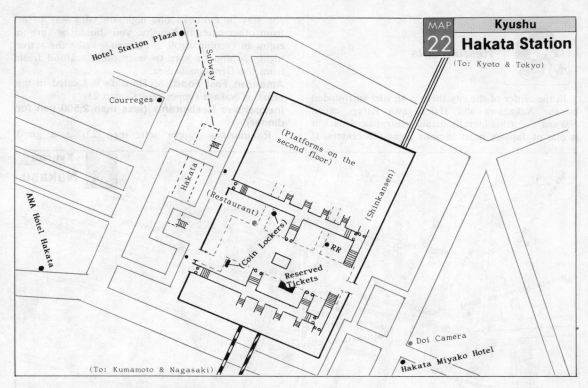

Map 22 shows the JNR Hakata Station, which is the terminus of the 735-mile (1,177 km.) long Tokaido-Sanyo Shinkansen bullet train that originates in Tokyo. Hakata is also the starting point of the major trains operating to many parts of Kyushu, such as Kumamoto and Nagasaki.

Places of Interest

Fukuokajo Castle 福岡城跡 **(upper left, map 21)**

Only a few gates and one turret still remain, but the castle grounds are on a 157-foot (48 m.) high hill that commands a bird's-eye view of the city.

Ohori-Koen Park 大濠公園 **(northwest of the castle grounds)**

The park is laid out around a large pond that is 1.25 miles (2 km.) in circumference. Several bridges provide access to the islet in the center of the pond.

Kushida Jinja Shrine 櫛田神社 **(middle right, map 23)**

Kushida Jinja Shrine is Fukuoka's most important shrine and is dedicated to the Shinto god Susano-o-no-Mikoto. The decorations used for the Hakata Yamagasa Festival (July 1-15) are on display in the museum attached to the shrine. They feature feudal era costumes and objects, and are colorful and elaborate but are no comparison to those on display in Karatsu (The museum is open from 9 a.m. to 5 p.m. Admission is 200 yen).

Restaurants

In the center of the city there is an islet surrounded by the Nakagawa and Hakatagawa Rivers called Nakasu (this literally means central sand bar); it is one of Japan's most famous night life centers. If you stay in Fukuoka one night on your way to or from other cities in Kyushu, you should be sure to enjoy an evening stroll in Nakasu — savor the active night life and be sure to taste some seafood fresh from the Genkainada Sea.

American Fast Food: McDonald's is located in the heart of Nakasu (upper center, map 23).

Inexpensive Restaurants (less than 2,500 yen for dinner)

Rokumeikan (upper left, map 23) is a good

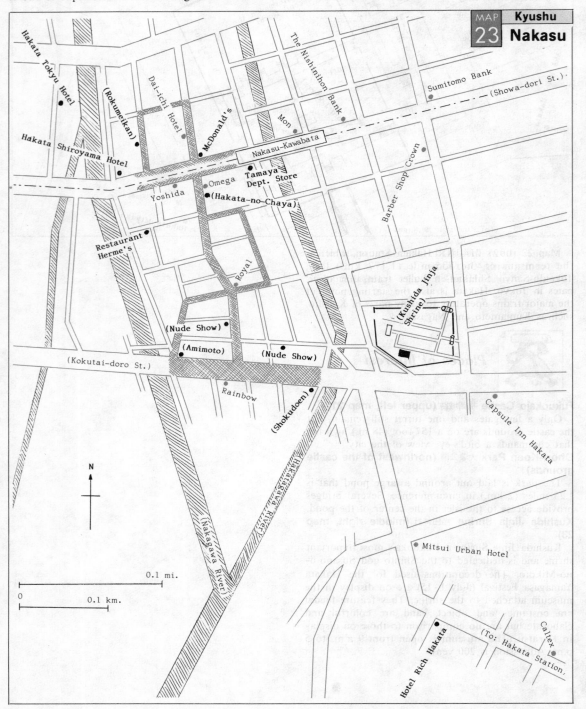

MAP 23 Kyushu Nakasu

Hakata Tokyu Hotel
(Rokumeikan)
Dai-ichi Hotel
McDonald's
The Nishinihon Bank
Mon
Sumitomo Bank
(Showa-dori St.)
Hakata Shiroyama Hotel
Nakasu-Kawabata
Barber Shop Crown
Omega
Tamaya Dept. Store
Yoshida
(Hakata-no-Chaya)
Restaurant Herme's
Royal
(Kushida Jinja) Shrine
(Nude Show)
(Amimoto)
(Nude Show)
(Kokutai-doro St.)
Rainbow
(Shokudoen)
Capsule Inn Hakata
N
0.1 mi.
0 0.1 km.
(Nakagawa River)
(HAKATAGAWA RIVER)
Mitsui Urban Hotel
Hotel Rich Hakata
Calex
(To: Hakata Station,

Chinese restaurant (650-1,500 yen per dish). **Restaurant Herme's** (upper left, map 23) serves spaghetti at 600 yen, stew at 1,300 yen and steak at 1,500 yen. **Hakata-no-Chaya** (upper center, map 23) has a number of yellow lanterns at its entrance. This pub-style Japanese restaurant serves a variety of seafood nabemono dishes ("Ishikarinabe," "Chankonabe," etc.) at 2,000-2,500 yen. **Shokudoen** (middle center, map 23) is a Korean-style barbecue restaurant (about 1,000 yen per plate).

Reasonable Restaurant (less than 5,000 yen for dinner)

Amimoto (middle left, map 23) is located at an intersection and is a Japanese pub restaurant, like Hakata-no-Chaya. If you want to try sashimi in addition to cooked seafood, Amimoto is a good choice.

Accommodations

HOTELS

First-class Hotels (20,000 yen and up for a twin room)

Hotel New Otani Hakata ホテル・ニューオータニ博多 (lower center, map 21)

   Address: 1-1-2, Watanabedori, Chuo-ku, Fukuoka; Phone: (092) 714-1111. The largest hotel in Fukuoka, with 436 rooms.

Nishitetsu Grand Hotel 西鉄グランドホテル (middle center, map 21)

   Address: 2-6-60, Daimyo, Chuo-ku, Fukuoka; (092) 771-7171. Popular among both Japanese and foreign business people (308 rooms).

Standard Hotels (14,000-20,000 yen for a twin room).

ANA Hotel Hakata 博多全日空ホテル (lower right, map 21)

   Address: 3-3-3, Hakata-ekimae, Hakata-ku, Fukuoka; Phone: (092) 471-7111. A high-standard hotel near Hakata Station (363 rooms).

Hakata Miyako Hotel 博多都ホテル (lower right, map 21)

   Address: 2-1-1, Hakataeki-Higashi, Hakata-ku, Fukuoka; Phone: (092) 441-3111. A 269-room modern hotel near the Shinkansen exit of Hakata Station.

Hakata Tokyu Hotel 博多東急ホテル (middle center, map 21)

   Address: 1-16-1, Tenjin, Chuo-ku, Fukuoka; Phone: (092) 781-7111. A standard Tokyu Hotel Group property (266 rooms).

Hakata Shiroyama Hotel 博多城山ホテル (middle center, map 21)

   Address: 5-3-4, Nakasu, Hakata-ku, Fukuoka; Phone: (092) 281-2211. A small, 117-room property right in the Nakasu nightlife area.

Business Hotels (less than 14,000 yen for a twin room)

Hotel Station Plaza ホテル・ステーションプラザ (lower right, map 21)

   Address: 2-1-1, Hakata-ekimae, Hakata-ku, Fukuoka; Phone: (092) 431-1211. A high-class business hotel near Hakata Station (248 rooms).

Hotel Rich Hakata ホテル・リッチ博多 (lower right, map 21)

   Address: 3-27-15, Hakata-ekimae, Hakata-ku, Fukuoka; Phone: (092) 451-7811. Another high-class business hotel with 178 rooms.

Hokke Club Fukuoka 法華クラブ福岡 (lower right, map 21)

   Address: 3-1-90, Sumiyoshi, Hakata-ku, Fukuoka; Phone: (092) 271-3171. A typical standard business hotel with 239 rooms in a quiet location.

東北

Tohoku

Tohoku, the northeastern part of Japan's main island, has always been the nation's least developed area, economically and culturally. Because of its severe winter weather and its mountainous topography, industrial development here has lagged far behind the economic miracle areas of the Pacific coast. But nature is unspoiled here, and the area has a beautiful coast. The area's natural beauties and the simple, warm hospitality of the people have long fascinated visitors. The area has also clung to its traditional crafts, which adds extra interest for those who make the trip to Tohoku.

The extension of JNR's north-bound Tohoku Shinkansen to Tokyo's Ueno Station has made travel to Tohoku much easier. I recommend the following two-night, three-day itinerary in Tohoku on a trip from Tokyo. To ease your travel in this area, take along only what you need and leave your big bags at your hotel in Tokyo. (See map 1).

1st Day: Tokyo — Ichinoseki — Hiraizumi (Chusonji and Motsuji Temples) — Ichinoseki — Sendai.

2nd Day: Sendai — Hon-Shiogama (Shiogama Jinja Shrine) — Boat ride in Matsushima Bay — Matsushima (Zuiganji Temple, etc.) — Sendai (or overnight in Matsushima).

3rd Day: Morning in Sendai (Zuihoden) — Tokyo.

- *If you don't mind arriving back in Tokyo in the evening, you can take the Tohoku Shinkansen late in the afternoon of the second day.*
- *You can also add a visit to Nikko to this itinerary. Take the Tohoku Shinkansen back to Utsunomiya, and then take the JNR Nikko Line to Nikko (Refer to the Nikko Chapter above for details).*

Transportation

The Tohoku Shinkansen 東北新幹線 operates from Ueno Station in Tokyo. Ueno Station 上野駅 can be reached easily from all parts of Tokyo by the JNR Yamanote (Loop) Line, the JNR Keihin-Tohoku Line, the Ginza subway line, or the Hibiya subway line.

As with the Shinkansens that run southeast from Tokyo, there are two types of trains on the Tohoku Shinkansen. The faster one, which makes fewer stops, is called "Yamabiko" (Mountain Echo), while the slower one, which stops at all the stations on the line is called "Aoba" (Green Leaf). Most Yamabiko trains run the whole distance between Ueno and Morioka (but several terminate at Sendai), while all the Aoba trains run only the shorter distance between Ueno and Sendai. Ichinoseki Station 一ノ関駅, your first destination, is served only by the Yamabiko.

All the Tohoku Shinkansens consist of 12 cars. Cars No. 1 through No. 4 have ordinary class nonreserved seats (Car No. 1 is non-smoking), Cars No. 5, No. 6, and No. 8 through No. 12 have ordinary class reserved seats (Car No. 8 is non-smoking), and Car No. 7 is a Green Car (first class, reserved seats). Car No. 9 has a buffet counter. When the train runs to the north from Ueno, Car No. 12 is at the front of the train, but Car No. 1 is at

Map 1 — Outline of Tohoku

(Map labels: To: Morioka, Chusonji Temple, Motsuji Temple, Ichinoseki, Morioka, N, 5 mi., 0 5 km., Nikko, Utsunomiya, Tokyo (Ueno), Furukawa, Tohoku Shinkansen, Matsushima Kaigan, Zuiganji Temple, Shiogama Jinja Shrine, Hon-Shiogama, Matsushima, JNR Senseki Line, Sendai, Pacific Ocean, To: Tokyo)

the front when coming back to Ueno. You should make reservations upon your arrival in Japan.

As the Tohoku Shinkansen trains approach stations, an announcement is made in both Japanese and English. Vendors walk through the cars from time to time with box lunches, beverages and snacks.

The following is the schedule for the major Tohoku Shinkansens. Only the Yamabiko timetable is listed for the north-bound trip because the Aoba terminates at Sendai and does not go to Ichinoseki. For the return trip I have listed both the Yamabiko and Aoba since you will be leaving from Sendai.

Ueno to Sendai and Ichinoseki

Train Name	Lv. Ueno	Ar. Utsunomiya	Ar. Sendai	Ar. Ichinoseki
Yamabiko-33	7:00 a.m.	7:47 a.m.	9:03 a.m.	9:36 a.m.
Yamabiko-39	8:00 a.m.	8:47 a.m.	10:03 a.m.	10:36 a.m.
Yamabiko-41	9:00 a.m.	9:47 a.m.	11:03 a.m.	11:36 a.m.
Yamabiko-45	10:00 a.m.	10:47 a.m.	12:03 p.m.	12:36 p.m.
Yamabiko-49	11:00 a.m.	11:47 a.m.	1:03 p.m.	1:36 p.m.

- The Yamabiko trains operate every hour on the hour, with the last train leaving Ueno at 8 p.m.
- If you don't have a Japan Rail Pass, the fare from Ueno to Ichinoseki is 10,800 yen (ordinary car reserved seat). The Green Car surcharge is 5,400 yen.

Ichinoseki and Sendai to Utsunomiya and Ueno

- You should take the Tohoku Shinkansen from Ichinoseki back to Sendai on the first day.
- As I mentioned above, if you add on a visit to Nikko after the Tohoku trip, take the Tohoku Shinkansen to Utsunomiya.

Ueno to Sendai and Ichinoseki

Train Name	Lv. Ichinoseki	Ar. Sendai	Ar. Utsunomiya	Ar. Ueno
Yamabiko-32	8:17 a.m.	8:48 a.m.	10:07 a.m.	10:53 a.m.
Aoba-204	—	8:54 a.m.	10:29 a.m.	11:22 a.m.
Yamabiko-34	8:58 a.m.	9:29 a.m.	10:48 a.m.	11:34 a.m.
Aoba-206	—	9:50 a.m.	11:30 a.m.	12:22 a.m.
Yamabiko-10	—	10:01 a.m.	—	11:55 a.m.
Yamabiko-38	9:58 a.m.	10:29 a.m.	11:48 a.m.	12:34 p.m.
Aoba-208	—	10:50 a.m.	12:30 p.m.	1:22 p.m.
Yamabiko-20	—	11:01 a.m.	—	12:57 p.m.
Yamabiko-42	10:58 a.m.	11:29 a.m.	12:48 p.m.	1:34 p.m.
Aoba-210	—	11:54 a.m.	1:29 p.m.	2:22 p.m.
Yamabiko-44	11:58 a.m.	12:29 p.m.	1:48 p.m.	2:34 p.m.
Yamabiko-48	12:58 p.m.	1:29 p.m.	2:48 p.m.	3:34 p.m.
Aoba-214	—	1:50 p.m.	3:29 p.m.	4:22 p.m.
Yamabiko-52	1:58 p.m.	2:29 p.m.	3:48 p.m.	4:34 p.m.
Aoba-216	—	2:50 p.m.	4:29 p.m.	5:22 p.m.
Yamabiko-58	2:58 p.m.	3:29 p.m.	4:48 p.m.	5:34 p.m.
Aoba-218	—	3:50 p.m.	5:29 p.m.	6:22 p.m.
Yamabiko-4	—	4:01 p.m.	—	5:55 p.m.
Yamabiko-62	3:58 p.m.	4:29 p.m.	5:48 p.m.	6:34 p.m.
Aoba-220	—	4:50 p.m.	6:30 p.m.	7:22 p.m.
Yamabiko-22	—	5:01 p.m.	6:13 p.m.	6:57 p.m.
Yamabiko-64	4:58 p.m.	5:29 p.m.	6:48 p.m.	7:34 p.m.
Aoba-222	—	5:50 p.m.	7:29 p.m.	8:22 p.m.

- Yamabiko and Aoba trains operate at similar intervals, with the last train (Yamabiko-76) leaving Sendai at 9:31 p.m. (arriving at Ueno at 11:34 p.m.).
- The fare from Ichinoseki to Sendai is 3,560 yen for an ordinary car reserved seat. A nonreserved seat is 500 yen less. Because the ride takes only 30 minutes, it is better not to make reservations in advance (The fare is cheaper and you can keep your schedule

Kokeshi dolls - typical Tohoku handicrafts.

flexible).
- The fare from Sendai to Utsunomiya is 7,300 yen (ordinary car reserved seat). A nonreserved seat is 500 yen less. The Green Car surcharge is 4,200 yen.
- The fare from Sendai to Ueno is 9,400 yen (500 yen less for a nonreserved seat and an additional 4,200 yen for the Green Car).

Hiraizumi

平泉

The Fujiwara family headed a strong local government in Hiraizumi from 1089 to 1189. A strong economy and political stability enabled three generations of Fujiwaras to nurture a level of culture comparable to that of Kyoto, and unequalled by any other local area. Chusonji Temple and Motsuji Temple are symbols of Tohoku culture in the medieval era. Yoritomo Minamoto, the founder of the first military government in Japan, defeated the fourth leader of the Fujiwaras in 1189, and the 100-year long prosperity of the north disappeared, never to return. The area is also famous for its lacquerware, and ironware, such as wind chimes and kettles. Many souvenir shops are located near the Chusonji bus stop and along the approach to the Temple.

Bus from Ichinoseki to Chusonji

A visit to Chusonji Temple requires a long walk on a hilly path. You should leave your bag(s) in a coin locker at Ichinoseki Station (The location of the lockers is pictured on map 2). Strangely enough, coin lockers in the station building are 200 yen, while those near the bus stop are 100 yen. The lockers can accommodate regular carry-on bags (So don't bring a big one with you! Put your bag(s) into the locker, shut the door, insert 100-yen coin(s) into the slot and turn the key to the left). The bus going to Chusonji operates every 20 - 30 minutes from early morning till early evening (around 8 p.m.), and leaves from stop No. 10 (lower left, map 2). Take a numbered ticket upon boarding. The fare is displayed on the board above and to the left of the driver's seat. The display changes as the bus travels along its route. Pay the amount indicated under the number of your ticket. Put your fare in the box near the driver when you get off (290 yen to Chusonji). The bus route is indicated with shaded red on map 3 and with a red dotted line on map 4 and map 5. The ride from Ichinoseki to Chusonji takes 26 minutes.

The JNR Tohoku Line operates between Ichinoseki and Hiraizumi almost every hour. However, because Chusonji Temple is not within walking distance of Hiraizumi Station (20 - 25 minutes on foot on a busy street), you still have to take this same bus, from Hiraizumi to Chusonji. Going this way saves only 180 yen and is much too time consuming.

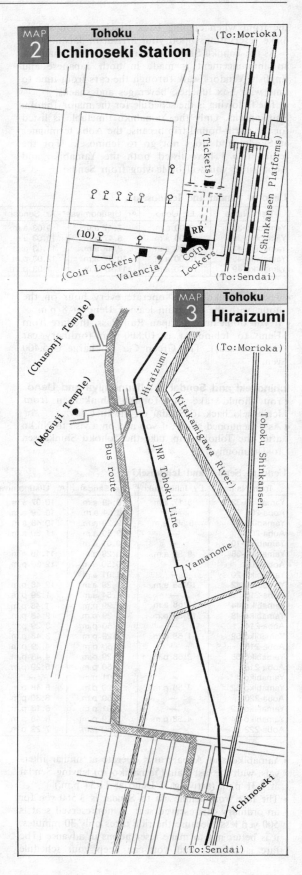

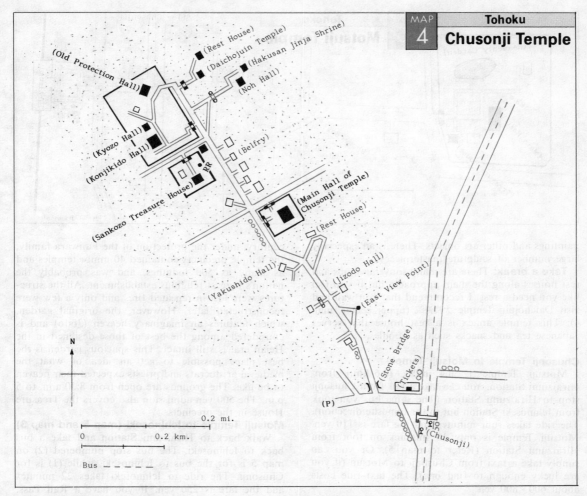

MAP 4 Tohoku
Chusonji Temple

(Old Protection Hall)
(Rest House)
(Daichojuin Temple)
(Hakusan Jinja Shrine)
(Noh Hall)
(Kyozo Hall)
(Konjikido Hall)
(Belfry)
RR
(Sankozo Treasure House)
(Main Hall of Chusonji Temple)
(Rest House)
(Jizodo Hall)
(Yakushido Hall)
(East View Point)
(Stone Bridge)
(Tickets)
(P)
(Chusonji)

N

0.2 mi.

0   0.2 km.

Bus - - - - - -

Chusonji Temple 中尊寺 (map 4)

Allow at least one and a half hours for this visit. The entrance to the main approach to Chusonji Temple is a stone bridge, which leads to a steep slope. Once you cross the bridge smoking is prohibited everywhere in the temple grounds.

Chusonji Temple was erected in the 9th century. It prospered under the reign of the Fujiwara family in the 11th and 12th centuries, and at its peak there were more than 40 buildings in the precincts (which actually cover all of one small mountain). Chusonji Temple lost most of its buildings to fire in 1337. Only Konjikido Hall (Golden Hall) and Kyozo Hall (Sutra Hall) survived the fire. Most of the other buildings were reconstructed in the Edo era. The 0.6 mile (1 km.) long approach to Konjikido Hall is shaded by tall cedar trees; the many small halls along this path add to the solemn atmosphere of the grounds.

East View Point 東物見台 (lower right, map 4) commands a good view of Mt. Tabashineyama and the Kitakamigawa River.

The Main Hall of Chusonji Temple 中尊寺本堂 (middle center, map 4) is located about halfway up the approach. Chusonji Temple is still active as a principal temple of the Tendai sect of Buddhism in the Tohoku region (The headquarters is Enryakuji Temple on Mt. Hieizan in Kyoto).

Konjikido Hall 金色堂 (National Treasure), **Kyozo Hall** 経蔵 and **Old Protection Hall** 旧覆堂 of Konjikido are located in the enclosed area at the end of the approach (upper left, map 4). The ticket office is at the entrance to the enclosure (8:30 a.m. to 5 p.m.). The 500 yen admission also covers admission to Sankozo Treasure House (upper left, map 4). Konjikido Hall, a small golden hall built in 1124, is coated with black lacquer and covered entirely with gold foil. It is especially famous for the delicate decorative art works of its interior; they testify to the high artistic achievements of the area in the 12th century. Konjikido Hall is contained within a larger concrete structure which was completed in 1968. The Old Protection Hall, which used to house Konjikido, has been moved to the north. Kyozo Hall, originally constructed in 1108 as a two-story building, lost its second floor to fire in 1337. The first floor was repaired and preserved.

Noh Hall 能楽堂 (upper center, map 4) is an important historical relic and testifies to the Temple's former preeminence in cultural activities. The Hall has an outdoor stage so that audiences can enjoy open air performances. Nowadays only one Noh play a year is performed on August 14.

Sankozo Treasure House 讃衡蔵 displays the temple's treasures, which include images of Buddha,

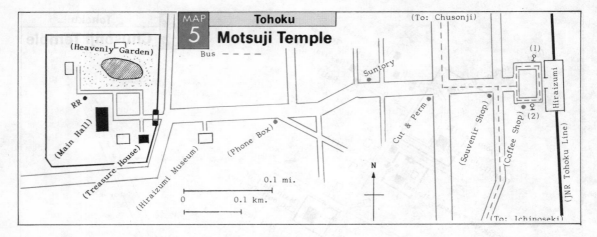

(To: Chusonji)

MAP
5

Tohoku
Motsuji Temple

Bus - - - -

(Heavenly Garden)

Suntory

(1)

RR

Cut & Perm

Hiraizumi

(Main Hall)

(Treasure House)

(Hiraizumi Museum)

(Phone Box)

(Souvenir Shop)

(Coffee Shop)

(2)

(JNR Tohoku Line)

N

0.1 mi.

0   0.1 km.

(To: Ichinoseki)

paintings and other art objects. There is an especially large number of sculpture masterpieces.

Take a break: There are many souvenir shops and rest houses along the main approach, but if you feel like you need a rest, I recommend that you wait and visit Daichojuin Temple 大長寿院 (upper center, map 4). This temple annex is a rest house that serves Japanese tea and snacks such as noodles.

Chusonji Temple to Motsuji Temple

Motsuji Temple is 0.4 miles (0.6 km.) from Hiraizumi Station. You can take a bus from Chusonji stop to Hiraizumi Station (The same bus you took from Ichinoseki Station but in the opposite direction). The ride takes four minutes and the fare is 110 yen. Motsuji Temple is only 10 minutes on foot from Hiraizumi Station (Refer to map 5). Or you can simply take a taxi from Chusonji to Motsuji (if you are lucky enough to find one). The taxi ride costs about 600 - 800 yen.

Motsuji Temple 毛越寺 (map 5)

Motsuji Temple was originally erected by the priest Ennin (Jikaku Daishi) in 850. In the 12th

century, under the protection of the Fujiwara family, the temple precincts contained 40 minor temples and as many as 500 lodgings, and was probably the nation's biggest religious establishment. All the structures were lost in repeated fires and only a few were reconstructed later. However, the original garden, which features an imaginary heaven (Jodo) and is considered among the best of those designed in the Heian era, is still intact. This spacious garden is the best place possible to get an idea of what the medieval aristocrats and priests expected their heaven to be like. The grounds are open from 8:30 a.m. to 5 p.m. The 500 yen admission also covers the Treasure House in the precincts.

Motsuji Temple to Ichinoseki (map 5 and map 3)

Walk back to Hiraizumi Station and take a bus back to Ichinoseki. The bus stop numbered (2) on map 5 is for the bus to Ichinoseki, while (1) is for Chusonji. The ride to Ichinoseki takes 22 minutes and the fare is 250 yen. If you have a Rail Pass, check to see if there is a convenient local train on the JNR Tohoku Line from Hiraizumi to Ichinoseki. For the schedule of the Tohoku Shinkansen from Ichinoseki to Sendai, refer to the Transportation section above.

Chusonji Temple.

Sendai

仙台

Toward the end of the civil war period (the end of the 16th century), a military genius named Masamune Date unified the smaller feudal lords of the Tohoku district and established a power base in Sendai. Because the capital at Kyoto was so far away, Masamune did not participate in the struggles or the bloody battles then being waged by those seeking central political power. He remained an influential feudal lord under Ieyasu Tokugawa, the first Tokugawa Shogun. The people of Tohoku still say that Masamune would have been the person to complete the unification of Japan if he had been born 20 years earlier and somewhere closer to Kyoto. This remark, regardless of its basis in fact, reflects the respect the people of the area still have for this one-eyed hero. Throughout the Edo era, Sendai prospered as the largest castle city in Tohoku under the reign of successive generations of the Date family. After World War II, Sendai was redeveloped as a modern city, but its quiet air of a feudal town, surrounded by thick green woods, has been preserved successfully. Even though Sendai lacks buildings of historical interest because of the devastation of the war, it is one of Japan's most livable cities. With its clean shopping arcades and generally pleasant atmosphere, it is also one of the most comfortable cities in Japan for an evening stroll. I recommend that you stay here for two nights. The city of Sendai has a population of 636,000.

Outline of the City

Sendai Station is a four-story building. The Tohoku Shinkansen platforms are located on the fourth floor. Exits are located on the second floor and the ground floor. If you want a taxi go down to the ground floor. If you are walking to your hotel, use the second floor exit. You will be surprised at the extensive maze of pedestrian bridges outside the station.

Sendai has two shopping arcades, as pictured on map 6 (shaded red). The arcade running east to west is called Chuo-dori Street 中央通り, and the one running north to south is called Higashi-Ichibancho Street 東一番町通り. Both of them are lined with department stores (such as **Daiei, Fujisaki** and **Mitsukoshi**), souvenir shops and restaurants. Many drinking spots and obscure cabarets are located on the streets to the west of Higashi-Ichibancho Street (indicated with red dotted lines). The area is completely safe; don't be afraid to take a look at this colorful night life zone and its jovial people. But if you are a woman alone don't stay in the area after 8 p.m., unless you want to find out how alcohol can inspire even shy country people to make shockingly indecent proposals. Stick to the shopping arcades after 8 p.m.

Government offices are located on the northern side of Jozenji-dori Street (upper center, map 6), and business offices are along Hirose-dori, Aoba-dori and Higashi-Nibancho-dori Streets.

Transportation in Sendai

Buses are the only means of public transportation in Sendai. The central part of the city can be reached easily on foot from all the major hotels. A subway, running north to south and passing Sendai Station, is under construction, but even when finished it will not be of any real use to tourists. Sendai's bus system is perhaps the most complicated one in all of Japan. There are more than 60 bus stops on the western side of the station. Even if you can read the destination names in Japanese, you really can't use the buses unless you also have a thorough knowledge of the geography of the area. Because you will probably visit only one or two places of interest in Sendai (because there really are no more than one or two), it is better to use taxis.

Shopping & Restaurants

Shopping

Craft Corner (middle center, map 6, in the Chuo-dori arcade) deals in a variety of handicraft items and antiques. **Shimanuki** (middle center, map 6, in the Chuo-dori arcade) also has many different types of Japanese dolls.

Restaurants

American Fast Food: McDonald's is located in the middle of Higashi-Ichibancho-dori arcade.

Restaurants

Florence and **Capri** (both in the middle center, map 6) serve Japanized Italian food. Spaghetti and pilaf are priced at 500 - 1,000 yen. **Sun Beam** (upper left, map 6) is a Korean barbecue restaurant and is recommended if you are starved for beef. Dishes generally range from 800 - 1,200 yen. **Tonkatsu Omachi** (middle center, map 6, on Aoba-dori Street) specializes in pork cutlet. A regular set menu meal costs 800 yen. The special "Gensui Katsu" is priced at 2,500 yen. **Tachibana** is an authentic, yet inexpensive Japanese restaurant on Chuo-dori Street (middle center, map 6). The first floor is a sushi restaurant and the second serves tempura. A sushi and tempura set menu combination is 1,800 yen. If you eat sushi a la carte, be ready to pay 5,000 yen. The plastic sushi displays at the entrance are a good landmark. **Isahachi** (middle left, map 6) is a robatayaki pub restaurant (on the basement floor).

Places of Interest

The following place(s) should be covered on the morning of the third day.

Zuihoden Hall 瑞鳳殿 (lower left, map 6)

Zuihoden Hall is a mausoleum of Masamune Date located on a small hill and surrounded by thick cedar trees. The original hall, a National Treasure, was a splendid structure with elaborate carvings and decorations but it was lost to fire during the war. The present building is an exact replica of the original. **Kansenden Hall** and **Zen-oden Hall,** the mausolea of the second and third lords of the Date family, are also located near Zuihoden. Both of them are open from 9 a.m. to 4 p.m. The 500 yen admission covers all three monuments.

If you have difficulty taking a taxi from Zuihoden back to the city, walk to Otamayabashi bus stop (lower left, map 6) and take an east-bound bus. Most buses terminate at Sendai Station.

Osaki Hachimangu Shrine 大崎八幡宮 (Outside of map 6, about 2 miles to the northwest from Sendai Station, optional)

Osaki Hachimangu Shrine (National Treasure) was built in 1607 at the order of Masamune Date, to offer thanks for the area's prosperity. This magnificent black lacquer building is typical of the designs of the time. The Shrine is located on a small hill, and is surrounded by a thick forest (9 a.m. to 4 p.m. Admission 150 yen).

Star Festival in Sendai in early August.

Accommodations

HOTELS
Standard Hotels (14,000 - 20,000 yen for a twin room)

Hotel Sendai Plaza ホテル・仙台プラザ (upper center, map 6)

Address: 2-20-1, Honcho, Sendai; Phone: (0222) 62-7111. 221 rooms in a quiet location close to local government offices.

Sendai Tokyu Hotel 仙台東急ホテル (middle left, map 6)

Address: 2-9-25, Ichibancho, Sendai; Phone: (0222) 62-2411. 302 rooms suitable for both business people and tourists.

Sendai Hotel 仙台ホテル (middle right, map 6)

Address: 1-10-25, Chuo, Sendai; Phone: (0222) 25-5171. A traditional Sendai property. Its 84 rooms were renovated recently.

Business Hotels (less than 14,000 yen for a twin room)

Mitsui Urban Hotel (Sendai) 三井アーバンホテル (upper center, map 6)

Address: 2-18-11, Honcho, Sendai; Phone: (0222) 65-3131. A good quality hotel for this category (212 rooms).

Hotel Rich Sendai ホテル・リッチ仙台 (middle left, map 6)

Address: 2-2-2, Kokubucho, Sendai; Phone: (0222) 62-8811. Facilities are comparable to standard hotels (242 rooms).

Sendai Washington Hotel 仙台ワシントンホテル (middle left, map 6)

Address: 2-3-1, Omachi, Sendai; Phone: (0222) 22-2111. A typical Washington Hotel, one of the largest business hotel chains in Japan (271 rooms).

RYOKANS
Inexpensive Ryokans (less than 12,000 yen per person with two meals)

Takenaka Bekkan 竹中別館 (upper right, map 6)

Address: 1-4-15, Honcho, Sendai; Phone: (0222) 61-2721. 33 rooms in a quiet location.

Takenaka Ryokan 竹中旅館 (middle center, map 6)

Address: 2-9-23, Chuo, Sendai; Phone: (0222) 25-6771. A 20 room property convenient to the downtown area.

Sumire Ryokan すみれ旅館 (upper right, map 6)

Address: 1-4-5, Chuo, Sendai; Phone: (0222) 25-8100. 15 rooms in a quiet location.

Isuzu Ryokan 五十鈴旅館 (upper right, map 6)

Address: 1-1-48, Kakyoin, Sendai; Phone: (0222) 22-6430. A small property with only nine rooms.

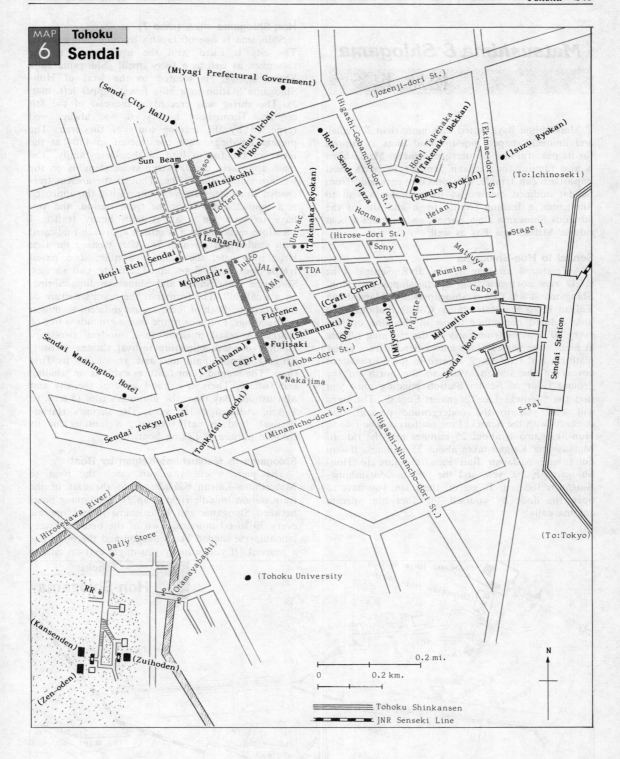

MAP 6 Tohoku
Sendai

(Miyagi Prefectural Government)

(Jozenji-dori St.)

(Sendi City Hall)

Mitsui Urban Hotel

Sun Beam

Esso

Mitsukoshi

Lotteria

Isahachi

Hotel Rich Sendai

McDonald's

Jusco

JAL

ANA

Florence

Craft Corner

(Shimanuki)

Fujisaki

(Tachibana)

Capri

(Aoba-dori St.)

Nakajima

Sendai Washington Hotel

Sendai Tokyu Hotel

(Tonkatsu Omachi)

(Minamicho-dori St.)

(Hirosegawa River)

Daily Store

RR

Otamayabashi

(Kansenden)

(Zuihoden)

(Zen-oden)

Hotel Takenaka

(Takenaka Bekkan)

Hotel Sendai Plaza

(Higashi-Gobancho-dori St.)

Takenaka Ryokan

Univac

(Sumire Ryokan)

Honma

Heian

(Hirose-dori St.)

Sony

TDA

(Ekimae-dori St.)

(Isuzu Ryokan)

(To: Ichinoseki)

Stage 1

Matsuya

Rumina

Cabo

Miyoshido

Palette

Marumitsu

sendai Hotel

(Higashi-Nibancho-dori St.)

Daiei

(Tohoku University)

Sendai Station

S-Pal

(To: Tokyo)

0.2 mi.

0   0.2 km.

N

Tohoku Shinkansen

JNR Senseki Line

Matsushima & Shiogama

松島，塩釜

Matsushima Bay, dotted with more than 200 small and uniquely shaped pine-tree-clad islets, is famous for its peaceful and picturesque scenery. Matsushima is also famous for Zuiganji Temple, Tohoku's most important Zen temple. The one day excursion from Sendai outlined below also incorporates a visit to Shiogama, a leading fishing town and site of the fabulous Shiogama Jinja Shrine, and includes a boat ride in Matsushima Bay as well.

Sendai to Hon-Shiogama

As pictured on map 1, the JNR Senseki Line 仙石線 runs northeast from Sendai stopping at Hon-Shiogama 本塩釜 (Main Shiogama) and Matsushima Kaigan 松島海岸 (Matsushima Coast) Stations. The blue colored commuter trains of this line operate every 30 minutes from early in the morning till late at night. The Senseki Line leaves Sendai from either platform No. 1 or No. 2, located in the northeastern corner of the station. Walk to the north on the ground floor of Sendai Station building until you find the "Senseki Line" signs in English. The signs will lead you to the underground passage that connects with the Senseki Line platforms. The ride to Hon-Shiogama is about 25 minutes and the ride to Matsushima Kaigan takes about 35 minutes. If you don't have a Japan Rail Pass, the fare to Hon-Shiogama is 280 yen, and the fare to Matsushima-Kaigan is 360 yen. To get off the train, you have to open the door by yourself — it does not operate automatically!

Hon-Shiogama 本塩釜 (map 7)

Shiogama is one of Japan's leading fishing ports. The city is filled with the lively spirit of the fishermen as well as a fishy smell! **Shiogama Jinja Shrine** 塩釜神社 is located to the west of Hon-Shiogama Station in a hilly forest (upper left, map 7). The shrine was erected at the end of the 8th century. Throughout history, it was always well respected by the leading lords of the area. The present buildings were constructed in 1704 at the order of the fourth lord of the Date family. The main approach, up 200 steep stone steps, is on the western side of the shrine. Though the ancient tree-shaded stone steps are very impressive, the approach is a long distance from the train station, and you have to walk on a street with heavy traffic. I therefore recommend a southern approach (indicated with shaded red on map 7). After passing the first large torii gate, the path is a quiet stone-paved traffic-free gentle slope up. There are two shrines, Shiogama Jinja Shrine and Shibahiko Jinja Shrine, on a small hill. The former is the main structure of the precincts. Both of them are magnificent vermilion red buildings. Entrance to the shrine grounds is free of charge. A small museum in a modern two-story building displays miniature festival shrines, swords, hanging scrolls, paintings and armor on its first floor. The second floor features exhibits on whaling and fishery. There is a good view of the city and Matsushima Bay from the museum's roof (8 a.m. to 5 p.m. Admission 150 yen). The shrine's Harbor Festival, held in early August, is famous for its colorful parade of fishing boats.

Shiogama to Matsushima-Kaigan by Boat

The pier, where you can catch the boat to Matsushima-Kaigan 松島海岸, is to the east of the train station (middle right, map 7). Sightseeing boats between Shiogama and Matsushima-Kaigan operate every 30 to 60 minutes. Two of the boats are very fanciful, one shaped like a dragon and the other like a peacock. If you're lucky you might end up on one

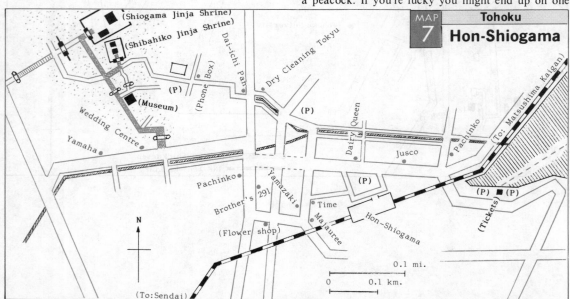

MAP 7 Tohoku
Hon-Shiogama

(Shiogama Jinja Shrine)
(Shibahiko Jinja Shrine)
(Phone Box)
Dai-ichi Pan
Dry Cleaning Tokyu
(P)
(Museum)
Wedding Centre
Yamaha
(P)
Dairy Queen
Jusco
Pachinko
(To: Matsushima Kaigan)
Pachinko
Yamazaki 291
(P)
(P)
(P) (P)
Brother's
Time
(Tickets)
(Flower shop)
Majauree
Hon-Shiogama
N
0.1 mi.
0   0.1 km.
(To: Sendai)

of them. There are two classes of seats on the boat. The first class fare is 2,400 yen, and the second class tickets are 1,200 yen. The ride takes one hour, and I was comfortable in the second class cabin (The frequency of operation is reduced in winter).

The boat cruises Matsushima Bay, skirting numerous small islands, all of which have been eroded into grotesque shapes by the waves. Oddly shaped pine trees that look like bonsai grow on each island. A newly constructed power station ruins the marine scenery at the beginning of the cruise, but for most of the trip you still see the artistry of nature. This is the scenery that thoroughly fascinated the brilliant Haiku poet, Basho, more than 300 years ago. You will see a number of bamboo sticks and logs on the surface of the water. The bamboo sticks are frames for cultivating sea weed, and the logs are used by oyster farmers.

Matsushima 松島

All of Matsushima's places of interest are located within walking distance of both Matsushima-Kaigan Pier and the JNR train station. You need about three hours to cover the area.

Godaido Hall 五大堂 **(middle center, map 8)** is located on a tiny island connected to the coast by a small bridge. It was originally built in 807 by Tamuramaro Sakanoue, a military leader who invaded the area at the order of the emperor. Masamune Date had the present hall built in 1600. The traditional architecture of the small temple complements the picturesque marine scenery. The inside of the hall is not open to the public.

Fukuurajima Island 福浦島 **(lower right, map 8) (optional)** is connected with the coast by a vermilion red pedestrian bridge. The island itself is a botanical garden (8:30 a.m. to 5 p.m. Admission 100 yen).

Zuiganji Temple 瑞巌寺 **(upper center, map 8)** is the most important Zen temple in northern Japan, and dates originally from 827. The present buildings were constructed in 1609 at the order of Masamune. Sammon Gate is the entrance to the main approach, which leads straight to the main temple precincts. You should turn to the right to see the numerous images of Buddha carved on the cliffs. In the olden days novices at the temple were set the arduous task of carving these images as part of their training. The ticket office is at the entrance to the main precincts (7:30 a.m. to 5 p.m. Admission 330 yen). The Main Hall, a gigantic wooden structure, houses masterpieces of carving and painting (the colors on the paintings are, however, a bit faded) that reflect the brilliant artistic trends of the early 17th century. The Hall itself and everything it contains are National Treasures. The Treasure House displays impressive Buddhist images and historical objects related to the Date family.

Entsuin Temple 円通院 **(upper left, map 8)** is also called Rose Temple because of the large number of rose bushes on its grounds. The mausoleum of Mitsumune Date, a grandson of Masamune, and the landscaped garden are worthy of special attention (8 a.m. to 5 p.m. Admission 100 yen).

Kanrantei 観瀾亭 **(middle left, map 8)** was used by the lords of each generation of the Date family for moon viewing parties on summer nights. The house

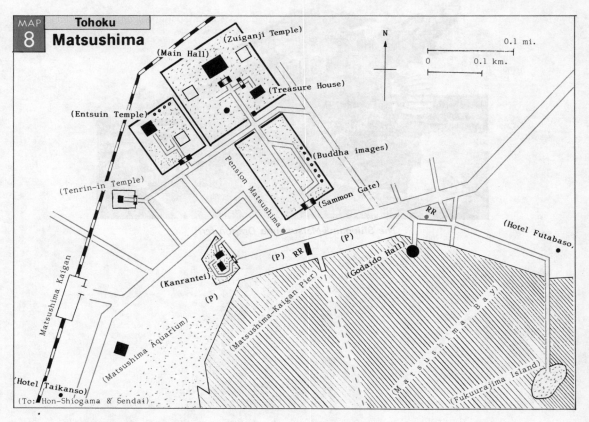

MAP 8 Tohoku **Matsushima**

N

0.1 mi.

0   0.1 km.

(Zuiganji Temple)

(Main Hall)

(Treasure House)

(Entsuin Temple)

(Buddha images)

(Tenrin-in Temple)

Pension Matsushima

(Sammon Gate)

RR

(Hotel Futabaso)

(P)

(P) RR

(P)

(Godaido Hall)

(Kanrantei)

(P)

Matsushima Kaigan

(Matsushima Aquarium)

(Matsushima-Kaigan Pier)

(Matsushima Bay)

(Fukuurajima Island)

(Hotel Taikanso)

(To: Hon-Shiogama & Sendai)

was originally a tea house in Fushimijo Castle in Kyoto, and was later presented to Masamune by Hideyoshi Toyotomi. Adjacent to Kanrantei House is Matsushima Museum, which features armor, swords, paintings, etc. of the Date family. The 150 yen admission covers both properties (8 a.m. to 5 p.m.).

Places for Lunch. There are a number of restaurants and souvenir shops on the main street along the coast. Eels are a specialty of the area. I know many foreigners who were pleasantly surprised the first time they tried eel. You might be too. Many quick lunches are available for 1,000-2,000 yen.

Matsushima-Kaigan to Sendai by Train

The JNR Senseki Line is the only train that serves Matsushima-Kaigan Station. Take the south-bound train to Sendai, the last stop. (This is the end of the second day of your Tohoku itinerary.)

Accommodations in Matsushima

These are added for those who would like an alternative to returning to Sendai for the second night of their Tohoku visit.

Standard Ryokans (12,000-20,000 yen per person with two meals)

Hotel Taikanso ホテル大観荘 (lower left, map 8)
Address: 10-76, Inuta, Matsushima, Miyagi Pref.; Phone: (02235) 4-2161. The largest property in Matsushima with 105 Japanese rooms and 14 Western rooms.

Hotel Futabaso ホテル双葉荘 (middle right, map 8)
Address: 35, Senzui, Matsushima, Miyagi Pref.; Phone: (02235) 4-3111. A 46-room standard property.

The Shiogama-Matsushima Dragon ferry.

Brief History of Japan

Pre-Historic Era

The Japanese archipelago separated from the Asian Continent about 10,000 years ago when the level of the sea rose at the end of the 4th Ice Age. According to contemporary Chinese documents, there were more than 100 small tribal communes scattered about Japan at the beginning of the first century. Large tombs, which were erected in the 4th century, have been found in many parts of Japan, and giant ones are located in Nara and Osaka. This supports the theory that of the many small "nations" led by powerful families at this time, the most powerful "nation" was located in the Nara-Osaka area. The establishment of what can be considered the first unified nation of Japan was achieved in the 5th century, in Nara.

Asuka Era (The end of the 6th century to the end of the 7th century)

Buddhism was introduced in Japan in the middle of the 6th century and provided a common spiritual basis for the organization of a centralized political and societal system. Horyuji Temple in the Ikaruga area of Nara was constructed around the end of this century. Though the original designs were changed slightly when the Temple was reconstructed in 670 after a fire, its scale and grandeur testify to the power and influence Buddhism had acquired in such a short period of time. The first Japanese Constitution, the "Seventeen Article Constitution," was promulgated by Regent Shotoku, whose portrait appears on each of modern Japan's 5,000 and 10,000 yen bills. (Since new bills were issued late in 1984, you'll only be able to see the Prince's portrait if you get some of the older, larger bills.)

Fujiwara Era (The late 7th century to 710)

A large scale capital was constructed in Fujiwara (south of Nara) in 694. An aristocratic political system and a tax collection network that extended to virtually every corner of the country were established. The East Tower of Yakushiji Temple in Nara is the symbol of the cultural achievements of this era. Its balanced beauty has been described as "frozen music."

Nara Era (710 — 794)

Japan's first permanent capital was constructed in Nara (a little to the west of the center of the modern city) in 710. To master the advanced science and culture of the Asian continent, the imperial court sent cultural missions to China; art treasures of India and Persia as well as those of China were brought back to Japan. Throughout this period, Buddhism, protected by the imperial family and the powerful aristocrats, grew in influence. The Great Buddha at Todaiji Temple in Nara, cast in 752, symbolizes this influence. Soon, the Buddhist priests extended their activities beyond the spiritual world and became involved in political affairs. Emperor Kammu moved the capital to Kyoto in order to rid the imperial court of their influence.

Heian Era (794 — 1192)

The new capital in Kyoto was completed in 794, and about this time, leading priests, among them Kukai and Saicho, began a reform movement within Buddhism. As part of their pursuit of spiritual purification, they opened training centers for priests in isolated mountain areas. Koyasan and Hieizan were locations of two of these new monasteries. For hundreds of years Kyoto continued to prosper and the city's imperial and aristocratic families enjoyed political and economic power. They were also the leaders, along with the priests, of cultural activities.

In the 12th century, economic development in the rural areas resulted in new power for local military leaders. The Taira family, based in western Japan, and the Minamoto family, based in the east, were the two most influential military powers of their time. Under the leadership of Kiyomori, the Taira family won major battles against the Minamotos, and then began its climb up the ladders of political power at the imperial court. Kiyomori became the prime minister, and members of the family occupied other important government posts. Kiyomori's daughter, Empress Kenreimon-in, bore Emperor Takakura a son who grew up to be Emperor Antoku. However, the Taira's prosperity did not last long. After the death of Kiyomori, the reorganized Minamoto force sparked revolts against the Tairas. After three major victories in the Inland Sea area, Yoritomo Minamoto seized the reins of power. The rapid ascent to power and the easy downfall of the Tairas have always symbolized what the Japanese regard as one of history's greatest lessons — that prosperity is like a bubble on the surface of the water, easily formed and just as easily broken, lost and forgotten. While the Taira family prospered in Kyoto, an autonomous government flourished in Hiraizumi, in the northern part of Japan's main island. The Fujiwara family, leaders of this local government, were also patrons of high culture, as symbolized by the Konjikido (Golden Hall) at Chusonji Temple and the Heavenly Garden of Motsuji Temple. After 100 years of prosperity, the Fujiwaras too were destroyed by Yoritomo Minamoto.

Kamakura Era (1192 — 1333)

Learning his lesson from the Tairas and the rapid deterioration of their military spirit once they joined the imperial court, Yoritomo established Japan's first independent military government. He made Kamakura, far away from the ruined imperial court in Kyoto, his capital. The simple and straightforward warrior spirit of the Minamoto family became the social norm, and the austere strictures of the Zen School of Buddhism gained countless adherents.

After the assassination of the third Minamoto Shogun, the political power of the Kamakura Shogunate fell into the hands of the Hojos, the family of Yoritomo's wife. In 1274 and again in 1281, the Mongolians who had established the Yuan Dynasty in China tried to attack Japan. These unsuccessful assaults were made at Fukuoka, on Kyushu, the southernmost island. Though the Kamakura Shogunate successfully defended the nation, the economic difficulties caused by the wars weakened its leadership. Emperor Godaigo rallied the dissatisfied warrior leaders from all parts of the nation and defeated the Shogunate forces in 1333, but this new imperial government only survived for three years, and another military leader, Takauji Ashikaga, established a new Shogunate in 1336, this time in Kyoto.

Muromachi and Azuchi Momoyama Era (1336-1603)

Though the Ashikagas centered their government in the Kyoto area, their rule over the rural areas did not last long. The financial power of local military leaders allowed them to remain independent from the Ashikaga Shogunate and to set up their own feudal systems. Beginning with the middle of the 15th century, there were frequent civil wars among local feudal lords who sought to expand their territory. The Ikko sect of Buddhism played an influential role in these wars, especially in the central part of the Japan Sea coast area. Members of this sect defeated the feudal lord in Kanazawa and established an autonomous government that endured for as long as 100 years. The famous Gold and Silver Pavilions in Kyoto were constructed by Shoguns of the Ashikaga family and are the most splendid legacies of the era. Flower arranging, tea ceremony and the Noh drama also date from this era.

In the second half of the 16th century, Nobunaga Oda, a minor feudal lord and brilliant military strategist from Gifu, near Nagoya, conquered neighboring lords and emerged as one of the nation's greatest military powers. In 1573, Nobunaga attacked Kyoto and defeated the Ashikaga Shogunate. After victories over other influential feudal lords, Nobunaga was on the brink of unifying the nation when he was assassinated in 1582 by his retainer, Mitsuhide Akechi. Another powerful retainer, Hideyoshi Toyotomi, a mere farmer's son who rose to a position of power, crushed Mitsuhide's rebel force, and then went on to complete the establishment of a centralized government.

In the period of peace that began with the end of the 16th century, all sorts of cultural pursuits flourished; it was a particularly rich and lavish era in the history of Japanese art. The gorgeous paintings of the Kano School are representative of the work of this era. Prototypes of the modern Kabuki and Bunraku puppet dramas also developed at this time.

However, the reign of the Toyotomi family did not last long. After the death of Hideyoshi, two top retainers of the Toyotomis, Ieyasu Tokugawa and Mitsunari Ishida, vied for power, and their struggle divided the other feudal lords. The two forces had a final decisive battle at Sekigahara, between Kyoto and Nagoya, in 1600, and Ieyasu's victory led to the establishment of a new Shogunate in Edo (modern Tokyo) in 1603.

Toward the end of the period of civil war, Christianity was introduced on Kyushu island. Because the Christian missionaries accompanied the European traders who brought advanced technologies and foreign products into the country, Nobunaga Oda allowed them to act freely, and the new religion spread, especially in Nagasaki and other trading centers of western Kyushu. Some of the feudal lords of that area became Christian and even sent envoys to Rome. It is estimated that Christianity quickly gained 700,000 adherents, but because the new religion was especially popular among the poor farmers who suffered from the heavy taxes and rigid caste system of the Shogunate, it was not acceptable to either Hideyoshi or Ieyasu. Christianity was officially forbidden by the Tokugawa Shogunate in 1613. The bloody battle at Shimabara near Nagasaki between the Christian farmers and the army of the Shogun was symbolic of the tragic destiny of Christians in Japan at this time.

Edo Era (1603 — 1868)

The third Tokugawa Shogun, Iemitsu, closed all the ports of Japan, except Nagasaki, in 1639 to shut out Christianity, and, at the same time, to monopolize foreign trade. Only Dutch and Chinese traders who did not have any connections with missionaries were allowed to trade at a secluded area in Nagasaki. This isolationist period, which continued for 225 years, until 1854, was also the longest peaceful era in Japanese history. By the middle of the 18th century, the population of Edo had increased to one million, the largest in the world at that time. Economic progress allowed even the common people to engage in cultural activities, and ukiyo-e (woodblock prints) and haiku (short stylized poems) achieved great popularity.

By the middle of the 19th century, the rigid feudal system had become a bar to development of a commercial economy. Though their social status was low, the merchants had great economic power and became underground supporters of a new, freer social system. In 1853, Commodore Perry of the United States brought his fleet to the port of Uraga, near Yokohama, and demanded the opening of Japanese ports for the supply of commodities to foreign fleets, and for international trade in general. The advanced technological level of the West that Perry and his sailors demonstrated helped make the people aware of the need for change. After civil wars between the conservative Shogunate forces, and those who wanted a new order (these included members of the imperial family and the innovative feudal lords of western Japan), the 15th Tokugawa Shogun, Yoshi-nobu, returned the reins of government to Emperor Meiji. This historic event of 1868 is referred to as the Meiji Restoration.

Modern Era (Meiji, Taisho and the current Showa Eras 1868—)

The new imperial government aggressively took the initiative in importing Western culture, techno-logy and social structures. Japan's new government also invested heavily in and promoted industrializa-tion. Despite the many changes that accompanied this modernization, the nation's traditional, unequal social structure survived. Sovereignty rested with the Emperor and, ultimately, he possessed all power. Only aristocrats could be members of the House of Chancellors and only men who paid a certain level of taxes were eligible to vote for members of the House of Representatives (Women gained the right to vote in 1925). After the tragedy of World War II, a genuine democratization took place in Japan. The Emperor was declared to be merely symbolic of the spirit of the nation, and elected officials, wielding all political power, ushered in a period marked by unparalleled efforts and crowned by the achievement of genuine social equality and phenomenal economic growth and success.

INDEX

Card 1

Station

下の電車または地下鉄の駅を教えてください

Where is the following train/subway station?
(Circle either train or subway and fill in the name of the station and the name of the line.)

Circle either one		路線名　Line Name	駅名　Destination
	Train　　Subway		
1	電車　　地下鉄		
2	電車　　地下鉄		
3	電車　　地下鉄		
4	電車　　地下鉄		
5	電車　　地下鉄		

Card 2

Ticket

下の駅までの運賃を教えてください

How much is the fare to the following station?
(Fill in the name of your destination and the name of the line you want to take.)

	路線名　Line Name	目的駅　Destination
1		
2		
3		
4		
5		

Card 3

Platform

下の電車の発車ホーム番号を教えてください

What is the platform number for the following train to the destination listed below?
(If the train is a local and does not have a name, write "Donko" in the train name column.)

	路線名　Line Name	電車名　Train Name	目的駅　Destination
1			
2			
3			
4			
5			

下の行先の市電またはバス乗場を教えてください

Where is the stop for the streetcar (or bus) going to the following destination?
(Circle either streetcar or bus and fill in the name of your destination.)

Card 5 Stop Street car Bus

Circle either one		目的駅　　Destination
1　Streetcar　Bus 　市電　バス		
2　市電　バス		
3　市電　バス		
4　市電　バス		
5　市電　バス		

私は下の目的地まで行きます
目的地が近づいたら教えてください

I am going to the following place. Please let me know when we near the destination.
(On the train, streetcar or bus)
(Fill in the name of your destination and show the card to a fellow passenger.)

Card 6 Destination

1		6	
2		7	
3		8	
4		9	
5		10	

下の目的地まで行ってください

Please take me to the following place.
(For a taxi driver)　(Fill in the name of your destination.)

Card 7 Taxi

1		7	
2		8	
3		9	
4		10	
5		11	
6		12	

Card 4 — Reservation

座席指定申込書
Application for reserved seats

If you have a Rail Pass, you can request reservations for JNR trains free of charge. Show the Pass with this form.
Your Rail Pass cannot be used for private railways.

乗車日 Date of Trip	月 (month)	日 (date)	人数 No. of Psns	大人 Adults ___ 枚	子供 Children ___ 枚

出発駅 Departure _____ Station	目的駅 Destination _____ Station

座席の種類 Class of Seat	(Check either one)	☐ グリーン車 First Class	☐ 普通車 Coach Class	☐ 禁煙席 Nonsmoking section, if available

第一希望 First Choice	電車名 Train Name	出発時間 Dep. Time	時 (hour) 分 (minute)
第二希望 Second Choice	電車名 Train Name	出発時間 Dep. Time	時 (hour) 分 (minute)
第三希望 Third Choice	電車名 Train Name	出発時間 Dep. Time	時 (hour) 分 (minute)

Card 4 — Reservation

座席指定申込書
Application for reserved seats

If you have a Rail Pass, you can request reservations for JNR trains free of charge. Show the Pass with this form.
Your Rail Pass cannot be used for private railways.

乗車日 Date of Trip	月 (month)	日 (date)	人数 No. of Psns	大人 Adults ___ 枚	子供 Children ___ 枚

出発駅 Departure _____ Station	目的駅 Destination _____ Station

座席の種類 Class of Seat	(Check either one)	☐ グリーン車 First Class	☐ 普通車 Coach Class	☐ 禁煙席 Nonsmoking section, if available

第一希望 First Choice	電車名 Train Name	出発時間 Dep. Time	時 (hour) 分 (minute)
第二希望 Second Choice	電車名 Train Name	出発時間 Dep. Time	時 (hour) 分 (minute)
第三希望 Third Choice	電車名 Train Name	出発時間 Dep. Time	時 (hour) 分 (minute)

Card 9 — Rest room

お手洗いの場所を教えてください

Where is a rest room?

Card 8 — Baggage

手荷物一時預り所またはコインロッカーを教えてください

Where are the coin lockers or a short-term baggage check room?

座席指定申込書

Application for reserved seats

If you have a Rail Pass, you can request reservations for JNR trains free of charge. Show the Pass with this form.
Your Rail Pass cannot be used for private railways.

乗車日 Date of Trip	月 (month)	日 (date)	人数 No. of Psns 大人 Adults ____ 枚 子供 ____ 枚 Children		
出発駅 Departure _____Station			目的駅 Destination _____Station		
座席の種類 Class of Seat	(Check either one)	☐グリーン車 First Class	☐普通車 Coach Class	☐禁煙席 Nonsmoking section, if available	
第一希望 First Choice	電車名 Train Name			出発時間 Dep. Time	時 分 (hour) (minute)
第二希望 Second Choice	電車名 Train Name			出発時間 Dep. Time	時 分 (hour) (minute)
第三希望 Third Choice	電車名 Train Name			出発時間 Dep. Time	時 分 (hour) (minute)

Card 4 *Reservation*

座席指定申込書

Application for reserved seats

If you have a Rail Pass, you can request reservations for JNR trains free of charge. Show the Pass with this form.
Your Rail Pass cannot be used for private railways.

乗車日 Date of Trip	月 (month)	日 (date)	人数 No. of Psns 大人 Adults ____ 枚 子供 ____ 枚 Children		
出発駅 Departure _____Station			目的駅 Destination _____Station		
座席の種類 Class of Seat	(Check either one)	☐グリーン車 First Class	☐普通車 Coach Class	☐禁煙席 Nonsmoking section, if available	
第一希望 First Choice	電車名 Train Name			出発時間 Dep. Time	時 分 (hour) (minute)
第二希望 Second Choice	電車名 Train Name			出発時間 Dep. Time	時 分 (hour) (minute)
第三希望 Third Choice	電車名 Train Name			出発時間 Dep. Time	時 分 (hour) (minute)